TOM
WILLS

Tom Wills, 1870, by William Handcock

TOM WILLS

First wild man of Australian sport

GREG DE MOORE

ALLEN&UNWIN

For Heather, Eve and Willem

Allen & Unwin
Sydney, Melbourne, Auckland, London

83 Alexander Street
Crows Nest NSW 2065
Australia
Phone: (61 2) 8425 0100
Fax: (61 2) 9906 2218
Email: info@allenandunwin.com
Web: www.allenandunwin.com

Cataloguing-in-Publication details are available
from the National Library of Australia
www.trove.nla.gov.au

ISBN 978 1 74237 598 4

Index by Fay Donlevy
Text design by Phil Campbell
Typeset in 10.5/14 pt Janson Text by Bookhouse, Sydney
Printed and bound in Australia by the SOS Print + Media Group.

10 9 8 7 6 5 4 3

MIX
Paper from
responsible sources
FSC® C011217

The paper in this book is FSC® certified.
FSC® promotes environmentally responsible,
socially beneficial and economically viable
management of the world's forests.

CONTENTS

CAST OF CHARACTERS

FAMILY

Sarah Alexander Tom's aunt. Sarah, Horatio's sister, was widowed by William Redfern, then married James Alexander and moved to London.

Sarah Theresa Barbor Tom's de facto.

William Ducker Long-time confidant of the Wills family and a man of considerable financial skill, he ran an auctioneer business in Geelong and became the mayor of Geelong. After Horatio's death, Ducker advised the family on matters of finance.

Jane Harrison Half-sister of Horatio Wills. Mother of H.C.A. Harrison, Mrs Harrison lived in Victoria Parade, Collingwood, where Tom spent considerable time in the late 1850s.

George Howe Married Sarah Wills (Horatio's mother) after the death of her first husband (Horatio's father), Edward. He was the first proprietor of the *Sydney Gazette* newspaper and was embroiled in financial disputes with the Wills family.

William Roope Roope was the husband of Catherine, sister of Elizabeth Wills. He was a trusted advisor in matters of finance and wool to the Wills family.

Catherine Roope Sister of Elizabeth Wills.

Edward Wills Horatio's father. He died when his wife, Sarah, was four months pregnant with Horatio.

Elizabeth Wills Mother of Tom, wife of Horatio.

Horatio Spencer Howe Wills Father of Tom and the most important influence in Tom's life. Horatio Wills was a newspaper publisher, farmer, politician, inventor, entrepreneur and adventurer.

Sarah Wills Horatio's mother.

Thomas Wills Tom's uncle and Horatio's older brother.

TOM'S SIBLINGS (IN ORDER OF AGE)

Emily Wills The second Wills child, Emily married her half-cousin, H.C.A. (Colden) Harrison.

Cedric Wills Like his brothers, Cedric played football for the Geelong Football Club. He worked on Cullin-la-Ringo from 1862.

Horace Wills Regarded by the family as the most gentle of all the Wills boys, Horace was a footballer of some note, playing with the Geelong Football Club during the 1860s. He worked on the family property Cullin-la-Ringo after Tom left.

Egbert Wills Youngest of the Wills boys and an exceptionally talented sportsman who excelled in athletics and football, Egbert played for the Geelong and Melbourne football clubs.

Elizabeth Wills Tom's sister.

Eugene Wills   Tom's sister, also called Eugenie.

Minna Wills   Tom's sister, also called Minnie.

Hortense Wills   Tom's sister and Horatio and Elizabeth's ninth (and last) child.

CRICKET AND FOOTBALL

James Mark Bryant   An Englishman who migrated to Melbourne and was more commonly known as Jerry, Bryant was a professional cricketer, footballer, publican and entrepreneur who played a role in the development of Australian Rules football.

Sam Costick   An Englishman and professional cricketer with various clubs in Melbourne and Sydney but most significantly with the Melbourne Cricket Club (MCC), Sam had most to do with Tom during the late 1860s and early 1870s.

Gideon Elliott   An Englishman and one of a clutch of professional cricketers admired by Tom. Of all the professionals, Gid (commonly called this) seems to have been closest to Tom. He played with numerous clubs but particularly Richmond and Melbourne.

W.G. Grace   The greatest cricketer of the Victorian era, Grace first brought an English team to Australia in 1873–74.

William Greaves   An Englishman and professional cricketer, like several other cricketers he was notorious for his demonstrative and untoward behaviour on the field.

William J. Hammersley   An Englishman, journalist, amateur cricketer, footballer, athlete and lover of the sport of horse racing. Hammersley left the most important public chronicle on the life of Tom Wills and wrote in *The Australasian* under

the title 'Longstop'. He played a role in the development of
Australian Rules football.

William Handfield   Tom's friend, Melbourne Cricket Club
member, intercolonial cricketer and slow bowler.

H.C.A. Harrison   Tom's half-cousin and brother-in-law; known
as Colden, the family called him Coley. He and Tom shared
a common grandmother. Harrison was regarded as the
champion runner of the colonies. During the 1860s he
emerged as one of the pre-eminent footballers in the colony
and captained the Melbourne Football Club. He oversaw a
major review of the rules of football in 1866.

William Hayman   Travelled with Tom Wills and the Aboriginal
cricket team during late 1866 and early 1867.

Charles Lawrence   An Englishman and professional cricketer,
Lawrence played with Tom in Ireland. He came to Australia
in 1861 with the first English team to tour Australia and
worked his way into the 1866–67 Aboriginal tour, later
usurping Tom's role by taking the team to England in 1868.

John Lillywhite   English professional cricketer and coach of the
Rugby School XI while Tom was there, Lillywhite was from
a distinguished cricketing clan.

George Marshall   An Englishman and professional cricketer in
the colony of Victoria.

Roland Newbury   Called 'Roley' for short, Newbury was the
pavilion keeper at the Melbourne Cricket Club and initiated
the 1866 Boxing Day match between the MCC and the
Western District Aboriginal team.

James B. Thompson   Journalist, amateur cricketer and footballer. A prominent member of the MCC, Thompson and
Hammersley were Tom's principal adversaries in squabbles
played out in the colony's press. He spread knowledge of

Australian football through *The Argus* and his involvement in developing the early rules was important in shaping the game's trajectory.

Richard Wardill   A brilliant polymath sportsman who excelled in running, football, cricket and rowing; a member of the Melbourne Cricket Club.

Unamurriman   The finest player in the Aboriginal cricket team of 1866–68; more commonly known as Mullagh.

FINDING TOM WILLS

I first came across the name of Tom Wills in a short article on the origins of Australian Rules football. Tom Wills had been bequeathed a lavish talent for the playing of games – he played cricket with virtuosity, challenging the constraints of that game, and was credited, more than any other, with creating the game of Australian Rules football. Towards the end of the article, my eyes settled upon a single line: Tom Wills had stabbed himself in the heart. In the early afternoon of a Melbourne day in 1880 he had committed suicide.

Curious about Wills, I wanted to know why his life ended that way – my starting point was his suicide. I went to the Mitchell Library in Sydney and searched the Melbourne newspapers for his obituaries. These gave me the first insights into his life. Wills was an alcoholic and his behaviour in the hours before his suicide suggested that he had been hallucinating. On the day before his death, 1 May 1880, Wills had been taken to the Melbourne Hospital and offered refuge, but had somehow managed to leave hospital and return home, where he took his life. I couldn't imagine anyone being allowed to leave hospital in that state. The only way to know how and why he left hospital was to locate his medical notes. In hope, more than belief, that such records still existed, I rang the Royal Melbourne Hospital,

long since made imperial. The boxes of patient records from
1880 had, indeed, been stored at the hospital and kept in a
backroom. When I arrived at the hospital, I was directed to a
room overfilled with heavy, unopened cardboard boxes. Inside
each box were leather-bound volumes of doctors' admission notes
from the nineteenth century. The boxes were not organised in
any particular manner – I would have to open each one and then
each bound volume of medical notes to find Tom's admission.

For five hours I peered silently into the lives of patients
admitted to the Melbourne Hospital until, without warning,
I found the notes I had travelled 1000 kilometres to discover.
Hasty and to the point, they recorded the essence of Wills'
mind as it unravelled: the telltale hallucinations and delusions
of alcohol withdrawal, recognisable and unchanged across
the century. At 5 p.m. Tom Wills had 'absconded' from the
Melbourne Hospital. The next day he was dead.

This single archival discovery suggested that other discov-
eries might be made, but before I delved further I needed to
know more about my man. This did not take long. Standard texts
on the history of Australian sport painted what was known of
his life. Born in 1835, Wills had been despatched by his father to
England in 1850 to study at Rugby School. His father, Horatio
Wills, was a man of hefty girth and even heftier ambitions for
his son. Tom excelled at Rugby School in sports; returning to
Melbourne in 1856 he became the transcendent cricketer in
the colony of Victoria. A sporting libertine, he was courted by
clubs and colonies throughout Australia. It was a safe bet for
the average punter to wage a shilling on any team captained by
T.W. Wills and, like a medieval prince swinging a cricket bat,
he travelled the country holding court on fields of his choosing.

In 1859 Tom Wills, along with three other men, sat down
in the backroom of a Melbourne pub and penned what has
become the most important and original document in Australian
sporting history. The ten rules they wrote established the basis
of Australian Rules football.

As I recorded what was known of Wills' life, it became clear that there were many gaps in his history. To research these gaps, I sent out one enquiry after another to locate archives in an attempt to unlock the secrets of his life. Letters, photographs and assorted archives were collected from across five countries; items were found in unexpected places. Of all the material I unearthed, nothing was more unexpected than finding Tom's schoolbooks from Rugby School. The mere fact that they had survived for over 150 years without any attempt at preservation was astonishing enough but it was *where* I found them that was most incongruous.

While searching for material on Tom Wills I visited Minerva Creek, a cattle property near Springsure, Central Queensland. The cattle station was run and owned by another Tom Wills, a descendant of the Wills family. The Tom I met lived in a modest bungalow on a property spanning 10,000 acres; nearby stood the original homestead where his mother lived. In the early evening, about 6 p.m., I was led into an old outhouse where I started looking at priceless letters written by Tom Wills 150 years ago. My Queensland host told me that the letters had been stored under the homestead for years. I picked up the letters, sat down on a bench, and spread them out on the vast rough-hewn table under a lamp. My only companions were the large winged insects that spun about the lamp and a seemingly endless supply of beer. I sat for hours on a hot Queensland night, with a can of XXXX at my elbow, reading the letters. To save paper, writers of the period often completed a letter in their normal horizontal script then turned the letter 90 degrees and wrote at right angles on top of the original letter. Some of the letters were torn and dates and phrases were missing at crucial points. Deciphering the letters took time. Not all the letters were in one piece so I moved the pieces, like tectonic plates, trying to find which piece went with which letter. When I looked at my watch it was four o'clock in the morning.

Later that morning Tom took me over to the homestead where his elderly mother lived. The homestead had seen finer days. It was dark inside despite the bursting Queensland sun. Dust covered the furniture and just about everything else I could see. While chatting to Tom's mother I noticed an old bookshelf in a corner, the kind you might see in a second-hand bookshop, draped with a torn curtain. I slowly drew back the curtain to reveal a line of books embalmed by the dust of Central Queensland. A puff of dust dispersed into the air and into my nostrils as I removed one book, *A History of Greece*. Written on the inside cover was:

> T. Wills,
> C. Evans,
> Rugby,
> Warwickshire
> March 14th, 1854

I could hardly believe what I was holding: I had found Tom's schoolbooks from Rugby. The pages of the book were difficult to prise apart and in some places were corrugated and stuck fast by water damage. Managing to free one page I turned it with a hesitant touch, but small flakes of paper, like the sloughing of skin, broke off and fluttered to the table. These textbooks had miraculously survived, connecting two alien worlds separated by 150 years and over 16,000 kilometres. From the black soil plains of outback Queensland I had my first glimpse of Tom Wills as a boy in England on the playing fields of Rugby.

I travelled to Rugby School looking for evidence of Tom's time there and amongst boxes of the boys' letters I came across a diary in which he kept an account of his cricket matches. In 1855, captaining his cricket team, Tom wrote of an incident that told me a great deal about his single-mindedness. Batting, he required ten runs to complete a century. Bent over his bat, Tom waited for the next ball. The bowler approached. The impertinent ball dipped and clipped his bat before it safely skidded into his legs. Or, so at least thought Tom Wills. Mr Soames, the Umpire, thought otherwise – out l.b.w. That evening, when Tom Wills

sat down to write his report of the game, he underscored with
some vigour his assessment of Mr Soames. Everything that
mattered to Tom was frozen in the instant that the ball had hit
his legs, waiting for the umpire's decision. Never mind that,
in the previous few months, the school had been flushed with
scarlet fever – a fourteen-year-old boy lay near death; another
lad had died. No, he never penned his private thoughts on these
matters. Sport occupied each moment of his thinking. He was
an unusual mix – thin-skinned and self-centred, yet generous
to the less gifted in his team. Peculiar was the word for Tom
Wills; just about everyone said so.

As I read his personal letters I could only feel intense
affection for Tom Wills. His thoughts were exhilarating and
infectious; his punning and disregard for the conventions of
sentence structure bordered on the thought-disordered. It was
hard not to love a man whose letters could so gloriously mock
himself and who immortalised Melbourne, in one of his manic
letters: 'Everything is very dull here, but people are kept alive
by people getting shot at in the streets.'

Tactless, he unerringly spoke his mind. A man of egalitarian
cut, Wills always sided with the underdog. A rapscallion for the
ages, he was not beholden to the conventions of the day; his
antics on the field were forgiven – his 'brain snaps' overlooked.
His taste for colonial beer needed no encouragement; alcohol
was a balm for his troubled spirit.

Wills emerged from his Rugby School chrysalis and in 1856, as a
21-year-old, returned home to the harsh Australian sun. Never
did a more beautiful athlete step upon the Melbourne Cricket
Ground. Tom Wills was an exotic intrusion into a dull world.
His life's work was about to begin. On the afternoon I discovered the medical notes that recorded the final hours of the
life of Tom Wills, I felt like I'd unearthed the remains of an
Australian *Titanic*. Here was our great sportsman – an expansive
and uncharted life – led by an unknown hand to a seemingly
inevitable end.

Tom Wills, c. 1857

PART ONE

1835–1862

What a son recalls of his father's love is often unsaid in the life of a man. When Horatio Wills pondered the head of his infant son, he would have considered that its size and shape were of importance. From its contours he indeed expressed optimism. Horatio thought the science of phrenology was worthy of notice, even in the movable bones that curved their way around his baby's head. With these considerations in mind, Horatio poured the lessons from his own life into the grasping hands of his infant son.

THE FAVOURED SON

AUGUST 1835–APRIL 1840

Tom Wills was born on 19 August 1835, on a sheep run on the Molonglo River, 180 miles south-west of Sydney. The first child of Elizabeth and Horatio, Tom lived his first four years on the plains next to the river.

The parents of Tom Wills were descended from convicts. Tom's mother, Elizabeth, was born to Michael Wyre and Jane Wallace, both convicts from Ireland who were transported to the penal colony of New South Wales for seven years. Wyre and Wallace married on 11 April 1815 at St John's Church, Parramatta, 15 miles inland from Sydney. Elizabeth was the middle of their three girls. When Michael Wyre accidentally drowned in 1823, all three girls were admitted to the Female Orphan School, Parramatta. Elizabeth was recorded in the admission register as being six years old and her surname was recorded as McGuire, the name she would keep until she married.

The Female Orphan School was established to civilise the colony of New South Wales. Girls came from all segments of the colony: free settlers, convicts and Aborigines. Looking up from the stone jetty on the Parramatta River, the girls could see a path that led from the river, rising along a hill towards

Elizabeth at the time of her marriage

the front entrance of the three-storey school. Outside the school walls were six acres of gardens in which grew flowers, fruit and vegetables for the girls' pleasure and sustenance. Routine and order marked days at the school. Mornings were devoted to reading, writing and needlework and after lunch to domestic instruction. Each morning and night the girls were mustered for Bible readings and prayer, and on Sundays they were taken by boat to St John's Anglican Church for worship.

At the age of twelve or thirteen most girls were apprenticed out, either into homes in the colony or to work as servants within the school. After five years, Elizabeth and her older sister Catherine were discharged from the school on 23 June 1828 and were apprenticed as servants within the school. Five years later, Elizabeth entered Mrs Jane McGillivray's Boarding School for 'a select and limited number of young Ladies, whose morals, comforts and education shall be attended to with fidelity'. Elizabeth's handwriting book from this year has survived:

Elizabeth McGuire, 15 years old
January 29th 1833

The art of Writing is one of the most necessary acquirements and greatest blessings that mankind can enjoy Ignorance and impudence are generally twins Careless habits retard our improvement generally Do not rashly that which you may repent Humility, that low sweet root, from which all Heavenly virtues shoot Modesty that unfolding ornament, adorned the maid Graceful manners distinguish the well bred Miss McGuire presents her kind compliments to Miss Thomson and requests the favor of Miss T's interesting

company to Tea this evening Indolence saps at the root of
virtue and happiness Let no one know your secret sentiments
be discreet Mildness is the proper characteristic of woman
Those who despise learning are unworthy of it Useful
employment produces happiness Endeavour to acquire a
graceful address Knowledge cannot be prized too highly
Improve the opportunities given you now True Philosophy
is only found in Religion Scorn falsehood as the greatest
meanness Be cautious how you give pain to those who
love you.

From Elizabeth's writing book, 1833

Elizabeth left Mrs McGillivray's and on 2 December 1833 married Horatio Wills, editor of the *Sydney Gazette*, after a courtship of eighteen months. She was, as far as can be reckoned, sixteen years old when she married.

•

Horatio Wills was born in 1811, the son of a convict. Or more correctly, Horatio was the son of a dead convict – five months before Horatio was born his father, Edward Wills, died in the family home on George Street, Sydney. The obituary in the *Sydney Gazette* described Edward as a man of respectability and integrity. But it had not always been so.

Edward Wills had committed robbery on the King's Highway in England and was sentenced 'to be Hanged by the neck until he be Dead'. The sentence was commuted to transportation for life to the colony of New South Wales and he arrived at Botany Bay on 26 July 1799, aboard the *Hillsborough*, with his wife and daughter. Although Edward and Sarah survived the voyage, nearly a hundred convicts did not: typhoid and cruelty saw to that. Edward Wills received a conditional pardon in June 1803 and a full pardon in 1810; soon, he and his wife Sarah were merchants of wealth and standing in Sydney. He died, only thirty-two years old, leaving five children and his wife four months pregnant with Horatio.

Sarah Wills remarried the next year. Her new husband was George Howe, owner, printer and editor of Australia's first newspaper, the *Sydney Gazette*. George died in 1821, followed two years later by Sarah. Horatio's older siblings, in particular the urbane and wise Thomas, cared for and mentored the young boy.

Horatio was apprenticed to George Howe's son, Robert, who had taken over the running of the *Sydney Gazette*. When he was little more than fifteen years old, Horatio ran away from work. Robert Howe immediately advertised in the *Sydney Gazette* to locate him; six months later he was back as an apprentice.

Horatio and his older stepbrother quarrelled repeatedly; it soon came to a head when Horatio, threatened with a whipping, brawled with Robert Howe. Horatio was struck over the eye; 'a severe wound'. Some months later, Horatio again fought with Robert Howe and a warrant was issued for Horatio's arrest. Always there for his younger brother, Thomas Wills arranged for William Charles Wentworth to defend Horatio when the impetuous adolescent returned to Sydney. Wentworth was one of the best-known barristers in the colony; however the magistrate was unmoved by Horatio's stories and ordered him to return to the *Gazette* office as an apprentice with the advice: 'You do not appear to have shown that subordination which an apprentice ought to do.' At sixteen, Horatio's personality was set. He was adventurous, even reckless, and had a temper, and he needed little material comfort to survive in life.

When his stepbrother died the following year, Horatio, released from servitude, continued to work at the *Gazette*, becoming the editor and printer. On the verge of turning twenty-one, Horatio wrote to his brother-in-law, Assistant Surgeon to the Colony, Dr William Redfern. Horatio had met Elizabeth not long before and seemed determined to marry and live a more stable life – a life also with ambition. Redfern replied on 31 October 1832:

My dear Horace,
I had the pleasure of receiving your letter . . . and rejoice to hear that you have sown 'all your wild oats' and that you are determined to become a sensible, steady, clever fellow. To become so only requires resolution. Stick close to your studies and the rest will be sure to follow. If you go on as you promise to do, you will be a credit to yourself, an honor to your relations, and a benefit to mankind. <u>Persevere!</u>

Horatio anguished over his limited formal education and was driven to pursue knowledge to compensate for what he felt he had been deprived of as a young man. It was not just a personal desire for self-learning – he advocated that colonists advanced themselves through science and literature. Before he turned twenty-one, Horatio established his own newspaper, the *Currency Lad*, and sought subscriptions 'to promote the cause of Literature in this Colony' and 'for the purpose of establishing a Public Library'. The library, he said, would be open to all free men, freed convict or free settler. There was to be no division among men. He believed a man should receive rewards in accordance with his abilities and industry. Horatio bristled with anger towards those born overseas who looked down upon native-born Australians, and wrote in the *Currency Lad*: 'Look, Australians, to the high-salaried foreigners around you! Behold those men lolling in their coaches – rioting in the sweat of your brow ... WE WERE NOT MADE FOR SLAVES!' But like many native-born Australians he looked overseas, particularly to England, for advancement in culture and business.

Horatio was well connected in Sydney and seemed to have every reason to remain there, but he and his young wife left to take up a sheep station, Burra Burra, on the Molonglo Plains next to the Molonglo River. Burra Burra rested on a bedrock of limestone and shale; in all directions grey-white outcrops of stone, like roughened shafts of bone, broke through the soil. It was a hard land for a birth. Seventeen months after Tom was born, he was baptised Thomas Wentworth Wills in the Parish of St Andrew's, Sydney. Horatio and Elizabeth named their first-born after Horatio's much-loved and respected brother, Thomas. His second name, Wentworth, was an unmistakable acknowledgement to William Charles Wentworth, the Cambridge-educated barrister who defended Horatio in court against Robert Howe. Wentworth – the son of the colony's chief surgeon and of a convict woman – had the qualities that Horatio valued and desired for his son: he was a statesman, explorer and fighter for the rights of the Australian born.

Life on the Molonglo Plains offered little comfort. In January 1839, soon after one of Elizabeth's several miscarriages,

Tom fell sick – 'poor little Tom was so dangerously ill' that Horatio and Elizabeth 'almost despaired of his recovery'. Tom survived. He had been a precious child before his illness, but now he was even more so. The uncertainty of further children for Horatio and Elizabeth, coupled with Tom's recovery from illness, deepened the bond between mother, father and child. In Horatio's eyes, this son whom providence had let live would have every advantage that Horatio had been denied. Most importantly, Tom would have a father.

In late April 1840, Horatio, Elizabeth and four-year-old Tom left the Molonglo River and overlanded south to Mount William, in the Port Phillip District of New South Wales.

A BOY IN A TENT

APRIL 1840–AUGUST 1850

The Wills family journeyed to Mount William, on the eastern edge of the Grampians mountain range, 140 miles north-west of Melbourne. It was here that Horatio took up land in November 1840.

Horatio settled upon Djab wurrung land, where over forty Aboriginal clans lived, sharing a common language. The main Aboriginal camps were sited on waterways: to the north flowed the Wimmera River and to the south the Hopkins River. Emu and rock wallaby were to be found on the plains and amongst the boulders; and in season the Djab wurrung clans consumed eels by the thousand at the fishing grounds of the Mount William swamp. Beyond the Djab wurrung land to the north and west were the Jardwadjali; to the north-east the Djadja wurrung and to the south the Dhauwurd wurrung. Although the Djab wurrung had an identifying language, much of their vocabulary was shared by these neighbouring clans. Many Europeans had difficulty hearing certain sounds of the Djab wurrung and were unaware of the subtlety of the language. Horatio, however, learnt to speak Djab wurrung and made the movements of his lips and palate mimic the hard and soft sounds. It had been four years since the first Europeans or Ngammadjidj had intruded into Djab wurrung territory.

In 1838 the Colonial Office in London had created 'The Port Phillip Aboriginal Protectorate'. The Protectorate consisted of a chief protector and four assistant protectors to oversee and record interactions between settlers and Aborigines. Chief Protector George Augustus Robinson visited the four districts of the Aboriginal Protectorate regularly, keeping extensive notes, and on several occasions visited the Wills family.

Robinson's diary of the period is a bleak collection of impressions and laments, of Aboriginal word lists and sketches. He recorded how sheep and cattle stomped upon the grass, driving away the kangaroos and denying the Aborigines a source of food. These heavy-footed farm animals damaged swamp vegetation where native women had previously dug for roots and delicate shoots and tubers. He recorded that Europeans had ransacked the Aboriginal fishing weirs and the secret hides the Djab wurrung used so cleverly to snare birds for food. He wrote that the skulls of black men were hung upon hut doors to intimidate natives, that rifles were fired repeatedly to warn and threaten, and that settlers rode horses through native camps to disorient and bully. Poisoning of natives was rumoured but hard to prove. Concealed from magistrates, vice and pleasure were controlled by the conscience of each individual man. Robinson recorded the pain of starving natives, syphilis, filth, death and a godless world of villainous acts by whites.

Robinson wrote words of hate at times in his journal, but never towards his natives. Oversensitive to slights, he was estranged from most of the European settlers he met; they saw the Protectorate as meddlesome and offered Robinson only begrudging assistance as he moved among the natives offering blankets, sugar, flour, fishing hooks and knives. Robinson documented many deaths – both Aboriginal and European. In January 1840 he came across a young Aboriginal man murdered by settlers:

He was lying on the opposite side of the creek. He was a
fine young man, apparently about 22 years of age, well made
and about 6 feet high. His face was of a light hazel brown,
resembling an half caste. His hair was black and resembled
that of the Otahetians. His back was cicatrized, having 2
rows one above the other. The ball had entered his back
and had passed completely through his abdomen. Part of
the intestines were protruding. His tongue was greatly
swollen and quite black, occasioned by his biting it in the
agony of death. His hand was clenched. I turned him over
and viewed him. Two kangaroo teeth, worn as ornaments,
were fastened to his hair. These I cut off and brought away
as a momento of the unfortunate victim.

In 1841, Robinson travelled near the settlement of Portland
where he met Governor Superintendent Charles La Trobe. La
Trobe told him of the recent murder of a settler:

They had received a letter last night of another horrible
murder committed at the Glenelg on a Mr Morton and his
shepherd. Mr Morton was represented as a gentleman, kind
and humane. The blacks it was stated had stretched the man
Larry out on his back and drove spears through the palms of
his hands and, the report says, they had cut the flesh off his
bones when alive and had eaten it and had eaten the flesh of
Morton. Morton was a respectable settler – an Englishman.
The particulars I learnt after I left the Governor.

Robinson first wrote of the Wills family when he was told that
natives had recently attempted to rape (or, in Robinson's words,
'to have connection with') and abduct Mrs Wills. Robinson
rode to Horatio Wills' station: a paddock under construction,
and two huts – one for the men, one for the overseer – and a
tent for the Wills family. Aborigines had murdered a shepherd
in the overseer's hut eight months earlier. It was raining hard
when Robinson arrived and Elizabeth emerged only briefly

from the tent where she and Tom, five years old, were living. Horatio was away. Elizabeth agreed to supply Robinson with some meat for that evening, then returned to the tent leaving Robinson in the rain. He dismounted and sheltered beneath an 'old tarpaulin' before going to see the overseer whom he found to be 'as uncouth as the rest'. Affronted, Robinson left Horatio's property dissatisfied with the level of respect and comfort offered him.

In his diary Robinson wrote that a native youth had told him: 'Thomson, Captain Bunbury, Captain Brigs and Mr Wills shot natives, plenty natives, "all gone too much boo white man".' Robinson continued and gathered further information, writing on 29 July 1841: 'Wills, Kirk and Rutter shot women who had infants and that the latter were left without milk. The attack was made on the camp, as far as I could learn, after Wills' man was killed.' There were other accusations made against Horatio in Robinson's diary:

Coom.ber.nin, F. shot by Wills
Mittecum, M. shot by Wills

Edward Stone Parker, an assistant protector under Robinson, visited Mount William the following year in March 1842, and offered a different view of Horatio Wills. Parker, unlike Robinson, spoke to Horatio: 'Mr Wills speaks well of the natives congregated at his station. They have been with him several months and make themselves very useful.' Parker noted favourably that Wills supplied the natives with food twice a day.

Horatio, in response to the conflict between Europeans and Aborigines, wrote an extraordinary letter to Governor Charles La Trobe in Melbourne. He told the Governor, truthfully, that the settlers had suffered loss of human life and property. And then, with understatement, he came as close as he ever did to admitting that he had killed Aborigines: 'we shall be compelled in self defence to measures that may involve us in unpleasant consequences'. Many men killed Aborigines near

Mount William. Most killed and kept quiet but Horatio felt compelled to hint of his sins of murder.

Robinson passed by again in April 1843. He had not forgotten his inconsiderate treatment two years earlier: '[It] was the second time I had called at that station and there was no person to speak to, that it was strange and to me unaccountable.' Horatio Wills, who was away in Melbourne when Robinson visited, was never again implicated in the murder of Aborigines.

•

Isolation fed Horatio's mind. A compressing volume of nothingness was broken only by his crate of newly consigned books purchased from Europe's bookstores and the occasional presence of the Aboriginal protectors. At the end of 1842, Horatio and his family moved to a new property, Lexington, a few miles north of the Mount William run, and on Christmas Day Elizabeth gave birth to Emily, the first of Tom's siblings. Horatio started a fitful diary that sometimes roared for pages in a single entry and then slept for months. The diary was a lamp that flickered beneath Mount William.

Horatio began this diary for seven-year-old Tom: 'Should the Almighty spare the life of my son, he will doubtless remember the circumstances connected with the first page of this journal.' He lovingly joked with his wife of Tom's amusing behaviour: 'my son Tom when about three years old was in the habit of keeping in his possession a vial, which he occasionally took to his mother, observing "a drop o' beer – long day!" the little guzzler! – mother's prototype!!!'

In his diary Horatio tried to explain the nature of man, laying out the follies of human life before his son. He instructed Tom to study human history and its vainglory and to submit gratefully to divine worship. Horatio uttered each line in his diary with the passion of a sonnet; there was not a timid moment to be had. The family lesson of self-reliance was repeated throughout and, to emphasise the urgency of this point, Horatio underlined each word separately so as not to allow a single word to escape the attention of his son: 'Never leave such things to others, Master Tom, when you can do them yourself.'

The Bible guided Horatio throughout his life and he read passages of the New Testament to Tom. But Horatio struggled to believe all that was written, and consulted authoritative texts to prove to himself its validity. The sins of man and the notion of an afterlife obsessed him: 'I am not at all convinced of the nature of the punishment to be hereafter awarded to sinners.' He fenced with his own scepticism but emerged as a triumphant Christian.

Horatio peered into his heart and looked for points of weakness. Before his eyes, vices small and large swarmed. He tasted his own spit – that foul swish through his mouth – and confessed his guilt. Smoking, he delighted, he had curtailed, for he had only smoked once in the past twenty-four hours but then lamented: 'I cannot altogether correct myself of the profane habit of vulgar swearing.' He examined himself until there was nothing to survey and declared that the heart of man was 'deceitful, above all things and desperately wicked' and rejoiced only on the day of the Sabbath, his day of relief from anguish. Horatio submitted himself to God and implored the world, implored himself and implored his son: 'Read carefully the whole of St John's Gospel . . . On this Gospel I build my life.'

Horatio, seemingly overcome by his exhortations, rested, and then continued to reflect pensively upon his son. Often, matters moved to the education of Tom. Horatio was teaching Tom the value of words and numbers but never forgot his own lack of learning: 'I now deeply vainly deplore my want of a mathematical and classical education. Vain regret! . . . But my son! May he prove worthy of my experience! May I be spared for him – that he may be useful to his country – I never knew a father's care.'

Horatio decided to send Tom to Melbourne to continue his education. Horatio's brother, Thomas, had overlanded from Sydney to Melbourne and was prominent in the finest social circles. Uncle Thomas was sophisticated and generous and enjoyed town life. He donated money to the Melbourne Hospital fund, was part of the organising committee of the Separation movement from New South Wales and his name appeared wherever men of influence gathered. He had lent some of his considerable wealth to Horatio to assist his brother in establishing himself as a squatter. A kind uncle, he could keep an eye on his young nephew Tom. In 1846 Tom entered the school of Mr William Brickwood in Little Flinders Street, Melbourne.

William Brickwood's School was regarded as one of the two best schools in Melbourne. The Oxford-educated Brickwood had a fine reputation and the sons of 'all the gentry' were sent to him. The school, for boys only, took day students and boarders. Boarders were charged 40 guineas per annum. It was one of the few institutions in Melbourne that offered a purely classical education – something which appealed to the classically minded Horatio.

In September 1846, eleven-year-old Tom played in his first cricket match, with two sides chosen from Mr Brickwood's pupils. Tom made a duck in both innings. The game, reported by the *Port Phillip Herald*, was played at Batman's Hill, the ground on which the Melbourne Cricket Club played. Cricket matches at Batman's Hill brought out the finest folk of Melbourne; carriages and ladies ringed the field. William Brickwood was a cricketer of moderate note – an early round-arm bowler when many cricketers simply bowled underarm – and had just been elected vice president of the Melbourne Cricket Club.

Brickwood ran his school in Melbourne for two more years and Tom was one of the thirty-eight boys in his care. On the final day of school in December 1848, the boys assembled for a prize-giving and farewell ceremony to their headmaster. The boys were quizzed in geometry, classics, recitation and arithmetic amongst other subjects, and prizes were awarded.

Lexington

Friends and family of the boys watched. Whether Tom's parents were present is not known but someone from his family most likely watched as the thirteen-year-old stepped forward to accept his second place in history and geography. Brickwood was moving to Brighton, near Melbourne, to join the Anglican clergy and due to his religious duties would not receive 'more than a very limited number of pupils' the following year. Tom was one of the twelve boys who went to Brighton.

Horatio and his family remained at Lexington, Mount William, while Tom was at school. Wool was Horatio's chief interest. He expanded his run of sheep, loading the wool on to drays to be hauled by bullocks to Geelong where William Roope, married to Elizabeth's sister Catherine, managed affairs for the Wills family. Roope measured the wool bales from Lexington, felt the wool's texture, examined its colour and packed it aboard steamers bound for London.

George Augustus Robinson made a final visit to the district surrounding Lexington in May 1847. He recorded seeing the occasional child of a European father and Aboriginal mother.

He also noted that black women worked in Horatio's fields but made a point of writing that he 'did not call' upon the family at Lexington. Robinson found a native boy on Horatio's property, a shepherd, 'some distance from the home station tending two flocks'. Robinson rode towards the boy who came naturally towards him. They talked. Robinson wrote down the boy's name and left Lexington and never returned.

Tom left Reverend Brickwood's school and went home to Lexington at the end of 1849. The Wills family had expanded. After Tom and Emily, there were Cedric, Horace and baby Egbert. His brother Horace remembered years later how Tom as a boy 'was thrown much into the companionship of aborigines, having no boy friends of his own age'. Tom's cousin Colden Harrison also remembered Tom's close relationship with the Aborigines of Mount William: 'My cousin, Tom Wills, at Lexington, was very clever at picking up their songs, which he delivered with a very amusing imitation of their voice and gestures, and could speak their language as fluently as they did themselves, much to their delight.'

Tom was to be sent to Rugby School in the English Midlands. Thomas Arnold had been headmaster of Rugby School until his sudden and unexpected death in 1842, aged forty-six. Arnold's intellect and enterprise had made Rugby the best-known and respected school throughout England. Education and the Church were his spheres of work. Ambitious, driven, earnest – these words were written about Arnold but they might also have been written about Horatio. Arnold sought to create a Christian school; the devil was his foe. Arnold looked for and found the devil's work within schools – drunkenness, falsehood, cruelty and bullying, active disobedience, idleness, the bond of evil. Thomas Arnold spoke of matters close to the heart of Horatio Wills.

There was a further advantage in sending Tom to England: Horatio's older sister, Sarah, could watch over him. Sarah had been married to Dr William Redfern; when Redfern died she married James Alexander, a merchant, and moved to live in London. Sarah was wealthy, loving and religious. She would look after her nephew. Tom could stay at her London home when on holidays from Rugby and be served by maids and ride in the family carriage – he could view London atop the horse and carriage that wealth provided.

Tom left Melbourne for England on 27 February 1850. He travelled alone. The Melbourne newspaper *The Argus*, reported that a 'Master Wells' was one of fifteen passengers aboard *The Lochnagar*, a barque of 300 tons under Captain Joseph Dalgarno. Tom wrote home about the voyage: the stormy nights; Simonstown at the Cape of Good Hope; coffee ground from burned biscuits; Captain Joseph Dalgarno. Dalgarno taught Tom the skills of knot making: to move one's fingers, nimbly; pull over and under; tug and release; to free one's self from the tightest of grips. There were skills for a lifetime to be learnt in knots.

After a voyage of some five months, Tom stared at the mouth of the River Thames cluttered with barges, frigates and merchant vessels: the maritime strength of the world's most powerful nation. The colony of Port Phillip was over 10,000 miles distant. Gravesend was reached; the day was fine; a light westerly blew. Tom arrived in London on 7 August 1850 and immediately wrote to his father.

COCK OF THE SCHOOL

AUGUST 1850–JANUARY 1853

The one great purpose for which boys are sent to Public Schools, is to prepare themselves by study, and the cultivation of their minds, for the duties of after life, for the duties of the learned professions, of the statesman, or of the gentleman.   *The Rugby Magazine*, 1836

The village of Rugby was situated 83 miles north-west of London in the county of Warwickshire, on the River Avon. Its elevated site afforded views of the surrounding countryside. When Tom arrived in 1850, it was a busy market town with just under 7000 inhabitants, with a substantial affluent middle class. Rugby, in the middle of England, was at the centre of a wheel through which all the major railway lines converged, connecting London with the industrial cities of Victorian England. From the Rugby railway station it was a comfortable stroll to the school – up a steady slope, across a bridge over the River Avon and then just beyond the village of Rugby stood the school, as it had since 1567.

In 1850, Tom Burn, a Rugby schoolboy, excitedly wrote home: 'The School seems to be considerably increased there are Shoals of new fellows.' One of those new fish was Tom Wills.

Although Tom commenced his schooling in the second half of 1850, it was in 1851 that he was formally registered into the school by another recent arrival, the Eton-educated Reverend Dr Edward Meyrick Goulburn, the school's new 32-year-old headmaster.

The 'sweet voiced' Goulburn was a conservative man, with the appearance of a watchful owl. A private man, Reverend Goulburn was unlikely to spark enthusiasm in even the fondest of admirers and as for sports, well, he was 'short-sighted, and therefore incapacitated from taking part in cricket and other games'. Conservative in manner, dress and religion, Rugby was unlikely to veer widely off course over the next five years.

The Boarding House of Master Charles Evans at 2 Watergate Street, Rugby, was one of nine houses at Rugby School. It would be Tom's home for the next five years. Charles Evans was in his late twenties and soon to be ordained as a minister. Well thought of by his peers and students, Charles Evans was a warm and generous teacher. One of Tom's schoolmates wrote: 'Evans is very jolly to me indeed on the whole, he is very strict indeed about being late and not knowing your lesson but as yet I have not incurred his displeasure.' The teachers at Rugby – all males – captured in the school photographs of the day were stiff and erect, rendering to perfection an image of the deepest solemnity.

Charles Evans, his younger sister Martha and seven servants managed the house and nearly fifty boys, ranging in age from eleven to eighteen. Tom was the only Australian boy in the house. Most boys were English, but there was a tincture of exotica – American, West Indian and now Australian. Evans, as was common among masters of the school, frequently invited small groups of boys to his rooms for supper, where they drank wine and sherry with their teacher. Charades, singing, parlour games and lengthy chats about school and life were all part of the evening's entertainment.

'*The School from The Close*'

The daily routine of the house was rigid. Boys were up at 6.15 in the morning and down to prayers at 7 a.m. Their first lesson, taken at a most unforgiving hour when minds were still thawing, finished at 8 a.m. Then it was breakfast, followed by a second lesson.

From Evans House Tom stepped directly on to Watergate Street, the main thoroughfare to and from school, several hundred yards distant. It was a broad street and, though rarely congested, a steady flow of schoolboys, teachers and 'townies' plied their way past one another and the flys, and other horse-drawn carriages that trotted alongside. Large elm trees with massive trunks and heavy boughs of emerald foliage offered the boys relief from the summer heat.

Small laneways trickled away from Watergate Street threading between private dwellings, inns and other Boarding Houses. Along one of these lanes lived Thomas and Hannah Townsend – 'Beerkeepers'. It was Mrs Townsend, with her four young offspring racing about her apron, who had most dealings with the Rugby schoolboys. Mrs Townsend boasted that her carefully brewed beer, when raised against the light, was notable for its clarity; more than a bit boiled and with a little added salt, it was not a breeding pond for cholera.

The Rugby School uniform was a peaked cap, a white shirt with a high stiff butterfly collar and ribbon knotted in a bow tie, a stylish winged dark coat and long striped pants. Most schoolboys were clean-shaven, but occasionally an older boy wore a moustache or beard. Walking to and from the school, it was easy to recognise the different personalities of boys by their deportment and manner. The 'swells or cocks' swaggered in the knowledge of having attained a universally admired position within the school. The most privileged was to be a member of the school cricket XI. Sometimes a thin elegant line of smoke could be seen rising above these boys, emanating from a short-stemmed clay pipe – the most popular smoking piece at school. The boys wrote of their affection for stubby brown clay pipes, which they nursed carefully within satin-lined cases, safely concealed in the breast pocket of their coats. This addiction was considered indispensable to the sporting boy or 'swell' and the stale aroma of tobacco that impregnated their clothing immediately identified them.

At the centre of the school was a slender clock tower with a domed roof. Extending from the tower on both sides, like the sweep of two large arms, was the main building: an imposing cream-stone facade, crested with a parapet, giving it the appearance of a fortress. To the left was the school chapel, standing in solitude and gloomily keeping watch over the green fields. It would be several years before the chapel underwent radical changes under the hand of the architect William Butterfield, and well before Butterfield travelled to Melbourne to redesign that city's St Paul's Cathedral.

It was late in the cricket season when Tom Wills picked up a cricket ball on the playing fields of Rugby, in his first week at school. When he did so and squeezed the hardness of the ball, this act impressed itself upon his mind and nearly twenty years later he could still recall the moment. At first he bowled underhand, with the sweeping action one might have used in lawn bowls, which was the popular style in Australia. But the fashion in Melbourne was unfashionable in England and it marked him as a backward colonial; he 'was told that style would not do for Rugby'. He adopted the latest style of bowling – a sweeping round-arm action in which his arm swung laterally and was never raised above the height of his shoulder. With his first delivery, using this new style of bowling, he hit the wicket and dismissed the batsman, and with the conviction of a religious convert Tom Wills declared: 'I felt I was a bowler.'

Each boy in Evans House was allocated a study. It was a refuge where the delicacies from home could be unwrapped at leisure, away from the prying eyes of boys who thought nought of intruding upon younger boys to bully and steal treats from home, and then scamper away, crowing of their conquests. Charles Kemp, a boy in Evans House alongside Tom Wills, wrote to his sister that he thwarted the bullies of the house who aimed to pry open his door, by attaching a powerful spring to the door hinge. George Melly, a former student, wrote in detail of his experiences of fagging at Rugby School in *School Experiences of a Fag*. Fagging was well known and an accepted system. Junior boys were prevailed upon to do menial tasks, typically gathering food or beer, for the more senior boys, and for some, life at Rugby could be miserable. George Melly wrote: 'In some [dormitories], floggings, smotherings, tossing in blankets, and every description of disgusting bullying, were of nightly occurrence.' There was fagging within the house and also out on the sports field. Tom supported fagging; several years later he commented in a letter: 'it is the good old system of fagging at public schools that makes numbers of gentlemen who are now at the top of the tree, what they are'.

A boy's study was typically cramped and the ceiling low slung. In it fitted snugly a chair, desk, bookshelf and a thermometer to monitor ambient temperature. The assorted quackery cures of the day lined the cupboard. A cricket bat might settle unobtrusively in a corner of a study, standing alongside a freshly greased cricket ball. A cricket ball could be purchased for seven shillings and sixpence, and grease applied to it to maintain its shelf life. Tom's study, though, was distinctive. He surrounded himself with objects that gave him comfort and connection to his settler's life in Victoria. His letters brimmed with requests for reminders of his home near the Grampians to be sent to him at Rugby to soften the loneliness of his first years in England. Letters, sketches, rocks, native birds from Lexington were all packed into his tiny study. When he wrote to his father and asked that the Djab wurrung 'native weapons' of war be posted to him, Horatio affectionately recorded in his diary that he had collected these weapons in readiness to send to Tom. But the most unusual and absurd idea was to transport two live black swans to Rugby. And, duly, two black swans, with elegantly curved necks poised in the shape of a question mark, were despatched from Melbourne for Tom's amusement. Both died in transit.

Rugby was divided into a Higher, a Middle and a Lower School. Progression from the Lower School through to the Upper School was based on academic performance and not on the age of the student. Tom entered the Lower School; Charles Evans was his private tutor. Boys fretted about their academic placement and progress. Nervous comments about the personality and fairness of their masters littered the boys' private letters and all, including Tom, strove to please their parents. He gushed to his father on 24 December 1850, just six months into school: 'the master says that if I improve as I have done during the last half, I will be one of the top boys'.

One hundred and fifty years on, scant clues remain of Tom's time in the classroom. The most evocative to survive are his personal textbooks – *A History of Greece*, *Histoire de la Revolution Française* and *Grecæ Grammaticæ Rudimenta*. The first – *A*

History of Greece – is crammed with Tom's scribbles: comments on the text under study or dates of lessons; teasing glimpses of half-completed messages of plans to meet persons unknown, at a certain time and place – a rendezvous. At the back of the book is a sketch in lead pencil, tucked away from inquisitive teachers' eyes, not much bigger than a postage stamp. Tom had sketched the head of a fellow boy at Rugby named Boyd. Tom wrote about him as one of the boys he played alongside in the Evans House cricket XI. William Boyd, the eldest son of a reverend, was headed for a career as an 'Iron Master' in industrial Newcastle, but Tom valued him as the cricket team's best longstop when playing against Arnold House.

Another book – on the rudiments of Greek grammar – is filled with the doodles of an uninterested adolescent. Circles and tracery ring words and sentences; the deep-brown ink of his scribble leaves an indelible trail of his drifting mind. Like schoolboys before and since, he wrote and rewrote his name in a variety of ways – some scrawled, others bold and self-important. Writing his name, it seems, was his favourite occupation.

•

For someone who controlled the interests of his son so keenly, Horatio made little contact in that first year of Tom's life at Rugby. In June 1851, Tom wrote home and ventured a complaint to his father: 'I have only received one letter from you since I have been in England.' Tom's first blush of homesickness slowly graduated into a deep loneliness over the next year and in his despondency brought together his thoughts on the strangeness of this new land that now absorbed his time. His senses became attuned to a darker light, softer vegetation and a continual dampness underfoot. Tom experienced the crisp snap of breaking ice as he walked across the Close to school and saw his first fall of snow layer the fields of Rugby. He joked, a little unconvincingly and with boyish naivety, of the wonders of a Christmas day in winter. He asked a friend from home, Luke Wilmont – who, like so many others in Tom's story, appears briefly and then disappears – to write and that 'it does me good [to] hear from any old friend'. At Lexington, the family gathered: Horatio, Elizabeth, their children Emily, Cedric and Horace. They were joined by Tom's cousin Colden Harrison. The boys and girls played and Horatio measured all their heights. The youngest boy, Horace, was just over the 3 feet mark. Emily was 4 feet ½ an inch and Colden, who was fourteen years old, reached just over 5 feet. Horatio was the tallest at 5 feet 7 inches.

Tom comforted himself by smuggling into a secluded corner of his mind the memories of Mount William and in his silent monologues recreated images of his family at home. His mother Elizabeth bustled with life while she plucked strawberries, while Cedric, barely seven years old, shot cockatoos on the property. Lonely and isolated, Tom asked his parents to write every detail, trivial or otherwise, about his family, then recorded, without bitterness, that he waited every day, expecting a second letter from his father and mother. Why no further letter had been received is unclear, for there is no suggestion that his parents were anything but loving and supportive towards their son.

In late June 1851, Tom returned to London to stay with his Aunt Sarah and Uncle James for nearly two months on summer vacation. His aunt and uncle took him to see the great sights of London: he was amused by Windsor Castle and attended the Great Exhibition at the Crystal Palace in Hyde Park so many times that he was 'quite tired of it'. Everything in London was magnified, and, being a boy prone to exaggeration, he could hardly contain himself, declaring to his Papa: 'The strawberries here are some of them as large as my fist . . .'

Unchained from parental expectation, he was cheeky to a fault. Impudent charm and adolescent provocation marked his letters, as well as glimpses of a budding sexuality and an interest in the female form, but he was prudent enough in these letters to not overplay his hand. Savouring his freedom during school holidays in London, he gave the first indication

that school work was not for him: 'My Aunt says to one Tom,
I hope you intend to work hard this half as if I have not been
working hard enough to please a saint, one thing I know is that
it does not please my health, I have been ill oftener the last
4 or 5 months than I have been for the last 6 or 7 years.' The
mere thought of being imprisoned in a classroom made him
glum. That high, stiff collar of the Rugby uniform had become
constricting on Tom. Just two months before his sixteenth
birthday, Tom was standing tall at 5 feet 8 inches – taller than
Horatio – and tipping the scales at 9¼ stone.

While Tom was enjoying London, Horatio and his family
moved into a new homestead on Lexington. Horatio surrounded
himself with mathematical instruments, books from European
bookshops, a French dictionary, texts on English grammar and
on geography, maps on his mantelpiece and the *Encyclopedia
Britannica*.

At the end of his summer vacation, and one day before his
sixteenth birthday, Tom penned a letter to Horatio that reflected
the divisions in Tom's mind. The first half of the letter was all
about duty to his father. Under instruction from his pious uncle,
with whom Tom had just attended the local Scots Church in
Bayswater, London, he scribbled in detail the sermon of the
day – The Gospel of St Luke, Chapter 18 – knowing that this
would please Horatio. At the end of this labour he reached what
truly pleased him: 'I am going to give you my cricket score of
runs and how many I have put out during the last six months as
I have a book with all my matches in.' The attention to detail
was assiduous. Line after line, Tom's writing analysed every
conceivable aspect of the games. How many times out; how he
was given out; his bowling figures – and all sprinkled with an
occasional wry aside. Boastful, proud and factual it marked a
style that would become familiar to a wider audience. In that
six-month period until August 1851, he scored 839 runs – more
than five times that of his nearest rival at Rugby.

Uncle James and Aunt Sarah in London maintained a watchful, if sometimes anxious, eye on their nephew at Rugby. When they could, they slipped into their letters the odd note from Tom's teachers: 'Mr Bloxam writes me in the highest terms of his [Tom's] attention and says he will shine in French and Arithmetic . . . he is deficient in Latin translation, and in consequence of this [he receives extra] a lesson in Latin, and English reading twice a week, and another lesson three times a week in Geography and writing.' Charles Evans, his private tutor and housemaster, penned a monthly report, which his uncle described to Horatio as 'gratifying to you'. In early 1852 his uncle wrote again that Tom 'returned to Rugby to-day in good health and spirits and quite ready for hard study'. It seems, though, that little of this family ambition penetrated Tom. His response was forthright: 'I know that if I work too hard that I will become quite ill. We hardly get any play during school time.' It was a statement Tom knew was nonsense. Playing games increasingly came to dominate everything he did at Rugby. Indeed, it is hard to imagine that he had time for anything else.

Towards the end of 1852, the annual athletics carnival at Rugby was held; the miserable winter weather saw the boys running in bare feet and shoes without spikes before a large crowd of spectators which was 'graced by a large assemblage of ladies who occupied the pavilion'. Tom kept a programme of the athletics events and carefully noted his performances in each event on the card before sending it home. Tom's name appears in most events: including the first, the 100-yards flat race, the best kick of a football and the longest throw of a cricket ball. About the 200 yards over twelve hurdles he wrote to his parents: 'We ran in four's or fives first and then all winners of each race went in for the prize.' Each detail in sport was important to Tom: how a game was conducted, its rules, its history and its winning. To beat Tom Wills was something a boy could write home about. David Hanbury, two years older than Tom, wrote to his parents of this day: 'The last race of all was the mile race ... five of us started, Owen, Wills, Fairbairn, Warneford and myself. We had to run rather more than seven times round a course of about 250 yards. Owen took the lead which he kept for the first two rounds, but on Owen getting the stitch I managed to be first in the fifth round and eventually won by about 20 yards ... I was perfectly thunderstruck as no one ever dreamt of my beating Wills or Fairbairn for a mile.'

During the winter of 1852 the grounds at Rugby were stripped back, returfed and levelled under the guidance of John Lillywhite, the English professional cricketer and coach of the Rugby School XI. Lillywhite was a distinguished player and teacher of the game, from the cricketing clan of Lillywhites who reached into all corners of English cricket over generations. Tom recalled his influence on many occasions. The imprint of John Lillywhite and Rugby School was stamped upon Tom until the day he died.

•

The cricket pavilion (Green Pavilion), built around the time of Tom's arrival at Rugby, still retains clues of Tom's presence. In the 1850s it was painted a deep green and set within a grove of tall elms. From the pavilion the cricketers looked directly onto the centre of Big-side, Rugby School's largest playing field. The match could be watched from the spacious front verandah while languishing on wooden chairs, or from within, through glass windows or wooden shutters. Sadly, for much of the late-twentieth century, the pavilion was neglected and left derelict. Its entrance had long been nailed over with boards; more like a dilapidated nineteenth-century cubby house than a cricket pavilion.

On entering this crumbling wooden hideaway today you leave behind the radiant sunshine of the present and enter the world of the schoolboy of the 1850s. The air is still and the smell of damp wood and rotting floorboards fills the mind and irritates the eyes. Little is visible in the gloom. The derelict

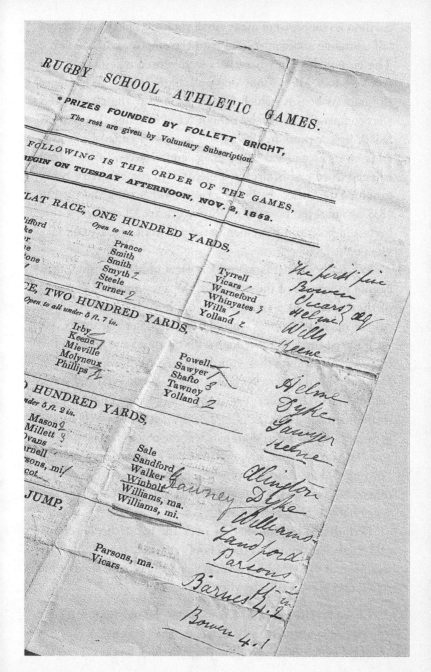

RUGBY SCHOOL ATHLETIC GAMES.

*PRIZES FOUNDED BY FOLLETT BRIGHT,

The rest are given by Voluntary Subscription.

FOLLOWING IS THE ORDER OF THE GAMES,

BEGIN ON TUESDAY AFTERNOON, NOV. 2, 1852.

LAT RACE, ONE HUNDRED YARDS,

Open to all.

Gifford
ke
r
one

Prance
Smith
Smith
Smyth 2
Steele
Turner 2

Tyrrell
Vicars
Warneford
Whinyates 3
Wills 1
Yolland 2

The first five
Bowen
Vicars
Helme
Wills
Keene

CE, TWO HUNDRED YARDS,

Open to all under 5 ft. 7 in.

Irby
Keene
Mieville
Molyneux
Phillips

Powell
Sawyer
Shafto 3
Tawney
Yolland 2

Helme
Dyke
Sawyer
Helme

HUNDRED YARDS,

under 5 ft. 2 in.

Mason 2
Millett 3
Ovans
arnell
sons, mi
cot

Sale
Sandford
Walker
Winbolt
Williams, ma.
Williams, mi.

Tawney

Alington
Dyke
Williams
Sandford
Parsons

JUMP,

Parsons, ma.
Vicars

Barnes 4.2

Bowen 4.1

pavilion is composed of many small rooms: a pokey jumble that fall upon one another, stuffed with the emptiness of 150 years. The cramped room where bats were stored measures only 4 feet by 6 feet. Hung along one wall, higher than eye level, are the honour boards, which list for each year the eleven boys who comprised the Rugby School XI. The name 'Wills', now faded, first appears in 1852. Each name is a rung of a ladder, and players ascend according to age and prowess. In 1853 Tom is listed third and is already a member of the executive being groomed for Office. In 1854 he rises another rung and then in 1855 assumes the position of Rugby cricket XI captain; a title he would hold and be remembered for until his last obituary was penned.

While these boards record the facts of his ascension, they cannot inform us of the struggles, the envy and the conquests of those years. As a sixteen-year-old boy, Tom was one of a pair of opening bowlers who obliterated opposing teams. He intimidated and cowed batsmen with his speed and bounce. But there were murmurs that Tom Wills and his bowling partner, Harman, threw the cricket ball rather than bowled it and at the end of the 1852 cricket season those suspicions found a voice in the national paper, *Bell's Life in London*. Rugby School was accused of achieving its dominance at the cost of fair play. Wills and Harman were publicly singled out as using an illegal style of bowling: 'Their collective bowling is much better than . . . the others; but (whisper) it is not fair: both the Rugby bowlers this year ought to have been called.'

Humiliated by this shadow over the name of the school, Old Rugbeians rallied to the school's defence. John Lillywhite was pressed to defend his protégés and the school, staking his reputation upon Wills' bowling style:

I have received several letters from the old Rugbaeans respecting a remark made by your correspondent 'Wicket' of the unfair bowling of the Rugby School bowlers. I can only say that the bowling of Messrs Harman and Wills, *the* bowlers, was perfectly fair, or the umpires at Lord's would have 'no balled' them; and, moreover, several gentlemen who stood umpires in matches last season at Rugby did not in any way broach the subject. I am professionally engaged by the school, and if gentlemen were less personal in their remarks, especially when they are ignorant of what they are writing about, they would do less injury to us cricketers. Trusting you will find a corner for this, I remain, Mr Editor, yours etc Princes-terrace, Caledonian – road, Islington, Jan 12, 1853. John Lillywhite.

Tom's mind swelled at a rapid pace and was congested with the sporting facts and figures of his craft. Detailed appraisals of himself, the state of the ground, players to watch – all of which brought immense joy to his heart – were savoured and transcribed, undiluted, onto the written page for Horatio.

Tom received a reminder of a distant life in a letter from his father, who wrote affectionately of a young Aboriginal boy from Mount William who had just visited the family. Before the 'black boy' returned home to Mount William, the boy approached Tom's mother and asked what had become of Tom:

Where Tom? Tom no quambie [come] here: when quambie Tom?' evidently much surprised at not meeting you he continued 'You show me Tom' – meaning the daguerotype likeness – He gazed upon it a long time – The old blacks, your friends, were fond of seeing it. They told me to send you up to them as soon as you came back.

The worlds inhabited by the favoured son and his father could not have been more different. As Tom played his first game at Lord's Cricket Ground, Horatio and his young family, having recently left their Lexington homestead, were living in tents pitched in the Geelong mud. Horatio was building a new house, Belle Vue, near Geelong. While Horatio shovelled the

mud from around his tent, his son's name was on everyone's
lips in England. The seventeen-year-old Australian, bowling
like a professional and batting like a gentleman amateur, had
just made Rugby School the most watched team in England.

The Governor, the title Rugby boys gave their fathers,
had invested a great deal in Tom. Expectations were high. For
Horatio, discipline, duty and responsibility guided one's life – to
suffer and triumph was the making of the man. Tom, for his
part, saw little virtue in suffering.

THE GOVERNOR'S DISPLEASURE

OCTOBER 1853–NOVEMBER 1854

Tom was late. Five or six minutes earlier the runners from his house had set off in pursuit of the two 'hares' along Barby Hill Road, just outside the school. By 29 October 1853, it was well into the season of 'Hare and Hounds', the name for cross-country running at Rugby School. On that particular soggy October day, Tom had been 'detained by French lessons' and missed the start of the Barby Hill run, but with lofty ease he soon caught and passed his fellow runners as they ascended Barby Hill. The boys in his house admired Tom as he ran 'beautifully all the way'.

Two of the faster runners in Evans House – Porter and Lomax – were the hares. The two boys carried on their run a long tubular canvas bag into which they stuffed shredded paper. With these bags strapped to their backs, Porter and Lomax set their watches, taking careful note of their starting time, and commenced the cross-country run from the Evans House gate. They turned onto Barby Road, up Barby Hill and then across the Rugby countryside, every so often plunging their arms deep into their canvas bags and sprinkling a little shredded paper over the ground to leave a trail.

The rest of the boys in Evans House were the 'hounds'. Nine boys ran as the hounds; one of whom, Tom, was still buried in his French class. The hounds were blind to the direction taken by the hares. After a number of minutes, the hounds set their watches and pursued the hares, following the trail of scattered paper. The object of the race was for the hounds to run the course quicker, if possible, than the hares. In 1853 eighteen-year-old Tom was the swiftest athlete in the school.

Running across the fields of Rugby was not easy, and the weather rarely kind. Rain was common and the lanes around the school – wet corridors lined by elms – dripped with water and were heavy underfoot. Not all the boys in the house started as hounds, some did not run at all. Wet weather was a strong deterrent and Headmaster Goulburn put limits on running in the wet, particularly on the younger boys who were watched carefully so as not to over-exert themselves. There were also competing events that took boys away from running; for Tom it was sometimes a cricket match, for others it might be a passing show or circus in town. So it was a variable mixture and number of boys who started the run; many of whom were blessed with more good intentions than speed.

The attrition rate was high: recently ploughed fields stopped boys in their tracks as their running shoes were sucked into the bog. Thick hedges that partitioned farms acted as human filters, and boys, entangled in their thorny branches, gave up and lay strewn on the ground. Clothes were ripped and tender skin was lacerated in pursuit of the hares. Enraged farmers sometimes stopped and apprehended boys, and in at least one of the runs a firearm was discharged in the general direction of the boys. Irate farmers fronted local magistrates with boys dangling in tow when the boys trespassed on their land.

The boys in Evans House recorded every 'Hare and Hounds' run and Tom's performance was a focus of their thoughts. When Tom took a wrong turn it was noted in the house report; when he made a mistake the others were likely to follow. Some days he ran beautifully, erect and rapid; other days, even he became bogged in the fields, was indecisive or misled by the cunning of the hares, making the wrong call for the boys following. Tom did not write about his cross-country running even though he figured prominently in the thoughts of the boys around him, and we can only guess at how these runs shaped his character. The runs almost certainly cultivated attributes that were to serve Tom well: fortitude, endurance and competitiveness.

As the boys neared the end of the Barby Hill course they ran along the footpath to 'Captain Hibbert's Park and along his drive to the Lodge Gate, near the Cock and Robin'. Despite being detained by a French class, Tom, at the pinnacle of his running abilities, was the second hound in. He had run the distance in forty-five minutes flat, quicker than any of the other hounds, and five and a half minutes faster than the hares. The boys ended the run at the Cock and Robin Inn on Dunchurch Road, where bread, cheese and jugs of beer awaited them.

There was a good reason for the boys to drink beer. In the year before Tom arrived at Rugby, the previous headmaster – Archibald Campbell Tait – noted an acrid aroma wafting in with the breeze through his office window. It was the smell of an open sewer that met and irritated Tait's nostrils. The village of Rugby had poor drainage and a foul water supply. That it had a notoriously high infant and adult mortality was no coincidence: 'The accumulated filth from the cesspools and ditches drained into the gravel bed of the town, and entered the water supply which was via wells and springs.' The town's water supply bred the bacteria that every now and then burst into epidemics of illness and crops of fatalities. When Tom Wills arrived at Rugby, the town was choking on its own filth.

The Rugby School boys had to decide what to drink to quench their thirst. To drink water or to drink beer? The boys sneered at the putrid house brew that washed down the chunks of salted beef that landed with a dull thud on their plates at dinnertime: 'the beer was such a very odd substance, you could only drink it if you were very thirsty, and swallowed it down without tasting it much'. Water might lead to illness and sometimes death; alcohol might lead to headache and drunkenness. One of Tom's school companions, Tom Burn, in his first week at Rugby, summed up his dilemma:

> I drank beer at dinner yesterday and in the Evening I had a headache, today I drank water and am now quite well – so I think that I have given beer a fair trial and must be content to drink water.

Rugby School, like other English Public Schools, brewed its own beer. 'Bottling the swipes' was the schoolboy name for bottling your brewed beer, and boys skilled in this craft were commended in verse and prose. Beer preoccupied their adolescent minds: its aroma, its hue, its subtle and intoxicating changes wrought upon the mind. The sporting rituals of football and cricket in particular were celebrated with beer. Such revelry and boisterous singing, though under some guidance from house staff, was accepted and seemingly plentiful.

House rules, both formal and informal, provided limits to alcohol use. Drunkenness, as distinct from drinking alcohol, was not sanctioned and could lead to expulsion from the school. Charles Kemp, who shared his time with Tom in Evans House, wrote to his mother:

> I regret to inform you of a most disgusting case of drunkenness that happened in our house yesterday. I chanced to be a witness of the awful spectacle; & I don't think I shall easily forget it. Goulburn came up to the house last night & has decreed that both the offenders shall leave on Tuesday, & I hope & trust it will be carried out.

•

From about this time Tom kept a diary of his cricket matches. A careful thinker about cricket, he spent time on these pages, though his handwriting was – as his batting – neglectful of style and indifferent to appearance. The diary opens with: 'The score was lost but Hanbury made his usual score of 10 !!!!!!!!!!!!!!' The same David Hanbury who had defeated Tom in a mile race in the school's annual athletics carnival. And just for emphasis, Tom, with characteristic flourish, added fourteen exclamation marks. Each match, laid out with detailed scores and commentary, was capriciously signed with a signature that wafted between T. Wills, T.W. and T.W. Wills.

Tom's sharp eye examined each component of a cricketer's play: where it needed redesign; when it worked well. He was generous but not over-generous when it came to dissecting himself, revealing an awareness of his burgeoning talents. He decided quickly, definitely, without reflection or supposition; nor did he consider another player's perspective: just his own unyielding view. His confidence in the correctness of his view, although narrow and obstinate, is seductive – the sort of boy you would like to have as captain of your team. And when Tom was wrong, played poorly or was bettered in a contest, at least in these private notes, he admitted as much. In his letters to his parents and later in life, Tom stretched stories to fit his desires. But here there was no stretching or reshaping.

Tom bowled fast and slow, he batted and kept wickets, and in the field his favourite spot of slip was his whenever he wished. Tom was stubborn and quarrelled with opponents when he felt he or his team were cheated. For Tom matches were won, or should have been won, even when they were lost, and he appreciated when and how the rules could be bent and shaped to win games. Not that he ever deliberately cheated – there was no suggestion of that. His standards were high and his frustration with others evident, but no more evident than his warmth and generosity to boys whom he sensed were not gifted cricketers, but nonetheless fought well. He emboldened the less gifted with his optimism and the genesis of an inspiring captain was clear in his words and actions.

These diary notes allowed Tom the privacy of an inner world to fantasise about what he might become, where adolescent thoughts were omnipotent and heroism a daily act. Tom cast himself as the great English cricket heroes of the day – such as William Clarke, the Nottingham underarm slow bowler. One of Tom's fellow students wrote: 'both [batsmen] soon succumbed to the bowling of Wills, who had put on slows, *a la Clarke*'. It was the sort of touch Tom liked. Bookwork was further than ever from Tom's mind.

Academic advancement in the Lower School relied on repetition and perseverance. Boys were 'called up' in class to recite lines or translate pieces of classical literature and ranked by performance. Some boys moved awkwardly through the vulgus, sticking every now and then with little idea as to which path to follow, and like an archbishop picking his way through a field of virgins, each step was a potential calamity. Wretched lines were the barometer of a boy's life. Tom Burn wrote to his sister: 'It only wants a week now to the beginning of the <u>Examinations so I am hard at work</u>, and have just been learning off <u>by heart 100 lines of Virgil</u>.' Andrew Johnston, a future Member of Parliament, reassured his mother: 'I have given up all thoughts of any play' and 'I have been stuffed up to the eyes in Roman history already'. In 1853 Tom sent home to his parents a monthly academic report that listed fourteen boys. The marks for all subjects were tallied and Tom topped this list. This looked impressive but the truth was that Tom was still puddling about in the Lower School – at eighteen, he was four years older than several of the boys on this report card.

By 1853 Tom had been a student at Rugby for three years but had moved up only a single form. A member of the School XI and a champion athlete, his sporting accomplishments were considerable, but his father's displeasure at his son's lack of academic advancement was clear. Tom was an easy target becalmed in the Remove, a lowly form in the Lower School. Exasperated and with the concentrated anger of someone who feels swindled, his father wrote:

MONTHLY REPORT.

The First Column contains the Names of the Boys and the Order in which they stand in their Class. The last Column shows the number of Marks total gained by each boy during the past Month, in Lessons, Exercises, &c., according to which they keep their places for the ensuing Month.

Names	Lessons, History, Geography, Euclid, Trigonometry & Scripture History.	Exercises and Verses.	Repetition.	Arithmetic.	Tables and Writing.	French.	French Pronunciation.	Marks Total.
1 Mills	880	162	880	770	195	408	170	3265
2 Phillips	681	273	610	680	200	341	190	2975
3 Dangerfield	631	144	420	385	145	236	160	2121
4 Hutton	694	182	235	525	140	210	125	2117
5 Wrigley	622	198	300	385	115	289	145	2055
6 Corbet	617	137	155	500	85	268	150	1912
7 Ireland	558	167	44	415	165	390	180	1909
8 Hatchell	575	128	265	455	70	231	135	1649
9 Prinsep	592	210	185	240	80	139	180	1626
10 Troup	551	93	80	295	95	225	130	1469
11 Molesworth	537	108	230	300	35	168	90	1468
12 Alston	509	176	165	210	50	140	80	1420
13 Hughes	556	104	434	0	0	232	80	1406
14 H. Jones	531	52	210	205	55	136	100	1289

You still however continue to write with a scrawl that would make a writing master eat his nails, and there are occasional errors in spelling and in the gramatical [sic] construction of your sentences at which I am much surprised. If you cannot write correctly now I am afraid you never will, and if you should after all my trouble turn out a dunce! You should at 18, with all the means at your disposal, be able to write in

English correctly and well – to write & talk French, and have a pretty fair knowledge of Latin – you must strive to accomplish this as soon as possible for you must shortly commence your studies for a profession. The law is the most honourable – the merchant also has a fair time of it. If you have brains take the law. Come out here 5 or 6 years hence a barrister. Remember that everything you do is for yourself, and if you do not succeed in life and obtain the reputation of a clever gentlemanly fellow, no one will be to blame but yourself.

[5]

GENIUS

NOVEMBER 1854–DECEMBER 1856

In early November 1854, Tom walked onto the football field at Rugby. He was one of ninety schoolboys lined up on one side of the field to play fifty Old Rugbeians in the annual football match between students and old boys. The reporter for *Bell's Life in London* noted of this contest: 'Wills, to the admiration of the spectators' rose above the swarm of boys and 'displayed an eel-like agility which baffled all the efforts of his opponents to retain him in their grasp'.

Rugby School played its own style of football. The game had evolved over several decades, and was played under rules devised by the boys. Several other prestigious schools, like Eton and Harrow, had their football games acknowledged in the press, and then barely more than an obscurely placed paragraph; in a game that might involve hundreds of boys, individuals were rarely named. Tom was an exception. He could exaggerate and extend the moment on the field of play, and drew eyes to himself through his skill and byplay. *Bell's Life in London*, December 1854:

'Football at Rugby'. A novel match was played on Monday, the 20th ult, between the Debaters and the School . . . On the School side the play of Wills was excellent, he quite

43

dodged the other side by his *slimy* tricks, which drew applause from the many spectators.

Football began in autumn and ended in winter. It was played on the field that stood beneath the Headmaster's Tower, separated from the school buildings by an unbroken line of elms. In winter, the night frost on the football field thawed slowly in the morning, revealing the grass well after the school clock had struck noon. When Tom arrived at Rugby a regular football competition had started amongst the House XX teams. Tom wore the Evans House football uniform: a peaked orange velvet cap and a jersey of orange and white horizontal stripes. The long-sleeved jersey, buttoned to the neck, tucked neatly into a pair of white flannel pants that narrowed at the ankles, continuing that sleek line to a pointed pair of high-heeled black boots. Formidable weapons indeed.

Players assembled like two lines of toy soldiers at the start of each football game. One team stood to the left of the midline

'Football at Rugby'

and the other to the right. A small cavity was dug into the Rugby earth at the mid-point of the field and into it was lodged the ball, steadied by a fingertip. The ball was a curious shape, neither sphere nor oval, but somewhere inbetween. Heavier than a modern ball, it was stitched at the seams with thick lace, the loose ends of which dangled freely. The team to kick off selected their finest kicker. From his boot, the ball shot into the sky until it reached its full height, and then fell towards the field into the arms of an opposition player. Depending on the number of players, several hundred boys might rush the catcher; the game was on.

Players swarmed across the field like bull ants whose mound has been prodded by the inconsiderate and inquisitive, sweeping the ball forward by fair means or foul. During a game, the tightly pressed bodies and furious whirring of legs concealed dirty tricks and retaliations. It took little with those formidable black boots to strip a flap of skin from another boy's shin just as cleanly as a carpenter's plane might on an unsuspecting length of wood. Grunts and shrieks were easily muffled by the noise of two hundred bodies groaning as one. The boys suggest they were nonchalant about their injuries, but snapped bones and boys being nursed either in their house or the hospital were not uncommon. Ointments and antidotes, and, of course, the occasional leech to suck up the sap as it flowed, were applied to the variety of injuries suffered. All this was cheerfully noted and documented in letters to parents and the house records.

The descriptions of play in the 1850s gave little sense of the tactics or even scores – and a game could be played out over many days. Indeed the rules of the schoolboys' game are almost impossible to comprehend, and changed constantly as the boys sought to refine them. Tom examined each point of play with a commander's eye, absorbing tactics and theory. At each end of the field stood unpainted wooden goal posts. The two vertical posts were about 12 feet in height and connected by a cross bar at 10 feet. The goals stood precisely 127 yards apart; we know this exact distance because it was recorded that Tom dashed over this length, from goal post to goal post, in the athletics carnival during his second year at school. The team that kicked two goals – the ball had to pass between the upright posts and clean over the cross bar – won the football game.

The great mass of boys were 'forward' players; they bullied and shoved the ball towards the goal, moving as a single mass across the field. Sprinkled amongst these 'forwards' sparkled the 'back players', or 'dodgers', who flitted in unpredictable dashes. These crafty players ran fast to elude tacklers, and, when caught, writhed and looped themselves about with rubbery arms to free themselves. Tom played as a forward and as a dodger but it was as a dodger that he rose to national attention in the press. And as for Tom's kicking, when the best runners in the school ran the ball in for a try at goal, it was Tom Wills who was summoned to kick. Tom's expertise as a kicker of the football was evident later in the colony of Victoria, where he was considered the longest drop-kicker of a football.

The game that Tom played at Rugby was played only amongst the boys at the school or between current pupils and Old Boys. No Rugby School football team existed during the 1850s. The boys wrote in their journals and letters a great deal about football; playing the game was a coming-of-age for the Rugby boys:

> . . . the consciousness that you have turned over a new leaf in your school life; that you have become in a sort of way the representative of your school and house on the arena of muscular strength or athletic agility . . . at football you must possess either muscular strength, or fleetness of foot, or true British pluck (the three points on which a Rugbeian prides himself most), to become even a tolerable player. And so you sit before your fire, looking idly on the genial flame, and occasionally seeking in the bottle by your side an additional stimulus for your imagination;

and . . . raise your eyes to where your cap is suspended above the mantelpiece.

It was just as well that Tom accustomed himself to the ferocity of football; he would need all his wiles to counter Horatio's accumulating frustration at his son's academic stagnation. Tom might even need the odd 'slimy' trick to squeeze past the old man.

•

Horatio's eyes in London – Aunt Sarah and her husband James Alexander – continued to watch over Tom. Aunt Sarah, a woman of wealth and inflexible religious devotion, showed a tenderness towards Tom that he did not forget, years later recalling her advice and encouragement. Sarah and James enjoyed their wealth; they could set Tom up just nicely, in England or Australia. All it required was for Tom to fall into line. But all was not well and even Sarah, with her loving tones, could not conceal Tom's poor academic progress. Sarah wrote to Horatio in 1854, just before Tom's nineteenth birthday:

> He is quite well, and I trust pursuing his studies with great attention. It would not be advisable to take him from school for some time yet. You are aware that he was very backward when he arrived in England, and he has much yet to learn, which could not be acquired with so much ease and advantage as at present, when no other occupation interferes to distract his attention.

In fact, Tom had received an offer from William Clarke, the entrepreneurial cricket professional whom Tom idolised. Clarke, in his mid-fifties, had formed a touring eleven – the All England Eleven – and had offered Tom the opportunity to join his cricket team and travel with him around the English countryside, earning his keep as a cricketer. It was a seductive offer but Tom did not leave school, remaining at Rugby for a further year.

His family continued to plot a suitable trajectory in life for an indifferent Tom. Aunt Sarah wrote: 'I am sorry that Mr Alexander will not have room for him at his office till he gets larger accommodation himself, but I am sure he will do his best to get him into an advantageous office, when his school studies are completed.' It was one of many attempts by family and friends to set Tom upon a career deemed worthy. Sarah went on: 'One most essential point is that he write a good hand, for no one would take him unless he did.' The scrawl that drove his father to distraction had become a common family objective to rectify. But in the end she fell back upon the Wills' tradition of emphasising personal responsibility: '. . . a great deal of observation and industry are necessary, and so much will depend upon himself'. With hope more than judgement she finished: 'Thomas appears to like the notion of being a merchant, and as I think he is naturally industrious, I have no doubt he will be a prosperous one. His general conduct is so good, that I indulge the hope that he will be a blessing to you and his mother.'

In the summer examinations of 1854 Tom ranked nineteenth from the bottom out of 166 boys but had somehow managed to drag himself from the Lower School into the Middle School. But by the end of 1854 a dark shadow passed over the school that expunged trifling concerns over academic performance. The Evans House archives record that a schoolboy, Watson, died from scarlet fever. The signature bright red rash and burning throat of the bacterial illness spread through the school. In Tom's house, Benjamin Ackers lay 'dangerously ill'. Goulburn promptly dismissed the school and Tom was back in London by early December.

When the students returned for the start of 1855 it was cold, even by Rugby's standards. Frosts were long and the ponds were congested with boys ice-skating. A dispute broke out between the boys and the 'town rabble' over the rights of the different groups over ice-skating, but was soon settled. Tom, still poorly placed in the Lower-Middle School, towered over the younger boys. One of these boys, William Erasmus Darwin, sat alongside Tom and studied French, and knelt and prayed with Tom in the Chapel. In four years' time, William's father would change the world with a book that began: 'When on board *H.M.S. Beagle*, as naturalist, I was much struck with certain facts . . .' No world within the British Empire was more unsettled by what these words suggested than the world of Horatio Wills, for whom the Book of Genesis had long given his restless soul the peace and certainty he needed.

As summer approached Tom was named the School XI cricket captain. Tom was the dominant bowler and batsman in the Rugby School team, but his lack of grace as a batsman singled him out as an unfinished product. Style counted for a great deal in Victorian England; and Mr Thomas Wentworth Wills, Esquire, was in need of polish if he was to receive complete approval when he stepped onto the grass of Lord's Cricket Ground. Tom was an emerging national figure and 'one to watch'. In April 1855 he received a letter from a stranger, a minister of the church, who asked Tom's permission to play in a cricket game with the Rugby students. The stranger did not use Tom's name; rather he simply addressed Tom as a 'fellow cricketer'. It seemed that was how England saw, and deferred to, Tom Wills. He had begun to learn his trade of captaincy. It was Tom's responsibility to square up cricketing accounts, organise fixtures and attend to scorebooks, but he had a less than precise attitude to matters administrative, not being blessed with a neat mind. Nonetheless, these tasks were part of the working trade of the captain and would allow him to instantly assume important playing and administrative roles back in Australia.

The time was looming when Tom would have to leave school. In August he would turn twenty: the Australian student was too old for school but untouchable as the school's most prestigious sportsman. By summer 1855, with his birthday imminent, he seemed to lose heart, sliding to bottom in his French exams.

Mr Bloxam's prediction in 1851 that 'he will shine in French' was not to be.

In his final week he captained the Rugby School XI team against Marlborough College. The following day he played his last game of cricket for Rugby as captain, defeating Marylebone Cricket Club at Lord's. The school – boys, masters and guests – assembled for the final time before summer break and were addressed by the headmaster. Edward Goulburn recorded that fifty Rugby boys had served in the Crimean War as officers and, with an economy of words, told his students that 'eleven had fallen as brave men desired to fall'. Goulburn announced a subscription to erect a memorial stained-glass window in the chapel to honour the Rugby dead.

T. W. Wills.

Only one daguerreotype of Tom has survived from his five years at Rugby; taken as he left school in June 1855. Kept by his younger brother Horace, it was shown in 1923 to a journalist with the *Evening Sun* and shows Tom, between adulthood and adolescence, with 'great chest development, and handsome'. His eyes are unusual – almond shaped, they burn with a pale light; his lower lip gently pouts, snared in a moment of petulance. His fellow Evans House students referred to Tom, in their farewell note, as captain of the School XI and, simply, 'the school bowler'. Their final written words were 'gone to Australia'.

The boys from Rugby, for so long tightly contained within a single embrace, dispersed. Benjamin Ackers survived his scarlet fever, and studied at Oxford – as did the bookish Andrew Johnstone, who learnt his lines of Virgil; both entered parliament. William Darwin settled comfortably as a banker and even more comfortably into the leather sofa at the Athenaeum Club in London. Frederick Prinsep, who studied Euclidean geometry with Tom, captained the 21st Hussars in 1853, serving with the Light Cavalry in the Indian Mutiny Campaign in 1858; and E.R.F. Vicars, who batted at six in the 1852 Rugby School XI, fought in Sebastopol, and then Burma and died there. Tom Burn, who favoured water over beer, son of a reverend, followed his father's calling and travelled to India and Burma, perishing in the service of his Lord having just made the age of thirty.

Three months after Tom had left school, news 'came of the taking of Sebastopol' in the Crimean War. The high-spirited boys in Evans House built a bonfire in the schoolyard to celebrate. They burnt boxes and assorted material until challenged by the sixth form on a matter of order, 'on which an extraordinary melée ensued'. Tom's housemaster, the likeable Evans, quelled the high jinks and concluded the proceedings in a most typical Rugbeian manner – wine all round for the boys and staff.

•

Tom remained in England for a further fifteen months before returning to Australia. He visited Rugby on numerous occasions and played cricket, football and ran across the fields in 'Hare and Hounds' just as if he had never left. Then in June 1856, twelve months after leaving the school, Tom stepped onto the fields of Rugby School for the last time, playing for the Marylebone Cricket Club. The Earl of Winterton opened the batting for Marylebone and was joined after the fall of the second wicket by Lord Guernsey. Tom Wills hit 22 runs in the first innings, driving a ball over the cricket pavilion and out of the ground for 6 runs. Tom was followed in the batting order by Mr Charles Du Cane, later to be Governor of Tasmania. The Marylebone Cricket Club won by 9 wickets.

Tom swept up and down England, playing cricket as he pleased. As a gentleman cricketer Tom played in the finest games: for the Gentlemen of Kent, the Marylebone Club, Cambridge University, several Rugby teams, the Gentlemen of 'Kent and Sussex', and just about any team that would have him – and there were few that did not. His hallmarks of persistence, stamina and competitiveness were honed; his body had filled out to a manly height of 5 feet 10 inches and the scales tipped 11 stone 2 pounds.

In Horatio's elaborate scheme for his children, Tom was to be the lawyer in the family. He would study at Cambridge, just like William Charles Wentworth, and return to Australia a professional man of eminence who would shape the colony. Or so Horatio imagined. Horatio had a personal connection with Cambridge University: his brother Edward had enrolled to study law in the 1820s. For generations it has been understood that Tom Wills had also enrolled as a student at Cambridge University, spending time at Magdalene College. This is only a partial truth. Tom did not formally enter Magdalene College nor any other college at Cambridge, but he visited to play cricket on Parker's piece and Fenner's ground – the two cricket ovals tucked into the south-east corner of the Cambridge campus. Tom played on these ovals with the Cambridge University team, although not enrolled as a student, during May and June of 1856 and also played a game for Magdalene College.

Tom's Cambridge flirtation gave him an aura of the educated young gentleman cricketer, which was to serve him so admirably when he returned to Australia. The game that really set Tom apart and enhanced his name was the Cambridge versus Oxford match. Over the years, fact has rolled into mythology. What *is* known is that Tom was present at this match and, Cambridge being one man short, the vacant position on the team was offered to him. Oxford agreed to Tom's inclusion. A keen observer at the time might have questioned how it was that Tom Wills was present at so many matches when it was noted that a team was 'one man short'. But regardless of his method, through good fortune or connivance, Tom artfully worked his way into the

Oxford–Cambridge cricket match, one of the highlights of the English sporting year. It was reported that Tom Wills, an Australian, not enrolled at Cambridge, was part of the first winning Cambridge team in four years.

Before Tom left England he met two men who would shape his life back in Australia. The first was William Josiah Hammersley, at Kennington Oval in Surrey, 30 July 1855. Tom played for the Gentlemen of Kent while Hammersley played for the Gentlemen of Surrey. Hammersley recalled the occasion years afterwards, when a professional cricketer: 'I forget which [drew his attention to] "that young fellow from Rugby, who plays with a 4lb. bat, and hits terrific".' Neither Hammersley nor Wills thought a great deal about this moment until they met again and 'shook hands in the pavilion of the Melbourne Cricket Ground' over a year later.

The second man who would influence Tom later in life was the English professional cricketer Charles Lawrence. Tom met Lawrence in the final months before returning to Australia, when, for reasons not entirely clear, Tom travelled to Ireland in August 1856. Lawrence was six years Tom's senior and played with the Phoenix Club in Dublin. Tom played in every game on offer for the month of his stay, where he was later remembered partly for his cricket, partly for the 'pranks' he played. Lawrence was a man with an expanded curiosity about the world and he, like Hammersley, would soon travel to and settle in Australia. Tom's last cricket game was on September 8–9, taking part in a United Irish team, after which he made his way back to England to prepare for the journey home.

The reason for Tom's return to Australia was probably his indifference to further study at Cambridge and his casual approach to money. Thrift, in his eyes, was not a virtue. He had cultivated a taste for spending money while he was at Rugby – Charles Evans had addressed the pupils in his house, concerned that some of them were leaning on their parents for money. The boys had their own phrase for this practice:

'drawing the Governor'. Tom had been indulged in England; Horatio wrote cheques to cover his profligate son's bills. And so it seems that Tom had spent freely, up and down the length of England, until, with no clear direction and having exhausted parental patience, he was called back home.

For the last fifteen months Tom had lived an accelerated lifestyle. He had been exposed to, and played with, the greatest cricketers of the age. It had been a relatively brief fling throughout England and Ireland but an important postscript to five years at Rugby School.

On 19 October 1856 Tom boarded the *Oneida*, a Royal Mail steamship of 2400 tons under the command of George Hyde, bound for Melbourne. The passengers included the new Governor for Victoria, Henry Barkly, and his wife and children. The steamship sailed past the West Coast of Africa, stopping at Cape Town before rounding the Cape of Good Hope and sailing across the Indian Ocean. The journey home took less than half the time it took to sail to England six years previously.

When Tom had departed in February 1850, Melbourne had a population of less than a day's attendance at the 1851 Great Exhibition in London. But while Tom was in England the world had converged upon Melbourne, passing through its narrow portal to the golden fields of Ballarat and Bendigo. Melbourne had changed beyond recognition – it was bigger, more ambitious and it sparkled. These words, so fitting for the Victorian colony, applied in even greater abundance to the man about to return. The *Oneida* docked on 23 December 1856 and Tom, voyage completed, took his first steps on Melbourne soil in nearly seven years.

THE SHRINKING AND EXPANDING
WORLD OF TOM WILLS

Belle Vue, built by Horatio, not far from the Victorian town of Geelong, was hardly the home of a man with grand designs – a simple long wooden bungalow, squatting close to the ground, whose front verandah looked out over paddocks that extended down to Point Henry. Belle Vue stood on 'The Point', as Point Henry was called, a notable local geographical feature: a narrowing extension of land that poked into Corio Bay. It had been the Wills' family home for nearly four years when Tom returned.

Belle Vue sat on over 300 acres of land. Blossoms circled the house in spring and orchards supplied cherry, plum, apricot, apple, pear and peach. Potatoes were grown, a fowl house supplied fresh poultry and eggs, and the family hung chunks of beef to dry in the cowshed. The clay from a nearby waterhole was moulded into bricks, hardened, and used to build a dairy. And moving in their own directions and at their own pace were cats, dogs, workers, washermen, and the Chinese, Irish and Scottish servants. The inner rim of the house and its gardens was surrounded by acres of mangolds and lucerne. And beyond the gardens, in the bush, the Wills boys and their friends shot

Belle Vue

teal, quail, cockatoos, hawks and wild cats, and fished for bream when they took a liking for that.

While Tom had been in England, his family had expanded. Six years earlier, Tom's brothers and sisters and his cousin Colden Harrison had stood against a wall at Lexington homestead and had their heights measured. Now Colden was fully grown and would soon be the finest runner in the colony. Tom's sister Emily had just turned eight when her height was measured; now fourteen, she was busy telling others what to do – her irritable personality was taking form. Cedric, whom providence had endowed with a look of perpetual dissatisfaction, was now twelve; Horace, of a more gentle disposition, had just turned nine; and Egbert, the youngest of the boys, was seven. The additions to the family – Elizabeth, Eugene and Minna – were all girls, and the littlest was twenty-one years younger than Tom. These small girls formed a distant world that Tom was never part of, and in letters he rarely mentioned them.

Horatio, driven by his interest in agriculture and local affairs in the Geelong region, had entered the Victorian Parliament the year before Tom came home and sat as a Member of the Legislative Assembly. He lived in Melbourne during the sitting of parliament but otherwise returned to Belle Vue to manage the farm and his family. Geelong connected Belle Vue to the rest of the colony of Victoria. To reach Geelong from Belle Vue meant a buggy trip along the Point Henry Road that curved around the Corio Bay. From Geelong, carriages, horses and bullocks went back and forth to Melbourne; the railway line, worked upon for years, linking Geelong to Melbourne, was soon completed.

Tom had changed since leaving Rugby. The unfinished lines of adolescence were gone. Still youthful, almost divinely so, his eyes were softer, more attractive, and his high forehead stretched to impossibly wavy hair. There was no petulance, perhaps just the hint of a smile brewing within those perfectly formed lips.

Tom's arrival in Australia had been expected by the Victorian cricketers. While Tom was in England, the first intercolonial cricket match between Victoria and New South Wales had taken place. The Victorians had lost. At the end of 1856, preparations were underway for a second intercolonial cricket match and Tom's reputation, having preceded him, suggested he would play. A trial match to select players for the Victorian team was to be held at the Melbourne Cricket Ground.

Playing cricket in Melbourne was different to playing on the fields of Rugby. The sun was brighter and surfaces rougher in the colony; there was no soft grass in Melbourne. Tom entered the pavilion of the Melbourne Cricket Club and 'shook hands' with William Hammersley, restarting their relationship from their first meeting in England. Tom stepped out onto the Melbourne Cricket Ground in the manner of one who fancied himself. Dressed in his Zingari costume of dazzling red, gold and black – a bird of paradise from Lord's – he naturally drew attention. In England I Zingari, a club of moneyed eccentrics, travelled widely in the pursuit of cricketing pleasure, bejewelled in their spectacular colours. For Tom, I Zingari was an ideal life to pursue: no work, exotic plumage and the attention of women. Down the flanks of Tom's Zingari flannels was daubed a flashing line of scarlet that gripped his buttocks and thighs. Here was the bolter from Rugby, pure and magnificent. A large crowd had gathered to watch Tom. Men admired and envied; women must have felt a sexual tingle as they studied his sculptured physique. It was an allure of which Tom was fully aware.

Tom was picked to play for the colony of Victoria against New South Wales and a practice match arranged for New Year's Day amongst the Victorian cricketers. Wills and Hammersley opened the bowling. Tom entertained, attracting the eye of the spectators as he stole runs from dull-witted fieldsmen. The crowds laughed at his awkward manner of batting. Tom kept his bat gummed to the ground, like a heavy clubbed foot, but he scored 57 not out and won the trial match for his team. The press highlighted that this was Tom Wills, oldest son of Horatio Wills Esquire, Member of the Legislative Assembly in the Victorian Parliament. Father and son were in the news a great deal that year. The press suggested that with the arrival of Tom Wills, the next intercolonial cricket match would be Victoria's triumph, a conclusion reached only eight days after Tom had returned from England. The Victorian cricket team, captained by William Hammersley, left for Sydney by the steamer *Telegraph* on 8 January.

The match took place on the Domain, public land that stretched between Parliament House on Macquarie Street and the bays of Sydney harbour. In preparation for the match, William Tunks, the honorary secretary to the New South Wales cricket team, requested a local butcher in Woolloomooloo to graze his sheep on the grass of the Domain. Men and women lined the perimeter in great numbers to watch the first day's play. Beyond the field a long line of tall terraced buildings, Richmond Terrace, reached towards Macquarie Street and the buildings of parliament. On the opposite side of the cricket ground the land rolled to Woolloomooloo Bay, a fingerling of water that inserted itself deep into the Domain parklands.

Beyond the inner ring of spectators rose a grassy slope where groups of women sat chatting in thick crinoline dresses that

FINAL RESULT!

BRADSHAW'S
CARD OF THE
GRAND CRICKET MATCH
VICTORIA V. NEW SOUTH WALES,
IN THE DOMAIN CRICKET GROUND,
WEDNESDAY, JAN. 14, '57, AND FOLLOWING DAYS.

Cards issued from the PRINTING MACHINE on the fall of each wicket.

NEW SOUTH WALES.

NO.	FIRST INNINGS. NAMES. HOW OUT.	RUNS.	SECOND INNINGS. HOW OUT.	RUNS.
1	W. G. Rees, leg before wicket b. Wills	28	c. Marshall, b. Hammersley	3
2	G. Howell, c. Bryant, b. Elliott	0	c. Marshall, b. Wills	0
3	H. Hilliard, b. Wills	20	b. Elliott	2
4	G. Gilbert, b. Wills	2	c. Bryant, b. Wills	31
5	J. M'Kone, b. Wills	1	not out	0
6	W. C. Still, run out	1	b. Elliott	9
7	O. Lewis, c. Bryant, b. Hammersley	3	c. Elliott, b. Wills	2
8	R. Murray, b. Wills	0	b. Elliott	8
9	Capt. Ward, R.E., c. Butterworth, b Wills	1	c. Coulstock, b Hammersley	13
10	E. Sadler, not out	5	c. A'Beckett, b. Wills	3
11	T. Lewis, c. Wills, b Hammersley	13	c. A'Beckett, b. Elliott	8
	Bye,1 ; L.B. 3 ; Wide, 1 ; No Balls, 1	6	B,3 ; L.B.1 ; W,; N.B.1	7

Total, first innings............ 80—Total, second innings...... 86

UMPIRES : For Victoria, Mr. C. F. Cameron ; for N.S. Wales, Mr. R. Driver, Junior.
SCORERS : For Victoria, Mr. H. Biers ; for N. S. Wales, Mr. F. Wyatt.

VICTORIA.

NO.	FIRST INNINGS. NAME. HOW OUT.	RUNS.	SECOND INNINGS. HOW OUT.	RUNS.
1	D. M. Serjeant, run out	7	b. O. Lewis	6
2	R. Coulstock, b. Captain Ward	0	b Ward	16
3	W. L. Rees, b. J. M'Kone	2	run out	0
4	E. A'Beckett, run out	3	c. and b. Ward	0
5	T. W. Wills, b. J. M'Kone	0	c. T. Lewis, b. Ward	1
6	J. M. Bryant, b. Captain Ward	23	c. Murray, b. O. Lewis	0
7	G. Marshall, c. Sadler, b. Lewis	13	c. M'Kone, b. O. Lewis	0
8	W. Hammersley, b. O. Lewis	10	b. O. Lewis	10
9	C. Cumberland, c. Still, b. Lewis	0	not out	0
10	R. Butterworth, c. Ward, b. O. Lewis	0	b Ward	0
11	G. Elliott, not out	2	c. Howell, b. Ward,	2
	Bye, 1 ; L.B. 4 ; Wide, 1 ; No Balls	3	Byes, 2 ; L.B. 1	3

Total, first innings............ 63—Total, second innings 38

Majority for New South Wales...... 65.

Published (by Authority of the Committee) on the Ground, by Gunton Taylor, Proprietor, of Bradshaw's Railway Guide. **PRICE SIXPENCE.**

rustled and brushed against the dry grass of the Domain and spread about them, folded like a range of mountains. Parasols offered movable shade and those who did not have such an item clustered in the speckled shade of the gum trees. Some men wore top hats of glistening black silk, hats so tall that they threatened to topple with a change in wind direction. Indeed, hats were a sign of social standing. And from a distance hats were seen in all their guises: some tall, some squat and round, others recently pulled out from a pocket were crushed and able to fit the shape of any noble or eccentric head.

For the moment, the town of Sydney slowed and concentrated on the match. Parliament was suspended and the Governor Sir William Denison made his way to the Domain. To the Macquarie Street parliamentarians who so eagerly left their offices to meet at the ground, this was an opportunity to reinforce their sense of superiority over the colony of Victoria.

The Victorians brought a modern style of play to the Domain. Tom took 10 wickets in the match; bowling fast round arm he teamed with Gideon Elliott, a Victorian professional and 'the fastest bowler' in the colonies. Tom was bowled second ball of his first innings by John McKone. McKone, the New South Wales opening bowler, bowled fast underhand, a style still considered old-fashioned. The Victorians regarded themselves as superior to the Sydney men and sniffed at McKone's antiquated action. The Victorian captain, Hammersley, remembered over twenty years later that it was 'the queerest match I had ever taken part in, as some of the Sydney men played without shoes, in their stocking-feet, and one or two of them even discarded those necessary articles and were in their bare feet!' The Victorians were cocky that day but despite their stylish play lost by 65 runs.

This was the second loss for the Victorians. The previous year there had been rumours that the Victorians were drunk on the field. After the second intercolonial match, there were again rumours that they tottered about the field soaked in alcohol and that 'some six or seven of the eleven, when they appeared on the ground, were not able to stand; in fact, that they were intoxicated'. Tom, prickly and oversensitive, wrote immediately to the press to defend the Victorian players:

> Now I really do not see what good people do themselves or any one else by bringing forward such uncalled-for and most ungentlemanly reports, to say the least of it. Now I have played in as many matches as any one in the colony, and know, or ought to know, what cricket is; and I will say I scarcely ever saw an eleven conduct themselves with such propriety as did the Victorians on this occasion.

Tom was bothered by more than charges of drunkenness. During the match, the Victorian player Gideon Elliott was accused of deliberately stopping a batsman from completing a run in direct disobedience of the rules. Tom would have none of this criticism of Elliott and supported his professional bowler: 'I consider him to have been quite justified in the way in which he acted towards Captain Ward.' Whether this meant Tom thought Elliott was perfectly justified in blocking Ward's path as he made for the run or whether Elliott did not deliberately thwart him is not clear. But this was to mark the beginning of Tom's public support towards not only Gideon Elliott but professional cricketers in general. When critics suggested that a better team could have been chosen, Tom dressed down the team's detractors. He detested the puffed-up dandies, the ornamental cricketers whose temperament was as brittle as fine bone china:

> Had one or two gentlemen who were asked to play, accepted instead of indulging in *picnics or some less worthy* pursuit, the *eleven* might have had a rather different *tale* to relate. A sea voyage, and three roasting days of a match, is not exactly what *some people would prefer*, to say nothing of getting SNUBBED on their return, after having nearly been scorched to death.

Tom Wills' name and his feats filled the pages of *Bell's Life in Victoria*, *The Argus* and the penny papers. He seemed to be everywhere at once. Cricket, which had seemed dull before Tom, now illuminated Melbourne. The newspapers spoke of Tom bowling sparklers, rippers, fizzers, trimmers and shooters. Balls skimmed and shaved, flew quickly and trimmed the bails; others were slow or sometimes dropped mid-flight, *à la* William Clarke, Tom's English hero, leaving a batsman perplexed at being bowled.

Tom could not have returned to Melbourne at a better time. The colony was obsessed with cricket, and cricketers' views and experiences were published in the press. The newly established *Bell's Life in Victoria*, based on its London namesake, printed everything Wills had to say and in the first two years after his return to Melbourne, Tom wrote or had written about him no less than fifty letters in the Melbourne press. Tom's voice was louder and heard more often than any other cricketer, for he had recently experienced, first hand, how English cricketers had engaged in public spats – played out in *Bell's Life in London*.

Tom made enemies – some in the press, some in the cricket clubs – but his prodigious talent swept any concerns away as clubs sought his services. Although he won games through his skills and leadership, it was also his unquenchable optimism that attracted clubs and individuals. Everyone wanted Tom; no one wanted him more than the prestigious Melbourne Cricket Club who, despite Tom playing his first club game with the Corio Cricket Club in Geelong, boasted that Tom had first belonged to them. Geelong ignored the Melbourne Cricket Club and always claimed him as their own. It probably mattered little to Tom; he played with both teams – and with anyone else who needed a cricketer. There was barely a day when Tom was not playing or practising cricket.

Tom made only occasional trips to Belle Vue. His brothers Cedric, Horace and Egbert – still just boys – longed to have their older brother as part of their shooting and fishing expeditions

Horace and Cedric

or to play cricket with, but they seldom saw him, more often reading about him in *The Argus* or *Age* or *Herald*. The boys idolised Tom. When Cedric was twelve he wrote to his sister Emily: 'I saw some lop eared rabbits in Melbourne about a fortnight ago for £5 a pair but Tom said that he would not give £5 for all the rabbits in the world.' That was it. If the finest cricketer in Victoria advised not to buy these rabbits then there was nothing else to consider! Then the questions and instructions poured from Cedric's pen. *Did Tom bring a cricket ball down with him? Did Tom bring a cricket bat? Tell Tom to get ready for hunting when he comes down next! Tom did not score many runs in Geelong. Where is Tom?* Beyond the small world the boys inhabited at Belle Vue, beyond the bream in the creeks, the teal to be shot, it was Tom who sat in the centre of their lives. To the three boys he was kind, generous, magical; an unblemished image of the ideal cricketer, an ideal brother.

In his first summer in Melbourne, Tom boarded at 165 Victoria Parade with his aunt, Mrs Jane Harrison, the mother of Tom's cousin Colden. The 'Parade', as Mrs Harrison's house was called, was a Melbourne base for the entire Wills family, including Horatio when parliament was in session. Victoria Parade, known to Melburnians as a road of dirt with puddles in the rain and a storm of dust in the heat, stretched through the inner suburbs of Fitzroy and Collingwood; from Mrs Harrison's Tom could walk to the town of Melbourne in a few minutes, where he had entered the law firm of James Smith and Robert Willan – a gesture of compliance with his father's desires. James Smith and Robert Willan were members of the Melbourne Club, a private gentlemen's club on Collins Street, and stepped in circles of considerable political and economic influence.

For Tom the cricket season never ended; it simply lay dormant. In winter, impatient for the newly planted English elms to bud, Tom wrote numerous and urgent letters to *Bell's Life in Victoria*. Through his letters over the next year, Tom Wills held an agitated public conversation with the colony of Victoria. He urged young cricketers (to whom he always cast a nurturing eye), to purchase the new *Victorian Cricketer's Guide*, then without pause, he chastised the secretaries of the various cricket clubs for keeping inadequate cricket records. He corrected, chided and praised, melodramatically challenging the colony: 'I trust that this time we will not allow the Sydney natives to write home and say, as proud Caesar of old, Veni, vidi, vici; but let us rather raise up Victoria's banner clear from any chance of defeat, and make ourselves perfect at all

Emily

points – and then Victoria's flag will wave proudly once more.'
The colony of Victoria, not allowed to forget Tom or his
passion, was bemused. His public letters sparkled and spat fire,
lighting up the dullest Melbourne day. As for his enemies, his
singular lack of awareness of how his obsessiveness aggravated
some about him was a weighty counterpoint to all his success
on the field. But for the most part it seemed that the common
man loved him.

Tom's private correspondence gives insights into his state of
mind during his first year back in Melbourne. In a letter from

'The Parade' on 17 September 1857 to Emily at Belle Vue, Tom started with his characteristic obscurity, then described a scene from the Harrison household that resembled a theatrical farce:

My dear Sister,

My dog's name is Nell.

I slept one night last week at the Parade & I was told to take my uncles bedroom & when I was just about to step into bed I heard a gentle tap at the door & I found that I had got another gentlemans room & I of course moved out & went into the next room where I was very [illegible word] to see a person in a night cap sitting up in bed & who also emitted several suppressed cries of astonishment – as who's that, what are you doing here – & for the life of me I could not open the door having a candle in one hand & all my clothes in the other – but at last I succeeded & who's room do you think I had got into? Miss Cavendishe's!!! [governess to the Wills girls] You say someone [illegible word] guess whilst I cut his hair of – off I should say. I think, excuse me – I was nearly stuck up again last night but I in a most valiant manner presented a pipe case at the ruffian & sd I wd shoot him if he did not keep off – at which he grumbled something and slunk off – & I was precious glad he did I can tell you –

Next came an unusual statement suggesting that there were times when Tom experienced the world in a depersonalised state. Like Alice having drunk her potion which made her shrink and expand, he experienced the world differently to those around him. That he smelt it, heard it, watched it go by with different senses, and not always senses that were pleasing to him: 'I have felt beastly bad this last week I do not know what I am standing on – & when anyone speaks to me I cannot for the life of me make out what they are talking about – everything seems so curious.' This seems more than a moment of normal confusion or playful writing; there is a note of distress, of

Victoria Pde.
E. Melbourne   Sept. 17th '57

My dear Sister.

              My dog's name is Nell –
I slept one night last week at the Parade
+ I was told to take my Uncles bed room
+ when I was just about to step into
bed, I heard a gentle tap at the door
+ I found that I had got another gentleman's
room + I of course moved out + went
into the next room where I was very
much'd to see a person in a night
Cap sitting up in bed + who also
emitted several suppressed cries
of astonishment – as who's that
what are you doing here – + for the
life of me I could not open the door
having a candle in one hand + all

matters beyond the control of his mind. What caused him to feel this way is unknown. Alcohol may have muddied his thoughts; or it is possible that his perplexity and altered sensory experience resulted from an epileptic seizure – certain types of seizure can produce the very symptoms described by Tom. Or perhaps this was evidence of an early mental instability due to a depressed or elevated mood. There is insufficient additional information in his letters to be sure of what was happening to Tom at this point but his discomfort is evident. The moment passed and so did his troubled recollections. Breezily he wrote of his resignation from the Melbourne Cricket Club after 'a row with some of the Members of the M.C.C.' and that he planned to join the Richmond Cricket Club. As it turned out, Tom did not leave the Melbourne Cricket Club. Towards the end of the letter he returned to the gentler teasing Tom of the first part of his letter, playfully admonishing his baby sister. He finished with a version of *Hamlet*, tossed in a pun and ended the letter as obscurely as he began:

> Will you be good enough to write or shall I stop wch [which] would suit you best? for I am beastly sick of writing a [and] getting no reply – 'There must be something essentially rotten in the state of Denmark' I fancy – I have to attend at <u>Court</u> tomorrow – not a <u>courting</u> case – but rather an Equitable one – how does the white Pony get on. My dog is such a nice one & as savage as a <u>bear</u> when on the chain & is a first rate watch <u>dog</u>. How is Miss of the <u>feline</u> tribe? It has been very warm here today in fact excessively so & very dusty '<u>My trousers & my coat</u>'
> how are all?
> Love & c & c
> & Believe me
> Your Devoted brother
> T.W. Wills

Perhaps his family knew how to decipher Tom.

The physical form of Tom's writing had changed from Rugby. No longer a shapeless shuffling line of ink, the words stood boldly, sloping backwards, as if the centre of gravity of each letter had dropped too low, and threatened to collapse upon the preceding letter. His elastic, unconstrained writing was in contrast to his father's economical script.

Tom's breathless, explosive and passionate language had developed into a peculiar stream of consciousness where lines of argument or considered opinions were not developed. His thoughts jumped about, breaking into defiant jabs. He used classical and Shakespearian allusions; cryptic asides and puns appeared everywhere. It was the language of extremes: everything was all good or all bad. The letters showed a mind full of energy and histrionic ideas without a centre and he often seemed in a state of perplexity, easily startled and ready to ride off furiously in any direction. The viewpoints of others never entered his thoughts, nor did he perceive how his behaviour or manner affected others. Although Tom's public letters to newspapers were often irritable or antagonistic, there is little that could be construed as malicious or hateful in his private letters. Humorous and impish, Tom revelled in being mysterious. Rarely did he allow others to glimpse his inner world – perhaps he had little understanding of it himself.

The letters of this period, from 1857 until 1860, revealed a remarkable mind. They were different from anything else Tom wrote and coincided with the greatest moments of creativity in his life. Buoyant and carefree, he seemed unencumbered with concerns that he should pursue anything but his own desires.

APPLAUSE, PROSPERITY, SOCIAL ACQUAINTANCE

OCTOBER 1857–JANUARY 1858

> If you are a man of leisure you will find more 'society' in
> Melbourne, more balls and parties, a larger measure of
> intellectual life – i.e. more books and men of education and
> intellect . . . all public amusements are far better attended
> in Melbourne; the people dress better, talk better, think
> better, are better . . . [and of Sydney] One feels quite angry
> with the town for being so unworthy of its site.
>
> *Richard Twopeny, English journalist*

In 1857 Tom spent time at 132 Lonsdale Street West, on the
western edge of Melbourne. The only name listed at this address
was a Miss Baird who perhaps took Tom in as a boarder; the
nature of his relationship to Miss Baird is unknown. Certainly
there was no shortage of boarding houses on the streets of
Melbourne and although not as conveniently located as Victoria
Parade, Tom could still walk to the Melbourne Cricket Ground
on the opposite side of town. He would have made this trip often.

On the corner of Lonsdale and Swanston streets stood
the Melbourne Hospital. In Elizabeth Street Professor Sohier
conducted his museum of phrenology where he displayed casts
of the heads of executed criminals, complete with annotations

on the incriminating evidence found in the bumps and dips of
their skulls. The professor advertised and invited the citizens
of Melbourne to come and have their own heads examined at a
price. Tom could have had his tempestuous crust looked at by
the professor for the cost of only five shillings. The law offices
where Tom worked – Robert Willan and James Smith: solicitors,
proctors and conveyancers – were situated in the fashionable
strip of Collins Street, between Swanston and Elizabeth streets.
Two doors down from Willan and Smith stood the private club
for gentlemen, the Melbourne Club.

Continuing east on Collins Street, Tom would have passed
nearby Parliament House, where, in the Lower House, Horatio
sat on his independent cross bench, declaring the Chinese to
be 'rice eating, opium-chewing Mongolians' and warning that
350 million were 'ready to pour in' and overtake the colony.
He demanded that the Chinese be run out of the gold fields of
Ballarat and Bendigo. Horatio's image of a Melbourne engorged
with wriggling, fecund Chinese was met with laughter. Just
beyond Parliament House, heading east along Wellington
Parade, the Richmond Paddock and the Melbourne Cricket
Club were only a few minutes' walk away.

The Melbourne Cricket Club pavilion was a modest timber
one-storey building, just under half a cricket pitch in length.
At each end of the roof was a gable prettily edged with wooden
lacework. You entered under a small covered verandah that
stretched the length of the building, where players and visitors
sat and watched the game of cricket. Surrounding the pavilion
were scattered native gums and casuarinas trees that grew on
the Richmond Paddock.

It was strange that this modest pavilion and the Melbourne
Cricket Club exercised such an influence on the minds of the
Melbourne public. Formed in 1838, only three years after the
founding of the colony, the MCC (or simply, the Club), as it
was referred to, had been in its present location for only four
years. Cricket was not as influential amongst the moneyed of the

city as horseracing, but the MCC was still seen as an exclusive organisation and dominated the administration of cricket in Victoria. Although an intercolonial selection committee was set up before each match against New South Wales, to try to represent all Victorian clubs, the MCC largely controlled the interests of cricket in the colony.

The Melbourne Cricket Club was a colony within a colony and within its conclave was a rookery of sorts, not of penguins or of seals, but of men. Along with the men of goodwill and integrity, the creative and industrious, were the cheats, the snivellers and the pole climbers. Some were young and self-centred; some competitive and touchy. By dint of wealth and connections Tom should have fitted in but he seemed not to. The politics of parliament were not to suit his father, nor did the politics of the Club suit Tom.

In September 1857, Tom was elected honorary secretary of the Melbourne Cricket Club, taking over from William Hammersley. This occurred only two days after Tom's letter to his sister Emily in which he had cocked a leg and declared he would leave the MCC for the Richmond Cricket Club. The week after Tom was elected as honorary secretary, Horatio Wills was elected to membership of the MCC.

Tom's life was lived within the fold of cricket, particularly the MCC. The men he met over the next few years at the Club became his companions, friends and detractors.

There was a caste system in cricket: amateur and professional cricketers were not considered equals. The ideal of the amateur cricketer, a cherished notion, was a gentleman who played the game for pleasure only and received no money from his club. Well educated, a man of business or in a profession, he was eligible to take a position within the club's administration – enhancing his already lofty status. On the cricket field, most amateurs saw themselves first as batsmen; bowling, particularly the arduous back-breaking fast bowling, was less commonly the lot of the amateur. They paid others to fill this role.

The lower caste – the professional cricketer – earned an income through playing cricket. They were generally poorly educated and were expected to behave in an ill-bred manner that confirmed their lowly status. The English wrote volumes on the image of the professional cricketer. The image was worthy; the attitude was condescending. There was a sense that the professional cricketer, despite his commendable skills, was crude and might poke a utensil deep into his gullet in company, smile his discoloured teeth, drink alcohol as his food and make conversation that was coarse and lewd. Sometimes a professional was described as livestock might be described, using the parameters of height, weight, sturdiness and age. Over winter a professional was put out to fatten up. Then there was the tricky area of manners, particularly his behaviour before his superiors, and his capacity to dress and present himself. A professional had to 'know his place' of inferiority.

The division between amateur and professional had been imported from England and, although the division was less stark in the colonies, it held significant sway. The MCC employed up to three or four professional cricketers each summer. Everyone else in the Club was an amateur and keen to remain that way.

Tom was a gentleman amateur. In England he was Mr T.W. Wills Esquire, the esquire a title for those who did not have an official title but by virtue of position or education were deemed gentlemen. In Australia, the suffix Esq., was occasionally fastened to Tom's name but it was a convention that did not flourish.

William Josiah Hammersley, amateur cricketer and nine years Tom's senior, was an important figure in Tom's life. For much of their early relationship they were friends, and Hammersley visited Belle Vue on numerous occasions. A wristy player who held his bat loosely, it was said by one of the Lillywhites that Hammersley walked rather than ran to the crease to bowl.

Cambridge-educated, with the elegant lines of a greyhound, Hammersley proudly wore his English heritage. He considered himself refined; Tom saw him as ornamental. His tendency to nap in quiet corners of the cricket field irked Tom. Hammersley displayed an overdeveloped sense of his imperial worth, feeling compelled at each opportunity to inform the colonials where they exhibited points of inferiority and how they might improve – presented with the air of a man who needed to carry out an unpleasant but necessary task. Criticism of his manner simply reinforced his beliefs. However, his natural facility to antagonise belied a well-concealed generosity; sometimes his bluster of imperial superiority seemed faked and he often wrote admiringly of the cricket skills of the colony. A lover of horseracing and athletics, Hammersley would later write for *Bell's Life in Victoria* and *The Australasian* under the name 'Longstop', becoming the most influential commentator on Victorian sport.

James B. Thompson was another amateur cricketer who influenced Tom – mainly in the first four years after Tom's arrival from England. Thompson was an all-round sportsman, a journalist of talent and wit. As sporting editor with the conservative *Argus* he held a position of some significance and, like Hammersley, was English born and had studied at Cambridge University. Neither Hammersley nor Thompson matched Tom's cricket skill. Other amateur cricketers of significance in Tom's life were: Richard Wardill, also English, an accountant and a champion at several sports; John Conway, only a boy when Tom was elected as honorary secretary but soon to become an all-round cricketer; Daniel Wilkie; Vernon Cameron, and Thomas Smith. These were the amateurs Tom played with: lawyers, journalists, teachers, merchants, accountants.

As for the professionals, Gideon Elliott was a fast bowler, faster than Tom but not quite as smart with the ball; and Jerry Bryant, slower than Elliott but steadier with the bat. Elliott and Bryant were publicans with hotels close to the Melbourne Cricket Club. George Marshall, another professional, was the best wicket keeper in the colony but he could also bat and bowl. All three – Elliott, Bryant, Marshall – were Englishmen, and played with the Melbourne Cricket Club for a good period of their careers.

Amateurs and professionals remained true to type. Professionals did not become amateurs and one would never suggest that an amateur become a professional. If, by chance, an amateur sportsman was mistakenly called a professional it was regarded as a slur. Tom had a natural allegiance to the professional cricketers about him. He was not the only amateur who supported the professionals but he did so more often and cultivated friendships with them. It was an egalitarian attitude that sometimes led him into conflict with the Club but attracted the admiration of the colony. However, he was not willing to relinquish the social advantages he received from his amateur status and his letters during this period revealed his views on the distinction between amateur and professional. Less than two months after he was elected honorary secretary, Tom wrote to the professional cricketer George Marshall informing him that he had been elected an honorary member of the Melbourne Cricket Club 'as an acknowledgement of your behaviour and as a compliment to you as being the best wicket keeper in the colony'. The intent behind the letter – to recognise Marshall's value as a cricketer – was supported by Tom and the Club. The wording of Tom's letter made it clear that it was not sufficient for Marshall to play well; he also had to behave well before honorary membership could be conferred. Similarly, when Tom's friend Gideon Elliott suffered a 'serious accident', a match was arranged to raise money. Tom wrote to *Bell's Life in Victoria* to support Elliott: 'The members of the M.C.C. must know that he has ever been a good and sober man on the ground, and is always to be found at his post when wanted by any member to bowl – hot or cold, all the same.' Tom's support was genuine and effusive but the phrase 'good and sober' betrayed his upbringing as a gentleman amateur. Tom might have admired the professionals as men and as cricketers but he was not one of them. For the moment Tom remained true to type.

After Tom's election as honorary secretary of the MCC, he wrote to William Tunks, the honorary secretary of the New South Wales Cricketers. This was a tricky letter. Tunks felt recent letters from Victorian cricketers in the lead up to the next intercolonial match had insulted him; there was doubt whether the matches would proceed. Tom wrote to an aggrieved Tunks to heal this rift. His first letter began nervously: 'I much regret there has been no notice taken of the Victorian challenge to play the New S. Wales eleven.' When sympathy and flattery were needed to soothe Tunks, he wrote: 'It gave me great pleasure to hear that you had taken the matter in hand and as I do think there is no one who has the game so much to heart as yourself.' Tom's letters were unusual, out of character, polite, almost obsequious. The disagreement between the colonies was smoothed over and the intercolonial game was arranged for the next year. For Tom, just twenty-two, it was a masterly performance in diplomacy, revealing that occasionally he was capable of manoeuvring like a clever courtier in a world of bickering self-opinionated cricketers.

•

A cricketer could play with several different clubs: membership of one club did not preclude a cricketer from playing with another club. Free to play with clubs of his choosing Tom travelled all over the colony. One week after he accepted the position of honorary secretary for the Melbourne Cricket Club he attended the Annual General Meeting of the Collingwood Cricket Club, held at the Clifton Hotel, managed by James (Jerry) Bryant, cricket professional with the MCC. Tom became a member of the Collingwood Cricket Club and some months later played against Heidelberg on 'the prettiest ground in the colony'. On an 'oppressively hot' day Tom took 7 wickets, playing a key role to defeat Heidelberg. There came an immediate cry to bar Tom from some games as his exceptional skills distorted the balance of play against weaker clubs. When he walked onto the field in such games, the cry 'All bets are off' was reported in the press. Betting on matches was rife and Tom's presence, often as a late inclusion, dramatically altered the odds. But all clubs still wanted him when it suited their cause. So he moved among them, slipping into any team of his choosing: Geelong, Melbourne, St Kilda, Collingwood and I Zingari. He had little time for anything else.

Tom recorded his experiences in a stream of passionate letters to the Melbourne newspapers: one, two, often more a week. His energy was boundless, and Melbourne's bowl too small to contain it. Tom was gifted but he also practised mercilessly and urged Victorian cricketers to practise their fielding without the indulgence of a net behind them, which he believed only encouraged laziness. Driven by a furious energy, it seemed Tom wrote more letters to the press in those two years than all other cricketers combined.

Tom's public letters irritated some cricketers, administrators and journalists, but his cricket talent protected him for years. Those most critical of Wills still admired his sporting abilities, even if it was the colder admiration reserved for those with excessive talent and confidence. Not that Tom was wrong or unmeasured in all his remarks – indeed, he was often right and quite logical – but he failed to allow his enemies room to manoeuvre and retreat with some grace, and his forthright tactics, which might have worked on the field, had limited value in life.

Tom, despite his elite position, always encouraged young players from less prominent clubs. He promoted the inclusion of country players in the Victorian team, which was not popular in the bigger metropolitan clubs, like the MCC, who felt they had the best players. Tom put colony ahead of club. He wrote with conviction of the importance of Victoria fielding its

best team but also, and more importantly, of embracing all men
with talent, not the privileged few. Whether it be professionals
or country players, Tom supported their cause. Precious few
did. Most cricketers and clubs thought it was simply a waste
of money bringing players from the small provincial towns
for practice, whereas Tom proclaimed to the colony: 'No, Sir,
I choose men for their real worth. I stoop not so low as to
choose a man because he may happen to be a friend of mine,
or a member of my club, or because he is a good man to *shout*.'

Tom's letters were popular and appeared weekly, sometimes
daily, depending on which newspaper published them, giving
the general public who would never enter the MCC a glimpse of
the politics of the Club. Or, at least, to see it according to Tom.
The average person regarded the MCC as elitist and inaccessible,
yet here was the honorary secretary of the Club talking about
professional cricketers as worthy and equal, about players from
Ballarat not from South Yarra, and whose challenging rhetoric
gave a voice to thousands who would never be heard or have
their letters printed in the newspapers. And for this Tom Wills
was adored. It is unlikely that Tom tried to win popular favour,
but this was the effect. Tom Wills was captain of a colony of
thousands of ordinary men and women before he was ever
named the captain of the Victorian XI; and soon he would be
that, too. It was only weeks before the next intercolonial match
to be played on the Melbourne Cricket Ground, in which he
would lead the Victorians onto the field.

The Chief Minister of the colony, William Haines, moved
to adjust the hours of parliament to allow parliamentary
members to watch the intercolonial match. Employers were
expected to release their workers during the hours of the
match. On the morning of the game, the Victorian and New
South Wales teams met for breakfast at the Richmond home
of the Melbourne Cricket Club president, Daniel Stodhart
Campbell.

The match commenced on 11 January 1858; the players of the two teams congregated on the ground just outside the pavilion, hitting practice balls. Wending their way amongst the players were the spectators who, on hearing the first clangs of a warning bell, began drifting slowly towards the boundary flags. Governor Henry Barkly arrived at noon; another few clangs of the bell, more drifting and then with the last bell the more inquisitive and sticky of the spectators finally made their way behind the boundary flags. They clustered around the perimeter of the ground: a finite space which at different points spilled over onto the field. Fifteen thousand spectators watched the game over the next three days. There was no time limit to matches in the 1850s and, theoretically, a game could stretch into weeks. But they never did. The nineteenth-century pitches were unpampered seams of earth and matches rarely lasted beyond three days.

Tom batted at position seven making 12 runs out of the Victorian total of 59: a moderate score at best. The New South Wales captain, George Gilbert, took the first hat trick in Australian first-class cricket that day: the first was Thomas Wray, an amateur from the Melbourne Cricket Club, followed by the professionals Gideon Elliott and George Marshall. At 3.30 p.m., the hottest portion of the day, the Victorian team, dressed in Cambridge light-blue shirts and white flannel trousers and caps, walked from the pavilion down the small set of wooden steps onto the ground.

During this match, Tom was etched in a lithograph: paused before bowling, about six to eight steps from the wicket. He is in a characteristic stance: a casual cockiness now so well practised that the origins of its contrivance from his sporting days at Rugby was probably long forgotten. But even in the still life, his figure was provocatively emphasised and would stir the interest of most. He took 5 wickets and New South Wales made 57 runs in their first innings.

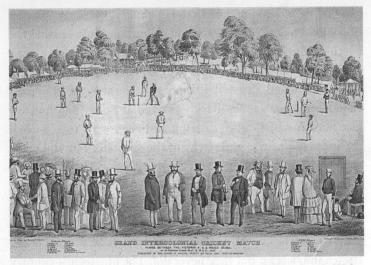

Intercolonial Cricket Match between Victoria and New South Wales,
January 1858

On the second day Tom walked out to bat without leg
guards – as was his practice. At the time, batsmen could choose
not to wear leg guards, more out of comfort than as an act of
defiance. During his innings he faced Oswald Lewis, a fast
underarm bowler who skidded the ball along the surface of the
pitch. Lewis bowled and the ball, hitting an imperfection in
the pitch, jumped and smashed into the soft flesh above Tom's
mouth. For a moment Tom lay unconscious; Dr Campbell
rushed out and attended him on the pitch. After several minutes
Tom rose, batted for another two hours, and at day's end was
49 not out. The Victorians made 238 runs, a figure not thought
possible in colonial cricket. The ring of spectators rushed the
field, throwing Tom onto their shoulders, and marched into
the pavilion. Victoria had all but won.

On the third and final day, Tom bowled to George Gilbert,
the New South Wales captain. He bowled a 'fast trimmer', a
ball designed to hit the top of the stumps; instead it hit Gilbert

near his waist. For a moment Gilbert stood, seemingly paralysed, and then snapped at the waist. He sank, his body folded in two, onto the pitch. Gilbert was carried from the ground. The Victorian papers commented that the New South Wales captain had been hit in 'a particular part of his person'. For those in the penny seats drunkenly swigging on swipes and nobblers, he was hit in the balls and good riddance. Gilbert, the only threat to Victoria, had taken 11 wickets as a bowler and top-scored for New South Wales in their first innings. Bruised testicles should have seen him out but when Gilbert limped back onto the ground to resume batting, Hammersley suggested Tom 'send in a sparkler' to test Gilbert's testicles. It was a private joke amongst Victoria's cricketers that Tom Wills could hit obstinate batsmen to soften them up. Perhaps it was simply the uneven surfaces of the time, but it happened enough to make cricketers consider its truth.

Victoria won the match; a German orchestra played and the MCC president welcomed all the players into the tiny pavilion. Campbell was gracious towards the defeated New South Wales team – he could afford to be. Into that modest thirty-foot pavilion were crowded some of the wealthiest and most powerful men in the colony, who celebrated what they privately believed: their colony was superior in all things. Tom had justified their opinion. Reports hint at a scene of scrambling politicians and influential members, the decorum broken in their haste to shake the hands of the Victorian cricketers – and in particular, Tom's. The following day Tom and the team travelled to the Toorak home of Governor Henry Barkly, for dinner and to receive formal congratulations on behalf of the colony.

In the midst of celebrating at the Governor's house, Tom rose to speak on behalf of the cricketers. He made an unusual and unexpected comment. He called himself a Sydney man, in reference to the colony where he was born. It was not a pointed or a malicious statement, and at the time it was probably forgotten within the flash of another bottle being uncorked, or lost in the jubilant jugs of wine that ripped down throats. The Victorians felt they owned Tom Wills, but Tom was not beholden to them and it was a sign that even in his moment of deepest attachment to the colony of Victoria, he belonged to no one in particular.

FOOT-BALL

JANUARY 1858–SEPTEMBER 1858

After the victorious intercolonial cricket match, Tom became embroiled in disputes on the field. He squabbled over the laws of cricket and was accused of unfair or unchivalrous play. When batting for St Kilda against the Richmond Club, 'he was floored by one of Elliott's balls, having incautiously retired to the tent to cheer himself with a glass of lemonade'. It was common knowledge that Tom was drunk when he batted that day. A series of blazing fights dogged him. Capricious and competitive, he captained the Collingwood Cricket Club while still playing for the MCC and St Kilda.

In the last week of February 1858, Tom and the Victorian team travelled to Tasmania at the invitation of the Launceston Cricket Club. The Victorians, captained by Tom, played a local Launceston team and won by an innings. Gideon Elliott took 9 wickets for 2 runs. The Launceston cricketers were displeased that the Victorian team included three professional cricketers – Jerry Bryant, George Marshall and Gideon Elliott – and held this to be an unfair advantage for the Victorians. The Launcestonians had wished to play only with amateurs and claimed the Victorians had broken an earlier agreement to bring only amateur cricketers. Tom was furious and disputed the Launceston claim.

The self-satisfied superiority of his cricketing hosts in Launceston angered Tom. They explained that it was impossible for the Victorian cricketers to meet the families of the Launceston cricketers as the Tasmanians were unable to distinguish who was a professional and who was an amateur. While the amateurs would have been welcomed into the homes of the Launceston families, the thought of welcoming the professionals curdled the Tasmanians' sensibilities. Tom pointed out the absurdity of the Launceston claim. If the professionals were unable to be distinguished from the amateurs – no blemish marked their body or tainted their behaviour – then why not treat them as men ought to be treated and regard amateur and professional alike? 'We have been in a strange land and forsaken' an enraged Tom wrote of Launceston. It was a slight Tom would not forget.

The following week the Victorians moved south and played a team from Hobart. On the last day of the match, Tom, bowling his fast round-arm deliveries, violently hit one of the Tasmanian batsmen three times on the right leg with such severity that the batsman was unable to run between wickets. The Hobart crowd observed with distaste Tom jump about exultantly when the cricket ball hit the batsman. It was suggested in the Hobart newspaper that Tom, in future, curb his delight in another's physical pain rather than squawk tastelessly like an excitable parrot splashing about in a waterhole.

Back in Melbourne, Tom told everyone his view of the welcome that he and his team had received in Launceston. The Victorians, who needed little excuse to look down their gold-lined noses at anyone, poked fun at the Launceston team and backed Tom.

Horatio Wills would have admired his son's defence of the Victorian professional cricketers in Launceston, if he had not been preoccupied with his own problems in the Parliament of Victoria. After three years Horatio Wills had found he did not have the stomach or gamesmanship for the theatrics of the parliament. Miscast in his role as a parliamentarian, his limited capacity to make public speeches, interest in phrenology and portly build were easy prey for circling satirists. When he asked the chamber if he might read his speeches rather than speak without notes, he was ridiculed. Each time Horatio rose to speak he experienced swelling tension across his chest and his mouth became dry, making it difficult for him to give his address. Horatio struggled with severe anxiety in parliament; though he did not avoid the task of speaking, he was, for the most part, a relatively peripheral figure in the years he sat in parliament. He had been regarded by the press as naive but enthusiastic when he first entered parliament. By his second month he was portrayed without pity:

> Mr. WILLS seems to possess in greater perfection than any other member of Council, the art of so framing his motions and his speeches that of necessity they come to nothing. It would be premature to condemn him as a permanently useless politician, indeed, because his faults may be curable, and his motives seem good. Up to the present time, however, he has been emphatically a blunderer.

By April 1858, parliament was not in session and Horatio was back at Belle Vue, relieved at temporarily escaping the derisive world of politics. The month of April gave Tom further access to those of wealth and influence in the colony. He dined with Sir George Stephen, a barrister and one of the few knighted men in the colony, and with members of the two Houses of the Victorian Parliament. The occasion was the Annual Dinner for the St Kilda Cricket Club, at which there was serial toasting and Tom was proclaimed the greatest cricketer in the land. When Tom rose to speak he flattered and warmed Sir George with his words and 'testified to the assiduity with which Sir G. Stephen and his "stool" attended the matches of the club'. Tom and Sir George lathered one another with praise; Sir George ended by saying that he never removed his stool upon which he sat to watch cricket when 'Mr. Wills was on the ground'. Tom was as well known in the colony as any man in that room, and certainly more loved by the people of Victoria. Knighted men and ministers of parliament knew that better than most.

Two months later, the Melbourne Cricket Club urgently convened a meeting – the Club was in debt. Tom did not attend. The delegates at the meeting accused Tom of unsatisfactory performance as the MCC honorary secretary and cited his 'continued non-attendance' at meetings. It was implied that Tom's poor administrative skills were part of the reason for the Club's debt. A resolution was passed that Tom forward the Club's books and papers relevant to his post as secretary if he intended to remain absent from meetings. On hearing these accusations Tom responded by writing a public letter, rebuking the Melbourne Cricket Club and rejecting the claim of his poor attendance at meetings. He wailed: 'If they had under gone one-half the fatigue or work for the Club that I have done this year they would not be quite so fast with their votes, not that I care for such a vote, but it shows the spirit of the Club to its best supporters, and if they carry on much longer in the same munificent manner, they will find themselves minus some of their best players.' Arguments with fellow members and threats to leave the Club were not new to Tom or the Club. No one knew what Tom might do, least of all himself.

•

Winter in Melbourne was a slow time. The pages of *Bell's Life*, which had sparkled with the argy-bargy of cricket, were deflated, and the advertised amusements as dull as the Melbourne light in June. Then on 10 July 1858, *Bell's Life* published the following remarkable letter from Tom. The editor wedged it below an entry on 'Pedestrianism' and above one on 'Billiards'.

WINTER PRACTICE

To the Editor of Bell's Life in Victoria

SIR, – Now that cricket has been put aside for some few months to come, and cricketers have assumed somewhat of the chrysalis nature (for a time only 'tis true), but at length will again burst forth in all their varied hues, rather than allow this state of torpor to creep over them, and stifle their new supple limbs, why can they not, I say, form a foot-ball club, and form a committee of three or more to draw up a code of laws? If a club of this sort were got up, it would be of a vast benefit to any cricket-ground to be trampled upon, and would make the turf quite firm and durable; besides which it would keep those who are inclined to become stout from having their joints encased in useless superabundant flesh. If it is not possible to form a foot-ball club, why should not these young men who have adopted this new-born country for their mother land, why I say, do they not form themselves into a rifle club, so as at any-rate they may be some day called upon to aid their adopted land against a tyrant's band, that may some day 'pop' upon us when we least expect a foe at our very doors. Surely our young cricketers are not afraid of the crack of the rifle, when they face so courageously the leathern sphere, and it would disgrace no one to learn in time how to defend his country and his hearth. A firm heart, a steady hand, and a quick eye, are all that are requisite and, with practice, all these be attained. Trusting that some one will take up the matter, and form either of the above clubs, or, at any rate, some athletic games, I remain, yours truly,

T.W. WILLS

Tom Wills was bringing his English schooling to Melbourne. Rugby School was the defining experience of Tom's sporting life; he played cricket in summer and football in winter. The time of the year when cricket stopped and football started was

Winter in Australia: Football in the Richmond Paddock

called the 'turnabout' by Rugby schoolboys. 'Turnabout' was
a ritual and cricket did not end until the captain of the cricket
team ended the cricket season and had his say as to when football
should commence. Tom Wills had been part of this changeover
of the seasons of sport for five years, and as a leading cricketer
he would have had a significant say in when turnabout took
place. He would do the same in Melbourne.

Two other factors probably shaped Tom's mind when he
called upon Melbourne to form a 'foot-ball' club. In 1855, the
year Tom captained the Rugby School cricket team, *Bell's Life
in London* published a letter that was, in tone and phrasing,
almost a clone of that written by Tom in Melbourne three years
later. The letter in *Bell's Life in London* urged the formation of
a rifle club and emphasised the importance of the defence of
England: 'Nothing could add so much to the national security
as a general knowledge of the use of the rifle.' There were
other letters of similar style written during the 1850s in this
sporting paper which could hardly have escaped the eye of Tom

who continued to read *Bell's Life in London* when he returned to Melbourne.

The final influence on Tom was his father. Horatio Wills sat on a parliamentary subcommittee to examine the colony's defences and soon, travelling to London on family matters, spoke to the Home Secretary on defence issues. Two weeks before Tom's letter, Horatio was linked publicly with the possible fortification of Corio Bay near Geelong. Rugby School, the newspaper letters in London and his father were the elements that shaped Tom's mind when he wrote his letter.

Advertisements appeared on Friday, 6 August 1858, in *The Argus* and *Herald*: a game of football was to start at noon the following day, Saturday 7 August, on the Richmond Paddock, just outside the Melbourne Cricket Ground. Forty Scotch College boys were to play a similar number from the Melbourne Church of England Grammar School, with a luncheon at the MCC pavilion. One team was to wear pink, the other blue. On Saturday morning, *The Herald* announced that there were no fixed rules for the game of football. Two umpires were to control the football match: Tom was one and the other was Dr John Macadam, the chemistry master at Scotch College. Macadam, born near Glasgow, had been in the colony for three years and was known and respected about town. Trained as a doctor and a skilled analytical chemist, he was a member of the Victorian Philosophical Society and was soon to be elected into the Legislative Assembly. With shoulder-length hair swept back over a high forehead and a neat, full beard, the dashing Macadam had the bearing of a nobleman.

Tom Wills had links to both schools. One of his employers, Robert Willan, was on the Melbourne Grammar School Council and had three boys at the school. And Tom's thirteen-year-old brother Cedric was a pupil at Scotch College and may have even played in the match.

Scotch College was a short distance from the Richmond Paddock – Cedric Wills and the other students could walk there in a few minutes. Several of the Scotch masters played football. One of them, Robert Morrison, was the younger brother of the Scotch headmaster, Alexander Morrison, and remembered by one of the boys as a footballer who was 'a fast runner and fair kick'. Thomas Smith, a teacher of classics, was tempestuous on the football field, favouring the technique of rabbiting. This was a rather violent tackle to bring down an opposition player who was running with the ball by suddenly bending down in front of the running player.

The headmaster of the Melbourne Grammar School, John Edward Bromby, had arrived in Melbourne in February and the school had opened in April, only four months previously.

Little is known about this day's football played on the Richmond Paddock, but we know that it and the few games of football played that year were closer to the game played at Rugby School than any other kind of football. On the Saturday evening, Bromby noted in his diary that the match had been 'fiercely contested for 3 hours' after which Scotch scored a goal and soon after that his own boys equalised. Evening fell and the day's play ended. What Tom made of this match on the Richmond Paddock is not known. He never troubled editors of newspapers with a letter and no private letters remain that recall this particular match. The game was continued on two subsequent Saturdays, ending without either team scoring again.

The voices of the boys who played during this early period of football are largely lost, but two or three have survived, recording the lingering strands of a lost conversation. One Grammar boy recalled:

> Our football-game had no rules at all. Tripping, elbowing, tackling, or anything else, was practised with impunity. I remember one tough little fellow who used to jump on the backs of taller boys and bring them down, and there were some who had more interest in counting the number of fellows they could trip than in trying to get the ball. There

was no limit to the number of players, or to the duration of the game, and masters used to play together with the boys.

Within a year of the football game against Scotch College, there were concerns voiced about the game's violence and several parents at Melbourne Grammar refused permission for their sons to play. A Scotch College boy recorded his memories when, as an elderly man, he remembered Tom Wills:

> It was in 1858 that the first real football was seen on the Grammar school ground when T.W. Wills brought a huge sewn many seamed round ball to show his brothers how to play the new English game, and it at once became popular.

Several games of football, conducted with little formality, were recorded in the winter of 1858 and players, moving among the few teams, played with whichever team needed them. Often men and boys played in the one team, though the dangers of this were apparent from the start to the participants. Apart from several school teams, there were the beginnings of adult teams but no suggestion of club structure and administration. Tom Wills was not the only person who organised these early football matches but his voice was the clearest and his is the name, more than any other, that writers of the time referred to in their portrayals of the Melbourne game of football.

On the last Saturday of September, Tom played in the final football match recorded in 1858, captaining the Melbourne team against South Yarra. At either end of the measured ground stood two goal posts and atop each post cotton handkerchiefs waved as flags. The football was a sphere 'neatly stitched'. Each side had twenty-six players. South Yarra wore blue shirts, Melbourne wore whatever they could, and all wore boots and full-length trousers. The betting favoured the South Yarra team. The game played that day, as in the previous games, was close in style to Rugby School football. In a full page of verse in the journal *Melbourne Punch*, only one player from the over fifty players on the field was mentioned by name: Tom Wills. Tom charged towards the goal leading a phalanx of his men. Melbourne kicked the only goal to win and the players adjourned to drink. The football season ended.

On the morning of this last football match, *Bell's Life in Victoria* reported that Tom Wills was no longer the honorary secretary of the Melbourne Cricket Club. Readers of *Bell's Life* learnt that D.S. Campbell, the president of the Club, was furious with Tom due to his lack of compliance with the Club's previous resolution that Tom return the minute books of his time as secretary. Tom cared little for the resolution and for the MCC; he failed to attend the Annual General Meeting at which he was replaced as honorary secretary. Perhaps it is a measure of his inadequate administration that, over 150 years later, the only minute book that cannot be located within the Club is from his time as secretary. Tom left the pile of junk he had collected as honorary secretary in a tin box in the pavilion, without any semblance of order. As if in a pique of rage, Tom gathered the Club's Zingari caps, cigars and pipes, spiked boots, cricketers' guides and minute books, and in one resentful heave threw them skyward to land in a spectacular shower of rubbish in the box. Hammersley recalled how the place was in chaos when Tom left.

Professor Sohier, at his Melbourne museum of phrenology, could have told President Campbell, William Hammersley and the other members of the Melbourne Cricket Club about the commotion in Tom's head. The forces of geology and volcanism were at work – Tom's skull bones, like the grinding and buckling plates of the earth's crust, were on the move.

Tom turned his back on the MCC and did what he had threatened to do one year earlier. He left the Melbourne Cricket Club and walked across the Richmond Paddock to find another club.

THE TREE OF LIFE

Professor McCoy, Melbourne University's first professor of natural science, collected his specimens carefully. In his specimen case was an insect collected from the Richmond Paddock, a phasmid, or stick insect, that measured 6 inches long. It was found camouflaged on a young gum tree, not far from the MCC pavilion. The first thing to strike the eye about this insect was its emerald segmented body; then its wingspan, which when fully stretched circumscribed a circle the size of a small dinner plate. All attention then rested on the colour of the wings: brilliant pink, a pink to bring delight to every little girl, a gift from the fairies. The semi-transparent wings, like tissue paper easily torn, allowed the insect to float from tree to tree in the Richmond Paddock. It had beautifully and perfectly adapted to life in the surrounds of Melbourne. The scientist in McCoy knew that this was the Australian insect *Podocanthus typhon* but he called it his 'Pink Lady'.

It was unlikely that Tom Wills considered anything more than cricket and football when he walked across the Richmond Paddock, the paddock to which he brought the rules of Rugby School football. This style of football would have to undergo changes to suit a new climate and landscape. The Melbourne rules of football did not come in a single stroke – rather, they evolved. The lesson of the 'Pink Lady' was that if a suitable niche could be found, life could adapt to the colony's conditions. That lesson, taken from the natural world, applied to all areas of new life in the colony: local environment and cultural isolation shaped change. The new football would have to adapt to the hard ground, the gravel surface and vast sloping land next to the MCC pavilion. The Richmond Paddock was a crucible of new life in the colony of Melbourne; new species, new ideas, new games were brought together to see what might survive and what would falter.

The Richmond Paddock shaped how football would evolve over the next few years.

TO BOWL WITH THE GODS

SEPTEMBER 1858–APRIL 1860

Act before you think was the creed by which Tom lived. He had left the MCC in a manner few men would have dared. Recklessly, perhaps courageously, he walked the 400 yards to play his cricket on the Richmond Cricket Ground, which stood in the same paddock as the Melbourne Cricket Ground. An appreciation of his own worth in cricket allowed him the freedom to move wherever he wished.

Gideon Elliott ran the Royal Hotel on Punt Road, opposite the Richmond Cricket Ground. In the coming year he built a small shelter on the ground to accommodate the Richmond Club members and guests. Elliott's little shed came to symbolise the Richmond Club's weaker social standing compared with the Melbourne Cricket Club. It was used as a bar and a dressing room, so cramped that players stumbled over one another when they entered and in summer the bodies huddled within sweated as one, giving off a collective odour.

In September 1858, Tom was unanimously elected president of the Collingwood Cricket Club. Richmond did not seem to mind but the Melbourne Cricket Club took great offence at Tom's libertine cricketing lifestyle. The MCC members never forgave Tom for leaving, and when the Richmond Club rapidly assumed

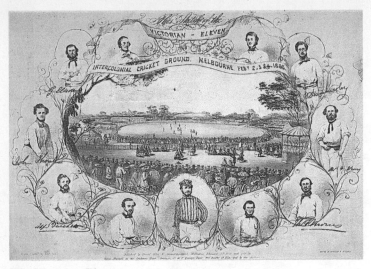

The Victorian Eleven

the position of the finest team in the colony, this grievance
turned into public criticism. James Thompson, the journalist and
disgruntled MCC member, wrote in his *Argus* column that Tom
had found a habitat in the Richmond Club more 'congenial' to
his nature. It was a cruel and public insult. Thompson's letter was
bait and Tom's enemies, the envious and the mediocre, gathered
about laughing and watched Tom's combustible brain crackle.

   The January 1859 intercolonial cricket match was to be
played on the Domain in Sydney. The colony of Victoria
expected Tom to win them matches; the chance of losing to
New South Wales seemed unlikely when Tom took the field.
He posed for a photograph with four other cricketers from
the team – Gideon Elliott, Jerry Bryant, George Marshall
and Barton Grindrod. Tom, beautifully attired and cradling
a cricket ball, appeared confident, almost insolent. The match
started with a storm and the rain rendered the field slippery.
On the first day Tom dislocated the top joint of his right middle
finger while attempting a catch. Apparently unaffected, he took

11 wickets for 49 runs, including the critical wicket of Oswald Lewis with the first ball of the last day, at a time in the match when the New South Wales team looked favourite to win. The Victorians won the match by two wickets.

Tom could do anything on the cricket field. He was recognised as the finest bowler and captain in the country, and when he fixed his mind to the task, he was a determined, cautious batsman who could hit the ball hard. Tom bowled fast round-arm, which frightened and hurt batsmen, and slow underhand lobs that flummoxed them – and seemingly every style or pace in between. He bowled the 4-ball overs with astonishing variety and could change from fast, to slow, to underhand lobs on a whim. He bowled whenever and wherever he wished and commonly bowled throughout an entire innings. As captain, he rarely needed to listen to other players' opinions and, according to Hammersley, when he did occasionally listen, Tom always followed his own mind.

Of all the paraphernalia that made up the game of cricket, it was the cricket ball that lay closest to Tom's heart. There were many places he could get hold of a cricket ball but the best known was George Marshall's Cricket Depot, Swanston Street, opposite the Town Hall. Anything to do with cricket could be purchased at Marshall's store: cane-handle bats, spring-handle bats, whalebone-handle bats, Zingari shirts, caps, belts and leg guards. Tom spent time there, wrote letters there. It was a popular point of congregation for the sportsmen of Melbourne. In 1859 Marshall advertised that he had in stock a new invention, a catapult, that flung cricket balls and was able to 'pitch the ball at any length unknown to the batsman, and at any pace'.

The cricket ball of 1859 was required to weigh not less than 5½ ounces, or more than 5¾ ounces; its circumference was regulated to not less than 9 inches, or more than 9¼ inches. Some might think the importance of the cricket ball inferior to that of the cricket bat. The amateur gentlemen did – eager to hold this piece of carved wood and stand erect. Their task was

*Left to right: Gideon Elliott, Barton Grindrod, George Marshall,
James Bryant and Tom Wills*

to bat well but more importantly to appear poised, masculine
and stylish. But Tom understood the value of the cricket ball; so
did the professional bowlers at the MCC who toiled obediently
under the sun for the amateur members. It is the cricket ball,
not the cricket bat, which should sit atop a pedestal. Without the
ball there is no thrust of one team against the other, no point
of contact or penetration, no potential for violence. Without
the ball nothing happens in cricket. The bat may glory in its
size and its varieties of wood, shaped and gleaming with oil,
but the ball has the simplicity and eternal beauty of the sphere.

A cricket ball records on its surface an entire match. A close
look at its leather covering – that red rind that encases a cricket
ball – will find marks scratched on its surface, imperfections

that are inflicted by the bat, the pitch and by every player on the field who touches the ball; marks invisible to the naked eye left by the bowler as he scratches at the ball with his fingernails, or plucks a loose thread or polishes hard. This is the bowler's scrimshaw, not carved on whalebone, but on the leather of a cricket ball.

Despite its apparent symmetry, no cricket ball is perfect. Each ball has a unique structure that gives it a distinct life. Bowlers sense this when they fondle a new ball, feeling how it might move or bounce. Tom may not have understood how a cricket ball obeyed the laws of physics but he was able to instinctively shift to that other world of the divine, where the few with true genius play sport. When he played cricket, it was not merely a game amongst mortals – Tom Wills bowled with the Gods.

•

At the end of March 1859 Horatio left for Europe, taking his three younger boys – Cedric, Horace and Egbert – to Germany for further schooling. Horatio remained in Europe for almost a year and on his return to Melbourne did not re-enter parliament.

Tom finished the cricket season by playing his last game for the Corio Cricket Club in Geelong. He wrote of the match to his father, who was now in London, and asked Horatio to pass the cricket scores on to Cedric, Horace and Egbert. Tom continued to pass on the results of his matches: invariably a list of successes watched by some of the most eminent men in the colony. It is difficult to say if Tom communicated these results for Horatio's approval, in the same vein as a younger Tom had sought Horatio's approval as a schoolboy at Rugby, but, regardless of his reasoning, Tom was keen that his father knew of his sporting life. Horatio read Tom's letter about the last match of the season and sent them on to his younger boys in Germany, telling them how proud he was of Tom. It was Horatio's idea to turn Tom into a lawyer but this was always a forlorn hope. Tom almost never mentioned his time with the solicitors Willan and Smith, other than a flippant remark or two, and it is hard to imagine, given his preoccupation with cricket and football, that he spent any time there at all. But for the moment, Horatio was content enough with his son's progress in the colony.

●

The Parade Hotel on Wellington Parade, with its smoking rooms, billiard tables and spread of sporting newspapers from London and the colonies, was a natural gathering place for the sporting men of Melbourne. Its licencee, Jerry Bryant, professional bowler for the MCC and an astute businessman, supplied the MCC with wines and beers. He boasted that he served only the finest of liquors, and, while this was a standard boast of hotelkeepers in Melbourne, it was rumoured that colonial-made beers were adulterated with impurities and that too much consumption sent a man mad. Bryant's hotel stood on the northern perimeter of the Richmond Paddock, 'only ten minutes walk from Melbourne'. Its proximity to the MCC with its clientele of sporting gentlemen was a stroke of entrepreneurial brilliance. It was only a short walk (or roll, depending on one's state of inebriation) from the Parade Hotel down the slope of the Richmond Paddock to reach the MCC pavilion, and there was always a steady line of customers making their way up the hill from the MCC.

On 17 May 1859, the first known written rules of Australian Rules football were agreed upon at the Parade Hotel. Four men decided the rules that day: Tom Wills, William Hammersley, James Thompson and Thomas Smith. Not a modest man amongst them. Thomas Henry Smith, classics master at Scotch College, recalled the exact day almost twenty years afterwards: 'Mr Wills, Mr Hammersley and myself' walked up the slope from the Melbourne Cricket Ground to the Parade Hotel. The fourth member, James Thompson, met the others at the hotel. According to Smith, the four men 'formed ourselves into a committee'. When the 'Rules of the Melbourne Football Club May 1859' were written and signed, Tom Wills headed the list of rule writers. The committee had been convened after a 'severe fight' and 'some smart raps exchanged, and a leg broken' on the Richmond Paddock. Skirmishes were common; 'hacking was permitted, and no objection was taken to spiked shoes'. It was customary for players to 'adjourn to the Parade Hotel close by, and think the matter over'. It is likely that the 17 May 1859 meeting was simply the most formal of these occasions when players met to consider the rules of the game.

The ten rules of the new Melbourne game were shaped by the football played at English Public Schools – Rugby, Harrow, Eton and Winchester. The four men made it clear that these English games were the starting point of their deliberations; Tom pressed strongly for the Rugby School football rules. Hammersley recalled: 'Tom Wills suggested the Rugby rules, but nobody understood them except himself.' James Thompson opposed certain features of the Rugby School game. He disliked carrying the ball by hand; the practice of 'place kicks', whereby the ball was placed in a shallow hole and then kicked; and the awarding of a free kick to a player who caught a ball from a kick. Despite Thompson's protestations over the next few years, these elements of the Rugby game were part of the Melbourne rules from the beginning.

Simplifying play and controlling excess violence lay at the heart of the new rules. Even Tom, who favoured the adoption of the Rugby School game, recognised the need for compromise. Hacking – the deliberate kicking of another player's shins – was banished in the Melbourne rules. The hardness of the ground on the Richmond Paddock also influenced Tom's thinking. He wrote to his brother Horace: 'Rugby was not a game for us, we wanted a winter pastime but men could be harmed if thrown on the ground so we thought differently.'

Tom brought the experiences of his Rugby schooldays to the early rules. He felt strongly about them and over the next

Rules of the Melbourne
Football Club
May, 1859

Officers of the Club
Committee
T. W. Wills Esq　　　T. Butterworth Esq
W. Hammersley Esq　—　Smith Esq
Alex Bruce Esq
Hon Treasurer
J Sewell Esq
Hon Secretary
J. B. Thompson Esq

twenty years tried to introduce more Rugby School rules into the Melbourne game. Although influential, he did not always succeed. Later, he would want a cross bar as part of the goals and he would also request that when a player received a free kick near goal, the best kicker in the team should kick for the goal. The practice in the Melbourne game was to give the kick to the player who was fouled. Tom, the designated kicker for goal for Evans House and the longest kick of a football in the colony of Victoria, would have used this change to his advantage. Neither of these changes were introduced into the Australian game. As for the shape of the ball, Tom's intransigence on this point was to win through. The issue of the ball's shape came to a head in 1860; James Thompson was Tom's main critic. Thompson, writing for *The Argus*, reported on the novelty of the oval ball at a meeting held in the pavilion at the Melbourne Cricket Club. Two weeks later, during a game between the Melbourne Club and the Richmond Club, the shape of the ball was raised again. Thompson objected to the oval ball but an obstinate Wills, captain that day of the Richmond team, demanded that the oval ball be used. Thompson wrote:

> Another drawback to an otherwise almost perfect afternoon's enjoyment was the objectionable shape of the ball, which was oval, and is said to have gained the prize at the Great Exhibition, besides being of the kind now in use at Rugby School. This class of ball may fly further than a round one, but assuredly, in nine cases out of ten, does not fulfil the expectations of the propeller, more particularly if there be any wind. Considerable dissatisfaction was expressed when the game began at the Richmond captain's [Wills] maintaining his right to the choice of ball, and a great deal more after the play was over.

The Melbourne rules spread quickly. Games were being played in Geelong in 1859, and by 1860 there were at least two football clubs in the Geelong region and probably many more that went unrecorded. George Glencross-Smith, Tom's friend at Point Henry, as an old man wrote to remind the public in a newspaper letter that it was Tom Wills who had brought the game of Australian Rules football to Geelong.

Over the next two years, Tom Wills became the most influential figure in football, playing against and alongside men with whom he played cricket. Most were amateur cricketers but the professional cricketers played as well. In football there was no distinction made; it was an egalitarian mix of players, something that might have pleased Tom. The names of Wills, Thompson, Smith, Bryant, Hammersley, Wardill and Harrison were often mentioned in the brief press reports on football. All had close links with the Melbourne Cricket Club. Tom played football at first for the Melbourne Club, usually on the Richmond Paddock just outside the Melbourne Cricket Ground, though occasionally games of football were permitted to be played on the MCG during these early years. Players moved freely amongst the teams; Tom played for Melbourne, Richmond and Geelong.

Of the early footballers, Tom Wills was regarded as the most highly skilled tactician and astute leader on the field. Competitive and aggressive, he was a dominant player whose long kicking was a potent source of goals. He experimented with tactics, improvised on the football field, and his original and competitive mind saw strategies and opportunities not previously seen. In one tactical leap, which foreshadowed the modern game, Wills, as captain of the Richmond Football Club, positioned his men down the football ground from defence to attack, instructing them to kick the ball directly to one another towards goal, and 'by this means succeeded in getting the ball safely landed between the posts'. On another day when his Melbourne team played the South Yarra team, there were fewer players than usual, allowing more space to run with the ball. He instructed his players to relinquish the conventional style of play, which was a mass of players clumped together shoving the ball forward, like Rugby schoolboys, asking them instead to exploit the lower number of players on the field and use the space by darting and running with the ball. Melbourne won. Tom's innovations were brilliant at a time of unimaginative manoeuvres.

Tom's cousin Colden Harrison first appeared in football player lists in 1859 and he drew attention for his speed on the field. Tom, among others, noting Colden's ability to sprint, 'insisted' that Colden compete in footraces. Within a year Tom remarked in a letter to his brother Cedric: 'Colden has turned out the best runner in the Colony.'

In the winter of 1859, Tom returned to board at Mrs Harrison's house in Victoria Parade and joined the volunteer artillery. Tom did not write about the early Melbourne football rules that he helped compose. Football, it seemed, was simply a recreation; rather, he kept writing letters on cricket.

Despite it being winter, there were still arguments in the newspapers about Tom and cricket – his lack of attendance at cricket matches, whether the MCG should be fenced and disputed umpiring decisions. In September, he was elected as vice president of the Richmond Cricket Club and, soon afterwards, to a committee for the Collingwood Cricket Club. In the same month Horatio purchased a book from a London bookstore as a gift for Tom, a dull piece called *A Handy Book on Property Law*, as a last attempt to lure Tom into a legal career. The pages remained untouched by Tom's ink and it is unlikely that Tom spent time on Horatio's gift. A few days after Horatio made this hopeful purchase, he wrote from London to his wife at Belle Vue:

Tell Tom that 'the greatest unwarrantable liberty' is not correct – 'The most unwarrantable' would be proper . . . I am so glad to receive your letters – so glad to receive Emily's letters – so glad to see Toms great improvement. He will yet be one of the first men in the colony if he tries.

Tom didn't need his father's criticism; he had enough critics in Melbourne to fend off. James Thompson was his sharpest foe. Wills and Thompson sat on the Victorian match committee in preparation for the next intercolonial match against New South Wales planned for February 1860. A practice match was arranged as part of the preparations and Tom was expected to captain one of the teams. The teams waited on the day but Tom did not arrive. In Thompson's eyes it was just the sort of irresponsibility he had tired of. Afterwards, Tom claimed that he was injured and could not take part in the match but Thompson scoffed and wrote in his *Argus* column: 'A tardy apology was brought over from the Richmond Ground, that Mr. Wills had hurt himself.' Thompson accused Wills of lying. It was a familiar refrain. In response Tom immediately resigned from the intercolonial match committee and sarcastically wrote of his accuser: 'Did the *Argus* reporter call a general meeting of the M.C.C. on Saturday to learn their opinion of me, or does he give his and their ideas from his private note book? (The one that incommodes his fielding I mean).' Thompson replied:

> Mr Wills – who I thought had by this time been taught that letter writing was not his *forte* . . . permit me to congratulate Mr. Wills upon having acquired something approaching to the first elements of English composition, an amiable eccentricity of which he has never yet been guilty, at least in his published correspondence . . . Mr. Wills declining from 'conscientious' motives to act upon a committee of which I am a member, is of itself so rich a gem, that no setting could improve its lustre.

Tom did play in a practice match in January 1860 at the Melbourne Cricket Ground. The temperature was over 100 degrees Fahrenheit and the sun and wind burned the players on the field. Tom Wills, choking with thirst, continued to play despite the remonstrations of others that he retire to the shade of the pavilion. Gideon Elliott and George Marshall had already escaped from the appalling heat. When Tom finally came in, severely dehydrated, exhausted, and distressed from the sun, the players laid him out upon a table in the MCC pavilion. A wet towel was wrapped about his head. 'I thought, really, it was all up with Tommy,' were the words of Hammersley, who had witnessed the scene.

Tom never boasted of his exertions that day on the Melbourne Cricket Ground, bowling throughout both innings. Why did he continue to bowl in that heat in a practice match when others about him fell? William Hammersley thought he knew the answer, recalling that a large crowd had gathered to watch Tom, and that Tom had felt an obligation to remain in the sun and perform for them.

Over 25,000 people attended the intercolonial cricket match in February at the MCG. Governor Barkly sat in his private box, elevated above the field of play to improve his view. Tom's mother Elizabeth and his sister Emily had travelled by train from Belle Vue to watch Tom, the Victorian captain. The oval was bare of grass in many places, the pitch was corrugated and dangerous, and a hot wind blew. Tom bowled, unchanged, in both innings. William Clarke, his hero from his Rugby School diary, would have approved. Tom scored 24 runs for the match, more than any other Victorian, and the Victorians won by 69 runs.

The evening after the victory, Emily watched Tom and the Victorian team walk on stage at the Cremorne Gardens, an amusement park near the Richmond Paddock, and receive a small medallion to mark their win – it was a tiny gold piece with a set of wickets and a cricket ball. Emily skited that 'Tom made a grand speech'. This was unusual, as Tom tended not to make 'grand speeches'; rather, his public words after a match were uttered with the pithiness of his father's phrasing. 'We licked 'em' was about the extent of his verbal eloquence, so different from his rambling and thought-disordered letters.

Afterwards Emily scolded Tom for losing a photograph of the Victorian cricketers: 'Tom has not one of those pictures of

the cricketers left. Not even for himself.' Her brother was careless but this was not severe criticism, for there was endearment
in Emily's tone. She forgave him. And most people repeatedly
forgave Tom. Despite Tom's raging letters and disputes with
fellow cricketers, it seemed no one took his recklessness and
spats too seriously.

After the match Tom posed in a bowling action for the
photographers, an action that many wished to examine more
closely, to observe the height of his arm and the straightness of
his elbow. There were murmurings that Tom's bowling action
was not entirely fair. He knew the rules better than most and
knew what could be bent to fit within the constraints of the
game. The disquiet over his bowling action had been voiced
when he was sixteen years old at Rugby School in England, and
had eventually followed him to Melbourne.

Cricket is a game that reflects deeply upon its history: rituals
are observed; precedents respected. This is no truer than in
the evolution of the action of bowling a ball. Lambert's 1816
Cricketers' Guide stipulated that: 'The ball must be delivered
underhanded, not thrown or jerked, with the hand below the
elbow at the time of delivering the ball.' In the early nineteenth
century a bowler kept his arm low, lower than his elbow, in a
kind of broad horizontal sweeping action. A further injunction,
in 1835, repeated that the ball must be bowled, not jerked, and
made it clear that the hand must not be above the shoulder in
delivery. This was still the law by which Tom bowled. Bowlers
strained within the confines of these anatomically bizarre rules
that sought to curb a bowler's effectiveness, although most
bowlers knew the law was absurd. William Caffyn, the great
Surrey professional, said that nine out of ten bowlers broke the
law at will by raising their arm above shoulder level.

Tom Wills dismissed the law and proclaimed that it was
unworkable: '. . . bowlers ought to be allowed to bowl as high as
they like, as long as they do not throw or jerk the ball . . .' Even
those bowlers who professed correctness of style practised their

craft with a thousand deceits. Bowlers in Melbourne, including Tom Wills, were caught between obeying what they regarded as a directive from Marylebone in London and their instincts. In 1860 the rule still read that the bowler could not have his hand above the shoulder at the point of delivery.

The point of contention regarding the fairness of Tom's bowling was largely whether his hand was raised above his shoulder as it swung to deliver the ball, though occasionally it was said he actually threw the ball. James Thompson wrote the following after Tom bowled for the Collingwood Club against the MCC:

> Wills, the migratory, was found in the Collingwood ranks, and, as usual, did great execution. A great deal of his bowling was, however, unfair in two respects – it was too high in the first place, besides bearing the closest possible affinity to a throw. The umpire for his side took no notice whatever of these continued improprieties, notwithstanding the repeated cries of 'No ball' from the pavilion, which was crowded with members of the club and their friends. This is by no means the first time this season that Wills, who ought to set a good instead of a bad example, has transgressed the tenth law. In the Intercolonial Match he put in a shy every now and then, and last week, at Emerald Hill, was frequently much above his shoulder. His motto seems to be, 'Get wickets, honestly if you can, but get wickets'. It is not to be expected that young bowlers, when they find 'the captain' sin with impunity, will be troubled with any rigid scruples, and bad habits will be acquired that will cost a whole season to get rid of.

Wills responded and accused the braying members of the Melbourne Cricket Club of selectively invoking the bowling rules when it suited their cause and mocked their capricious embrace of his talents: 'when the Sydney men fell fast before my bowling, there was no cry raised then by these members and their friends of no ball; oh, no, sir, it would not at all have suited them, not it; but when their pet club gets into difficulties, they have no lack of friends to shout and bellow "no ball . . .".' Despite the cries to do so, no umpire had called Tom for an illegal bowling action.

Although Tom still wrote letters to the press, his letters no longer flowed unrestricted and his influence was less prominent. In a bigger and more complex Melbourne than four years earlier, Tom's voice – still an insistent, provocative one – was now less easily heard.

A FATHER CALLS FOR HIS SON; EXPECTATION IS FULFILLED

APRIL 1860–OCTOBER 1861

'Tom has now retired from cricket,' Horatio announced to his family. Tom and Horatio were preparing to leave Victoria to take up another family property in Central Queensland. The property, Cullin-la-Ringo, was over 200 miles inland from the Queensland port of Rockhampton.

Horatio had summoned Tom to join him on the trek to Cullin-la-Ringo, and Tom did not resist travelling with his father to Queensland though there were good reasons to do so. Melbourne fizzed with the news that the first English Cricket XI might visit Australia before year's end. Private letters speculated on the team's arrival and public letters were full of what the English might make of the colonies. Tom, the best cricketer in the land, heard the news from all directions. Even Cedric, at school in Germany, had been aware of the impending visit by the English team: 'I have heard a good many persons say that the All England 11 are going over to play the Australians so tell Tom he may look out for getting a licking if they do.'

Every cricketer in Melbourne anticipated the visit of the Englishmen. Tom wrote to his cousin Colden Harrison and wondered if enough financial backing had been found to get the English team to Australia:

How about the All England Eleven – 6 of one & half a dozen of the other I suppose to their coming out – & . . . being able to raise the necessary subsidies – eh? Your aff cousin.

Horatio was not indifferent to his son's cricket. He boasted: 'I think our men will beat the English eleven. They would surely do so if Tom played. The Sydney people are delighted that Tom is not to play against their eleven this year.' Horatio did not disapprove, but cricket was not a way of life for someone moneyed. Tom, undoubtedly, would have captained the Victorian team against the English. It was an opportunity that might never arise again, but when the English

Horatio Wills

team walked out upon the Melbourne Cricket Ground, the best player in Australia would be 2000 miles distant in the Queensland bush. Why would Tom travel to Queensland on the cusp of his greatest moment?

One might have expected some reaction from Tom to his father's directive to accompany him to Queensland. Perhaps a stubborn moment or a plaintive declaration that he wished to remain in Melbourne. Tom had no end of comments or lines that he had used over the years, but instead there was nothing; Tom went to Queensland when he was asked by his father. For a man who railed at every moment in his public sporting life, this seems surprisingly meek. 'I have entirely given up cricket so you will not hear of me playing again in the Grand Matches.' This was a typical Tom declaration: expansive, with a touch of hysteria, and not entirely true.

Tom may have declared that he was finished with cricket, and so echo his father's wishes, but there were rumours in Melbourne that Tom had agreed to return from Queensland to play in Melbourne against the English team. To this end a committee in Melbourne had pledged sufficient funds to pay Tom's expenses from Queensland. Tom had also considered that, if Melbourne was too far away, then Sydney was not, and he became a member of the Albert Cricket Club, Sydney, for the summer of 1861–62. Horatio might have thought that Tom had given up cricket but Tom had arranged to play in both Sydney and Melbourne.

Apart from the visit by the English Cricket XI, there was little to keep Tom in Melbourne. His departure from the law offices of James Smith and Robert Willan caused him no discomfiture. With charm he informed his brothers in Germany that he was leaving the law to head bush, waving away any trifling family concerns: 'the law wont pay here now' he told them with an insouciance that came so naturally to him and which infuriated those around him. Tom's words were a deft deception, for there is no inkling that he was ever interested in the law – apart from appeasing his father's ambitions. It was a clever defence by Tom to say that the law would not pay, rather than acknowledge his own discontent and lack of commitment. It was a ploy Tom used frequently: to place responsibility upon something or someone else. It seemed to come so naturally that one wonders if Tom was even aware of it. The fault was never his own. The prospect of a career in law had now ended. Tom's amateur sporting contemporaries were men of a more conventional tilt: Richard Wardill was an accountant; William Hammersley and James Thompson were journalists; Colden Harrison was a public servant; Daniel Wilkie and Richard Driver were lawyers. But the dull refuge of financial and social convention held little to entice someone not of an orthodox bent of mind like Tom.

Perhaps there was a woman (or women) who might hold Tom in Melbourne? He rarely mentioned women in his personal correspondence, so he surprises when he wrote to Cedric of an unnamed woman: 'I am not yet <u>spliced</u> to the young lady in Sydney nor yet likely to be as she has got married to some one else – so that's all off but I must look out for someone else.' When his friends Gideon Elliott and Jerry Bryant married, Tom simply made the comment: 'Elliott is married so is Bryant' in a tone bleached of emotion, not bothering with whom Elliott and Bryant married. Tom noted the marriage of his friends with resignation and acceptance; a phase in life that one was expected to pass through. For a man not beholden to convention, marriage, the most stringent convention of all, was a dubious prospect. Tom's lack of self-examination and his egocentricity offered him immense freedom in pursuing his interests, whether that was women or sport. It seemed unlikely a woman would ever tie Tom to Melbourne.

In the months before Tom and Horatio left for Queensland there was disquiet with Tom amongst the family. The problem was money. Or more specifically Tom's infinite capacity to allow money to slip through his fingers. He struggled with the convention of marriage, and also failed at another pillar of convention – saving money – again at odds with his father who maintained his account book with precision.

In the financially responsible hands of Horatio, the Wills family rarely struggled for money. Over the previous decade, family money had flowed to Tom, unchecked; however, Horatio knew of Tom's lack of prudence with money and took steps to manage this. A pragmatic Horatio penned a fresh will in the days before Tom and he left Victoria; in so doing he separated his love for his son from the measures needed to protect the family estate. Horatio wrote: 'In the event of my said son Thomas Wentworth Wills misconducting himself' the trustees of the estate were authorised to remove Tom from the management of the station and if that be the case, Tom 'shall not participate in the final distribution of my estates as aforesaid but in lieu of his part or share shall receive for the term of his natural life the yearly sum of One hundred pounds and no more'. Cautious, reliable and measured, Horatio ensured Tom's welfare while protecting the estate. These were shrewd preparations by Horatio. His action showed a care for his son borne from a love that was as practical as it was affectionate, and it revealed Horatio's deep understanding of his son's personality.

In the six months before their departure from Melbourne, Horatio had despatched Tom to learn the station crafts of a squatter. Tom worked every day at a blacksmith, next to the White Horse Hotel on the Queenscliff Road near Point Henry. He worked with anvils, bellows and glowing hot tongs, and learnt how to shoe horses. His hands rapidly blistered: a wonderful preparation for Queensland cooed Horatio, predicting that Tom's large and bony hands were well on the way to the thickened insensitive skin needed for shearing. Next Tom was sent to the property of Alex Anderson at Skipton in Central Victoria and, to Horatio's pleasure, learnt to work the shears.

At the end of January 1861, Tom and Horatio departed Melbourne by steamer for Sydney and then continued to Moreton Bay in Queensland. Emily travelled part of the way with them, stopping at Sydney. Horatio was taking a caravan of people and supplies with him: trusted work companions from Belle Vue, bullock drivers, shepherds, and their wives and children. From Moreton Bay this gathering of Victorians would travel through inland Queensland to Rockhampton and then on to Cullin-la-Ringo. The steamer *Telegraph*, bearing Horatio and Tom, arrived in Moreton Bay, Queensland, on 27 January.

In South Brisbane, on 5 February, Horatio and Tom assembled people and items of exploration and settlement: men, women and children; five loaded drays; over a hundred rams and 'a large number of dogs, including five half-bred bloodhounds intended specially for the protection of the party'. Horatio planned to travel from Brisbane to Toowoomba and then to the Darling Downs where he would collect over 10,000 sheep. Horatio's fortune in Queensland would be intimately linked to the price of wool in England. The cost of inland transport from Brisbane was a heavy debt and only the price of wool in England could offset this expense.

Horatio split his men into four teams; drays pulled by bullocks transported the party inland. A heavy wooden, flat-topped vehicle, each dray was laden with two tons of goods – each rotation of the wheels a laceration upon the earth. Because of their unwieldy bulk, drays could be easily bogged or smashed. There were thirty-two bullocks to lug five drays over a 600-mile route and wooden yokes locked firm the drays to the bulging neck muscles of the bullocks. Mostly the bullocks pulled the drays; other times they pushed; and sometimes they pushed and pulled together.

Three days after leaving Brisbane this armada of vehicles passed through Ipswich, moving on to Toowoomba when death hit: one bullock, one dog and one man. The man drowned. Food was hard to find and the travellers were frugal; rations were calculated. Wallabies that zipped through the bush were shot and fed to the dogs. Men could starve in the Queensland bush. Horatio had told his boys in Germany a story about Peter Macdonald, from whom Horatio had purchased Cullin-la-Ringo. Macdonald, on a trek into the Queensland bush, became lost and raving mad from starvation. He had survived by stuffing tadpoles and lizards into his mouth, and when he had the luck to shoot an emu he latched his teeth onto its long neck and sucked its blood. Three weeks out of Brisbane, Tom and Horatio felt the ache of the absence of meat. Tom shot a paddy melon and slit it down the middle. The sweet paddy melon, with its conical-shaped head and soft brown eyes, dropped ungarnished into their open mouths and welcoming bellies to settle a keen hunger.

The caravan left the lowlands to the west of Brisbane and ascended the mountain range, reaching a height of 1800 feet.

They passed through forests of massive trees that reached towards the heavens, whose trunks were draped with twisted vines. Bush ticks were everywhere in the scrub; succulent and bloated, they bit hard into the skin of travellers leaving red, swollen marks.

On the Darling Downs Horatio and Tom collected over 10,000 sheep, staying briefly with the squatters who lived there. This was the last call where hunger was easily satisfied and liquor taken in – beer for Tom; wine for Horatio. The mob of sheep was cursed and cajoled forward through the scrub, moving northward to Rockhampton.

There was no specific type for an Australian pioneer but somehow Horatio seemed the most unlikely of men. Corpulent in build, a student of French grammar and English literature, he was part evangelising Christian soldier and part accountant. He carried into the Queensland bush a revolver, a rifle slung over his shoulder and a flask of shot. But he backed his boast of self-sufficiency by making calico tents for the less practical among his group. Horatio, with the eye of a needlewoman and the brow of a yeoman, stitched and slashed his way into the heart of the country. On 30 March Horatio wrote that he expected to reach Rockhampton in seven weeks.

Rockhampton – a steamy pit of sea, sand and heat – sat next to the Fitzroy River. Horatio was held up there in late June by heavy rains and made the decision to take a different route to Cullin-la-Ringo. Rivers, gullies and interminable ranges were crossed as they moved slowly away from the coast. At night it was cold, cold enough for Horatio to wrap about him a great grey coat and to warm his fingers as he prepared to write letters to Elizabeth at Belle Vue.

Tom and Horatio wrote to Cedric, Horace and Egbert before their trek to Queensland. Tom, warm, loving and wry, always obliged his brothers when they requested small gifts. They never forgot those kindnesses from Tom. Horatio's ambitions for his country had not faded. He urged his three boys: 'Go ahead all of you – Hurrah for the Australians! Beat all others my boys! God bless you.' Cedric was to be his chemist and to live in France to study 'the vine' before returning to Victoria: 'the vine and its juices will be your profession – excel my boy'. Horace would be his lawyer now that Tom had failed him: 'the law – you will shine there – if you try – you will try won't you?' And little Egbert – his course was not yet determined. 'Lose no time,' he exhorted his young boys, 'because you must in a great measure depend upon yourselves for getting on in the world.' Dutifulness to one's father, schoolteacher and God was Horatio's trilogy of obedience for his boys.

Cedric, Horace and Egbert were curious about the trip to Queensland and, in the manner of young boys, showed more exuberance than knowledge or taste. They were particularly curious about the Aborigines, about whom they had their own German teaching: 'Mr Thomas said the other day that the most wonderful thing in the world is that the Australian blacks climb up trees by sticking their big toe nails in to the bark.' And that 'blacks were more like monkeys than anything else he said they had no calves to their legs . . .' A colonial newspaper had recently ridiculed an Aboriginal runner as having only his toenails to dig into the turf in a foot race against a European runner with spikes. The boys wrote of their father's adventure and little Egbert, ten years old, nervously remarked that their father had 'brought the little gun with him to shoot the wild blacks'. They wanted to know how many blacks were met and if they had fought with Horatio. But their father revealed a conciliatory attitude to the Aborigines he might meet in Queensland: 'Mr Macdonald (Peter) tells me that the blacks he saw on a late excursion beyond our run were a fine lot of fellows and very kind to him and his party. We'll try to keep friends with them.' Horatio was aware of the violent fighting between local Aborigines and settlers in the Cullin-la-Ringo region, and wrote of the need for vigilance. The new self-governing colony of Queensland employed a Native Police force of Aboriginal men commanded by Europeans to 'disperse' gatherings of Aboriginal people. Bombastically, Horatio directed his children: 'Always remember, boys, in an enemy's country to keep rifles clear and powder dry!'

As they moved closer to Cullin-la-Ringo, Horatio and Tom began sleeping beneath a tarpaulin tent that was open at both ends. They burnt a small pat of cow dung as they slept, to keep mosquitoes at bay and to generate warmth. A year before, Horatio had travelled to Queensland to purchase Cullin-la-Ringo. On that occasion the nights were also cold but Horatio and his men had feared that lighting a fire might attract Aborigines. But Horatio's desire for warmth had eventually overcome his fear and he slept near a warm blaze with his gun cocked. He recalled that on one night as he slept next to the fire: 'the dog gave a growl and I heard a footstep behind my mia mia, but jumping up revolver in hand saw nothing. The grass was very high & thick and blackfellows can put themselves away very cleverly.' Usually a cautious man, Horatio Wills was capable of the risky, impulsive act.

At Point Henry, there was anxiety amongst the women at Belle Vue about Tom and Horatio's safety. They wrote letters, welcomed visiting clergy, picked fruit from the orchard, and all the while chatted and joked nervously about the trials facing Horatio and Tom. Horatio knew that his trek to Queensland was risky and he even hinted at the possibility of his own death. To his sons he wrote: '. . . let me be pleased with you all before I die, should it please God'. In a sentence he burdened their conscience with an impossible request.

Horatio and Tom were closely connected in many ways – their language had come to resemble one another's over the years and Tom's thread of narcissism, his flair for conflict and his prickly creative temperament were characteristics shared by his father. In the eight months spent in the Queensland bush no bitter or angry words flowed between Horatio and Tom. Horatio wrapped his arms about his son. 'I take care of your son,' he wrote to Elizabeth, 'for I am always up very early generally an hour before day – make up the fire – boil a pot of tea – which we bolt between us – go after our horses and then the bullocks – after which breakfast and off!' Horatio had accepted the disappointment of his son's failure to study law. Linked by blood, hunger and affection, the trek was a reconciling between father and son.

The caravan moved north in the Queensland haze, passing through Rainworth Station, managed by Jesse Gregson, about 20 miles from Cullin-la-Ringo. Gregson, a young man in his early twenties, had only arrived in the area several months before. A private mail service reached Gregson's every two weeks and he promised to keep Horatio's mail until it could be collected. The land they moved through was thinly wooded, with long flat stretches of tall dry grasses and clumps of tea tree and clusters of thorny bushes mixed with wood of more value to the new settler. There was bloodwood for splitting into slabs to erect a hut, and spotted gum for the construction of hurdles to pen in the sheep. And there were creeks and wells to replenish the thirst of man and beast.

Departing Rainworth on 3 October, they crossed over Separation Creek, the boundary between Gregson's property and Cullin-la-Ringo. Horatio wrote and declared to his wife, relief mingled with triumph: 'Thank Heaven! Cullinlaringo at last!' Camp was settled next to the shaded cool of a creek bed with running water. From the campsite looking north, beyond the creek and above eye-line of the prickly shrub of the camp's edge, the observer saw a stretch of grass without end. Mr Cave of the Native Police arrived to meet Horatio and brought news of the birth of a girl, Hortense Wills – Horatio's ninth child. Unaware of his wife's pregnancy, Horatio lovingly chided his wife: 'Oh Bessie, Bessie – what a rogue you must be to keep me in the dark!'

Horatio's skin boiled under the Capricorn sun; he had arrived months later than planned. And it was quiet, apart from the occasional banging together of a sheep yard or the splitting of a slab of wood to erect a hut during the cooler periods of the day. The local Aboriginal tribes could be heard, a shout every now and then, and a return call from beyond the scrub. Every so often small groups of men and women entered the camp and a strange game of half-understood gestures and mimicry took place between settler and Aborigine. A garden fence was erected by the settlers and a patch of ground cleared for melons and pumpkins.

Seven days after arriving at Cullin-la-Ringo, Tom took two men, a team of bullocks and two empty drays back to Albinia Downs, to collect provisions. Tom left on Sunday 13 October and retraced his path to Gregson's and then a further 40–50 miles to Albinia Downs. Meanwhile, on 17 October, on the far side of the globe, the English cricket team drank champagne at the London Bridge and prepared to leave for Melbourne. Tom reached Albinia Downs and collected the supplies. Returning with the loaded drays, Tom and the men had to haul the drays up a steep dry creek bed that formed a stony staircase. The bullocks wedged their cloven feet into the rocky ledges of the creek bed in order to reach the top.

It took Tom seven days to make this trip to Albinia Downs and back to Cullin-la-Ringo. When he returned to the camp his father and eighteen other settlers were dead.

THE PRIDE OF QUEENSLAND

OCTOBER 1861–JULY 1862

Here and there, the dry grass was matted with blood. The sticky coagulated patches marked where each man, woman and child had been attacked and had slumped to the earth. Weapons of war – boomerangs, nulla-nullas and spears – lay scattered and broken. They were killed on 17 October, three days before Tom's return. The dead had been buried; quick smart, too, in that Central Queensland heat. Horatio, now close to his Maker, a position he had fervently sought in life, was respectfully given a grave to himself carved from the earth. Most of the other settlers were arranged in a vast burial pit – one large hole held them all. There was grief but no time for grieving. In the newness of life without his father, bewildered and concussed by events, Tom urgently wrote to his cousin in Melbourne, Colden Harrison: 'My dear Coley, I have not time to go into particulars I can only say that <u>all</u> our party except I have been slaughtered by the black's on the 17th. I am in a great fix <u>no men</u>.'

At the point of greatest need in his life, Tom wrote to Colden Harrison. His mind unhinged, his normal protective mechanism of disarming jocularity was disabled. It was no coincidence that Tom, not a man to communicate his fears to anyone, wrote to Harrison – both sublime athletes, their bond was forged from shared ability and respect as much as their common bloodlines. In the letter, he referred to one of the murdered men, George Elliott, the brother of Tom's friend and fellow Victorian cricketer, Gideon Elliott: 'Tell Elliott [Gideon] that poor George was killed close to the tents & had a small <u>switch</u> in his hand that he used to drive the sheep with, I have his pouch now. <u>All clothes of all sorts</u> gone – Flour sugar & tea not touched but blankets Zingari shirts & Beds all gone.'

There was nothing in this letter to Colden Harrison that was teasing or cryptic. Gone was the playful Wills of old. The script is physically contorted, in sympathy with the pain of the writer. This was the writing of a man distressed beyond the capacity of human tolerance. Tom made his first plea: 'I want a <u>good</u> man up here that thoroughly understands sheep please to let Mr. Roope know it I have given him <u>particulars</u> but urge him to send me a good <u>overseer</u> . . . We are all stripped to what we <u>have on</u>.'

The first settlers to arrive found a scene of devastation; the campsite resembled the death scene of a shipwreck with debris washed ashore and the offerings strewn into the distance:

Some of the women were found with their sewing in their hands. The cook was close by his fire; the children were by their mothers. Immediately outside the camp, one of the bullock-drivers, who had been engaged drawing in logs for the sheep yard, was found dead by his bullocks, with his whip in his hand. The team was still yoked, and three of the bullocks strangled. Another man who he had assisting him was also found dead . . . Baker and son and third man, evidently made a struggle for their lives. They were putting up a tent at the time the attack was made, and they used the tent poles in defending themselves. Their bodies were very much mutilated, one of the men having his leg nearly cut off with a blow from a sharp instrument . . . The whole place was a total wreck. The only things left at the camp were the sugar, tea, tobacco, flour, and some pieces of iron and zinc. The boxes and cases were all broken open, and everything was taken away, amongst which were blankets, a quantity of books, crockery, tools, axes, adzes, knives, some white-handled daggers, regatta shirts, trousers, clothing of every description, and other articles ...

Wills reeled off the dead, like a team of cricketers, to Colden: 'H.S. Wills, D. Baker Snr, Mr. D. Baker Jnr, Mrs. Baker, Elizabeth Baker, Iden Baker (a Boy) & an infant, – 8 months old, G. Elliott, P. Mannion, Mrs. Mannion and 3 children, E. McCormick, C. Weeden, Jas. Scott, Henry Pickering, George Ling & a man called "Tom" engaged at Rockhampton. Alive T.W. Wills, Jas Baker, E. Kenny, P. Maloney, John Moore & Wm Albery.' The loved and well known were sprinkled amongst the unfamiliar. Thousands of sheep that the party had coaxed, bullied and cajoled across the Central Queensland plains from Moreton Bay were scattered throughout the bush. Wills needed men and protection – and needed them immediately.

Tom completed his letter to Colden Harrison on 24 October. It was stamped in Rockhampton on 2 November; passed through Brisbane on 9 November; reached Colden at Victoria Parade in Melbourne on 19 November; finally arriving at Belle Vue, Point Henry, on 20 November 1861.

The first person to come across the murders was Edward Kenny, one of Horatio's shepherds. The illiterate Edward Kenny recorded a deposition the day after the attack, while sheltering with Jesse Gregson at nearby Rainworth Station. This man without letters implicated a careless Horatio:

I ... am a shepherd in the employment of the late Mr. Wills. We arrived on Mr Wills' station Collinaringo [sic] about a fortnight a go. the Blacks came up to the station two or three times but as they appeared quiet no notice of them was taken. Mr Wills used to carry a revolver but although he had plenty of firearms none were served out to any of the men . . .

In the initial stages, Jesse Gregson offered the helping hand of a neighbour, providing Tom succour and comfort and men to reconstruct the Wills property. Gregson left Tom at the station to manage the stock and offered him a place of refuge at Norwood, near Rainworth. Tom, with gratitude, accepted Gregson's offer. While Tom rested, Gregson led a reprisal party to hunt down those responsible for the killings.

From Gregson's, Tom wrote on 26 October and implored the Colonial Secretary in Brisbane for a detachment of Native Police to be stationed at Cullin-la-Ringo for his protection: '. . . be quartered there as otherwise it would be impossible after the above events to get <u>men</u> to stop unless <u>so</u> protected. The widow and orphans of the late H.S. Wills join me in my prayer.' But his urgent requests, though justified, went unfulfilled.

The full knowledge of the slaughter was yet to penetrate the thickets of the bush. The remote location of the attack had at first paralysed and then distorted the information that was transmitted to the outside world. Information trickled slowly into Rockhampton. From there it was transferred instantaneously to Melbourne by the modern marvel of the telegram. Mrs Catherine Roope was gardening, having just finished her breakfast, when the first message of Horatio's death arrived at Belle Vue. Eugene Wills, Tom's seven-year-old sister, called Mrs Roope to inform her that her husband, Mr William Roope, was on the back verandah, agitated. Mrs Roope could not make out her husband's incoherent and hurried message and brought him inside to settle him. He explained he had just read a telegram that brought news of the death of Horatio Wills; he then broke down and cried 'like a child'. Reverend Campbell, who had arrived at Belle Vue with Roope, 'read a portion of Scripture from the Bible and offered up prayers to the Almighty very suitable to the occasion'.

Dozens of telegraph messages were sent – each with only part-information of what had happened; some were misleading. For the family in Victoria, huddled about these fragmentary telegrams from an alien land, it took weeks to piece together and decipher, and then to accept the fate of Horatio and his party. These two telegrams convey the ambiguity and incorrect details telegraphed:

> Horace Wills, Mrs Baker, daughter and two (2) children, Mrs Manion and three (3) children & Scott murdered on (20th) . . . instant by blacks. Tom Wills safe.

> Horatio Wills, Momas & eight others murdered by blacks at Rockhampton. Send word to friends immediately steamer for Rock-hampton next week . . . Word 'Momas' may be 'Thomas'.

News of the attack was reported in a disjointed, frenzied manner and there was an urgent desire for clarification by the family. There was uncertainty as to whether Tom Wills had survived. Stoically, Elizabeth suggested that the news might be in error. It was not, after all, the first time such deaths of Queensland settlers had been mistakenly reported. The distance from Queensland allowed her to recreate in her mind alternative explanations and cling to the most slender of hopes that her husband was alive. Fearfully, the Wills family in Geelong and Melbourne received the news. Elizabeth read what she regarded as a comprehensive account on 20 November – a full month after her husband had died.

Elizabeth never travelled the 2000 miles to visit Horatio's grave. There would be no headstone or burial gathering to give substance to the family's grief. They would have to deal with their grief without the physical presence of their lost father. Christian teaching had always been a powerful explanatory force for the Wills family, and as grief engulfed them, the family, or at least the women in the family, took solace in shared religious convictions and reassuring rituals.

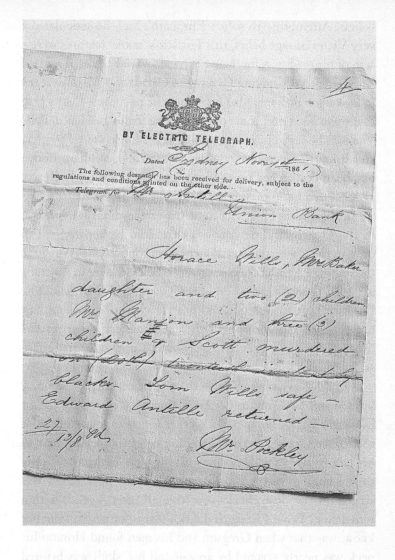

In the face of death, the task for any Victorian-era family with pretensions to Christianity – and the Wills family had more than pretensions – was to find meaning in that death. A family friend, Pastor Archibald Crawford, advised Elizabeth to find meaning 'for the fateful blow' and to hold fast to her

beliefs. Attempting to soften Elizabeth's loss, he articulated a
very Victorian-age belief, that Horatio's 'noble' features were a
sign of his readiness for 'being carried away'. Elizabeth advised
her young sons studying far away in Germany: 'We must learn
to look upon it as intended for some wise purpose – Let us pray
that some good may come out of it.' The family residence, Belle
Vue, was besieged by clergy, and Bible readings offered comfort
and strength several times a day. Meanwhile, William Roope
had been despatched on the long journey to Cullin-la-Ringo,
as requested by Tom, leaving Belle Vue on 10 November.

In the midst of his grief came the extraordinary suggestion
in the Queensland newspapers that Tom be approached to
captain the Queensland cricketers in a proposed match against
the visiting English cricket team. 'The best cricketer in Australia
is now a Queenslander,' cried the *Queensland Guardian*. The
English, as it turned out, did not travel to Queensland, but
not even the murder of his father and eighteen other settlers
dissuaded some from viewing Tom as a cricketer first and a
son second.

On 20 November, Elizabeth, now accepting of her new
burden in life, wrote to her boys Horace, Cedric and Egbert
in Germany. She composed a picture for their young minds of
their father, locked in time, standing erect and defiant next to
his tent in the seconds prior to his murder: 'he had only time
to fire one out of the four barrels when the poor fellow was
struck on the dear cheek (you have all often kissed) with a
tomahawk'. What Elizabeth did not reveal, or perhaps did not
know, was that when Gregson and his men found Horatio his
neck was nearly severed by an axe and his 'skull was bruised
and dreadfully beaten with waddies'. Her future warnings to
Cedric and Horace, when they laboured upon the Queensland
property several years later, did not diminish over the years:
'. . . you will be careful about those horrible blacks – you can't
be too watchful'. To each warning about those 'blood thirsty

wretches' she attached a maternal commandment to do as she said in the name of their father's memory.

The grieving family formed a collective view of the reasons for the murder of Horatio, and in this view, Horatio remained unblemished by accusations of inadequate vigilance. To the family, Horatio was a victim of cowardly, unwarranted aggression. Emily, for whom bitterness was a birthmark, saw a saintly Horatio, flawed only by his unquestioning trust towards the local Aborigines. Cedric, now sixteen, and with the naivety of an adoring young brother, wrote in a letter to Tom: 'but I am almost certain that if you had been there it would not have happened, poor Papa trusted them too much. If I am not mistaken they did not put them in coffins when they buried them but if they did not I suppose you have seen to that.' Meant to be comforting, it raised the issue of whether Tom experienced guilt over his absence from Cullin-la-Ringo on the day of the murders. But this remains unknown. Tom throughout his life was not prone to introspection in his letters, and guilt, perhaps the most confronting of all emotions to commit to paper, was an internal experience he denied or, more likely, bypassed unrecognised.

Tom Wills reacted with a raging hatred towards his father's killers. His anger sprang from a desire to avenge his father, and from an anxiety borne from mistrust of the Aborigines near Cullin-la-Ringo. In his first letter to Colden Harrison he had cried for a revenge party of 'good resolute men that will shoot every black they see'. This was rapidly answered. Jesse Gregson had already led a raid of retribution against the local Aborigines in the first days after the murder of Horatio Wills. At that time Tom had remained at Gregson's station and was not part of the raid. Cedric wrote and asked Tom in an excited adolescent fashion: 'Were you one of the eight who attacked the blacks camp the Tuesday after it happened?' Another party of settlers, led by Peter Macdonald, was assembled at Rockhampton, at a rowdy public meeting, to pursue the attackers on horseback.

Estimates of the numbers killed in the first Gregson reprisal and in the reprisals that followed vary. The precise details have been mired in deception and hysteria.

Despite Tom's calls for revenge, there is no evidence that he rode with the pack in pursuit of his father's killers. This was not from want of liberal encouragement to do so by his family. An exultant Emily wrote to her young brothers in Germany that 300 blacks, 'Gins and all' had been slaughtered and added with relish, that they were 'hunted like wild dogs'; then, as an afterthought, not of contrition but from habit, she added: 'I hope you read your bibles often.'

Tom never articulated a conciliatory attitude and was not sympathetic to the plight of the Aborigines near Cullin-la-Ringo station. He sarcastically branded them as 'inoffensive/harmless blacks' in a bitter personal rebuke to local settlers who argued the case in favour of Aboriginal rights.

Mr Dutton, a settler on Albinia Downs, was an object of Tom's anger. The views of Dutton and the small number of settlers who publicly sympathised with the injustice meted out to local Aborigines only served to nettle Tom. Their public letters were a defiant counterpoint to Wills' own letters damning those who wished to protect the Aborigines. Three months after the attack Tom wrote again to the Colonial Secretary:

> I know for a fact that several of the late murderers of my father & party are at this moment in at Mr Dutton's station . . . If murderers are thus to be protected I cannot see how a man is to be sure of his life for a minute in a country like – for these men come in for protection & then again in a little while sally out and commit some foul deed & then return to where they know they are safe.

Consumed by rancour, he wrote home to his mother that a group of settlers had recently encountered a small gathering of Aborigines near a river. There was no suggestion of hostility from them. But in their haste to depart, as the Europeans approached, the Aborigines left intact their fishing nets. Tom, displaying a wrath his mother would have heartily approved of, was bent upon destroying Aboriginal property to inflict suffering for its own sake, '. . . they <u>came</u> on a mob of black's but they all got away in a <u>crack</u> leaving their fishing nets behind & they did not destroy them – great fools I told them for not doing so.'

The local and intercolonial press had openly accused Horatio of neglecting warnings to take due care on his property and that the fault for the deaths lay at his feet. Though personal depictions of him were invariably positive, there was explicit and implied criticism of Horatio for his lack of vigilance. 'On new runs the blacks are invariably hostile and Mr. Wills fell a victim to placing a mistaken confidence in their apparently friendly disposition.' Official letters suggested that Horatio, at least to the administrative eye, was regarded as being too lax in keeping the Aborigines at a distance.

Such insults were not to be tolerated by Tom Wills and he leapt to defend his father's memory and honour, springing from his corner in pugilistic pose. With characteristic flair, he shot off a string of letters to newspapers locally and beyond Queensland. The letters were dramatic, with his distinctive extravagant underlining for emphasis. For once, such dramatic effect was well placed. Tom's was a lone voice in support of his father. He thanked those who proffered help and uncompromisingly abused those who did not. Privately, however, Tom Wills lamented that he had warned his father before the attack to be mindful of the need for firearms. But in public his stance was to shield his dead father. This was Tom Wills at his finest:

> In the first place, without entering into details, the BLACKS *were not encouraged about our place*, and in fact had only been up *once* prior to the final attack, and if there had been a castle on the *Run*, they would have all been killed in like manner, for each man *had* his *lot*. All the guns, &c were

loaded and at hand for immediate use. No man would carry them although I asked them to do so – saying that the blacks would not harm a stick.

In the second place, *Mr. Cave and his police* were not at the rescue of our property two days after the affair happened – they did not even arrive on the Run till nine clear days after. Some people, Sir, have a convenient mode of perverting the truth:– I owe the recovery of my property to seven of Mr. Gregson's *shearers*, three of whom were on the Run the *next* day collecting the stock. Give honour, Sir, unto whom honour is due:– their names are as follows – James Leather, Peter Benedict, Duncan McLean, William Baxter, Joseph Clarke, George Ghan, and Thomas Hughes. They willingly left off work, and would not leave me until I was comfortably settled here at Norwood. Mr. Gregson was also indefatigable in his exertions, and rendered me, and still continues to render me, all the assistance in his power.

I hear also, Sir, that some *old woman* has been laying down the *law* through your medium as to what we *ought* to have done &c. How easy it is, Sir, to put things on paper. We ought to have huts up &c. How much more likely a small party is to be murdered than a large? – and how are these huts to grow without men? I never knew them to fall off trees yet. *Old men*, Sir, must not teach their grandmothers &c.

I hear also, Sir, with regret, that some persons calling themselves gentlemen have already been speculating as to the amount the *Run is to be had for.* Such people must rejoice then at such an opportunity being given them; but, Sir, in this case, they will not have the pleasure of even seeing the Run, if I can help it. The young bird is not deficient of some of his lamented father's pluck, as they may find, some of these odd days.

A testy Wills scorned what he regarded as mischievous accusations against his father, repudiating the widespread claim that the Aborigines were encouraged about the station. On the counterattack, he declared that the local tribes were informed that they could hunt for game, if they did not interfere with the sheep; and that firearms were at the ready in his father's tent and not quarantined from the men.

At times when his defensive guard slipped, Tom implicated his father's cocky disregard for the situation. When Tom left the camp prior to the attack, he had offered Horatio his loaded revolver because Horatio's was damaged. His father scoffed at Tom's wariness of the local Aborigines, dismissively replying 'there is no danger'. Twenty-two years later, William Hammersley recalled this nonchalant misjudgement by Horatio in one of his many conversations about Tom Wills:

> The old gentleman was a shrewd man of business and looked well after Tommy, . . . Tom Wills has frequently told me that he never trusted the natives, but always carried two six-shooters and often warned 'the governor' to do the same, but the old man prided himself on being able to manage the blacks from his experience of them gained in Victoria, and said they would never harm him.

Jesse Gregson also claimed, many years afterwards, that he had advised Horatio to pass out his firearms to his men rather than leave them on the drays but Horatio responded that he 'knew all about blacks before you were born' and dismissed Gregson's concerns. He recalled Horatio's attitude towards the Aborigines: 'Old Wills had treated them kindly giving lollies to the children, handkerchiefs to the gins and tobacco to the men. Not a trouble or dispute of any kind had occurred.'

Tom also remembered these meetings when the settlers arrived at Cullin-la-Ringo: 'A few of the natives then came up to the camp to look at the white "maries" (women), as they call them. One of the black women wanted to exchange her piccaninnie for the overseer's wife's baby; but of course the white woman did not see the point at all.'

There were various explanations put forward at the time to account for the murder of Horatio and his party. Tom did not articulate his reasons for the attack, but years afterwards Cedric Wills made the following claim:

> Before the arrival of the Wills's on Garden Creek, where the murder was committed, the blacks were collecting on the Nogoa River at the foot of Separation Creek, with the object of attacking Mr. Jesse Gregson, the first owner who stocked Rainworth and who with a detachment of native police had shot some blacks for the supposed stealing of sheep prior to the arrival of our party. My oldest brother Tom, who came out with the party, but who happened to be away with two teams and the drivers at the time of the murder, told me, 'If the truth is ever known, you will find that it was through Gregson shooting those blacks; that was the cause of the murder.'

Cedric recorded that an Aboriginal boy had confirmed this story for him and that the attack on Cullin-la-Ringo was an act of revenge for a previous aggression by Jesse Gregson. Cedric speculated that Horatio was mistaken for Gregson by the Aborigines. These claims were later denied by those who knew Gregson.

Publicly, Tom continued to dress down his father's critics. But of all the letters written by Wills, perhaps the most revealing was when, stripped of all bravado, he had written to Colden in the days immediately after the killings, blurting out in the very opening sentence: 'if we had used common precaution all would have been well . . .' In this sentence we have the clearest evidence that Tom rued Horatio's disregard of his son's advice to be more aware of the dangers about them.

Meanwhile, as the family wallowed in Horatio's idealised image, their distress and dreams were focused on Tom – now the head of the family. Tom wrote: 'So go to work "<u>Tom</u>". Remember your poor dear Father's words and work like a man

– by God's blessing so I will.' These words enshrined Horatio and imprisoned Tom. It was through Tom that Horatio's legacy was to continue, or so the family assumed; Tom, however, was never up to the challenge. He assumed the heroic mantle of reviving his father's dreams, boasting of the promising future of the station. Emily wrote to her brothers in Germany that 'Tom says he has made a vow over Pa's grave that he will stick to the station and Cullinlaringo will be the pride of Queensland yet.' Tom declared to his mother: 'I shall fear no one and do to my best what is my duty . . . my Father that God trusted me & I only act now as if he were himself present and could approve of what I do . . .' Tom's proclamations were dutiful and brave, comforting words for his family, but the objective evidence reveals them as platitudes to appease his mother – vainglorious promises went unfulfilled. All the while, he struggled with the loss of his father.

At several points in the ensuing years, we glimpse how the slaughter of nineteen people, including his father, and the back-breaking solitude affected and reshaped the mind of Tom Wills. How the human mind and body responded to a traumatic experience was poorly appreciated in 1861. Some of the first medical descriptions were emerging on the other side of the world in the American Civil War, where a young physician, Jacob da Costa, treated the men brought in from the battlefields of Fredericksburg, Virginia. Dr da Costa noted that some of the most disabled soldiers had sustained no physical wounds; it was not human flesh, but human spirit that had buckled after witnessing death on the battlefields. The sweating victims – strapping young foot soldiers – told da Costa of a sense of suffocating as they slept, of an overvigilant nervous system and of wild dreams, reliving the experiences that aroused them. Palpitations were frequent; their sleep was 'jerky'. Pains struck about their heart; dimness of vision rendered them infirm. But most of all they experienced the thumping of an 'irritable heart'. Of all the proffered treatments, only one was indispensable:

sleep. This could be achieved only by removing the soldier from the prodding of disorder and fear. Without this, little hope was held for recovery.

But Tom Wills was not going anywhere, and Dr da Costa was half a world away from the Queensland scrub and the sleep he prescribed was something Tom could ill-afford. Sleep, in Tom's fearful mind, was the one state that rendered him vulnerable to the enemy. And the enemy was not so much the stealthy tread of hostile tribes but rather the hellish images conjured in his mind. Two months after the murders, his sister Emily relayed the following to her brothers in Germany about Tom: '. . . poor fellow he says he never felt so changed in the whole course of his life . . .' More than a hundred years later, we can only speculate on Tom's inner world. We know that the intruding unwanted memories returned, as they had done for the young soldiers from Fredericksburg. Outsiders saw Tom with a body strapping and firm, but the thumping of his irritable heart at night, visible to none, would occur for years. Three years after Cullin-la-Ringo, nightmares still stalked his mind. He let this slip to Emily on one of his visits to the family at Belle Vue in

early 1864: 'Tom dreamt a man was murdered on the station . . .'
The fault line was deep and his mind was quarantined with
memories that struck at him from unseen corners.

For periods Tom Wills lived the life of a shepherd on the
station. Sandy Blight, a curse brought to Australia by early
Europeans, rendered him blind in his left eye at one point
for weeks. He lived a life of fear and hypervigilance after the
murders, scanning the horizon for further attacks on settlers.
Each attack and killing sensitised Wills, stripping back whatever
protective coating he had grown since his father's death. His
fears were neither histrionic nor exaggerated. Following the
murder of an isolated shepherd, Tom wrote of his life: 'I have
now to watch sheep at night, – having only three hours sleep
– and attend from daylight till dark in the shed.'

Nine months after his father's death, Wills sat alone in a
shepherd's hut and wrote to his mother. Wrapped tightly on all
sides by the melancholia of isolation, Wills voiced his fear of
dying in Queensland. Horatio was now gone and his direction
in life was to be determined by no one but himself. That was
always the strategy of greatest risk for Tom Wills.

Tom Wills, c. 1863

1862–1880

'HE SAID LITTLE BUT THOUGHT THE MORE,
AND WHEN PUT OUT, AS ALL CAPTAINS ARE AT
TIMES, AND MUST EXPECT TO BE, HIS USUAL
WAY OF VENTING HIS TEMPER WAS NOT BY
ABUSE, BUT BY TWISTING A PET CURL IN HIS
BEARD OR BITING HIS THUMB NAIL TO THE
QUICK. IF HE HAD ANY JEALOUSY TOWARDS A
RIVAL, IT WAS AS A BOWLER, BUT, AS A RULE,
HE WAS QUICK TO RECOGNISE NASCENT TALENT
AND THE FIRST TO ENCOURAGE IT.'

WILLIAM HAMMERSLEY

GOD PRESERVE ME
FROM A SYDNEY MOB

JULY 1862–MARCH 1863

Horatio's death cut loose Tom's mind. It was station life that concerned Tom now and it was how he would be judged, on this plot called Cullin-la-Ringo, 2000 miles from Melbourne. Horatio had recalled for his boys the image of the previous owner of Cullin-la-Ringo, Peter Macdonald, munching on tadpoles to thwart starvation. Men lost weight in this land, lost condition, as one might observe in a prized animal, until what was left was sharper, more elemental, stripped to whatever was needed to survive. All spare produce and bodily flesh were pressed into this purpose.

The Queensland sun whittled Tom's flesh during the day; mosquitoes stabbed and sucked at night. The heat and isolation and flies and dust ate at more than a man's body. Fences preoccupied Tom's mind – fences to repair, fences to build, fences that penned a man. Brains were important on this property, and organisation, but it was mainly muscles that were needed. Every day. Muscles that bulged and knotted like those in the necks of the bullocks tearing at the earth around Tom and his men. Muscles for blacksmithing, shoeing, chopping and lugging.

William Roope, despatched to help Tom, had arrived at Cullin-la-Ringo on Christmas Day in 1861 and assumed control of the property. Roope had been a senior colleague of Horatio's in the Victorian Parliament and a steadfast advisor in matters of wool. Elizabeth trusted Roope. Roope was to be the steadying hand on Tom's shoulder.

William Roope and Tom Wills quarrelled from the start. In Tom's eyes, Roope was a ditherer: 'He was a manager – yes a manager of old women no more just as fit as any old doll to manage a station.' They argued about everything; on alcohol, not easily procured so far inland, they were divided. Roope kept two casks of porter and wanted to exchange this alcohol for money but Tom saw no point in that. Sarcastically, he muttered to his mother that Roope 'actually gave me a glass full & says he will sell the rest . . . I think he might have given me a few bottles of it as it would do me a world of good at present'.

Roope tolerated Tom and the station for only six months and he left in June 1862, two months before lambing. Tom condemned Roope as a malingerer and a hypochondriac: 'I am glad Mr. R. has gone he is too slow for this work. I hope if they send another he will be an active man & not 61.' Catherine Roope, who lived with the Wills family at Belle Vue, received her husband's vexed letters from Cullin-la-Ringo and wrote in her diary that Tom 'behaved exceedingly ill' and that her husband left the property because of 'Tom's misconduct'.

Perhaps Tom should have made more of Roope, tried to work with him, for when Roope left Cullin-la-Ringo Tom was alone again. He sulked to his mother: 'Really [I] do all the work & bear the brunt of everything and someone else gets the praise.'

It was the seasons of the sheep – lambing and shearing – that set the station's tempo. Shepherds sat in their huts, watching their mob of sheep, then wandered about on foot and horse to count their flock. Woolsheds were constructed and a wash pen built across a creek. Once cut, the wool was loaded onto waggons that ground their way to Rockhampton, Tom's only point of connection with the outside world. Horatio's training for his son – learning to shoe horses and work a pair of shears in his large hands – was all put to use by Tom for life in Queensland. But nothing could have prepared him for Cullin-la-Ringo.

Shearers threatened to strike but Tom managed that. He could handle working men; it was his great strength. However, money was needed to pay the shearers' and shepherds' wages and the cost of fencing seemed never to be met. The continuous questions that flowed from his mother and the trustees rattled about his brain. *What was the London price? How much to transport wool to Rockhampton? When to sell and when to buy? When to cheat and when to lie?* Money, that most wretched of stuff, filled the pages of letters between Cullin-la-Ringo and Victoria.

Cullin-la-Ringo was a community of men. There was no woman for Tom on Cullin-la-Ringo except those that occupied his dreams, and he complained of having no one to mend his clothes; his loneliness tried him. His mother sent him boots and pants, sometimes new, but usually they were hammered and stitched old ones. The rituals of civilised Melbourne life, once taken for granted, were longed for on the station. On 8 June 1862, Tom wrote of his 'best dinner' for eighteen months – roast mutton, preserved potatoes, rice, jam and pickles. Scurvy, with bleeding gums and dank breath, was reported at Gregson's but Tom had lime juice to ward this off. He grew vegetables and fruit, and sold them to other settlers: jams, lime juice and pickles. Tom ran frantically between selling produce from the property and working in the yards. He surrounded himself with animals – a pattern throughout his life – cats, puppies, chickens and goats meandered around Cullin-la-Ringo. Dogs snapped at Tom's heels. He liked their company.

The memory of Horatio suffocated Tom. The words of a dead man lingered and rested heavily upon him. Tom knew it served his purpose to foster the image of a heroic Tom doing Horatio's work. He wrote to his mother: 'I know well it will be so – but thank God, I do my duty to my poor Father & I'm content & I hope to live to see the day when Ced & myself get our share & then we will thank <u>no man</u> except our <u>poor</u> dear <u>old</u> <u>Father</u> . . . I wish you would keep my letters to you – they may be of use some day, no one knows what <u>persons</u> will do.' This was Tom's first hint that there were problems on the station. What he wanted kept safe in those letters, and why he needed them, he did not explain.

By July Roope had gone and the nights were cold and ice was 'nearly an inch thick in the mornings'. When the sun rose and warmed the earth and opened the cracks deep beneath the black plains, the snakes and other creatures that sought refuge within those deep hollows slithered into the sun to hunt. Tom wrote: 'Had a very narrow escape from a snake trod on him and felt him twisting round my leg.'

There were moments of resurrection of Tom's cheeky spirit; a burst of what had previously blossomed. In such a moment he teased his mother: 'We have 4 mountains near the <u>old camp</u> named <u>Horatio</u>. Spencer. Howe. & Wills and one Mt Elizabeth a beauty . . .' Whether Elizabeth's colour deepened to her son's flattery she did not say. She fretted that there was no woman to tend to her son; but no woman, she vowed, was to be sacrificed to those 'wretched blacks'. The station must be first secured. Cedric arrived back from Europe in July and was sent to Cullin-la-Ringo. He was just seventeen years old. On 19 August Tom turned twenty-seven; Elizabeth baked a cake at Belle Vue, as she did every year for her son, and

Elizabeth

her younger daughters – Elizabeth,

Eugene, Minna and Hortense – gathered about and ate the cake in honour of Tom.

Soon after Tom's birthday, rumours drifted to Victoria, not the kind the Wills family wished to hear, suggesting that Cullin-la-Ringo was a poorly run station. In response, the trustees in Victoria appointed an agent in Queensland to closely watch the property. It was the agent's task to ensure that the property was well run and made money. The trustees were interested only in the miraculous pastoral alchemy that transformed physical work into profit. Tom would be judged not by the labour and suffering of station life but by the number squeezed through a pen that told the trustees whether the station ran to a profit or a loss.

The trustees of Cullin-la-Ringo kept a watchful eye on Tom's handling of finances. Not all the money spent was fully accounted for and it was noted that some cheques drawn by Tom had little to do with the property. The antipathy between Tom and the trustees grew with every mislaid cheque. Sensing their critical assessment, Tom wrote with bravado to appease his mother, bragging that 'A Mr. Dance a squatter . . . says my yards are the best in Queensland and he is going to erect yards after my plan. My father met him several times on the road, He says that the run in 10 years hence could not be purchased for a 100-000£, the best in Queensland.'

In September 1862, Tom wrote to the Attorney-General in Brisbane: he wished to become a local Justice of the Peace. His tone was irritable and disrespectful – not the manner to please a bureaucrat. The following month on 30 October he wrote again, in a more conciliatory tone:

> I take this earliest opportunity of asking your pardon & correcting myself in my last to you, I Sir, of course supposed that the Ministry appointed J.P's not as I have been informed by a party of gentlemen who are designated in this district by the name of 'the Club'. You must know Sir, that we on the Nogoa are divided from Mr Gregson's

by a <u>range</u> & all on the Nogoa waters are <u>Victorian</u> men.
I can now, Sir, understand the spirit of their working, in
our own immediate district we have not a single J.P. & the
consequence will be that we shall have to trot <u>miles</u> for
justice whereas our friends on the other <u>side</u> are all <u>JP's</u>.
I will add a list of those immediately in this neighbourhood.
Messrs Major & Jeffray (Nogoa) . . . Our great fault is that
we are unfortunate in being 'Victorians'. Apologising for
my former epistle,

I remain Sir,
Your obd^t servant,
Thomas W Wills.

P.S. I shall in all probability be in Brisbane about the beginning of Dec & I then may be able to place before you our
position here.

•

Tom's face had sharpened; his cheekbones sat high and exposed,
and his skin was drawn taut. His eyelids clamped to form
a horizontal slit – a squint wide enough to see through but
sufficiently narrow to exclude the sun – and his once pale skin
appeared as if he had lingered too close to a furnace. It was a
darker face, harder.

The world was passing Tom by. The first English cricket
team had arrived in Melbourne and played cricket over the
summer of 1861–62. They played cricket and returned to
England, leaving the impression of a team that engorged
themselves on spires of wine and mountains of food. If Tom
had been in Melbourne some of this adulation and attention
would have been his. Not all of the English cricketers returned
home; Charles Lawrence, born in Middlesex, stayed and joined
the Albert Cricket Club in Sydney. He set up his tobacco and
cricket goods store in George Street, selling cigars, snuffs, pipes
and offered smoking rooms for the sporting man. In Victoria,

Tom's cousin Colden Harrison played football on the paddock next to the Argyle Hotel in Geelong and the Melbourne Football Club continued to play on the Richmond Paddock. Little had changed in the Melbourne game of football since Tom had left for Queensland. Jerry Bryant, George Marshall and Sam Cosstick were the current professional cricketers employed by the MCC while Gideon Elliott had left for the Middle East to prospect for gold. William Hammersley continued to pontificate about the colonials, and no-balled the professional cricketer William Greaves for an illegal bowling action. Insults were exchanged and umpire and bowler marched about with much self-righteousness until Hammersley left the ground. James Thompson had left Melbourne for Bendigo and was playing cricket and football, and working with the *Bendigo Advertiser* as a journalist. Stranded in Queensland, Tom received the occasional *Bell's Life in Victoria* and might have read about those events in a world 2000 miles from Cullin-la-Ringo. If he had, he would have seen his name mentioned many times. In Melbourne Tom was never forgotten.

At the end of 1862, there was an expectation that Tom would return to Melbourne and play cricket for Victoria against New South Wales. Tom's family also anticipated his arrival at Belle Vue for Christmas. Egbert and Horace, recently returned from Germany, arrived at Belle Vue looking for Tom as did Jimmy Baker, one of the survivors from Cullin-la-Ringo, whom Tom had taught how to fire a pistol. All the young boys milled about Belle Vue waiting for Tom, trailing around an anxious Elizabeth. But Tom did not arrive for Christmas.

The Melbourne newspapers reported that Tom had been 'detained' on his way to Melbourne. This was curious, even more so when it was noted that Tom was playing cricket in Sydney. He had paid the one pound subscription to become a member of the Albert Cricket Club. Tom played in a white straw hat, blue shirt and white trousers, and he opened the bowling alongside the captain – the English professional Charles

Lawrence whose preference for a bowtie and polka-dotted shirt
set him apart from the rest of the team. Then surprising news
reached Melbourne that Tom had promised to play for New
South Wales in the next intercolonial cricket match – a coup
because it was widely assumed that whomever Tom played for
would win the match. On hearing this rumour, Emily gently
admonished her brother: 'You turncoat.'

Tom eventually arrived in Melbourne on 9 January aboard
the steamer *Wonga Wonga*. Stepping off the steamer he was
confronted on all sides by the claim that he had promised to play
for New South Wales in the next month's intercolonial cricket
match. Tom dismissed the claim but all the evidence suggests
that he had agreed. Two weeks later the New South Wales
cricketers, irritated and waiting for Tom to return to Sydney,
met at Charles Lawrence's Cricket Depot in George Street.
The secretary of the New South Wales cricketers urgently
telegraphed Tom Wills to confirm his availability to play. The
match was less than two weeks away.

Tom had arrived back in Victoria but he did not travel to
Belle Vue, even though he had not been there for two years.
Rather, he returned to the sporting field and the Richmond
Cricket Club. Tom did not play for New South Wales, and the
relieved and now confident Victorian cricketers elected him
captain for the next intercolonial match.

When the Victorian players were selected, George Marshall,
the best wicket keeper in the colony, refused to go because of
his business enterprises. Reluctantly, and with some ill will,
he was pressured into travelling to Sydney. Marshall's bad
mood was aggravated when, on the way to Sandridge Pier, he
was thrown from his horse and carriage. The steamer trip to
Sydney was wretched, taking a lengthy three and half days.
Marshall telegraphed that it was a 'disgusting trip' and that
he, Tom Wills, William Greaves and Richard Wardill were
all dreadfully seasick. The Victorians arrived late, with the
game due to start the following day. The Victorians requested

a day's rest to recover from their trip; the New South Wales team refused.

The game on the Domain started as scheduled, on 5 February, and when the players reached the Domain it was thick with police, a portent of events. Victoria won the toss and fielded. Tom Wills bowled fast and with unearthly accuracy. Problems occurred on the second day of the match after lunch with the New South Wales team in their second innings struggling at 4 wickets down for 11 runs.

Sydney Jones, batting for New South Wales, left his crease after facing the last ball of the over. George Marshall took the bails off and appealed to the Victorian umpire who gave Jones out. Then the New South Wales batsmen appealed to the New South Wales umpire who said Jones was not out. The New South Wales team claimed that the ball was dead as it was the end of the over, and that the Victorians were already in the process of changing fielding positions. The Victorians denied this and the teams argued. Marshall had a record of 'sharp practice'. In the previous intercolonial match he had also removed the bails, the batsman then being allowed to continue, but neither the spectators nor the New South Wales players had forgiven Marshall.

Ernest Docker, playing for New South Wales, recalled that Marshall was the best wicket keeper of his day but 'an ill-tempered man, and he disputed the decision, left the ground in defiance of his captain, and refused to go on with the game'. The crowd, stirred up, booed the Victorians, and threw objects at the players and rushed the field. Tom, leading his team off the field, was struck in the face by a stone. The Victorians immediately returned to their quarters in the city.

That evening the Victorians met at Tattersall's Hotel, arguing with one another and disagreeing upon the course of action. Eventually at 8 p.m. Tom wrote to Charles Lawrence, the New South Wales captain: the Victorians consented to continue the game on the proviso that both umpires were removed. The Victorian umpire, and the professional players George Marshall and William Greaves, furiously and famously left Tom Wills and returned to Melbourne. On the third and final day of the match, Tom walked out on the Domain with only eight of his team. Tom Wills top-scored in both Victorian innings; Charles Lawrence played brilliantly, taking 14 wickets. New South Wales won the match by 84 runs.

In the speeches after the match Richard Wardill was the first to speak on behalf of the Victorians. When Tom spoke he was less diplomatic. He was criticised in Sydney for having made a false promise to play for New South Wales and criticised in Melbourne for losing and for what the Melbourne press saw as his insipid behaviour in continuing the game. Tom denied all accusations until there were none left to deny.

After the match, Tom Wills and George Marshall penned angry letters to the *Sydney Morning Herald*. Tom wrote:

> Before we started from Melbourne we were informed that there would be a row about the match; but at the same time I may be allowed to say that I have never played up here yet without there being a row, . . . We have allowed the 'mob' to win, but not the cricketers . . . The wicket was put down, and an appeal was made, and the decision was given against him; and *no appeal* by Mr. Jones, and consequently Mr. Driver [New South Wales umpire] had *no* right to say I called over. Sir, he had no right to open his mouth without an appeal to him by the batsman, who is the only one entitled to make an appeal from the other umpire's decision . . . This conduct, on his part, seemed to excite the mob, who at once commenced to hoot and yell like very demons, backed up, I must say, by many individuals in the grand stand, who, I believe, are called by misnomer gentlemen, and who ought, if educated, to have attempted to soothe the troubled waters rather than lend themselves or their example to excite further an already over-excited crowd of uncontrollables. Had not this point

arisen at the time it did, we, without a doubt, would have won the match; but as soon as I found that the 'umpire's' decision was not taken . . . I left the field, together with my Eleven. We were then followed by *a mob*, and some of us were literally stoned, others *sticked*, and others *peached*: and when we left the ground had to be escorted by policemen out of the Domain – very barbarians would never permit such conduct towards their greatest foes, let alone their *visitors*. Mr Marshall, I *consider*, in one point, was quite justified in leaving, as I consider had anything gone against New South Wales, his life really would have been endangered. I myself and others, have since been insulted over and over again. I never did *promise* to play for New South Wales, and why, therefore, can I be called turn-coat . . . As to my present statement, I for one do not think that Victoria will ever send an Eleven up here again.

When Tom returned to Melbourne he was met with suspicion and accused of behaving weakly. Marshall and Greaves were praised by some for refusing to continue the match; others were angry at them because their behaviour might be seen as unbecoming, not a Melburnian trait so they thought. Tom Wills was held responsible for Victoria's humiliation. Suspicion about his alleged interest in playing for New South Wales confirmed in some minds that Tom had not acted in Victoria's interest. But what really bothered Victorians the most was that they had lost to an inferior team, an inferior colony.

At a meeting of the Victorian cricketers held at Marshall's Cricketing Depot in Swanston Street, Tom was called upon to recount what happened on the field and to explain why he continued to play the game. He maintained that the New South Wales batsman, Jones, was out. Marshall, of course, concurred. Each member of the Victorian team gave his version. It was loud and histrionic, confirming what was already fixed in their minds – the righteousness of the Victorian case.

Within Tom's circle of friends the Sydney players were regarded as 'regular cowards and cheats'. George Glencross-Smith wrote with indignation: 'Someone threw a stone and it hit Tom in the face and Marshall dare not move out of his hotel for being murdered. Someone in the crowd gave Huddlestone a blow with a stick.' Emily, with all the relish of someone who loves a stoush, wrote excitedly about it and sent Cedric in Queensland the newspaper reports of the match and the rioting.

Melbourne journalists wrote a great deal about the match and the class of men in the two colonies. Victorians held themselves to be the superior breed. Sydney men, the Melbourne press condescendingly argued, showed a distinct tendency towards 'excitability'. It was true that Sydney men could be played with in cricket, dined with and even bred with. But Melburnians did not need to conjecture long before settling on the fact of their superiority over the men from Sydney. And even if the readers in Collins Street smiled at these teasing suggestions in the press as the froth of the day, there was an assumption of its correctness. When Tom Wills suggested that he might play for Sydney the astonished reaction in Melbourne had sprung from a deeply held conceit, which was barely camouflaged by intercolonial diplomacy.

Each colony rearranged the evidence to suit their opinion, then, convinced of the correctness of their position, tucked their view beneath their arms as if it was a spanking new cane-handle cricket bat and turned their backs on each other, refusing to play cricket for two years.

As for Tom, he left Melbourne and headed bush. He had sex on his mind.

LEAVING CULLIN-LA-RINGO

FEBRUARY 1863–APRIL 1864

Julie Anderson was known as one of the gentle Anderson sisters from Barrigal, near the town of Skipton in Central Victoria. She and her sister Sarah spoke softly: 'a thing so much admired in women, is eminently exemplified in these two young ladies, in quiet manners they very much take after their father who is very amiable'. Julie and Sarah were the daughters of the 'very amiable' Alex Anderson. It was Anderson who had taught Tom how to hold sheep shears before he and Horatio had trekked to Queensland. Tom's interest in Julie had been noted four years previously by William Roope: 'a sly fellow' he had whispered to Horatio.

The Anderson girls were regular visitors to Belle Vue and Egbert and Horace, on holidays from Scotch College, were invited to the Anderson farm. They were teased endearingly by Mrs Anderson, who spoke of Tom as her prospective son-in-law. It seemed settled – Tom was engaged to be married to Julie Anderson. Both families approved. But through all the matchmaking, Julie's name did not appear in any of Tom's surviving letters.

Tom headed to Skipton in March to see Julie. Before he left Melbourne, he wrote to his brother Cedric at Cullin-la-Ringo, deriding the New South Wales cricket team as having 'cheated us' and then boasting with playful self-deprecation: 'I made 25 & 17 not out either Inns [innings] pretty good for a muff eh?' Once the important matters were written, Tom made a passing reference to getting married and his plan to take his wife to Queensland. In this he was less animated than in the account of his batting score in the last intercolonial match and at no point did Tom mention Julie's name. Although Tom had been down from Cullin-la-Ringo for two months, this would be his first trip to see Julie Anderson – a negligent attitude to courtship in the mind of his sister Emily. She sniffed her dissatisfaction with Tom's preference for cricket over courtship: 'I don't know whether Tom intends taking unto himself a wife but I don't think he has been to Andersons since he came down which I should resent if I were the young lady.' Tom told everyone that he planned to take a wife but his casual manner suggested he had capitulated to expectation rather than desire.

Alex Anderson treated Tom as his prospective son-in-law, offering to send a man up to Queensland to assist Tom with his work. Anderson was a sincere, unworldly man whose writing suggests he was more at ease holding a sheep's crutch than a pen. At the end of one of his letters to Tom, to underline his daughter's affection, he wrote: 'Julie has been writing all afternoon to you, so I shall close.'

While Tom was in Queensland, Julie and Tom wrote to one another a good deal. None of Tom's letters have survived, but we know he wrote every two weeks because Julie reassured him that this was sufficient for her. Julie Anderson enshrined Tom in distant Queensland: 'I don't expect more, it is very good of you to write so often . . . it seems a very long time since I saw you . . . I am sorry Tom to hear that you have not been well.' Julie wrote pages on her domestic duties, of farm life and the weather: 'I have had my tea but cant say it has done me much good as yet . . . I am longing to get your next letter . . . You are such an awful long way off. I hate to think of what a number of miles there are between us . . . I don't remember finding fault with you for not writing often Tom. I am just content I hear from you once a fortnight.' Which was just as well because her letters on darning, tea making and the weather were unlikely to arouse even the most passionate admirer. Julie was available but perhaps more virtuous than desirable.

Tom remained at Skipton with the Andersons for five or six weeks, frustrating his family who had been expecting his return to Belle Vue for three weeks. Tom had promised to return to Queensland but failed to do so and the trustees of Cullin-la-Ringo wanted to see him. His friends raised their eyes at Tom's lengthy absence from Cullin-la-Ringo: 'Tom is up the country yet, he is taking a good spell of it,' wrote George Glencross-Smith.

Tom finally left the Anderson farm at the beginning of May, just in time to play in the first football match of the Geelong season. The games were few and without a structured competition. The local paper, the *Geelong Advertiser*, heralded the first game: 'Australians against the World'. Tom captained the 'Australians', a team of native-born sons, against 'The World', a team of men born overseas. The 'Native' team wore a slip of blue ribbon to mark their origins and play started at 2.30 p.m. on the paddock next to the Argyle Hotel. After the 'Natives' scored the first goal, matters deteriorated and when more quarrelling occurred after a disputed goal, Tom and his 'Natives' left the field in protest, clutching the ball tighter than their sense of entitlement, leaving the World team alone on the field. The following week Tom left for Cullin-la-Ringo, but before leaving, he promised his brother Egbert that he would return for Christmas to play the All England Cricket XI and to marry.

Elizabeth managed the money for the family at Belle Vue. She wrote out her expenses carefully in an exercise book, recording each item of cost – a practice Horatio would have beamed over. A haircut cost 1 shilling, a pair of scissors 1 shilling

6 pence, and a trip to Melbourne and back by train cost 16 shillings. She recorded giving Tom the occasional pound note, as well as shelling out money for Tom's expenses: subscriptions to the Geelong Football Club (5 shillings), Melbourne Cricket Club, Corio Cricket Club and Richmond Cricket Club. Not to mention shirts, Zingari caps (7 shillings and 6 pence) and boots – new and old – that needed repair. This detailed family budget provided by Elizabeth was the kind of account that the trustees of Cullin-la-Ringo expected Tom to provide for the station. None had been forthcoming.

It was with relief that Elizabeth wrote on 19 May that Tom had started back to Queensland taking with him two more men – an old shepherd from the family's days at Lexington and a bullock driver. Before Tom left Belle Vue the trustees impressed upon him the need for economy at Cullin-la-Ringo. Uncle Thomas sat in with Elizabeth and Tom as the trustees explained the financial state of the station. Tom's uncle visited Belle Vue regularly and when he could, suggested strategies to improve the station. Elizabeth, 'dreadfully anxious' about Tom drawing large cheques, bore the burden of his flippancy and lack of care with money. Clutching her breast, seeking an antidote to her rattled nerves, she exclaimed to her God and family: 'We have all taken to Homeopathy.'

Tom travelled back to Queensland by steamer, along with his friend George Glencross-Smith, and played 'putting rings on a peg' on the steamer's deck. On arrival in Brisbane they walked about the town's streets. George was astonished at the Aborigines he saw: 'you meet them every two yards you go in the place, they are not a bit like the blacks in Geelong, they are long legged beggers and <u>boots</u> and <u>hat</u> is [their] principal amount of clothing, <u>thats all</u>.' The next day Tom was finally sworn in as a Justice of the Peace in the Supreme Court in Brisbane on 27 May 1863. He swore an Oath of Allegiance 'to Her Majesty Queen Victoria as Lawful Sovereign of the United Kingdom of Great Britain and Ireland, of this Colony of Queensland'. And then signed his name.

Tom arrived at Cullin-la-Ringo in August 1863 – he had been away from the property for nearly eight months. On the day before Tom's birthday, Elizabeth wrote him a loving maternal letter and, for the moment, was not concerned with Tom's misdemeanours. She wrote of her concern for his painful knee, which should be wrapped. It was if she was speaking to a child of ten rather than a man of twenty-eight: 'it would do your knee good if you were to try a bandage about it & with the addition of a little turpentine [rubbed] to it'. Her relationship with Tom was still very close and unlike any she had with her other children. In the following weeks Tom sketched Cullin-la-Ringo station and sent it to his mother, to her delight.

The month after Tom's return, a nearby settler was speared by local Aborigines through the neck and died. Victorian newspapers reported these attacks with eye-catching phrases and drawings that depicted terrified Europeans awaiting the stealth of the blacks. And each time the memory of Horatio's death was rekindled for the family. Tom, always primed for these assaults, sent letters of condemnation to the Queensland press. On 17 September he wrote on the inadequacies of the Native Police deployment and on those who criticised the settlers:

> The black police are well enough to chastise after an act, but they do not seem to be a preventive force at all, it seems to me they are located badly, instead of being placed in the beat of blacks, they are out of it. Murders are invariably committed when they are at the furthest extremity of their rounds, and consequently it is some days before they can be put upon the tracks of these bloodthirsty villains. I suppose your Brisbane saints will still cry with a long face – Oh pity the poor inoffensive blacks, I wish they would just step up here, and see a place whilst the babies of the murdered men are above ground, if that sight would not turn their

Cullin-la-Ringo

hypocritical cry, they ought to be put at the bottom of a well
to get cool, and give them time to reflect. If they too think
that the blacks can or are to be civilised, why do they not
come in 'propria persona', and undertake the reformation.
Oh, no, sir, this would be coming too close to the point. You
would find that business arrangements would not allow of
their absence. Yet they can fill the papers with preposterous
stuff about blacks whom they do not understand, and call
every squatter who protects his own life and the life of his
men a murderer . . .

Almost as soon as Tom had arrived at Cullin-la-Ringo, he
prepared to leave again – to return to Melbourne to play cricket
over the summer. Negotiations in Melbourne to organise the
annual intercolonial cricket match between New South Wales
and Victoria had failed. The New South Wales cricketers wanted
an apology from the Victorian team for the letters written by

Tom Wills and George Marshall in the aftermath of the riotous game. When the Victorians refused to apologise, New South Wales organised to play Queensland. Ironically, the Queensland cricketers wrote immediately to Tom at Cullin-la-Ringo, asking if, now that he was a Queenslander, he would consent to play for the Queensland colony against New South Wales. The Queensland papers gloated when Tom, 'the champion cricketer of the colonies', agreed to play after the shearing season had ended at Cullin-la-Ringo, anticipating he would be elected captain.

Tom would agree to play with anyone who asked. But Queensland was not the centre of cricket in the country – nor was Sydney. Only Melbourne offered the finest cricket matches and this summer the All England XI, captained by George Parr, were due to arrive in Melbourne in the middle of December. So after just three months at Cullin-la-Ringo Tom left for Melbourne, leaving Cedric again in charge of the station.

Tom departed Cullin-la-Ringo, with a haste that suggested little regret, and made his way across Central Queensland towards the coast. As he travelled to Rockhampton, the Queensland press announced plans to lure the English cricket team to Brisbane. On 12 December Tom Wills was named in the Queensland cricket team to play the English, if indeed the English could be persuaded to travel to Brisbane. In Melbourne Tom was picked in the first cricket match against the English team – the English XI would play a Victorian XXII at the Melbourne Cricket Ground. Whether the Victorians were aware of plans by the Queenslanders to purloin the best cricketer in the country is unknown. Even had they been aware, it is unlikely they would have considered that such an attempt could compete with their own plans for Tom.

Emily wrote to Cullin-la-Ringo on 17 December to tell Cedric the English cricket team had arrived in Melbourne: 'I suppose Tom will soon be down now as he was leaving then. The All England Eleven arrived last night and were escorted to Melbourne in great grandeur today at noon.' All the Melbourne talk was about the England XI and anyone who read the newspapers in Melbourne knew that Tom Wills was coming home.

Tom made Rockhampton on 15 December, but missed the steamer to Sydney by twenty-four hours and was forced to bide his time in Rockhampton, a place he loathed: 'a Brute of a hole'. The English were making their final preparations to play the Victorian XXII captained by George Marshall. The first match was to start just after the New Year. Tom left wretched Rockhampton and breathed hard: 'I shall have a hard race for the first match.' But making the match after his delay was impossible.

Tom's dash from Cullin-la-Ringo to Melbourne to play cricket fascinated the English. This was surely the journey of a madman. The English wrote about Tom's race for the match in the gentlemen papers and cricket magazines of London – Tom

Wills, of Rugby and Cambridge fame, crossed the breadth of Australia to play cricket. It was part admiration, part amusement. They were an odd lot these colonials in Australia, and Tom Wills was the oddest of the lot.

When Tom arrived in Melbourne he shot straight from the steamer to the Melbourne Cricket Ground. By the time Tom arrived, the match between the All England XI and the Victorian XXII was three days old. On the fourth day, the word that Tom was at the ground spread; the crowd waited and watched until he emerged from the Melbourne Cricket Club pavilion. Walking on to the MCG, Tom heard the familiar sound of adoration.

As the English moved about the colony playing cricket, Tom was at their side. The trustees, exasperated, wanted Tom back at Cullin-la-Ringo. Frustrated, Elizabeth approached William Ducker, Horatio's old merchant confidant, and her accountant. The sober and industrious Ducker was requested to sort out the financial mess on the station and assess Tom's culpability. Tom's elusive and slippery manner to date had been met with some forbearance, but he was found to be still drawing cheques for his personal use while claiming them as station expenditure. Once this deceit was exposed, he was asked not to leave the colony of Victoria until he presented himself before the trustees to explain his behaviour and resolve the financial affairs of the family property.

Tom was expected to marry Julie Anderson on this trip. His brothers and sisters wrote and chatted about it. Elizabeth, however, was less sure that a respectable woman should live on Cullin-la-Ringo. Tom's Aunt Sarah, who had cared for him on his vacation breaks from Rugby School, prayed fervently for Tom's marriage and his salvation; and not in that order. She wrote to Tom from London and sent his fiancée jewellery as a wedding gift. Aunt Sarah prayed that Tom might live a life of virtue. The fear that Tom might not enter everlasting life after his death drove her sentiments: he must obey and bend his will to the Lord and seek salvation in everlasting life. But no puritan thread ran through Tom's heart and his devotion to scripture was considerably less than his devotion to *Bell's Life in Victoria*. While he made reference to prayer and Christianity in his letters, Tom gave the impression that although he might have believed in the faith, it was not part of his daily thinking. This did not hold back Sarah who thrust upon Tom all the religiosity of the Wills dynasty in preparation for his marriage: 'His letter addressed to you and to us all, in His own book the Bible. In it you will find direction to guide you in every duty, and to put you in to the right path and if you offer up to Him sincere and heartfelt prayer . . . By this time I hope you are a married man . . . made up your mind, with Gods help, to perform all the solemn duties you have pledged yourself to perform . . . children . . . to train them up for the Lord, so that when your time of departure may come it will not be an eternal separation but that we may meet again in Glory.' Sarah repeated Horatio's commandments about duty: 'Let me beg of you to continue to be a dutiful son to her [Elizabeth], and to remember your dear father's dying instructions to you all, to exert yourself to the utmost for her and your brothers and sisters interest.'

In January 1864 while Tom was playing with Ballarat against the English team, his mother wrote to Cedric:

Mr Morris was out here on Sunday to tell me something of importance. Mr Anderson had been down to see him and the consequence is Tom is not likely to be married for a very long time to come. Mr A has heard something not at all in Tom's favor. So Mr Morris wished me to write and advise him [Tom] to return to the station without any loss of time. I do not expect he will even go to Skipton this time. Tom would act for himself in all things so now he must now also bare the blame of all things himself. I rather pity him but at the same time he is to blame . . . for he had not yet given an account of how the money was spent [that] he had given him when last down here – he is really like a child with money – not to be trusted with it.

Tom had done something to inflame the mild Alex Anderson. Tom's marriage was off; letters crisscrossed from Melbourne to Belle Vue to Brisbane to Rockhampton to Cullin-la-Ringo, full of whispers about his bad behaviour:

Cedric: So Mr. Tom has got himself into disgrace has he? I wonder what it was that Mr Anderson heard about him?

Selina Johnston to Emily: I know how unhappy you must feel at what has occurred I did not think Tom would have behaved so to you all but I will not say any more of him because I fear it will distress you.

Pussie Glencross-Smith: I suppose you have heard by this time that Tom's engagement is <u>broken</u> off. Tom Board told me he had a letter from Skipton, and it said it was broken off, and that Mr Anderson was in a great rage with Tom. I had a letter myself today saying it was true so you will not have a Mrs T.W.W. at present at Cullin-la-ringo . . . I believe the committee of the Intercolonial match are going to write and ask Tom to play for Brisbane. What a shame of him to go and run up bills at the hotels, I suppose the <u>station</u> will not pay them.

Another letter, written before the engagement collapsed, implied that Tom had either received love letters from a woman or women other than Julie Anderson, or that if these letters were from Julie, his behaviour was less than honest:

J.H. Norcott to Cedric: To give you a hint of how a person may be deceived I could have perused some love letters from [and here the letter is torn and words are missing] to yr brother which had fallen into other hands!!!

And as if to confirm an illicit world and a juicy hidden life that Tom kept as his own, Norcott finished with a revelation that doubled as a threat: 'Of course I did not but this will show you that yr brothers most trusty toady's, can & are acquainted with all his secrets & private affairs.'

There is no mention by Tom in any surviving letters of what happened and why his engagement collapsed. In fact he seemed to not let matters impede his return to cricket at all. He spent January travelling the Victorian countryside with George Parr, Julius Caesar and G.F. Grace – younger brother of the more famous William Gilbert Grace – and the rest of the English cricket team. The English melted in the summer heat and choked on the dust. Tom played for Bendigo, Ballarat, Ararat and Maryborough as the English team played and drank their way through the country towns of Victoria. Ignoring the trustees who wanted him to return to Belle Vue and explain the station's ledger, Tom went on to New Zealand with the English cricketers.

The steamer *Alhambra* left Sandridge Pier and arrived in Dunedin, Otago, on the south island of New Zealand, in the early hours of Sunday 31 January. Over 20,000 immigrants had recently headed towards the gold diggings of Otago, many of them Victorians. Elizabeth, despite everything, felt sympathy for her son:

Tom did certainly arrive in Victoria but he has not shown his face amongst us – or even sent a line of writing. I expect it is all owing to his marriage being put an end [to]. You may be sure it was a great blow to him for he started from the station full of hope of having everything finally arranged & returning a new man. I suspect also, that was his reason with joining the cricketers, & going off to New Zealand just to drown his cares. I am exceedingly sorry for what has happened, for I know well it would have been the making of Tom & a pleasure to us all had he been married this trip.

New Zealand was another month of pleasure with rounds of morning champagne, afternoon claret and a flurry of cricket matches in between. The English, fawned over by the New Zealanders, travelled by coach and six horses, winning just about everything. Tom moved about with the English XI, umpiring the first match and then playing for the local sides until the end of the tour. In the final game, Tom played with a XXII from Otago and became involved in a dispute on the field. One of the Otago players, a 'Mr Maddock', left the field in protest at Tom's poor bowling, insinuating that Tom deliberately bowled in a manner to assist the English. The accusation appeared in the *Otago Daily Times*. Tom, from whom such a public insult might once have drawn a barrage of letters, had time for only one. Swelling with indignation, he wrote from the Provincial Hotel, Dunedin, to the newspaper's editor, denying Maddock's view of the dispute. Tom criticised the poor quality of the local team's fielding rather than his own bowling and, scoffing, suggested that Mr Maddock might like to have tried bowling himself, '*a la* ten-pin alley style'. To establish his position of moral superiority, Tom added that the accusation against him was a gratuitous insult to the English XI. Tom signed himself as captain of the Otago XXII, a designation noted the following day in the paper as somewhat unusual considering that Tom was neither a member of the local club nor a resident. It mattered little for within a day Tom and the All England Eleven left for Melbourne, from where he travelled to Belle Vue to face his mother.

Elizabeth's tolerance for her son's behaviour had lessened but she struggled to condemn him. The family was told that Tom's signature meant nothing in Queensland and that cheques that bore his signature alone were not honoured. With profound understatement, she wrote to Cedric: 'It seems a very difficult matter for Tom to keep accounts.' Even when the evidence of his financial ineptitude and deceit was overwhelming, Elizabeth's tone was more tolerant than vindictive, exhibiting tenderness and

pity towards Tom. Perhaps the love for her first-born had blinded
her to an honest assessment but Elizabeth drew the line at Tom's
selfishness when he requested that his young brother Horace, only
sixteen, be taken out of school and despatched to Queensland to
help on the station: 'Tom states very strongly the benefit it would
be to the station if he had Horace but I say no. Tom has had all
the benefit of a good education so he must allow his brother a
little.' Elizabeth, seeking to maintain a united family appearance
to the outside world, wrote to Cedric and told him to keep Tom's
misbehaviour to himself; she measured father against son and
found Tom wanting. The letter was a turning point for Elizabeth:

> Tom is not near the man for work as your poor father was he
> would never complain of what he did for us all . . . I wish the
> station was out of debt so that something could be done to
> the grave & have a coffin made for his poor bones . . . Tom
> has done very wrong in drawing upon strangers when last
> in town. Mr Ducker told me he was puzzled to know how
> Tom had paid his way down – for they had written to tell
> him in case he made up his mind to come down he was to
> get £20 from Mr Johnstone but it appears he came away
> without it & I suppose this is the result of drawing on the
> agents in Rockhampton . . . Tom is dreadfully childish with
> regard to money & he knows the many bills both here & in
> England his kind father had to pay for him, but he cannot
> expect that indulgence now. He must work for it . . .

Elizabeth prepared to enact Horatio's wishes, as laid out in
his will, and remove Tom from Cullin-la-Ringo; her husband's
premonition that Tom might not handle station life had proved
accurate. More letters passed between Tom's mother and the
trustees about Tom's deceit with money. William Ducker, who
had been called in by Elizabeth to help manage the situation,
wrote to Cedric: 'Your brother has been to New Zealand with
the cricketers – and I believe is daily expected back. The trustees
nor myself, have not yet seen him, since he left the station. You

Horatio's gravesite

may rest assured that the interest of the Estate generally will be well watched over – and no irregularities in finance matters in any way will be sanctioned.'

When Tom returned from New Zealand, not everyone was waiting to criticise him. Horace was delighted that his older brother was back and hoped he might get him free tickets to watch the English cricket team and avoid paying the half-crown admission. Even Horace and Egbert knew of Tom's untrustworthiness. Horace wrote to Cedric: 'Mama has bought you a nice album but will not trust it with Tom [in] fear he might lose it.' Another time Elizabeth cautioned against Tom being allowed to take firearms from Belle Vue to Queensland: 'I am undecided about the Pistols. I should not like to send them up by Tom in case some wrong should happen [to] them.' Perhaps it was just recklessness, for Tom had a facility for losing things, but the implication was that objects slipped through Tom's fingers in exchange for money.

In early 1864, Mr Morris and the other trustees dismissed Tom from Cullin-la-Ringo. His sister Emily, who had for

some time been dismissive of Tom and on occasions hinted
of her brother's sneakiness, celebrated his fall. Tom's future,
she guessed, would be that of a professional cricketer – not an
option she regarded with pride. Emily wrote:

> Hip Hip Horrah Mr Morris . . . on Friday afternoon . . . told
> Ma that Tom had resigned at least Mr Morris made him and
> is not going back to the station again. I wonder what he will
> do? Turn professional cricketer I suppose. I wonder if Ma
> will say anything to Tom about it? And will Tom loaf here
> or . . . to Melbourne and go to the bad . . . I feel so relieved
> since I have known of his dismissal . . .'

Tom remained in Victoria, continuing to follow the English
team and to play cricket. He was 'unanimously' elected as
captain of the Victorian XXII to play the English at the MCG
in April, at the end of the English tour. It rained and the game
was drawn. William Caffyn, the champion English batsman and
barber, was courted by the MCC and remained in Melbourne
to become a professional cricketer. The rest of the English team
returned home; Tom went back to Belle Vue.

Elizabeth's relationship with Tom was complex and changing.
In response to her son's behaviour, she was sometimes angry,
sometimes pitying and sometimes expressed a sense of guilt
over her role in his development as a man. She understood with
profound sensitivity the impact of the loss of Horatio upon
Tom, a loss which she, of course, shared; and she often called
upon her memory of Horatio's words to help soothe and guide
her in understanding Tom: 'unfortunately for him, he lost his
poor fathers services too early. Your father used to say himself
Tom worked well – but he required one to guide him – who
does not? Everyone feel[s] the want of a <u>good one</u>.'

THE MAN WITH NO CLOTHES

APRIL 1864–DECEMBER 1865

People carry all sorts of little lies in their pockets – slippery
fishy explanations that they know are not true; small parcels
of distorted information; facts rearranged to satisfy their
conscience. Tom had collected these all his life, with ease and
little self-reflection.

In April 1864 Tom wrote to Cedric giving his version of
why he had left the station. It was a brief letter that concealed
what would have been a difficult and accusatory meeting: 'Mr
Morris, Mr Ducker my mother & self had a grand meeting
the other night & it was ultimately decided that I should not
return to the station.' Tom implied, disingenuously, that he
had contributed an equal say in the decision rather than being
dismissed. The trustees enacted Horatio's prophetic words: to
remove Tom from Cullin-la-Ringo in the case of misconduct.

Tom remained at Belle Vue. It was a house of women with
his mother and, in descending age, his sisters, Emily, Elizabeth,
Eugene, Minna and Hortense. Tom's three brothers were living
elsewhere: Cedric was at Cullin-la-Ringo, Horace and Egbert
at school in Melbourne. Tom had yet to explain to the trustees
how he had spent money on the station. William Ducker,
the family accountant, asked Cedric to examine the ledger

books on Cullin-la-Ringo and to report back. Ducker was not convinced that Tom had told the truth about his spending and wrote: 'Sometime since your Brother sent me a list which he said he made up from the Station Ledger but I cannot make it correspond with the cheques and orders he has drawn on the bank & on Mr Roope . . . The trustees would be willing to take the bank account as correct but it does not show for what purpose the money is spent whether for wages to the men or for your Brother's private account.' Ducker did not openly accuse Tom of stealing money from the station but each line implied that this was the case. Tom continued to make excuses and his mother wrote more words of hope, and concern: 'Tom remains quietly here. Yet I hope he may stay till he gets something to do & not get himself in any further debt. Mr Ducker told me Tom was waiting for his papers & box to come from the station before he could square up the accounts. I wish he had them down for he has not a shilling to buy clothes with untill [sic] he knows how he stands with the Trustees.'

Tom's expulsion from Cullin-la-Ringo was murmured about within the family, and letters between family members chirped with suppressed excitement about Tom's bad behaviour. Emily was Tom's persecutor: 'Tom is at the Point I wonder how long he will stay there. I don't like being in the house with him. I do write to the Andersons. They have not said a word about Tom's behaviours, but I did last time I wrote.' Tom never mentioned his failed engagement to Julie Anderson but Emily was ready to remind everyone of her brother's untrustworthiness: 'If you knew how Tom is despised by all who know anything of him . . . Poor Ma would be terribly cut up if all her sons turned out like her first born and the station would never pay if some of the family were not to help work it. I believe Tom's debts exceed his share in the station I wonder if he intends to loaf on Ma always. He never even helps in the garden but reads novels and sometimes plays Foot Ball or Cricket.'

Then, in the winter of 1864, Emily wrote to Cedric a single astonishing line about Tom: 'I believe his wife is a very bad woman & was when he married her. I hope you wont say anything to Ma about her.' Tom was married – to an unnamed woman not approved of by his sister and whose behaviour and perhaps existence were to be kept secret from Tom's mother.

So who was the 'bad woman' that Tom had married? It is likely that Emily was referring to a woman called Sarah Theresa Barbor. But Sarah Barbor, or Sally as Tom referred to her, was already married. Tom's 'marriage' was no marriage at all. He had chosen a woman not only unpresentable to his family but one whom he could not marry. Sarah Barbor was a mysterious figure in Tom's life – there are no surviving photographs of her, she was relegated in letters and in life to only the occasional comment and her name was frequently misspelt in the private and public documents that recorded her existence.

Born Sarah Duff in Ireland, she married Samuel James Barbor on 15 August 1857 in Dublin. Four months later, on Christmas Eve, Sarah, nineteen years of age, and her husband stepped off the *Lillies* and into the city of Melbourne. Her husband, described as 'a gentleman' on their marriage certificate, was twenty-three. If the unnamed wife was Sarah, it is likely that Tom met her either in the early months of 1864 or perhaps on his previous trip to Victoria in 1863. By 1864 Sarah was separated from her husband – he had started another relationship with a woman who was pregnant with his child.

What Tom's family knew of Sarah and the nature of their 'marriage' is not clear. There are very few surviving letters that mention him in the second half of the 1860s, and a further complication is that Tom wrote very little about the women he courted and even less about his emotions towards them. Over the next six years Tom's mother did not mention Sarah Barbor in any of her correspondence, nor any other woman associated with Tom. It is possible that Elizabeth was not even aware of Tom's 'wife' during these years, even though some of Tom's siblings knew of her existence. It is also likely that Sarah remained in Melbourne away from the family and Elizabeth, as Tom moved between Melbourne and Belle Vue.

For the rest of 1864 Tom drifted between Belle Vue and Melbourne following the currents of football and cricket. Emily remained furious with him and did not talk to him for months on end, but for Tom's male friends his return to Geelong was a joy and they wallowed in his tales of Queensland: 'Tom has [been] telling me some yarns about eels almost as large round as your body in the nogoa, and a fish he calls "Barrimundi".'

Tom wrote to Cedric in Queensland and sent him a copy of *Bell's Life in Victoria* that featured Tom in the Melbourne Athletics Sports carnival on the Melbourne Cricket Ground. Tom, matched against the best kickers of the football in the colony, boasted to Cedric: 'I won the drop <u>kick</u> (£2.2) kicking 173 feet . . . Colden won the high jump (30/-).' Tom had a detached interest in Cullin-la-Ringo and even included some advice to Cedric: 'Last year's wool brought from 1/8 to 1/10 per lb – what <u>awful</u> bosh Mr. J wanting to shear in grease and have it <u>scoured</u> after . . .' A few more comments on sheep, shearing and carriers of wool and he was finished with advice to his brother. Tom never talked about his misdeeds nor gave a sense of being bothered by them, but he was angry at the trustees of Cullin-la-Ringo for listening to men's 'yarns' about him, moaning: 'I was so thoroughly disgusted at being told after doing ones best to get a good increase, that one had done nothing at all.' But no one heard his voice – a voice that self-pity had entered. And then, suddenly, the moment of gloom evaporated from the page and he ended: 'There will be a good time for us yet Ced old chap – I am thinking of going up to Sydney to stay and I am expecting a job from there. Anything to pass the time away.'

The opening match of the 1864 football season took place on Saturday 21 May on the Richmond Paddock. Tom was to captain the best fourteen players of the Melbourne Football

Club against Colden Harrison's team of the next best twenty players from the club. In the end, Tom did not turn up and Richard Wardill took his place as captain. For the rest of the winter Tom played football in Melbourne and Geelong.

Emily recorded in her letters some of the football games, particularly the play of Colden Harrison. Her interest was raised because Colden had been courting her. After approval from Elizabeth, Emily married Colden Harrison in November at the Point Henry church. Tom was there and wrote a long letter: 'On Thursday last the 10th Emmy & Colden were married – there was a grand arch made at the last gate down the lane for them to pass under . . . George Smith eat so much at the Lunch that he got tremendously sick. Uncle Thomas was present . . . Mr Rennie was to have been present but on Wednesday he played a match against the North Melbourne & he kept wicket. I hit him in the eye with a ball & he could not see, we gave them a good dressing.' Tom's letter regarding Emily's marriage suggested no irritability towards his sister, but despite her new-found status as Colden Harrison's wife, Emily remained cold and distant to Tom.

Towards the end of the year Tom, now twenty-nine, appeared discontented with the ordinariness of his life. Privately his mother despaired: 'I am afraid he will hardly be able to get away from this for debt – someone or the other is continually after [him].' Elizabeth bemoaned her son's aimlessness and sought help from the heavens. The fault, she thought, lay in his obsession with the game of cricket, and for the first time she confessed to others that she suspected that Tom would never earn a shilling. Tom was tired of the gossip about him and looked for somewhere other than Victoria to live. Although he rarely seemed to appreciate how others suffered as a consequence of his actions, he never gave the impression of malice nor did he seek revenge or influence. But now with summer near and cricket about to start, Tom needed a place of refuge. Like an artist seeking patronage he sought out the Melbourne Cricket Club.

On 21 November he sent a chit to the MCC:

Dear Sir,
Your notice of my election to the M.C.C. duly to hand I
shall be down for Saturdays match &c. I shall not be able
to pay my subscription till the beginning of the new year.
I suppose that will be all right?
I remain
My Dear Sir
Yours very Truly
Thomas. W. Wills.

Tom had no money to pay for an MCC membership (2
guineas) and if Biddle, honorary secretary of the Club, had
consulted Tom's mother she would have confirmed that Tom
had not a single shilling to buy clothes. Tom's note to Biddle
was breezy stuff. Pure Wills. His presumptuous 'I suppose that
will be all right?' had the tone of a man who knew it would be
all right. And Tom's presumptuous tone was matched by the
pressing solicitude of the MCC to take him back – the Club
desired its greatest player as much, perhaps more, as Tom wished
to return. He was to play alongside Richard Wardill, the newly
elected captain of the Melbourne Cricket Club, and also managed
to play with the Geelong and Richmond clubs. This time, the
MCC allowed Tom his wanderings. In December, he bowled
for the MCC against South Melbourne. William Hammersley
was batting that day for South Melbourne and doing rather
well – perhaps too well – until, on 41 runs, Tom bowled and hit
him severely on the left elbow, ending Hammersley's innings.
It was a blow that was not forgotten by either man.

Tom returned to the MCC as an amateur cricketer but the
professional cricketers in the Club were still his closest allies.
Within a week Tom came to the defence of the professional
Jerry Bryant, alleging that the brilliant amateur fast bowler John
Conway had assaulted Bryant. Tom wrote an indignant letter on

Bryant's behalf but had the composure not to completely forget the status of the amateur. Even in his moment of aggravation, Tom made sure that he referred to Conway as Mr Conway; Bryant was simply Bryant.

28th November 1864
W.C. Biddle Esqe
Hon Sec M.C.C.
Dear Sir,

It is with pain that I have to request that you will bring before the committee of the M.CC an enquiry into the conduct of Mr. John Conway who in a <u>most</u> <u>cowardly</u> + ungentlemanly way did make an attack upon one James M Bryant on Saturday last in the M.C.C. Pavilion, not even contenting himself with having acted in a dastardly manner, but did afterward <u>boast</u> of his <u>deed</u> in places of Public resort in the City of Melbourne. Such <u>conduct</u> if not thoroughly investigated + the offender <u>punished</u> <u>as</u> <u>far</u> as the <u>Rules</u> of the Club will allow is <u>not</u> calculated to <u>raise</u> the standing of the leading Club of the Colony. It has been my painful but I think most necessary duty to make this complaint + I trust it will be thoroughly investigated.
I remain
Dear Sir
Yours Obly
Thomas W. Wills

Elizabeth was vexed by Tom's long absences and unemployment: 'He told me when he left just before Christmas that he was going to see one of the members and try to obtain a situation – but it is impossible for anyone to interest themselves for him so long as he gives himself up to the cricket field. I do despair of Tom ever doing any good for himself.' Then, in the timeless manner of maternal self-deception and hope, she continued: 'it is really a pity for I do not think he is in reality bad – but mixing with bad companions and I only wonder by this time he does not see the folly of it – I have no doubt but your brother Tom would have been thoroughly reclaimed had your poor father been spared.'

During the cricket season of 1864–65 it was rumoured that Tom was one of six Victorians going to England as part of a cricket team put together by Charles Lawrence. Nothing more was heard of this. In April 1865 the Melbourne Athletic Sports were held at the MCG before the Governor and his wife and 7000 spectators. Tom won the drop-kick contest, kicking 163 feet to beat Colden Harrison's 155 feet. Tom's reward was 3 pounds 3 shillings, not enough to pay his debts.

In May, Tom attended a meeting of the Melbourne Football Club at the Higgs Royal Hotel on Punt Road in Richmond. It was the usual incestuous group: Tom Wills, Richard Wardill, William Hammersley, Colden Harrison and a few others. Richard Wardill, perhaps the only sportsman to rival Wills in skills across a range of sports, was unanimously elected secretary and treasurer of the Melbourne Football Club. Tom was elected on to the Melbourne Football Club committee alongside Colden Harrison and William Hammersley. Wardill proposed another review of the rules of football as played in Melbourne. When it was suggested that this be carried out by a subcommittee, Tom objected and urged that the rules be sorted now; he had an aversion to committees interfering. Tom Wills 'strongly advocated' that a horizontal cross bar, 8 feet from the ground, be fixed between the two vertical goal posts – to kick a goal, a player must kick the ball over this cross bar and between the vertical posts without touching the wood. The vote on Tom's proposed amendment was tied and the chairman was called upon to cast the deciding vote. Mr Shoosmith cast his vote and Tom's proposal was defeated.

In the winter of 1865 Tom Wills and Colden Harrison were amongst the best-known footballers in the colony and often captained their teams. They played football on the Richmond

Paddock and occasionally, when granted permission, on the Melbourne Cricket Ground. The Melbourne and Geelong clubs were the strongest in the colony. Colden Harrison, now entrenched in the Melbourne Football Club, had lived and played in Geelong several years earlier. When the two best teams in the colony played each other, the clubs brawled openly about which team 'owned' Tom and Colden. The *Geelong Advertiser* complained about the conduct of the Melbourne club; it was believed that they had barred Tom and Colden from playing for Geelong. The newly elected Melbourne Football Club secretary, Richard Wardill, wrote a public letter to defend his club. Colden Harrison remained with Melbourne and his name was fastened to that club until the day of his death, over sixty years later. At the end of winter Tom Wills, the first captain of the Melbourne Football Club, left and never returned. From that point all his football was played with the Geelong Football Club. *Bell's Life in Victoria*, in considering Tom's loss to the city of Melbourne, made the point that the finest leader of men on the football field had left the metropolis.

Tom's life had returned to its familiar routine: football in winter, cricket in summer. Alcohol and tobacco were constant features of both sports. In the instruction manuals to young cricketers, advice was dispensed on the protocol governing drinking alcohol and the types of alcohol to consume. It was considered that 'heavy alcohols' might affect a young batsman's 'eye' for the ball. Spirits in particular were regarded as dangerous, and a batsman who ignored this advice and drank spirits could expect a deterioration in his performances. Light wines were viewed as optimum and were served in some matches before, during and after a day's play. The most common smoking device found on the cricket fields of the colony was the small clay pipe. Some observers of cricket objected to these pipes, but smoking on the cricket field was an essential accoutrement of the colonial cricketer. When articles were written objecting to this habit of smoking, it was not the 'dirty habit' of inhaling a bit of 'cutty' or 'weed' that was objected to, but rather the immobility and carelessness of fieldsmen distracted by their smoking. 'How many a good catch has been missed by the smoke of a cigar getting in the eyes of the fielder, or by the hurried attempts to stow away a pipe!' Tom smoked his little clay pipe on the field and in the MCC pavilion. He would sit in the pavilion watching cricket, fingers characteristically entwined in his beard, his face, settled in meditation, shrouded by smoke from his fiery pipe. Tom held, admired and coveted his small clay pipe. But if you were Tom Wills, son of Horatio, you did not merely caress your pipe on the field, you made it part of the entertainment as you drank and smoked and bowled all day. And so it was when Egbert, still at school at Scotch College, watched Tom play in Melbourne in December of 1865: 'Tom got drunk the other day when he was playing in a match in Melbourne & he kept himself on bowling all the time with his slows, he had a short clay pipe in his mouth and was kicking up a fine to do and making the people laugh.'

•

The cricketers of Victoria and New South Wales finally settled their differences and made arrangements to resume their inter-colonial contests, which had not taken place since the spectator riot of February 1863. The next intercolonial match was set for Boxing Day 1865 on the Melbourne Cricket Ground but problems were brewing within the MCC.

William Caffyn, the MCC's English cricket professional, was disgruntled. Rumours reached the MCC that Caffyn had made derogatory comments about the MCC. Caffyn denied the rumours. Initially, he had demanded an exorbitant salary of 400 pounds per annum but settled for 300 pounds per annum and assistance with his barber business. As the first year of his contract neared its end, William Caffyn, or 'Billy' Caffyn as he was more commonly known, had not received all the money owed him. He wrote to the MCC, asking to be released from his contract to allow him to play cricket in Sydney. Caffyn was a brilliant all-round cricketer whose characteristic bodily twitch as the bowler approached was well known. The MCC was loath to let Caffyn go to Sydney with the intercolonial match so near but could not afford to retain him. 'Billy the Barber' bolted for Sydney to play cricket and cut hair, establishing a hairdressing salon on George Street near the Sydney Town Hall. Publicly the MCC maintained equanimity but, within the pavilion, telegrams scuttled about and were read by committees that spoke of Billy Caffyn's duplicity. But that was not the Club's only problem.

Sam Cosstick, another MCC professional, also headed to Sydney – 'that refuge for destitute cricketers' as Hammersley wryly observed. Cosstick had been refused employment over winter at the MCC because there was no money to pay him. In Sydney they could pay him what he wanted. These were not the only defections – with the intercolonial match between New South Wales and Victoria imminent, Victoria was stripped of some its best cricketers.

Tom was asked to lead this emasculated Victorian team. Three years earlier, after the riot and a defeat, Tom was blamed for everything and there had been suspicions as to which colony he favoured. There was some anxiety about the Victorian team but this was obliterated by the sound of bitter squabbles coming from the MCC pavilion.

Tom Wills was elected captain of Victoria and Charles Lawrence was elected captain of the opposition. The match commenced on Boxing Day and the visitors, brimming with imported talent, batted first. In Tom's third over he bowled and hit the New South Wales batsman Kellick, who, although in severe pain, recovered but needed a runner to continue – no victory would be easily achieved. New South Wales scored 122 runs in their first innings. In Victoria's first innings Tom batted late and resumed on the second day when a hot wind blew across the scantily grassed MCG and the sun shone through the early heat haze. Players left regularly 'to liquor'. Iced wines were served in the cricketers' tents; cooling claret was the favoured drink. Tom batted for two-and-a-half hours until the end of the Victorian first innings and was the last man out.

The Victorians had added 132 runs for the last 2 wickets, finishing with a total of 285 runs, a score that had not been seen before in these matches. Tom top-scored. The man whose batting style drew mirth from observers as his bat stuck to the earth like a dead stump made 58 runs. Weary, he did not bowl until relatively late in the second innings, taking six wickets in the match. Victoria, the team from which everyone had defected, won the match by an innings and 20 runs.

Tom was chaired from the MCG upon the shoulders of his players, that sweetest of altitudes for a sportsman. Tom Wills, the native-born cricketer, had defeated New South Wales with its two All-England players, Billy Caffyn and Charlie Lawrence, and the other defectors. Victoria didn't need them – they had Tom Wills; that was enough. A thick press of bodies met Tom in the pavilion, including the governor. Tom had seen off one governor – it was Governor and Lady Darling who greeted Tom. All the colony's eyes were upon him. Melburnians even mumbled about forgiving Sydneysiders their cheating ways in the previous intercolonial match. Sydney grumbled about Tom's shying with the cricket ball. Melbourne would have none of that.

But very few in this throng of people could know what had happened to Tom this year. This was the Tom Wills who was married in the eyes of his family but not married at all; who was chased out of Geelong by people for money he owed; who drank and played merrily on the field and whose family was more distant than ever. Neither Governor Darling nor his Lady could see that beyond the adulation, Tom Wills was a rubble of imperfections.

Sometimes a man who belongs to no one belongs to everyone.

[15]

HAVE NOT THESE BLACKS
NAMES OF THEIR OWN!

JANUARY 1866–FEBRUARY 1867

The victory in 1865 drew all eyes to Tom and he was enticed
to all points of the colony, playing cricket until nothing more
could be played. At summer's end he withdrew from cricket and
returned to his mother and sisters at Belle Vue.

On 8 May 1866, Colden Harrison, captain of the Melbourne
Football Club, chaired a meeting of the footballers of the city
of Melbourne at the Freemason's Hotel to review the rules of
the game. Tom was not at the meeting; his move to Geelong
had rendered him peripheral to development of football in
Melbourne. On that same day, another event quietly took place.
The minutes of the Melbourne Cricket Club included one item
that would change the course of Tom's life: 'It was agreed to
allow R Newbury the use of the ground for two days during the
month' for a match 'with the native black eleven'. It was the first
reference to a proposed cricket match between an Aboriginal
team from the Western District of Victoria and the Melbourne
Cricket Club. The unusual request had come from the lowly
Roland Newbury, the pavilion keeper at the Club.

Roland Newbury knew his place at the Melbourne Cricket
Club: he cut the grass, tended the bar, pruned the shrubs and

181

cultivated the flower gardens for the members and their ladies who paraded before the pavilion. Roley, as he was known, was also a cricketer of sorts for the MCC, pitching in as wicket keeper and bowler at times. He lived in a world between the two classes of cricketers at the Club – he could never aspire to the world of the gentleman amateur cricketer nor was he skilled enough to be a true professional cricketer. But it was the vision of this obscure in-between man – to bring a team of Aboriginal cricketers to Melbourne – that would stop the colony.

In August, three months after the first intimation of a match between an Aboriginal cricket team and the Melbourne Cricket Club, *Bell's Life in Victoria* announced that Tom Wills would travel to the Western District to coach the Aboriginal team. Only five years had passed since his father had been murdered and Tom's unforgiving voice towards the Cullin-la-Ringo Aborigines was still evident in family letters. How could Tom possibly coach a team of Aboriginal cricketers?

Roland Newbury's motivation was to make money. Tom's need to earn money was hardly surprising for a man whose life now rested upon the capacity to make a living from cricket. Tom was well known to Newbury through the Melbourne Cricket Club but neither Newbury nor Tom acted on behalf of the Club. In the past, Tom had played cricket with anyone who asked, and now he could do so with an Aboriginal team and make money as he played. Beyond this, Tom's personal reasons for coaching an Aboriginal team remain a mystery.

Although Tom was called an amateur cricketer, he did what all of the finest amateurs did: behaved like a chaste amateur while receiving money for playing cricket. Even his Melbourne Cricket Club membership fees were paid by the Club. In the last intercolonial match Tom received 20 pounds for 'travelling expenses', a euphemism for Tom being paid to play. The amount of 20 pounds was in excess of his travelling expenses but it was acceptable and maintained the illusion of a gentleman cricketer.

When this excessive payment to Tom became public knowledge there were derisive comments in Sydney.

Tom tried his hand at making money by arranging a cricket match between the Victorian team and one from South Australia, but his impetuosity outstripped any business sense. He asked for too much money and did not bother to consult his fellow Victorian cricketers. When the South Australians declined, Tom's inept efforts were released to the press in Melbourne. Tom had offered to take a Victorian team to South Australia for 470 pounds; when he did not get a response he reduced this to 220 pounds. The Melbourne press chuckled at 'Master Tommy' in a manner that suggested a familiarity with his bungled but benign money-making attempts.

Though he still looked like an amateur from the outside, and he maintained his amateur status, Tom Wills had become what his sister had said he was destined to become – a professional cricketer. His coaching and playing with the Aboriginal team was the point when he openly earned money from cricket.

One month after his appointment to coach the Aboriginal team was announced, Tom wrote to Horace on Cullin-la-Ringo. After sweeping a gossip's eye over Melbourne and passing judgement on the scandals of the metropolis, he reverted to a familiar theme – one of bitterness and fear towards the blacks at Cullin-la-Ringo. He berated unwary settlers near the station: 'it would have served them right for allowing the blacks to come in after all the warnings they have had'. But Tom seemed to draw a distinction between the Aborigines of Victoria and those of Queensland – none of his correspondence about the cricket team even hinted at the antipathy he still felt towards the Cullin-la-Ringo Aborigines. Horatio's murder was remembered widely in the colonies so public comment on Tom's decision to coach a black cricket team might have been expected, but it was largely left alone by the press, perhaps out of respect for a dead man.

On 20 November Tom Wills boarded a steamer to Portland, from where he travelled overland to Lake Wallace, 80 miles west of Mount William in Western Victoria. The Aborigines Tom was about to coach came principally from the Jardwadjali language group. The Jardwadjali shared over 90 per cent of its language with the Djab wurrung people, with whom Tom had played as a boy at Mount William and whose language he was familiar with. When Tom arrived at Lake Wallace he wrote in a letter: 'The blacks shape well. I give them six hours a day, good hard work . . . This is a fact, not bad, eh? Mullagh is a fine bat. The blacks field splendidly and by the 26th they will be good average bats.' Hammersley wrote of Tom's letter in his *Australasian* newspaper column and it spread throughout Melbourne. Tom's letter was more than a message; it was a tactical strike. Whether Tom thought his team could win is unknown, but his principal tactical weapon was the MCC's ignorance of the Aborigines' capabilities. No one in Melbourne knew how good or bad the Aboriginal team might be, but if Tom could create uncertainty by boasting of his team's prowess, then his team might just win. It was a weapon a clever captain might use to destabilise a more powerful opponent by creating anticipatory fear amongst the opposition. Tom Wills, middle-weight street fighter, was needling and inveigling his way into the anxieties of the cricketers he was about to play. It was a brilliant stroke.

Tom had mentioned the Aboriginal cricketer, Mullagh, in his letter to William Hammersley. Mullagh was Johnny Mullagh, also known as Unamurriman, the finest of the black players. Sensitive and self-conscious, Unamurriman was originally a groom on Pine Hill, David Edgar's station that lay between Edenhope and Harrow. He then worked for John Bryan Fitzgerald on Mullagh Station where the whites named him Johnny Mullagh. Like all the Aboriginal cricketers, he was burdened by a European name of convenience.

The Aboriginal men who made up the team at Lake Wallace, near Edenhope in Western Victoria, worked on stations in the area. Several were well known on the cricket field and their names featured in cricket reports in the local newspapers. The European station owners introduced the Aborigines to the game of cricket or at least nurtured their interest in the game. There were Thomas Gibson Hamilton on Bringalbert Station, north-west of Edenhope; David Edgar of Pine Hill Station; Edgar's neighbour, John Fitzgerald on Mullagh Station; and William Hayman of Lake Wallace, Edenhope. It was Hayman who, in August, had despatched photographs of the Aboriginal team to Melbourne and who planned to join Tom Wills in taking the team to the Melbourne Cricket Ground.

Melbourne and Geelong received reports of Tom Wills and the team he was preparing for the Boxing Day match. The messages were few from Lake Wallace but those that emerged served to stimulate expectations as to how the Aboriginal team might perform. Tom Wills was the only name familiar to the people of the colony and, when it was announced that he talked to the black team in 'their own lingo', he became linked forever to the team. In the minds of the populace it was Tom Wills and the Aboriginal cricket team.

On 30 November, a fete was held in Geelong to raise money for the St Paul's Bell fund. The local Mechanics Institute overflowed with people passing through the various stalls, and in the middle of a stall selling poultry stood a photograph of Tom Wills and the ten Aboriginal cricketers which was to be raffled that evening to the curious citizens of Geelong. The photograph of well-presented men with black skin and their white captain excited even the dullest imagination.

Tom Wills, William Hayman and the team left Lake Wallace in two coaches and headed towards Dunkeld, 80 miles away. They left the small town of Dunkeld at five o'clock in the morning on Thursday, 20 December and arrived at Skipton at midnight. The team was refused permission to bed at the hotel – it was said because of the late hour of the team's arrival. There was no suggestion that Tom Wills or William Hayman were treated differently to the Aboriginal team and, most likely, all remained in their coaches overnight. On Friday morning, they arrived in Ballarat where the team assembled and practised, drawing favourable comments from onlookers. That evening they caught the train to Melbourne, arriving at midnight.

When the team arrived for practice at the Melbourne Cricket Ground, all eyes were upon Unamurriman whose batting evoked admiring glances as colonial eyes passed over his smooth and elegant movements. In batting, everything is a matter of geometry: eyes, angles and lines. Unamurriman stood erect at the crease; apparelled in leg guards, belt and gloves, he seemed built from segments. He precisely aligned these segments to play each shot. The smooth movements of Unamurriman were partly a gift from the heavens but not entirely; his movements had been ground into a perfect state by years of repetitive practice.

Outside the Melbourne Cricket Club pavilion, Tom Wills and the team posed for a photograph. Tom was the only player

Aboriginal cricket team, December 1866

wearing a cap, which he tilted over his balding head. What hair he possessed seemed uncombed, thrusting rudely out from beneath his cap. His left hand, curved like a set of pincers, nipped at the top of his coat and, in the absence of buttons, drew together the edges. His generally dilapidated appearance gave him the look of a man who had just tumbled from a rubbish bin. To his left stood Unamurriman, Johnny Mullagh to the spectators. Slim with an aristocratic stance, fine boned and of a chocolate complexion, Unamurriman's reserved expression articulated all that Europeans thought distinguished in portraiture. The ten black cricketers surrounded Tom – encased in heavy European clothing, vests buttoned with obsessional care from neck to waist, each black face wore the solemnity of a judge. Tom Wills was about to walk onto the Melbourne Cricket Ground with ten black magistrates.

Andrew Newell, a spectator at the MCG, recalled the 'fearfully hot' Christmas Day preceding the match. Welcoming sweet zephyrs twirled through the Richmond Paddock on Boxing Day as '5 or 6 thousand people' came to see the 'novelty'. Newell almost certainly summed up the private thoughts of the thousands present when he later wrote: 'Tommy Wills whose father was killed by them captaining and coaching them!' Until now, the team of Aborigines had dwelt only within the imaginings of the people of Melbourne, nurtured by the occasional note sent by Tom from Lake Wallace. By the time they had reached Melbourne, the sympathy of the colony was with the Aboriginal team in their match against the MCC, a club that remained beyond the reach of most colonists. The moment Tom Wills and his team walked onto the field, the white colonists aligned themselves with the Aboriginal cricketers; ten men of a dispossessed race, in a common grievance against what the Melbourne Cricket Club symbolised.

The bell sounded and the ground was cleared for play at noon. After three hours the Aboriginal team completed their first innings for a lowly 39 runs. As each dismissed Aboriginal

December 1866: Tom is far left, W.E.B. Gurnett is wearing the top hat.

batsman left the field and made their way through the gate to the pavilion, curious spectators gathered about the gate to scrutinise more closely their facial features and physique. When Richard Wardill, the Melbourne Cricket Club captain, walked to the crease, the Aboriginal cricketers gave him three 'British' hearty cheers. The MCC won the match by 9 wickets but it was Richard Wardill's 45 runs that created the victory.

The Melbourne Cricket Club may have easily won the game, but the whispers throughout the colony spoke of their ungraciousness. Prior to the match, Tom Wills had requested that his team field first rather than bat before such a large

crowd at the start of the first day. The MCC refused. Their refusal of what seemed to the average man a most reasonable request promoted further sympathy for the black team. More skulduggery surfaced when it was discovered that the MCC had strengthened its ranks with cricketers who were not even members of the Club. Losing was something the MCC had never taken to with grace, and the thought of losing to a team of Aborigines would not have been tolerated. Wills spoke defiantly and publicly of his disgust with the MCC's treachery, and there was not a man or woman in the colony who was not aware of the events.

As the Aboriginal matches extended beyond Boxing Day, Roland Newbury's moment was over. Virtually unheralded at the time, Roley was discarded until his name settled as an obscure historical footnote in the history of the Aboriginal team.

While Tom and the Aboriginal team played in Melbourne, the annual intercolonial match between Victoria and New South Wales was being played in Sydney. The intercolonial game, normally the highlight of the season, was a dull affair next to the exotic Aboriginal match. The much-depleted Victorian team lost and there were stories of the drunkenness of two Victorian cricketers, Sam Cosstick and William Greaves. On their return, Cosstick and Greaves were summoned to appear and give evidence before a Melbourne Cricket Club committee. The two professionals were charged with 'insulting several of the passengers' on the steamer to Sydney; being seen 'drunk on the streets of Sydney on Christmas Eve'; and that alcohol had rendered them unfit for play. An absence of memory marked the evidence they tendered before the MCC committee. The Melbourne public wanted nothing to do with its white Victorian cricketers. All eyes were on Tom and his ten black men.

How did Tom's mother and his siblings react to their son and brother coaching a team of black cricketers? One might have expected anger and condemnation towards Tom but there was none. Elizabeth and the family seemed to regard the Aborigines of Cullin-la-Ringo differently from the team that travelled with Tom. Tom was not criticised or made to appear guilty of abusing the memory of his father. In December, his mother casually noted to Cedric in Queensland: 'He is away at present beyond Portland. He is training 11 blacks for a cricket match to be played in Melbourne on Boxing Day.' Likewise Horace noted in passing: 'I heard the other day that Tom was going to England with the black cricketers, I don't know if the report is true or not.' No anger; no aggrieved family sensibility, although the family continued to write savagely about the Cullin-la-Ringo Aborigines for many years. Horace wrote a few years later:

All the blacks are off to see the 'devil' and I only hope he
will keep some of them. The native police officer told us he
would not let any of the strange blacks stay in the district
and he intends shooting some as soon as he can get a chance.
I hope he gets some of the old ones from here.

On 3 January 1867, Tom Wills, William Hayman and the
black team left Melbourne by train for Geelong where, upon
arrival, they were immediately 'objects of considerable curiosity'.
After a game against the local club, which the Aboriginal team
won easily, Tom with characteristic lack of forethought took his
team to Belle Vue to see his mother:

> You will see by the paper I send that we had the company of
> the 12 black cricketers to dinner on Sunday. Tom brought
> about 17 here without any notice so you may be sure we had
> a good long table besides two side ones – they are thinking
> of taking them to England & Tom will go with them.

Any disapproval Elizabeth felt was reserved not for the
Western District Aborigines, but for her son who arrived at
Belle Vue without warning. The local newspaper reporters
were interested more in the behaviour of the Aborigines than
any other aspect of the lunch. The manner in which they
held their cutlery and addressed other guests at Belle Vue was
analysed with the objectivity one might scrutinise a wild animal
undergoing domestication. Manner and deportment were the
barometer of civilisation; dining at Belle Vue, the team bore
the imprint of fine cultivation and won approval. To be a 'quiet'
black was to commendably know one's place. The team departed
Mrs Wills' that evening and boarded the train to Melbourne.

Rumours of the team possibly travelling to Sydney and then
to England continued. Tom Wills had written to Hammersley
from Lake Wallace of an unwelcome entrepreneur insinuating
his way into the management of the Aboriginal team. Tom
gave no name but it is almost certain that Tom was referring

to Captain W.E.B. Gurnett, ex-soldier, who had appeared in
one of the two photographs of Tom and the team in front of
the MCC pavilion at the Boxing Day match. Although three
and a half inches shorter than Tom Wills, in the photograph
Gurnett wore a top hat that elevated him above all the players.

On 8 January 1867 in the rooms of Thomas Pavey, solicitor
to the Melbourne Cricket Club, a document was signed that
contracted the Aboriginal team to travel overseas under the
management of Gurnett. It was suggested that the team may
travel to England, Scotland, France, Ireland and any country
thought suitable by Gurnett – even the United States and China
were proposed. It was unusual for Aborigines to be offered any
kind of contract, however, it was profoundly unbalanced in
favour of the entrepreneurs. The contract legally bound:

> William Reginald Hayman First part
> Messrs Unamurriman and others Second Part
> And William Edward Brougham Gurnett Third Part

Each cricketer was named: their Aboriginal names were
followed by a second name that linked them in some way to
their appearance, their environment or anything that tagged
them to make them identifiable to their European employers
in the Western District.

Unamurriman commonly known as	Johnny Mullagh
Yellana	Johnny Cuzens
Unaarriman	Harry Jellico
Murrumgunarriman	Jemmy Tarpot
Bullenchanach	Harry Bullocky
Arrahmunyarrimun	Peter
Pappuijarrunin	Paddy
Balkinjarrunin	Sundown
Tallachmurrmiun	Dick
Mijarruk	Lake Billy
Cungewarriman	Billy Officer

Bilvayarrimin	Watty
Brunbunyah	Tommy Redcap
Lingurgarrah	Harry Rose
Bripmuarriman	Charley
Jungagellmijuke	Dicky Dick

An X was placed next to each Aboriginal name to represent their signature, then Gurnett and Hayman signed the deed. The contract stipulated that Unamurriman, Yellana, Bullenchanach and the other Aboriginal cricketers 'shall in all such cricket matches exercises and sports comport and behave themselves in a sober and proper manner to the satisfaction in all things of the said William Edward Brougham Gurnett' and 'behave with such sobriety and regularity as shall be necessary to the proper and effectually carrying out and performance of the said Cricket Matches exercises and sports'. Gurnett agreed to pay for the Aboriginal cricketers' board, clothing, travelling expenses 'suitable to their condition in life', and provide 'the sum of seven shillings and sixpence per week for pocket money', and at the completion of the tour to pay each player the 'sum of Fifty pounds'. William Hayman was to receive his travelling expenses, lodging, percentage and profits, and 1000 pounds when the team returned to Australia.

The Melbourne press reported that the Aboriginal players, Gurnett, Hayman and Wills had met and signed the contract. Curiously, when the contract is examined, Tom's name does not appear. It is inconceivable that Tom's omission from the contract was an oversight. The most likely reason was that Tom Wills and William Gurnett were competing with each other to take control of the tour. Whether Tom chose not to sign a contract or was deliberately excluded by Gurnett is unknown. Nonetheless, it was agreed that Tom would receive travelling expenses, a weekly allowance and an unspecified sum on the team's return to Victoria. But for the moment, in the colony of Victoria, it was assumed that Tom, like the

pay to each of them the sum of Fifty pounds &c &c
And the said William Edward Brougham Gurnett
doth hereby also covenant and agree that it shall and
may be lawful for the said parties hereto to play and
carry out a Cricket match in the said Colony of Victoria
previously to their departure therefrom under whatever
auspices the same may be advertized provided that he
the said William Edward Brougham Gurnett shall
receive and be paid one half of the net profits resulting
from or gained by the same Provided nevertheless and
these presents are upon this express condition that if
any one or more of the persons constituting the said
parties hereto of the first second and third parts shall
fail neglect or refuse to comply with any one of these
covenants conditions and agreements hereby on his or their
part to be observed and performed then these presents
and all matters and things herein contained shall as far
as concerns the person or persons so failing neglecting or
refusing as aforesaid be absolutely null void and of
no effect — **In witness** whereof the said parties
to these presents have
hereunto set their hands and seals the day and year
first above written —

Signed Sealed and Delivered   William Reginald Hayman (L.S.)
by the said William Reginald Hayman   The Mark of
in the presence of   ×   (L.S.)
    Thomas Pavey Sol: Melbourne   Unamurriman or Johnny
    Jno D. Lynch Clerk to the said   Mullagh
    Thomas Pavey   The Mark of
Signed Sealed and Delivered by   ×   (L.S.)
the before named Unamurriman   Yellana or Johnny Cuzens
or Johnny Mullagh Yellana or   The Mark of
Johnny Cuzens Unaarriman   Unaarriman or Harry Jellico (L.S.)
or Harry Jellico Murrumgunarrum   The Mark of
or Jemmy Tarpot Bullenchanach   Murrumgunmarriman or Jemmy (L.S.)
or Harry Bullocky Arrahmunyarrimin Tarpot
or Peter Pappinjarrimin or   The Mark of
Paddy Balkinjarrimin or &c   Bullenchanach or Harry Bullocky (L.S.)
Sundown Jallachmurrimin or   The Mark of
Dick Mijarti or Lake Billy   Arrahmunyarrimin or Peter (L.S.)
Cungewarriman or Billy Officer   The Mark of
Bilvajarrimin or Watty by   Pappinjarrimin or Paddy   (L.S.)
their respectively making their   The Mark of
marks hereto and acknowledged   Balkinjarrimin or Sundown (L.S.)
in my presence the before written &c   The Mark of
                                          ×
                                    Jallachmurrimin or Dick   (L.S.)

Aboriginal cricket contract

to be the respective act and deed
of each of them And I hereby
certify that the contents of the said
Indenture were previously to such
Execution explained to them and
that the nature and effect thereof
were at the time of such execution
by each of them understood by the
said Unaarurriman or Johnny
Mullagh. Yellana or Johnny Cuzens
Unaarriman or Harry Jellico
Murrumgunarriman or Jemmy
Tarpot Bullenchanach or Harry
Bullocky Arrahmunjarrimin or
Peter Pappinjarrimin or Paddy
Balkinjarrimin or Sundown
Jallachmurrimin or Dick to
Mijarrk or Lake Billy to
Cungewarriman or Billy Officer
and Bilvayarrumin or Watty

The mark of Mijarrk (L.S.)
or Lake Billy

The mark of Cungewarriman
or Billy ✕ Officer (L.S.)

The mark of Bilvayarrumin (L.S.)
or Watty ✕

The mark of Brunbunyah
or Tommy ✕ Redcap (L.S.)

The mark of Lingingarrah (L.S.)
or Harry ✕ Rose

The mark of Bripmuarriman (L.S.)
or Charley ✕

W. E. B. Gurnett (L.S.)

The mark of Jungagellinyuke (L.S.)
or Dicky ✕ Dick

Thomas Pavey
Sol.
Melbourne

Jno. D. Lynch
Clerk to the said Thomas Pavey

Signed Sealed and Delivered
by the said William Edward
Brougham Gurnett in the
presence of
Thomas Pavey
Jno. D. Lynch
Clerk to the said
Thomas Pavey

Aboriginal players, was contracted to William Gurnett. To emphasise his claim to the team, a cunning Gurnett wrote to Sir Redmond Barry, Supreme Court judge and pre-eminent figure in Melbourne, and ingratiated himself as a reputable entrepreneur.

Two days after the contract was signed, Bullenchanach was found drunk in the streets of Richmond and arrested by Constable John Evans Long. Bullenchanach was fined 5 shillings, which, the local Richmond newspaper reported, was paid by his 'instructor' – this may have been Tom but no name was given. The report of Bullenchanach's drunkenness and arrest was reported only in the local Richmond newspaper, but in this single report the stereotype of the degraded savage emerged: 'Although an expert in the cricket-field, when sober, it was apparent that with liquor in, he was not a whit better than any other drunken aborigine.'

Tom and his team's every step were keenly observed. For some, they were best dissected from a distance: playing lawn bowls on Victoria Parade, Fitzroy, or parading in horse-drawn coaches. The more English the activity undertaken by the Aborigines the more gasps of satisfaction and the louder the applause from the colonials. For the most part, commentary was gracious, although the words 'novelty' and 'freakish' were never too far away. Physical attributes were acknowledged and there was open admiration of the team's courage on the field. Description of their physical features was linked to particular attributes: swift of foot, sharp eyes and elasticity of limbs marked the Australian native. Care was taken to draw a line between the team's physical prowess and their mental capabilities – opinion was divided, with some proclaiming them as intelligent as Europeans, and others saying they displayed an intellectual level no higher than an animal.

Tom's association with the team amused some onlookers and was the source of numerous jokes. In the Bendigo press it was reported that Jellico (Unaarriman), the team jester, upon asking a gentleman 'to teach him to read and write English, as he was going the grand tour . . . was referred to Mr Wills as a good schoolmaster. Jellico promptly replied. "Whats usy Wills. He too much along of us. He speak nothing now but blackfellow talk."' The colonists loved it.

Tom was sometimes described as a 'Native' of Australia; a term used to described Australian-born Europeans but also the term used for Aboriginal Australians. The use of the term 'Native' blurred the distinction between Tom and the team. Usually this was inadvertent but sometimes it was done with deliberate intent and could work either for or against Tom depending on what was portrayed. The quick-witted Hammersley, always on the lookout for ways of undermining the colonial stock, had once chortled:

> Natives (not aboriginals, though there is often very little difference between the two), and those who have been brought up in this colony, have a very vague idea, if any at all, of the state of society at home, and the broad line of demarcation that exists between classes . . .

The initial voyeurism, tinged with self-conscious embarrassment, gave way to admiration and, in a rare moment of equality, the team had come to be regarded as Victorians first and blacks second. From Geelong, there was kinship with Tom – a 'Geelong man', not just a Victorian. Of course, some colonials desperately wanted to see the team fail and Tom to look a fool. But something was happening in the colony beyond the realm of cricket. There were deeper reflections on how the tour might bridge the worlds of black and white, and with each round of applause, the reflections of a Melbourne society that had tidied away an uncomfortable history grew more disturbing. An unwelcome past was resurrected. How was it possible to enjoy and feel at one with this team of Victorians, knowing that colonial society owed its existence to the destruction of Aboriginal life? Some colonials responded with guilt and anger at past European cruelty and wrote letters to the press. Some, restating a sense of European superiority, banished the team from consciousness by ridiculing them. Some just watched, curious and bemused.

Tom had played cricket and batted with knights and dukes; Victorian Governors had squeezed his hand with joy; Chief Secretaries had embraced him. But somehow the Boxing Day match in Melbourne with the ten Aboriginal cricketers was cast at an altitude unknown in sport in the colony. A moral thread ran through this match that rendered the name of a radiant Tom Wills on everybody's lips. In a stroke 'Mr Wills' was all the Europeans of the colony, purified and decanted, and locked in a single body; and communicating with Aborigines in their language, he enchanted the colony and promised a miracle. One colonist was moved to write a public letter to Tom:

To T. Wills, Esq.
PER FAVOUR OF THE EMPIRE

Sir, – Although you may not be fully aware of the fact, allow me to tell you that you have rendered a greater service to the aboriginal races of this country and to humanity, than any man who has hitherto attempted to uphold the title of the blacks to rank amongst men. You have shown that the aborigines did not deserve the foul treatment they have received at the hands of the whites; that they were capable of improvement; and that they could rise high when an opportunity of rising was afforded them. Your success is a standing reproof to the civilising system we have hitherto adopted; and if you take your intelligent aboriginals to Britain, where men have learned from us to regard the ancient races of this country as no better than brutes, a cry of shame will ring from one end of civilised Europe to the other against our injustice and brutality. Your's are not picked men; for long ago the men you would have picked have been shot down like dogs by the usurpers of their hunting grounds, who, led on by the demon of greediness and gain, wantonly destroyed the old occupants of their runs, and held humanity so cheap that they proved themselves, and not their victims, to be the very basest of God's creatures. Now, you will come in for no inconsiderable share of this well-merited odium, if you appear to our fellow countrymen at home to treat with ridicule your aboriginal team. And you will appear to deserve your share of this reproach no more effectually than by continuing the practice of nicknaming your men. Have not these blacks names of their own, that you call one Tarpot, another Bullocky, and a third Lake Billy, Cuzens, Peter, or Dick-a-Dick? At first the blacks will appear ridiculous; but the first impressions will soon wear off, and all the ridicule will, eventually be levelled at yourself. Finish properly the work you have commenced, and cause our barbarian nicknames to give place to the more legitimate and euphonious names by which your men are all known to each other, and by which they were called when they received the spear at the age of manhood in the secret meetings of their nearly obliterated tribes. For your own sake I recommend this step as well as for the sake of the country which, like myself, you have the honor to be

A NATIVE

The colonies were not the only ones transfixed with Aboriginality. The news of the tour had spread to Rugby School and the boys wrote in their school magazine about Tom: 'We are sure Mr. Willes [sic] would be much gratified if a match could be arranged between his team and the School Eleven.'

The team played further matches in Melbourne and travelled to Victorian country towns – winning in Bendigo, losing in Ballarat. Tom and Unamurriman were the team's standout players. When the Tasmanian team arrived in Melbourne in the middle of January, Yellana and Bullenchanach became the first

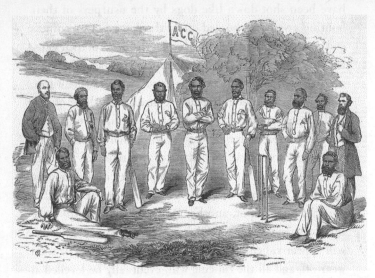

Captain [Wills], Officer, Sugar, Jellico, Cousins, Neddy, Mullagh, Bullocky, Tarpot, Sundown, Peter, Umpire

Aborigines to play for Victoria; Unamurriman was frequently ill and unable to play for Victoria against the Tasmanians. The team was courted and letters were written to Tom Wills, William Gurnett and William Hayman seeking the Aboriginal team to play matches in Victoria, Queensland and New Zealand. Each win reinforced the team's skill and each display of impeccable manners drew forth comments on their noble characters. As affection for the team insinuated its way into the heart of the colony, men associated with the team from their earlier days in and around Edenhope squabbled over who had taught the blacks the game before Tom Wills coached them. Towards the end of January, Tom Wills and the team sought refuge from the public's demands just outside Melbourne in the hamlet of Heidelberg. The team remained there for two weeks of rest. Bilvayarrimin fell seriously ill with 'measles'; Dr Bleeck, a local surgeon, was called in to care for him and the Aboriginal team.

As the team prepared for Sydney there were moments of disquiet in Melbourne. Some commented on the unnecessary haste in spiriting the team to England, and Gurnett's seductive charms were insufficient to camouflage his empty purse. He had promised prizes to the winners of an athletics contest held on the MCG after the Boxing Day cricket match which were not forthcoming; his creditors grew suspicious of delays in repayments. Then Richard Brough Smyth, from the Office of the Central Board for the Protection of Aborigines, wrote on 12 February to the Chief Secretary of the colony proposing that the tour might simply be a trick of greedy men – taking an Aboriginal cricket team and 'exhibiting them for profit in England', and when the cricketers 'ceased to be a source of profit they will be cast adrift and left helpless and destitute'. He wanted the venture stopped unless there was a more adequate guarantee for 'their proper maintenance'.

Two days later Tom Wills, William Hayman, William Gurnett and the Aboriginal team made a swift exit for Sydney aboard the steamship *City of Melbourne*. Almost three weeks earlier another name had appeared amongst the sprawl of entrepreneurs – Charles Lawrence, the English professional who had remained in Sydney after the first English tour of 1861. When the Aboriginal team, with Wills as captain and coach, arrived in Sydney it was Charles Lawrence who greeted them. Tom and his team stayed at Lawrence's Pier Hotel, Manly Beach. The first cricket match against the Albert Cricket Club, captained by Charles Lawrence, started on 21 February. In the middle of the match, when Tom walked out onto the Albert Ground, he was arrested and threatened with gaol.

[16]

A LOT OF BLACK SAVIDGES A
PLAYING AGAINST XTIANS

FEBRUARY 1867–AUGUST 1867

Tom's arrest was unexpected but the events that led to it began seven weeks earlier, on New Year's Day.

On 1 January, one week before the Gurnett contract was signed, Tom Wills had telegraphed a Sydney businessman, J.C. Jarrett, to arrange a match for the Aboriginal team on the Domain parklands for the middle of January. This was Tom's plan, separate from any venture Gurnett was arranging. In effect, Tom and Gurnett were competing to control the Aboriginal team. Tom's Sydney representative also sent a letter to the New South Wales Lands Minister seeking approval for the use of this parkland. This letter was passed on to the trustees of the Domain for consideration on 4 January. The New South Wales Cricket Association then considered Tom's application and on 7 January, still before the Gurnett contract was signed, it was agreed 'that this Association has no objection to act with Mr. Wills provided a suitable arrangement can be come to'. Tom Wills concluded an agreement to play in Sydney with his Aboriginal team before any contract had been signed with William Gurnett. Soon afterwards, Gurnett became aware of Tom's plans.

Things went wrong almost immediately for Tom. The Aboriginal team did not leave Melbourne in time to meet the date arranged by Tom and Jarrett to play on the Domain. When Tom and the team had still not arrived in Sydney by 18 January, Jarrett and another businessman, W. Penman, ordered the dismantling of the grandstand and fencing that had been erected on the Domain. They were irate and out of pocket, and the Sydney public were incensed. The Domain was public parkland and there had been loud objections to Tom Wills being granted use of these lands to make money for personal gain. Wills' breach of contract with his partners Jarrett and Penman was made public through the press. Openly embarrassed, they took legal action and sought damages from Wills, as was reported in the *Sydney Morning Herald*:

> The grand stand which was erected in the Domain for the convenience of spectators of the Intercolonial Cricket Match, and which was allowed to remain upon the understanding on the part of the authorities that it would be required for spectators of a match to be played between the eleven Victorian aboriginal cricketers and a team of Sydney whites, is now being removed, together with the fencing, the engagement entered into between Mr. Jarrett and Mr. Wills, to have the aboriginals in Sydney to play a match on the 17th, 18th, and 19th of the present month having fallen through; and we understand that some law proceedings have been commenced by the former to recover from the latter the expenses incurred by entering into a contract for re-erecting the fencing, advertising, etc., on the alleged breach of agreement. It appears that the 'darkies' are now under the management of Mr Gurnett, and arrangements have been made for playing a match on the Albert Ground in the course of next month. In the meantime, it will be a relief to those of our citizens who are accustomed to promenade in the Domain, to find the unsightly structure removed.

When Tom arrived in Sydney, he was introduced to Messrs Jarrett and Penman and disclaimed any liability on his part. Penman and then Jarrett issued a writ against Tom, which led to his arrest on the first day of the cricket match against the Albert Cricket Club. Tom's arrest was brief, as Charles Lawrence and Mr J. O'Brien of the Tattersall's Hotel became security for him and he was given eight days to resolve his differences with Jarrett and Penman. The match continued, with Tom playing, and ended two days later.

The cancellation of the Domain Aboriginal match had been reported in New South Wales and Victorian papers in the weeks before Wills, Gurnett, Hayman and the team left Melbourne. Tom must have known of the problems he would face in Sydney but perhaps he ignored the possible consequences, as he had done so often before. His failed attempt to arrange this match provides an understanding of why he did not sign the Gurnett contract: he had been in competition with William Gurnett as an entrepreneur, from the time of the Boxing Day match.

How this dispute between Wills and Gurnett was resolved within the troupe is unknown but there was never a suggestion that Tom would not captain and coach the team. To ensure there was no error in understanding who was managing the Aboriginal team, William Gurnett wrote to the *Sydney Morning Herald* to publicly reinforce his role as manager of the team and sole entrepreneur: 'There seems to have arisen a misunderstanding with reference to Mr. T.W. Wills's position with the Aboriginal Eleven, which I think it my duty to correct.'

The court permitted Tom to travel with the team on 28 February to Maitland, north of Sydney, where the team, as everywhere else, was ogled. Several of the Aborigines donned lavender-coloured gloves and promenaded on the streets. After their match against a local cricket XI, Tom Wills, William Hayman and the Aboriginal players attended the opera on Saturday evening at the Olympic Theatre in a private box, at the invitation of the Maitland community. The cricketers, Tom included, were presented to the audience, stepping on stage to the throwing of bouquets and endless cheering.

When Tom returned to Sydney he put forward to the Supreme Court a compromise solution to his legal problems. While this compromise was considered by the plaintiffs Jarrett and Penman, the court ordered that Tom be gaoled. Jarrett and Penman accepted Tom's compromise and he was released from custody, the matter taking less than a day. Tom paid 35 pounds for the breach of contract and all legal costs.

William Gurnett was not so fortunate, and his worsening financial problems came to a head when his creditors in Melbourne tracked him to Sydney and he was arrested. No one came to save him and he was imprisoned in Darlinghurst Gaol in Sydney.

Gurnett, it turned out, was a confidence trickster with a record of fraud. He was a swindler, a study in psychopathy, not burdened by a conscience. Smoothly spoken, an impresario with an empty wallet, he was one of Australia's first international cricket entrepreneurs. It was the aroma of money that drew Gurnett towards the Aboriginal cricket team. Gurnett, an exquisite pedlar of deceit and a top-hatted viper, had gently hoodwinked the colony into thinking he cared for the Aboriginal team, but it was revealed that Gurnett never had the money to make the journey to England and had lied to everyone, including the MCC, from the beginning. With the promised trip to England now a false hope and Gurnett revealed as a shyster, the tour lost its way. Fifteen months later when Gurnett was received into Pentridge Gaol, it was recorded that he bore three scars – one on the bridge of his nose, one above his right eyebrow, one on his forehead; and those hazel eyes that had deceived many appeared 'turned in a little'. In an age when such marks were not discounted, these stigmata were enough to condemn him.

Travelling to England now seemed impossible but the tour continued throughout New South Wales, albeit less triumphantly. Wills had been inextricably linked with the Aboriginal team since the Boxing Day match in Melbourne, but after his arrest his association was less clearly imprinted in New South Wales. Charles Lawrence, opportunistically, began to take an increasing role in managing the team and was a stabilising factor on the tour.

Lawrence, seven years older than Tom, was a small man with a trimmed, goatee beard. Nimble and neat, fastidious even, he was well organised, and, unlike Tom, never forgot where he began and ended. A man of some considerable curiosity with a love of learning, he recorded his thoughts in his diary. Towards the end of the tour, Lawrence captained the team and Wills played under him – a sign of Lawrence's growing influence. Years later, Charles Lawrence claimed that one of the reasons he had remained in Australia after the 1861 English tour was to 'make a fortune' by teaching 'the Blacks' cricket. 'I had seen the Blacks throw the Boomerang and Spears . . . if I could teach them to play Cricket and take them to England I should meet with success, this impression never left my mind . . .'

Sydney cartoonists parodied the black cricketers: stripped of their clothes and drawn with silly vacant grins, they ran about the field with arms and legs cocked at hieroglyphic angles; or they were drawn with the face of a gorilla rather than that of a magistrate; and they were laughed at: 'At FOUR O'CLOCK the Aboriginals will display their proficiency in the arts of civilisation, by throwing the Boomerang, standing at the Bar, Wine Vaulting.'

The last game, with team morale low, was played in late April on the Albert Cricket Ground in Sydney. Its purpose was to earn enough money for the team to return home. Charles Lawrence had emerged as the team's leader; Tom was barely mentioned in reports of the game. Tom, William Hayman and the Aboriginal players tottered back to a wet Melbourne. There was no cheering on their return – the exotic was now commonplace, indifference displaced curiosity. A disorganised, waterlogged tour concluded with a dreary affair in the mud of the Melbourne Cricket Ground in May. The Melbourne press had almost forgotten the team and Tom barely rated a mention as the tour fizzled. He returned to Belle Vue and was playing football in Geelong within two weeks. Hayman and the Aboriginal cricketers slowly, in dribs and drabs, returned to Edenhope.

Bilvayarrimin, known to the colonials as Watty, died in an open-topped cart as it trundled towards Edenhope. The inquest into his death was held on 15 May at the Lake Wallace Hotel where William Hayman recalled for the coroner:

On the 27th of April he left Sydney in good health and spirits, he did not suffer from, seasickness. On the 4th of May about 10 p.m., he was very drunk in Melbourne, he had to be carried to bed. On the 7th inst he left for Portland, in good health, – on the 8th inst, he played cricket at Portland, and with a deal of more exercise than usual and got drunk that night. He was then carried to bed. On the 9th started for Coleraine he was then under the influence of liquor, about 10 miles on the road he remained behind the waggon and when he overtook us, he was very drunk – he was abusive to everyone and then got out and walked with Paddy – and Tarpot. The deceased and the two last mentioned did not overtake us but camped with a bullock and came up to us next morning at the Green Hills. He then had a good breakfast at the Green Hills, and came on with the whole party. About 1½ pm he called at an Hotel on the road side where the deceased eat apples . . . and drank, beer, he was not drunk from the effects of the beer, about six pm he had tea at Coleraine . . . The next morning he started with the whole party for Lake Wallace. During the whole of that time he did not complain, I did not see him alive since. I saw him drunk about six times but not on succession, he was very fond of liquor always and excited when drunk. I think deceased was about 33 years of age.

It was said that Bilvayarrimin died from lung disease and
that 'his lungs were diseased sufficiently to cause death which
was immediately caused by the bursting of a blood vessel in
the lungs'. Mounted constable Thomas Kennedy was present
at the Lake Wallace Hotel at the reading of the inquest. Three
months later, in August, when Charles Lawrence prepared to
take the Aboriginal team on a tour of England, Kennedy wrote
of his concerns of the care in store for the Aborigines:

> Twelve of them are now mustered and since their advent
> here the majority of them have been drunk and consequently
> a nuisance to the better conducted inhabitants. As the
> promoters of this cricketing scheme take no steps to check
> the supply of liquor – and the constable very often absent
> from his station is almost powerless to stop or detect the
> parties who supply them, the consequence is a great deal of
> drunkenness and other disorderly conduct – three of them
> are now locked up on those charges.

By the time of Bilvayarrimin's inquest, Gurnett was out of
Her Majesty's Gaol in Darlinghurst and was living in Melbourne.
Meetings were held to see if the creditors would 'allow Gurnett
to keep his furniture, clothing, beds, bedding, and tools of
trade'. It would not be long before Gurnett saw the inside of
gaol again. When the haphazard tour folded and Gurnett's
humbug had been revealed, there was no invective privately
or publicly directed at Wills, who was seen as much a casualty
of Gurnett's trickery as the Aboriginal team. And at no point
was Tom held responsible for behavioural problems amongst
the team, nor was there a single reported incident where Tom
exhibited drunken behaviour with the black players. Tom was
protective of his team and regarded Unamurriman as equal to
the most capable batsman in the colony. As he had been towards
cricketers all his life, he was fair and understood and appreciated
the Aboriginal players' skills, but like others, he also saw the
team as a way to earn money. Tom Wills rarely referred to the

Aboriginal team in his surviving letters. Beyond a paying job and an ill-fated attempt at entrepreneurship, he never gave the impression through word or deed that he considered the broader social and political context of the tour. The voices that were not heard throughout the tour were those of the Aboriginal players. It seems no one asked what they made of the enterprise – or if they did, the answers were never recorded.

MR WILLS TAKES A JOB

JULY 1867–JANUARY 1869

Professional cricketers did not live long. They were expected to die in their thirties or forties. Poor living conditions for some, abuse of alcohol and tobacco for others, shortened their life expectancy. For the next three years Tom Wills lived his winters in Geelong and summers in Melbourne. And after the winter of 1867, Tom Wills first played as a professional cricketer with the Melbourne Cricket Club. It would be wrong to say that he chose to earn money from cricket, but there was nothing else Tom did, and nothing else he could do. For nearly twenty years, he had bowled, batted and fielded and thought of little else beyond the boundary.

However, Tom presented a dilemma for the Melbourne Cricket Club. He should have been called a professional cricketer as he was contracted to the Club and paid a weekly wage: just like a professional. But there was uncertainty within the Club as to how to regard their finest player – the problem was Tom's background as an amateur and a gentleman.

Tom was English trained and educated. In England, an amateur cricketer was bestowed the title Esquire, and to write a player's name leaving off Esquire was to insult that man. Tom was always Mr Thomas Wills Esq. in England. Although rarely used in Australian sport, it was still a courtesy title for gentlemen; what constituted a gentleman was never exactly clear, but birth and education were important. Tom's English training was an important point in establishing his superior breeding. Tom knew this and had exploited his advantage when he returned to Australia.

Tom flashed his *carte de visite* in Melbourne and let it be known that his cricket coach had been John Lillywhite, one of the clan of Lillywhites, of Rugby School. Tom had brushed through Cambridge, played with bucket loads of Esquires, sprinklings of Reverends, the Earl of Winterton, Lord Royston (there was more than one Lord who played with Tom), the Honorable this and that, and had bowled to Dukes and had batted with knights. Now he was asking for money to play cricket in Melbourne.

Tom didn't quite fit anywhere. His untidy apparel could be overlooked; his disorganised thinking gently smirked at. But his background, that was another matter altogether. Could a man touched by Rugby and Cambridge, and who had played with the froth of gentility, possibly become a professional cricketer with the Melbourne Cricket Club?

To an outside observer the status of the amateur and the professional seemed distinct, but the separation was never as clean as might be imagined. For several years, Tom had received extra money for excellent performances and his cricketing clothes and equipment were paid for by the club, as was his membership subscription. All this was done while Tom maintained the status of an amateur. But as the various payments to Tom increased and he refused to have a career outside of cricket, it became clear that Tom's status was somewhere in between an amateur and a professional.

Of those in the colonies who imposed their opinions on such matters, the amateur cricketer William Hammersley was the loudest. He believed that amateurs and professionals needed to be separated from one another, as if contagion was a risk. Hammersley detested the manner in which, at the MCC, professional cricketers addressed amateurs by their Christian names. He moralised that this was contamination gone too far, and all would suffer and slide into a muddy egalitarianism – a future that horrified Hammersley.

Tom's attitude to the amateur and professional cricketers around him was neither simple nor consistent. He judged a man, and a cricketer, by his intrinsic worth and abilities, not his title, but he had also been content to enjoy and exploit the privileges of his amateur gentleman status. Tom was not comfortable moving towards the status of a professional, although all his life he remained a supporter of the professionals' worth and causes. When chided over his professional status, he angrily defended himself and the integrity of professional cricketers from his critics, but it seemed that some of Tom's fury was directed towards himself. Despite his defiant public words, Tom struggled to fully accept his changing status. It was a contradiction with his professed egalitarianism that frustrated and angered him. His public letters suggested that he should have accepted his professional status; he resented his inability to do so.

The Melbourne Cricket Club wrestled for a description of Tom that satisfied their desire for maintaining appearances, and in the spring of 1867 they gave him the title of 'Tutor'. In that way the club could avoid calling him a professional. So when Tom rejoined the Melbourne Cricket Club in 1867–68 he did not argue with his title and became a professional treated not quite like any other professional. Of course, everyone knew it was a sham to call him a tutor rather than a professional cricketer, but somehow it looked less grimy, less of a fall from a favoured status. There was one further difference that made it clear Tom was treated with distinction: professionals were never called Mister; in fact they were usually shorn of just about everything except their surname. Not for tutor Tom Wills – in the minutes of the MCC he was Mr Wills, 'Tutor' to the Club. And Esquire, too, could be his, if he wanted it. And sometimes he did.

So when Mr William Handfield – honorary secretary of the MCC – wrote to the private secretary of the Victorian Governor in October 1867, he could invite the governor to the opening match of the season at the Melbourne Cricket Ground, to enjoy a match between the first XI 'with professionals' against fourteen young players with Mr Wills. It was Mr Wills as amateur who attracted most attention whether it was governors or blacksmiths.

Having dispensed with the issue of appearances, not a small matter to either Club or person, Tom negotiated with the Club for money. Handfield wrote to Tom at Belle Vue:

> Mr dear Sir
> I have been instructed by the Committee of the Melbourne
> Cricket Club to enquire if you are willing to take an engage-
> ment as Tutor to the Club for six months commencing on
> the 1st Oct. The salary which the Committee would be
> prepared to pay you would be at the rate of £3 per week,
> & your attendance would be required upon the ground
> on practice days from 3 o'clock pm until sundown – Two
> professional bowlers will be engaged by the Club, Cosstick,
> & Greaves, the former chiefly for 1st eleven players & the
> latter exclusively for others.

Tom's letter of offer was different to the letters the Melbourne Cricket Club sent to its professional cricketers, Cosstick and Greaves. For a start, Tom was never simply called 'Wills' like Cosstick and Greaves, and Cosstick and Greaves were never addressed as 'Sir'. The offer to Tom was more of a request as to whether he might consent to play for the MCC. And there were no qualifying phrases about behaviour in Tom's letter. When Sam Cosstick and William Greaves were offered contracts they were typically informed that payment was conditional on their 'satisfactory conduct'. And finally the club's professionals were

expected to tend the pitch and till the soil of the flower beds
and top-dress the oval. Tom would have to do none of that.
Tom played cricket and that was all.

In September 1867 Tom received a letter from Charles
Lawrence. Lawrence had financial problems – his estate had
been surrendered to the courts and he was bankrupt. Lawrence's
money problems did not concern Tom, but he was resentful
upon hearing that Lawrence had resurrected the Western
District Aboriginal cricket team and planned to sail to England.
Tom was not included. An irritable Tom wrote to William
Hammersley telling him of Lawrence's plans but Tom could
do little. Lawrence usurped him as captain and coach of the
team and set about touring the colony, as Tom had done nearly
twelve months before.

The intercolonial cricket match against New South Wales
was played in late December 1867 on the MCG. Tom captained
the Victorians. On a perfect wicket Richard Wardill, the captain
of the Melbourne Cricket Club, scored the first century recorded
in matches between the colonies: 110 in the first innings. Then
came a Melbourne dust storm and rain of biblical force. In the
end, Tom took 9 wickets, Wardill hit the winning run and the
Victorians won by 7 wickets. After the Victorians' victory, Tom
replied in the after-match speeches: 'Thank you gentlemen,
and [expletive deleted] . . . I'm very glad we licked 'em.' The
professional bowlers at the Melbourne Cricket Club – Sam
Cosstick and William Greaves – might have warmed to that
utterance. Tom was sounding more like them by the day.

Tom Wills had to protect his income. Sam Cosstick and Tom
Wills often worked upon the MCC together in matters relating
to money, and usually with success. The minutes of the Club
reveal that they scrounged for money, and fought and prompted
the Melbourne Cricket Club at each turn. They bargained in
tandem; when one received an increase or concession the other
immediately wrote and sought the same. In late March 1868,
the MCC wrote to Tom and Sam Cosstick to 'dispense with the

services of Mr T.W. Wills as professional tutor and S. Cosstick as professional bowler to the Club'; first Cosstick then Tom wrote and complained that the full six months of their contract was not yet up. The MCC recanted and paid them for their full six months. Tom finished his first period of six months paid work on 19 April 1868.

After his first summer as tutor to the Club, Tom received a letter from William Handfield, the honorary secretary of the Melbourne Cricket Club – a title that had once been Tom's. Handfield was a friend to Tom within the politically treacherous world of the Club. In this private letter, Handfield laid out his respect and admiration for Tom, and of the personal debt he owed him for his assistance over the summer:

> I cannot refrain from expressing to you my sense (personally) of the value of your services to the Club during the season now drawing to a close – I myself have derived considerable benefit from your instruction & can testify to your unwearied exertions in the hours of practice – Further I attribute the general success of the Club in matches this season very much to your excellent coaching advantage derived from the fact of your playing for the Club in most of their principal matches & I hope that the Club may be fortunate enough to be able to secure your services again next season.

Handfield also expressed his sentiments in the Club's annual report, which was published in the Melbourne press, writing admiringly of Tom and telling everyone that, in Tom Wills, the Melbourne Cricket Club had the best bowler in Australia and, perhaps, there was none better in England.

Handfield's words of affection told another story of the relationship between Tom and the Melbourne Cricket Club. Tom had been associated with this Club since boyhood, when, at the age of eleven, he first played alongside William Brickwood, his school headmaster and also the vice president of the Melbourne Cricket Club. True, there were belligerent clashes between Tom and the Club, but, just as often, he was embraced. There were many individuals who supported Tom, and for his part he accepted what the Club had to offer. The title of 'Tutor' might not have been just a matter of saving face, or even recognition of Tom's amateur past – perhaps there was more than a note of sympathy and understanding for Tom. None of this was ever speculated upon in the minutes of the Club. What was said in those 'lengthy discussions' in the pavilion was stripped until only a single line remained that recorded Tom's appointment at the start of the summer and his dismissal at summer's end.

For the next four years, each summer Tom wrote to the Melbourne Cricket Club and enquired if the Club had money to use his services as bowler and batsman. The Melbourne Cricket Club thrived over this period and the Victorian XI was the finest team in the country. Club and colony rode high. Handfield, Tom's friend and admirer, knew why and was not afraid to tell the colony, the Club or Tom. Tom Wills, tutor not professional, was back coaching and bowling and batting at the Melbourne Cricket Club.

•

In winter Tom returned to Belle Vue and played football exclusively for Geelong, often as captain, but not always. His younger brothers – Egbert, Cedric and Horace – also played for Geelong during this period. Egbert was the best of the trio. Fast and slender, a hurdler of grace, he became known as a talented footballer in Geelong and Melbourne. Horace and Cedric played whenever they made trips down from Cullin-la-Ringo.

On 1 July 1867, Tom boarded the train in Geelong with his football team and travelled to the Richmond Paddock to play the Melbourne Football Club, captained that day by Colden Harrison. Egbert played alongside Tom. Drinks and lunch were taken in the Melbourne Cricket Club's pavilion. During the second half of the match Tom grabbed the football, and moving to kick, was set upon and thrown down, landing on one of the numerous footpaths that crossed the Richmond Paddock. His face hit the ground hard and play was stopped while he was carried from the field, unconscious. Tom was tended to, emerging some time later with his head wrapped in bandages. His face was a bloodied knot of a thing: one eye was 'in total darkness', one eyebrow scraped clean off his face and the skin on his chin nearly shaved to the bone. Geelong won the match, Tom was praised for his captaincy, and, just for a moment, Melbourne took notice of him again as a footballer.

TOMMY WILLS! TOMMY WILLS!

MARCH 1869–DECEMBER 1870

A cricket team is a federation of men, not always equal or harmonious. Prior to each intercolonial cricket match, the teams elected their captains; for over a decade his fellow players had chosen Tom as the Victorian captain whenever he was one of the team.

The intercolonial match between Victoria and New South Wales took place in early March 1869 and was played, for the last time, on the Domain parkland in Sydney. On the eve of the match, the Victorian players met to elect their captain. The players elected Richard Wardill. That evening Tom wrote to Wardill, refusing to play under him or, indeed, anyone else; he would only play if he were made captain. A telegram was despatched to Melbourne: 'Wardill has been elected "skipper", and Wills declines to play under his generalship.' The players met and resolved to play without Tom. Later that evening Tom wrote again to Wardill, retracting his previous impulsive decision not to play.

The following day, Tom took the field with the rest of the Victorian team. Wardill was out to the first ball of the match; Wills took 7 wickets in the second innings and Victoria revealed a new bowler – the tall Frank Allan. Tom liked the look of

Allan, describing the colonial find: 'He comes on you like a big spider, all legs and wings.' Allan took 8 wickets in the first innings. Victoria won by 78 runs.

Tom did not solicit favours from the journalists who wrote about cricket; an act of honesty in the eyes of the average man in Melbourne and an act of naivety to those politically motivated. If Tom had political nous he might have managed William Hammersley better. Hammersley, through his sporting column in *The Australasian*, had provoked and taunted Tom for years, criticising his impetuosity, his bowling and sometimes his manners. When Tom had stupidly fought with Wardill over the captaincy, Hammersley grabbed the opportunity to humiliate Wills. Oozing self-righteousness, Hammersley contrasted Tom's position as a tutor to the Melbourne Cricket Club with that of Wardill's noble and lofty amateur status. He claimed that Tom's position as a paid servant of the club was a good part of the reason that the Victorian cricketers had not voted him captain. Hammersley also had his own ideas about what qualities a captain should possess – qualities he did not see in Tom. Wills, he wrote, had lost his 'moral ascendancy over his men' and misbehaviour had lowered the tone of the team to the colony's discredit.

Wounded by Hammersley's sneering words in *The Australasian*, Tom wrote immediately to the Melbourne *Leader*:

MR WILLS AND HIS DEFAMERS

Sir, – Will you permit me space to offer a few remarks in reply to several articles and letters that have appeared concerning me in your Collins street contemporary? I will not sit quietly by and see myself run down in the manner referred to without a few words of explanation, and, besides, I shall not submit to be made a stepping-stone for any man. In an article appearing in the *Australasian* of the 13th March, I am decidedly made the stepping-stone for Mr Wardill, and he is made to appear all that is perfection. Innuendoes, too, are made and allusions concerning my private life, which concern no one in the cricket field . . . If I chose I might easily retort upon the man whom the writer in the *Australasian* wishes to exalt at the expense of my down fall. I might simply refer to his conduct after being elected captain, and the night prior to the match. The *Australasian* writer says:- 'Mr Wardill has the entire confidence of the cricketing community,' but he cannot shove this statement down my throat, for I do not really know a more unpopular man outside his club amongst the cricketers of the colony. He also speaks of the chances I had, etc. I think that the writer (for I fancy I know him) had better not call the kettle black, for the pot is not far off . . . Victoria may yet be glad to get me; but my answer is, *never more, ve victis.*

Thomas W. Wills

When a committee of the Melbourne Cricket Club met later that month in the pavilion to review the intercolonial match, it sought evidence on Tom's behaviour. Tom's petulance in Sydney had angered many in the Club where both he and Richard Wardill played. Whatever private thoughts they had, the members of this committee agreed to pay Tom extra money for his steamer passage, his uniform and the personal account Tom gave them for his private expenses on tour. Despite everything, Tom had taken wickets in Sydney and won games for the colony and the Club.

Three days later Tom was summoned to give evidence on another matter. He was called before the match and ground committee of the Melbourne Cricket Club. Sam Costick was in trouble. The pavilion keeper at the MCG, Mr Treen, listed the complaints against Costick:

1. Creating a disturbance in the Pavilion and Bar.
2. Threatening Mr Treen unless 'he acted in accordance' with the wishes of the professionals.
3. A disrespectful manner towards members of the MCC Committee.

4. That Sam Cosstick was found 'by the secretary lying drunk in the committee room on Thursday the 1ˢᵗ April at half past six o'clock in the evening'. On this latter point, no attempt was successful in rousing Cosstick from his insensible drunken state.

Cosstick denied all the accusations except that he had been found insensible from drink in the committee room. He called upon Tom as a witness.

Tom frustrated the committee with carefully worded responses: 'Mr Wills was questioned on the subject at Cosstick's request . . . but his evidence only went as far as supporting Cosstick's denial of having made any disturbance or said anything disrespectful of any member of the Club <u>as far as he knew</u> . . . it entirely failed, did not even attempt, to touch upon the principal charge'. Tom made no reference to the alleged threats by Cosstick against Mr Treen, the pavilion keeper, and although his evidence did not incriminate Sam, it did not help as much as Sam might have expected. That Tom defiantly kept quiet on some matters showed his support for Sam, the put-upon professional cricketer, but his deliberately vague answers made it clear to the MCC committee that Tom knew more than he admitted. The committee ruled unanimously that Sam Cosstick was forbidden to enter the pavilion.

A professional cricketer's life turned on his health and his employer. After Sam Cosstick was found sodden in the Melbourne Cricket Club committee room, there was a further disagreement over money. When it was suggested publicly that Sam was discontented at the Club, he knew his employment was under threat and so wrote to *The Australasian* newspaper: 'I have nothing to complain of in the treatment I have invariably received from the committee of the Melbourne club . . . I have always treated the hon. sec., the office bearers, and the members with the respect due to them, and I have always endeavoured to do my duty as a bowler.' Cosstick's letter was part explanation, part submissiveness and part defiance. It was an act repeated by professionals to keep their income.

In early 1869 Tom announced that he was leaving Victoria to return to the family property, Cullin-la-Ringo, in Queensland. Before the last intercolonial match, Tom had suggested that he had plans to leave Victoria and in the aftermath of the match, humiliated and ill-tempered, he impetuously and defiantly wrote that even if Victoria wanted him again as a cricketer, he would not return to them. Testimonials were arranged; cricketers gathered and money collected. Such testimonials were common, organised to financially assist cricketers in their life beyond the sport. The papers in Melbourne and Geelong farewelled him; William Hammersley stopped sniping and wrote a beautiful though bittersweet biography of Tom in his sporting column; then nothing more was heard.

By September, Tom had still not departed for Queensland and it was rumoured that the possibility of an English team visiting next summer kept him in Melbourne. But that was not the reason Tom remained in Victoria. William Ducker, the family's accountant, made it clear why Tom did not travel to Cullin-la-Ringo in a letter he wrote to Cedric: 'Your mother has been very dissatisfied about Mr TW Wills and at her request he was written to that the station could dispense with his services and requesting him not to proceed to Queensland.' Tom Wills told everyone he was leaving Victoria but he was not going anywhere. He would remain and play cricket in Melbourne. Tom expressed no further thoughts on the matter, simply turning up to play cricket in Melbourne and Geelong and returning to his job as professional tutor with the MCC at 3 pounds per week. The Melbourne Cricket Club took him back; they always did while he was still of value.

The following month, November, the Corio Club of Geelong and the Melbourne Cricket Club prepared to play one another. The two clubs fought over which team would have Tom. The MCC wrote to the Geelong club that they had 'no objection to the Corio Club playing fifteen men if they desired it' but they could not have Tom. Through the eyes of the MCC, Tom was worth five men.

During the summer of 1869–70, Tom was living with Sarah Barbor in the Melbourne suburb of South Yarra. The Aboriginal cricketers Unamurriman and Yellana joined Tom as paid bowlers with the Melbourne Cricket Club, receiving one pound per week plus board at the Melbourne Cricket Ground. In February the Aboriginal bowlers fell ill and Tom was left to bowl every day at practice with little assistance. Tom complained to his mother: 'I am awfully tired every day, because the two darkies have been bad nearly every day, so I've had to do all the work and the weather has been awful and is fearful today also.' Of the ill Unamurriman, Tom wrote: 'Mullagh went home on Monday, I don't think he will live a month.'

The 'fearful' sun that beat down on Tom's brain concerned his mother. Severe exposure to sun was believed to induce a kind of colonial madness and in Sydney, Dr Norton Manning, a man who tended the mentally ill at his Tarban Asylum, wrote: 'The sun here is responsible for much brain disturbance . . . five per cent of the total cases (of insanity) are attributed to it', adding, 'after an attack of sunstroke alcohol is an absolute poison . . . A person who has once suffered from sunstroke must be either a teetotaller or a lunatic. There is, I believe, no middle standpoint.' Cricketers and their followers expressed similar views. When the cricketer George Marshall died, aged thirty-nine, it was said that he suffered 'softening of the brain, caused by slight sunstroke received while playing his favourite game under a midsummer sun'. Tom would need to take care.

Tom wrote from Melbourne to his mother but there was no mention of Sarah Barbor. He wrote mainly of what he needed: 'I shall take the trousers down tomorrow to the steam boat' – Tom was probably asking his mother to repair his clothes. Of his little sister, Elizabeth, he asked her to make him a cap in the MCC colours: 'I wish you would ask "Bessie" to be kind enough to

make me one for the <u>match</u> red–white & blue.' He complained
that merchants in Geelong were not telling the truth about
his debts, but by now it seemed that everyone knew Tom was
loose with the truth where money was concerned: 'Brights bill
is quite a <u>myth</u>,' he complained, 'because Mr Ducker paid him
up to the last thing I had – I only had since one pr of trouser
8/- for shearing. The day I left for Melbourne I wished to get
Crimean shirts but he would not let me have them unless I paid
cash – I never <u>go there</u> again.' The shearing Tom mentioned
occurred on one of his occasional trips to Belle Vue. Tom Wills
was thirty-four, captain of the Victorian cricket team and the
country's finest cricketer, but was still dependent upon his
family, like a child.

Tom was elected captain for the next intercolonial match
against New South Wales. It was played at the Melbourne
Cricket Ground in February 1870, and the Victorians won by
265 runs. Tom played modestly taking only 3 wickets while
Charles Lawrence captained New South Wales for the last
time, but the game was chiefly remembered for accusations
of throwing the cricket ball by both teams. The New South
Wales team had included the Aboriginal bowler Twopenny. Tom
and Twopenny were accused of throwing and it was rumoured
that Twopenny was included to counter Tom's 'chucks'. The two
bowlers were compared and, hypocritically, the Melbourne press
found Tom's technique more acceptable because his throwing
was better disguised: 'Undoubtedly Wills throws sometimes,
but there is some decency about it, some disguise.' At the end
of the game, Charles Lawrence publicly criticised the Victorian
bowling. Tom said nothing.

The accusations of Tom's throwing, which had never stopped
over the past decade, were now more insistent. Throwing was
seen as a cowardly act, an act designed to physically hurt a
batsman and gain an advantage. But if a bowler won matches for
club or colony then neither club nor colony looked too closely.
Victoria kept winning because they had the best player in Tom

Wills, cowardly or not. Tom travelled with the Victorian team
to Tasmania and captained the team against a Tasmanian XVI
in Launceston in the middle of March. The Victorians won
easily though not without comment on Tom's bowling style.

It was not only the merchants of Geelong who wanted
Tom's money. Tom wrote to the MCC claiming that on the
recent trip to Tasmania he had been threatened with arrest
for moneys owed from four years earlier. The amount was not
large, but enough to be remembered over that time: 3 pounds
9 shillings 6 pence. His letter, read before the committee of
the Melbourne Cricket Club on 22 March 1870, stated that a
Mr Jones of Launceston claimed Tom owed money for food
and drink supplied. Tom, defiant in the face of this accusation,
responded that he had paid the money but his word was doubted,
and over two months later the MCC committee paid the money
on his behalf.

At the end of May 1870 Tom wrote to Cedric that he planned
to remain in Melbourne for winter. Tom threw a suggestion
into the air and half-attempted to catch it: 'I really believe that
the best place after all and the most salubrious will be Fiji.'
Dreamily, he suggested to Cedric that the climate appealed to
him and that he might consider growing cotton – not that any
such suggestion ever counted for more than a passing thought
with Tom. Increasingly alone, and seemingly tired, Tom ended
his letter to Cedric as an old man might have: 'Write old boy
when you have a few minutes to spare.'

William Ducker, now the Mayor of Geelong, wrote to Tom
and offered him a permanent way out of his financial debt.
He suggested that Tom sell his stake in Cullin-la-Ringo to
his brother Horace and then secure his money with a trustee,
to thwart any 'creditors who might annoy you'. Ducker's plan
was that Tom then receive a regular interest to live on from
the principal. Tom, who knew enough to understand that this
was a secure option, sold his stake in Cullin-la-Ringo to his
brother Horace for 1550 pounds. The regular payments might

have allowed him to return to his amateur status, but whether the amount he received was sufficient to do so or not, Tom remained a professional cricketer.

Before the end of 1870 Tom Wills posed for a full-length portrait, painted by Irish artist William Handcock. Handcock is an obscure figure in Australasian history; he lived for a period in Dunedin on the south island of New Zealand and left only subtle brush marks of his time in Melbourne that are not easy to find. Handcock was dying when he painted Tom, but was probably unaware of the fact. He may have felt a roughened patch on his tongue, a thickening that grew and was prone to bleeding every now and again. Handcock died the following year from cancer of the tongue, at the Melbourne Hospital.

William Handcock chose to paint the portrait in oil, a medium not typical of his work. Painted in his cricket whites, Tom wore the colours of the Melbourne Cricket Club on his belt and cap. It is the most famous image of Wills. Finally we see the colour of Tom's light-brown hair, his white skin and pale blue eyes; he does not look like an athlete, more like a middle-aged lawyer with a liking for a nobbler. His white flannels and shirt conceal a body one stone heavier than a decade before, not overweight, but perhaps sagging around his middle. His head and neck, like a scruffy periscope, poke out from his collar which is secured by a bowtie, and on his head sits a red cap, like a pillbox hat. The cap, which was exhibited by the Melbourne Cricket Club over fifty years later, has a fanciful blue and white trim. Tom's long thin nose is reddened and coarse and flanked by equally red cheeks, betraying his liking for drink. It is unknown who commissioned the Handcock painting and where it was kept after completion, but fifty-three years after it was painted *The Australasian* reported that Hugh Trumble, MCC secretary, had purchased the portrait (from whom is not stated) and donated it to the Melbourne Cricket Club. And there it remains.

Circumstances had changed little for Tom: winning matches, envied and admired, the captain of Victoria, the 'finest' player in the country. The writers in the newspapers who taunted him were correct, of course. Tom had no idea how to look after himself; others had done it for so long. Melbourne rejoiced in Tom; songs were written and lustily sung about him: butchers, blacksmiths, doctors, journalists; the whole bloody colony crammed into the same stinking beer-soaked room, swaying around an upright piano, roaring with delight, and singing . . .

TOMMY WILLS! TOMMY WILLS! TOMMY WILLS!

He led a somewhat jolly life, since as a youth he'd scout;
He's seen all kinds of players in, he's seen them all go out;
At Rugby he was captain, he bowl'd on the Surrey Hills;
I have a weakness, I confess – it is for TOMMY WILLS,

Chorus:
I'm safe to win when I begin, TOMMY WILLS, TOMMY WILLS;
Bowling fast or slow the same, TOMMY WILLS, TOMMY WILLS;
Come, my boys, let's all go in, TOMMY WILLS, TOMMY WILLS;
Fast or slow, I'm sure to win. Hurrah for TOMMY WILLS.

TOMMY WILLS! TOMMY WILLS! TOMMY WILLS!

They were probably singing in the MCC pavilion bar as the paint dried on his portrait.

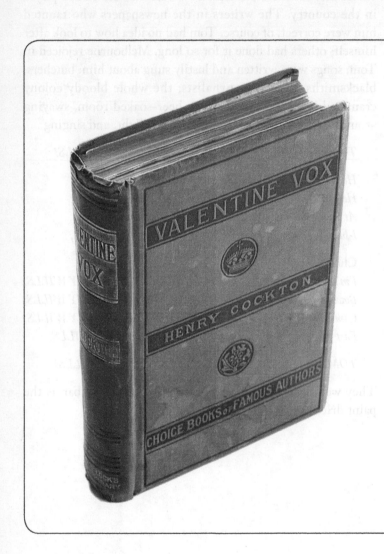

THE ART OF FORGERY

Tom had a favourite book: *The Life and Adventures of Valentine Vox, The Ventriloquist*. He read from this book at a series of weekly meetings at the Point Henry Schoolhouse, next to Belle Vue, to help raise money for the school. Tom, the local celebrity, chaired the meetings. People gathered with their amateur talents to perform for a good cause: some men sang, some played musical instruments. When Tom read *Valentine Vox* on stage, the schoolhouse overflowed with people and the crowds laughed in convulsions at the stories he read. The hero of Tom's book, Valentine Vox, had a gift. He had a genius for ventriloquism. Vox made people laugh; he drew attention and applause. Vox liked a lark, a bit of mischief. Tom knew this story well.

Valentine Vox was a master of forgery – in his case, the forgery was ventriloquism. Tom's skill lay in the art of throwing a cricket ball without detection. The trick of throwing in cricket, like throwing one's voice, was to never conduct the forgery too often, just when it was needed.

SATAN'S LITTLE HELPER

> For Mr. Wills to no-ball Mr. Wardill for throwing is like
> Satan reproving sin.
>
> *William Josiah Hammersley*

Tom and Sarah were living together in Argyle Street, South Yarra, a street of simple brick and wooden houses where bootmakers, law clerks, butchers, tailors, ironmongers and a soapmaker lived. Tom Wills, a self-described 'cricketer' for the purpose of the local council, rented a four-bedroom weatherboard cottage wedged between Alexander Byth the ironmonger and William Phillips the tailor.

Elizabeth visited Tom and Sarah, taking the train to Melbourne from Geelong. The family letters indicate that Elizabeth believed Sarah to be Tom's wife, apparently still unaware of her de facto status. She fussed over her children, giving advice liberally on suitable wives for her sons, and watched over the family fortunes of Cullin-la-Ringo. She dispensed her now regular warning to Cedric and Horace in Queensland not to permit Aborigines to 'collect in large numbers about you so that they may prove too strong for you and at last refuse to move away', adding to prick their conscience, 'my mind can never be at rest while any remain near the place'. Although Elizabeth had never fully accepted Tom making a living as a professional cricketer, she was fond of him, deeply, but had long since stopped dispensing maternal advice to him. It had rarely done any good.

It was Tom's fourth season as tutor to the members of the Melbourne Cricket Club, still gathering some of the privileges of the amateur while being paid a salary. Over the years, the title 'Tutor' was used less for Tom; it was now commonplace for Tom to be called a professional with the MCC. Whether Tom should be allowed the privilege of playing as an amateur cricketer was debated before the intercolonial game between Victoria and Tasmania. The Tasmanians had once again requested that only amateur cricketers take part in their match. Tom was unlikely to have forgotten that in 1858 the Launceston cricketers had failed to shake the Victorians' hands and refused some players admission to the Cricketers' Ball because they found it impossible to distinguish amateur from professional. It was decided that Tom would umpire the game for payment rather than play; Victoria won by 10 wickets.

Two weeks later, Victoria prepared to play New South Wales on the Albert Cricket Ground in Sydney. Tom was elected as captain of the Victorian team without controversy.

Arguments against Tom's bowling action were gathering strength and voices hardening against him. Hammersley collected and articulated these arguments against Tom more clearly and more determinedly than anyone else. The balanced equation of cricket was corrupted in Hammersley's eyes by 'chuckers', and that year Tom had bowled balls that pitched and sprung with such violence that they regularly jumped over batsman and keeper directly into the arms of the longstop. To physically wound a batsman was one way of getting him out. Hammersley's *Australasian* pointedly wrote of Tom: 'If I cannot hit your wicket or make you give a chance soon, I'll hit you and hurt you if I can. I'll frighten you out.'

The Victorians defeated New South Wales by 48 runs. Tom top scored in the first innings, 39 not out, but his bowling provoked comment. In the weeks beforehand, his critics in the press suggested that he might be called for throwing in the match against New South Wales. The criticism had some impact upon Tom as he bowled only 9 overs, taking one wicket in the first innings, and did not bowl in the second.

Tom was displeased with his bowling in this match. Describing himself as 'stiff' on the field, his body creaked as he stooped to field the ball. Writing in the 1871 *Australian Cricketers' Guide*, he implied, for the first time, that his skills were fading.

It was not only Tom's bowling that provoked the sly words of sharp-eyed critics – more than the ball was seen to sway; Tom's gait lurched, suggesting to the spectator that the claret had been swigged a little too heartily. The days were hot and the players drank their fill and more. As the *Sydney Punch* remarked on 11 March 1871:

Ye Cricket Match

I think it was stuttered the Melbournites led,
And hiccuped, 'Our fellows are going ahead
In spite of (*hic*) Wills and his "swingers".'

But I cannot wind up without hinting of pale
Bottled brandy and liquors like porter;
Ye knights of the bat with a droop in the tail,
If ye wish for the future to win without fail,
Remember when next in a match you regale,
Though the 'swells' of the senate grow gay upon ale,
'Tis wiser to stick to pure water.

As the cricket season progressed, nothing more was said of Tom's bowling action or of his drinking on the field. The season seemed to be gently closing with no further controversy.

•

On 25 March 1871, Tom stepped onto the East Melbourne field in a club match between the Melbourne Cricket Club and the East Melbourne Cricket Club. Richard Wardill captained the MCC and Tom opened the bowling for Melbourne with his medium-fast round arm deliveries before a crowd of 500 spectators. In the third over, the umpire, Samuel Hopkinson, no-balled Tom for throwing. There was a brief stir on the field and in the crowd, but it was a small event in a small match and Tom continued to bowl without hindrance.

Afterwards, the gossip on the streets of Melbourne was that there were things more crooked than Tommy's arm. Two letters, written anonymously, appeared in the press claiming that the no-balling of Tom for throwing had been concocted before the match. The anonymous letters accused the honorary secretary of the East Melbourne Cricket Club, Mr A.E. Clarke, a burly intimidating man with ambitions for his club, of grooming the teams' captains and the umpire into no-balling Wills:

> Was it after Mr. A.E. Clarke had so affectionately shaken hands with him that he discovered 'the crank' in Wills's delivery? Was it after Mr. A.E. Clarke had called the M.C.C. captain, Mr Wardill, into the pavilion and told him that it was resolved to put down throwing, and that he had better agree with the E.M. captain to give orders to the umpires to that effect? Was Mr. Hopkinson aware that Mr. Clarke had had a conversation with Mr. Wardill, and was the hint given him to 'no-ball' Wills?

It was rumoured that Clarke, desperate to enhance his own team's status, wanted to defeat the Melbourne Cricket Club by whatever means he could. There were also suggestions of heavy betting on the outcome of the game and that the attempted removal of Tom as a bowler was part of this scheming. The public accusations were not denied and Tom, not for the first time, felt that he had been set up to fall. There was brief public ill-ease about the men in the shadows who had manipulated the game, but this ill-ease soon passed as the cricket season ended.

In April Tom boarded a steamer for Sydney to play a single-wicket match, a game with modified rules, typically with one to four players on each team. Although cricketers sometimes played down the gambling aspect, money was made from these games, and Tom was always looking for money-making ventures. The participants were three Victorians – Tom, Sam Cosstick and John Conway, against three New South Welshmen – Dave, Ned and Charles Gregory. There were rumours of death threats against the Victorians and suggestions of gambling were rife. Tom negotiated an earlier start to this game but 'for reasons best known to himself, he either declined or forgot to acquaint his confreres with this arrangement', provoking an irritable Conway to chastise him. Tom did not bowl in this single-wicket match – a decision made after Dave Gregory from New South Wales was no-balled for throwing. The Victorians lost a close game. At the conclusion of the match, the players and spectators were last seen and heard rambling down George and King streets drunkenly singing with all their might – *Rule Britannia* and *God Save the Queen*. Somewhere in all of this was Tom.

Tom made little contact with his family as the cricket season ended. His mother wrote to him in South Yarra and later mused how strange it was that she never heard from her son anymore. The ruse of the marriage to Sarah Barbor continued and when Horace enquired of his mother about Tom and Sarah, he wrote: 'Did you see Mrs T.W.W. when you were up in Melbourne?' Elizabeth continued to urge her sons to marry and reflected with satisfaction that her youngest son Egbert, who followed a more conventional trajec-tory, was now a teller in the bank with a recent salary rise. Horace, at Cullin-la-Ringo, asked with the same eagerness and intrigue as he had from Germany when he was a schoolboy:

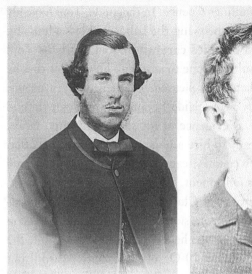 

Egbert   *Horace*

'Is Tom going to be a professional bowler this year?' Even Tom
didn't know the answer to that question, but must have wondered
if scrutiny of his bowling action might ban him from the game.
How much money he might earn from cricket – for bread to
chew and beer to quaff – would depend on the straightness of
his arm as it etched an arc across the sky.

In August 1871 Tom turned thirty-six. In that month New
South Wales proposed to the MCC to 'debar professionals' from
future intercolonial matches – potentially disastrous news for
Tom. The MCC refused the proposal and, on the 16 October,
an MCC committee met to choose the professional bowlers for
the next cricket season. They had before them two letters of
application – one from Sam Cosstick and the other from Tom
Wills – but the Club had money for only one bowler. Knowing
that he might not get re-employed by the MCC, Tom sent
letters to Adelaide, Ballarat and Geelong cricket clubs. He also
completed *The Australian Cricketers' Guide 1870–1*, a cricket

guide he sold for 2 shillings 6 pence. In the guide, Tom foolishly admitted to sometimes throwing the ball, a reckless admission that his critics and enemies carefully noted. Perhaps Tom thought nothing could be done to stop him bowling or that he could still take wickets as he pleased, whether he threw or not. He wrote repeatedly to Adelaide hoping for employment and sent over his guide as evidence of his status and importance. Adelaide was not ready to hire a bowler and declined his offer. Tom could bowl for a country team if he wished but he preferred to await the MCC's judgement.

The Melbourne Cricket Club met to consider the applications for the position of professional bowler. An initial decision in favour of Sam Cosstick was held over for four days while the decision was reviewed. On 20 October, Richard Wardill put forward the motion to employ Sam Cosstick; William Handfield put forward an amendment favouring Tom. It was put to a vote and Tom lost two votes to six. Those who voted for Sam Cosstick included William Hammersley and Richard Wardill. Tom would now have to scavenge for employment elsewhere.

It might appear that Tom had been overlooked for the job because of his cantankerous behaviour, excessive drinking on the field and the problem regarding his bowling action. But it was unlikely that any of these factors were the chief reason. No, the reason for Tom's demise was all about winning and prestige. The task for the Melbourne Cricket Club, as it was for all clubs, was to win games. Tom had helped them do this for the past fifteen years but Sam Cosstick was now the superior bowler. Clubs have always explained away the behaviour of players who win them games – they tidy away and excuse drunkenness and excesses, seeing no need to take a moral stand until it is expedient to dispose of a player. Even Tom had concluded that Sam had been the better bowler in 1871. He might have borne the coarseness of the cricket professional but Sam simply took more wickets. For all of its noble gesturing, the MCC cared about winning more than anything else. Sam would stay; Tom would go.

Despite Tom's application for employment being rejected by the MCC, he never wrote an angry word about Sam or criticised Sam's appointment. Tom's egalitarian attitude and his understanding of Sam Cosstick's burden was admired by the colony. Tom acknowledged Sam's skills. With a wife and a brood of children, any loss of money, injury or illness would have exposed Sam's family to great suffering. Tom, unlike Sam, did not know his place – neither amateur nor professional – but by the end of 1871, the 36-year-old Tom knew his skills were declining. Tom and Sarah left South Yarra and looked for a place to live in Geelong.

The day after the Melbourne Cricket Club rejected Tom's application for employment, William Hammersley wrote an article in *The Australasian*, justifying Tom's demise:

> Chucking, or throwing, is usually resorted to by those who, from some muscular deficiency, are unable to keep up the pace of their bowling. There was a time when Mr. Wills could 'bowl' almost as fast as Cosstick can now, but, like many bowlers before him have, I suppose, he is getting stiff in his biceps, and cannot put the pace on by legitimate bowling as he once could. A throw enables him to do so, and it is just this increase of pace, from the medium of a fair bowl to the fast of an unfair throw, that so often gets rid of a batsman.

Tom wrote to the Melbourne newspaper, *The Leader*, to defend himself before the public. He questioned Hammersley's courage and skill and pronounced, more for the benefit of the readers than his adversary: 'Mr. "Longstop" [Hammersley's pen name] no doubt will chuckle and crow when he learns that I'm no longer the coach for the M.C.C. but I can inform him that as long as I am given health and strength, so long shall I endeavour to play the game.'

Until the Melbourne Cricket Club rejected his services, Tom had spent his summers in Melbourne. Without employment he moved to Geelong and purchased a house in Upper Skene Street, in the heart of the town, not too far from his mother – a buggy trip around Corio Bay to Belle Vue. Elizabeth visited them and wrote of Tom and Sarah. She did not badger him, give advice or goad him to do his duty.

The details of Tom's finances are unclear but William Ducker and his Uncle Thomas assisted and offered advice. Some of his share of the family estate, 1550 pounds, was invested in real estate for him and several properties were purchased in the Geelong area. If Tom had handled his finances well, he could have lived a reasonably comfortable life. But that was never the case.

Tom and Sarah's new house was a four-bedroom brick cottage, a step up from the weatherboard at South Yarra. It was a modest dwelling, but spacious enough for Tom and Sarah on the inside, and two large flapping geese and a chicken run on the outside. They lived next to William Barnard, a labourer who grew produce on his block; on the other side was a stretch of vacant land with a rusty iron shack; and beyond this lived a blacksmith. It was a convenient location, near the train station and 'just past the football ground' – the paddock on which the Geelong Football Club played opposite the Argyle Hotel. As summer approached, Ballarat and Geelong squabbled over the discarded Tom; both hoped to sign him up. On 7 November 1871 Tom started as the Corio Cricket Club professional. Tom was openly called a professional cricketer in Geelong though he still had qualms about that status. For the rest of his life, in local government residential records, he never called himself a professional cricketer, rather a 'gentleman'.

There was just one further incident before year's end, a year that had started calmly, which centred on the definition of a lost ball during a game of cricket. Points of contention on cricket law arose periodically in the press. Tom, who regarded himself

as more knowledgeable than most on the laws of the game, was
unable to resist being lured into the dispute, especially on this
occasion as it involved some of his old adversaries – William
Hammersley and Richard Wardill. It all started when Richard
Wardill wrote a letter complaining that his side, the MCC, had
lost a game because of a lost ball:

> A ball was hit by Mr. Ford [Melbourne] over the fence into
> the road. In fielding the ball Mr. Goldsmith [EMCC] fell
> and was unable to return it. The batsmen ran eight runs,
> which were duly scored. Subsequently I am informed that the
> umpire (Mr. McPherson) said that 'lost ball' was called, and
> directed the scorers to alter the score from eight to six runs.

Wardill claimed that the ball was not lost, just simply beyond
the reach of an injured fieldsman, and that the score should
have remained at 8 runs, allowing the MCC to win the game. A
seemingly trivial incident had roused players from all around the
colony to write in with their versions. Naturally, Hammersley,
as protector of all things MCC, wrote and agreed with Richard
Wardill. Tom, who had not forgiven the MCC, Hammersley
and Wardill for his loss of station, wrote that the MCC was
at fault. He rattled off a series of lost-ball variations from his
games at Rugby and Cambridge:

> Whilst playing a match on Parker's Piece, Cambridge, in
> 1856, a gentleman fielding long leg and going after a ball
> accidentally ricked his knee joint, and could not get to the
> ball. 'Lost ball' was called and allowed, although the ball
> was in sight . . . A lost ball was given at Rugby, in 1855, the
> ball lodging in a fork of a tree, visible to nearly all the field.
> In fact, the protest against 'lost ball' should never have been
> lodged, for *no committee* could alter the umpire's decision . . .

The spat was about more than a lost ball. It was about what
divided one man from another; what separated a smug MCC
from the distant Corio Cricket Club. Hammersley saw himself

as a spokesman for the Melbourne Cricket Club, knowledgeable on all matters in colonial sport. It was intolerable to Hammersley that Tom Wills, in provincial Geelong, should argue against him. Hammersley emphasised his superior English connections: 'I was a member of the Marylebone and Surrey clubs; constantly during the season on both grounds, Lord's and the Oval, knew well nearly every gentleman and professional cricketer of any note' and then he went on to demean what he regarded as an insolent Wills: 'and yet I never but twice saw Mr. Wills during his English career'. So ended 1871. The next intercolonial was three months away and Tom, slightly desperate, shot off challenges to play cricket for money.

The intercolonial cricket match against New South Wales was set for late March 1872. Speculation centred on whether Tom would play for Victoria and, if he did, whether he would be called for throwing. Hammersley continued to condemn Tom's bowling action. Partly he was driven by his disapproval of what he regarded as Tom's breach of the rules, but his antagonism went deeper. Tom had a natural affinity with colonial egalitarianism and, despite his occasional throwing of the cricket ball, he retained the affection of the people – something that Hammersley struggled to comprehend and which increased his frustration.

A fugitive from Melbourne, Tom was feted in Geelong with allies everywhere. Each word was recorded; each step amplified; each opinion believed. He radiated over-confidence when asked about the upcoming intercolonial cricket match, boasting that a colonial team would beat the best England had on offer, or at least 'give them a tying up'. Horatio could not have scripted this better.

The Melbourne paper, *The Leader*, spoke out most strongly in favour of Tom. It was a weekly newspaper like Hammersley's *Australasian*, and the two papers saw themselves as direct competitors, so supporting Tom might help Tom but it was also good for business. *The Leader* took issue with each of

Hammersley's points. It was as much a brawl between two newspapers as it was between two men. The MCC, *The Leader* claimed, was without Tom 'demoralised and incapable to meet teams [and] at the mercy of second rate clubs. The best cricketer in the colony has been banished to Geelong . . .'

The question of whether Tom would be included in the Victorian team was soon answered. An MCC team travelled to Geelong to see if Tom's bowling was worthy of selection for the intercolonial match. Against a strong MCC team, captained by Richard Wardill, Tom bowled brilliantly, taking 8 for 26 off 191 balls. At the end of February, he boarded the train with his team and travelled to the St Kilda Cricket Ground. He took 10 wickets on the first day and his performance was shot around the colony. The Geelong press crowed; his enemies in Melbourne made excuses. There was no doubt Tom would be selected and most likely captain the Victorian team.

Tom was not oblivious to the speculation that he might be no-balled in the intercolonial match but, seduced by twenty years of fame, perhaps he considered that nothing could stop him bowling as he wished. What Tom expected as he led his team onto the Melbourne Cricket Ground remains unknown but some in the colony knew what was to come.

Before the game, a curious set of meetings had taken place. The purpose of those meetings was to 'check the very objectionable and unfair system of throwing' and certain 'arrangements' had been made for the umpires to 'carry out the strict letter of cricket law'. When Tom came to the crease, Umpire Sellars no-balled his first ball. On 30 March 1872, Tom Wills became the first cricketer to be called for throwing in intercolonial matches. After two overs he stopped bowling – three balls had been ruled as chucks – and did not bowl again. Tom, uncharacteristically, did not protest wildly on the field; perhaps he knew there was little point. Despite Tom not bowling, the Victorians won by an innings.

Hammersley breathed with the self-satisfaction of someone who had been publicly vindicated. Tom returned to Geelong and wrote angrily from his nest between the station and the football ground, not pausing to consider the wisest course of action: 'For the last two years a certain writer in *The Australasian* has been constantly writing down my bowling, saying, why not call Wills a most deliberate shy.' Tom did not have to name Hammersley. Then publicly he reiterated that 'a meeting was held by certain representatives of New South Wales and Victoria . . . virtually wanting them to no-ball Wills at any price, and to have carried out the agreement properly the umpires would have to have signed a written contract'. Neither Tom, nor anyone else, named the gentlemen involved but he implied that Hammersley was either an active architect of the plot or had seduced others to his line of thinking. Either way, Tom blamed Hammersley.

Underlying the rift between the two men were the old tensions about origins and class. Tom went on: 'Gentlemen, because they have come from England, think they can force anything upon us poor natives, but thank God we are not such fools as they take us for.' At this point in the letter Tom lost his way, constructing an argument that no one could follow: 'What good has this attempt at no-balling done? None at all – in fact throwing in future will be all the go . . . No balling has never done any good either at home or here.' Tom's rage and prickly sensitivity rendered his thoughts illogical and the absurdity of this argument escaped him. Perhaps he was past caring.

In early May, as the cricket season ended, Tom and his teammates took part in a fundraising match in Geelong. They rubbed burnt cork over their faces, parodying the Aboriginal cricketers that Tom had coached. The Geelong press called them 'stunning darkies'; the Melbourne press called them 'ludicrous'.

Tom faced an uncertain winter in Geelong. Winters offered little comfort to the professional cricketer – only a lucky few obtained work mowing, mending fences, and cutting and rolling grass in readiness for the next season. Then, at the beginning of

August, Tom woke to find himself a wealthier man. His uncle, Thomas Wills, had died on his Kew estate in Melbourne. His uncle's shrewd mind and astute real estate investments from the colony's earliest days had made him one of its wealthier citizens. Uncle Thomas' will was big, over forty pages, and as his estate was settled, it revealed that Tom owed his uncle a considerable amount of money, which was later paid. In a late change to his will, Uncle Thomas had, thoughtfully and generously, tried to ensure his nephew's welfare by giving Tom a part share in a property.

Tom's good fortune became known in Geelong and the *Geelong Advertiser* wrote that Tom, with the money from his uncle's will, might 'resume his place among the gentlemen cricketers of the colony'. His situation, known to many, was broadcast sympathetically: 'His many friends will be delighted if the statement turns out to be correct, as the former captain of the Rugby men has for years had to make a hard fight for a living.'

In December 1872, the Melbourne Cricket Club, despite recent disputes with Tom, staged a benefit game to raise money for him. Most professionals could expect to have one or two of these games held to raise money for them but Tom had made a habit of them. Over one month later, Tom wrote from his home in Upper Skene Street to his friend William Handfield, the honorary secretary of the MCC, acknowledging the small amount of money from the match:

My dear Sir,

I beg to ackge receipt of cheque for £5–4 – 6. Many thanks for same – Please accept personally my sincere thanks for the trouble you took with reference to my match and be good enough to convey to the Committee of the M.C.C. my thanks for their kindness in letting me have the use of the Club Ground.

I Oblige

Yours very Sy.

Thomas W. Wills

Tom had not used this kind of language for many years; not since, as a young man and recently returned from England, he had negotiated with the touchy William Tunks. In the past, when the Melbourne Cricket Club needed Tom, he had not been so careful with his language, but now he showed some awareness of the importance of cultivating those who could improve his survival as a cricketer. The MCC responded generously: they paid Tom his money, compensated him for the train trip to Melbourne and gave him a further 3 pounds, the equivalent of one week's bowling.

In the last days of 1872, an unusual cricket match was arranged in response to Victoria's repeated intercolonial wins. Victoria played a combined team of thirteen players from New South Wales, South Australia and Tasmania. Although Tom had been called for throwing in the last intercolonial match, he was still regarded as Victoria's best captain. Wills was selected in the Victorian team and the players, with no hesitation, elected him captain. It was expected that if he bowled he would be called for throwing.

Tom was cautious when he came on to bowl. Bowling slowly his arm was straight, but as his deliveries increased in speed Tom was called for throwing. The game was a disaster for Wills. The cocky Victorians lost and Tom was blamed for embarrassing himself and the colony. For the first time in Tom's career, there was little dissension. Hammersley circled his limping prey, writing mercilessly that 'Victoria played virtually only 10 men, as Wills was of no use whatever'. He moved beyond the realm of cricket, striking at the heart of what he saw as Tom's wayward personality: 'I think that no man should be elected captain in a cricket match about whose ability to first "captain himself" there is any doubt.'

Tom Wills was the most prominent, the most enduring and the most outspoken of all the bowlers who were accused of throwing, and it appeared that he would be made to shoulder the burden. For many years his throwing of the occasional ball had been openly acknowledged in the colony, and even he outrageously admitted to it in his 1871 *Cricketers' Guide*. Tom's English training, amateur status and talent had long quarantined him from criticism. It was only now, when he tried to bowl his faster balls, that the 'crank' was revealed in his arm. Tom Wills' competitiveness probably blinded him from reaching the conclusion of those around him who saw his bowling as cowardly, as the refuge of the cheat.

After he was called for throwing in this combined match he wrote letters to Hammersley at *The Australasian* but the editor refused to publish them. He managed to get his letter published in *The Leader*. In a gross misjudgement, Tom was critical of his team, when the faults lay with him. Tom began obliquely, as he often did, casting a line to *Hamlet*:

> There's a divinity doth shape our ends,
>   Rough-hew them as we may.

I shall feel exceedingly obliged if you will allow me space to make a few comments on an article, written by one 'Longstop', in the columns of your Collins-Street contemporary, in which he makes pretty free use of my name, and I may here remark that the same writer has for the past three years been in the habit of writing me down whenever he could possibly get a chance, and whenever he thought it would do me an injury, allowing me no opportunity of replying in the columns over which he presides; but really every cricketer knows the man, and how very contemptible he is. Did he not try to cast cold water upon the late match, and allude to the Sydney players as professionals (as if it were a dishonest profession)? I can remember the time when 'Longstop' would have been hard up indeed if it had not been for the poor contemptible professional cricketers . . . I once had the pleasure of playing under 'Longstop' as captain in an 'Intercolonial', and a bigger old woman never held the position, yet forsooth he talks about the captainship of the

late match, etc Allow me to inform him that it was not the
bad generalship that lost the match, but the bad batting,
the worse fielding, and the miserable bowling. What could
anyone do in such a state of things? However, just to annoy
him, I will strive next year to be good enough to occupy
the same position, and try to win, even as I did on the
late occasion, although he seems to think different; and
furthermore, I will captain a team with anyone in the world,
bar none. The greatest mistake I made was not going in
earlier each innings, for I was in far better form than fully
one half of the team.

Tom's vainglory was reminiscent of the period after he had left
Cullin-la-Ringo, ten years earlier.

Hammersley, in closing out these public letters of abuse, did
so with personal insults and sarcasm, using his close knowledge
of Tom's family and schooling:

Tom Wills indulges in one of his periodical vulgar
attacks on me . . . He commences with the quotation from
Shakespeare . . . though what it has to do with what follows
I cannot see, unless to explain how his parents intended that
he should be a lawyer and a gentleman, but that Providence
ordained otherwise, as his brains were so shallow and his wits
so blunt that nature interposed and resolved on his being a
professional cricketer – and a very honourable profession,
too, Mr. Tom Wills, certainly. I am not at all surprised if
you, Sir, have refused to insert Mr. Wills's letters if they
were at all like what appeared in last week's *Leader* . . . In the
course of a few years, when Mr. Wills has been to school
again, he may be able to write a decent, gentlemanly letter,
and then, perhaps, the editor of *The Australasian* may be
more kind to him.

You have been a good cricketer, no doubt; a middling
bat, and a very ugly one; but as a bowler you would have
been played out long ago had the umpires 'no-balled' you

as you should have been, and will be now if you try your
dodges on again ... I will give you a little parting advice,
Mr. Wills. You are played out now, the cricketing machine
is rusty and useless, all respect for it is gone. You will never
be captain of a Victorian Eleven again, that you may be sure
of. You are really an old woman now, like 'Longstop'. Settle
down, quietly at Geelong, dear Geelong. Eschew colonial
beer, and take the pledge, and in time your failings may be
forgotten, and only your talents as a cricketer remembered.
Farewell, Tommy Wills.

Tom threatened legal action. Like two cockfighters clasped
together by unholy claws it needed a heavy hand to pluck them
asunder. Hammersley, having disturbed Tom's heart, retracted
himself from Tom's affairs, returned to his box at the Melbourne
Cricket Club and coiled up within its embrace. Tom Wills would
not trouble him again; that trill in Geelong was now too distant.
In the life of the colony in 1873 this was a diversion, a topic of
gossip that had entertained Melburnians; even if many thought
Hammersley was correct, they didn't take to him much: he was
too pompous by half. The common man claimed Tom as their
own and viewed Hammersley as a smug, prickly bastard. To all
who watched with a voyeur's eye and read with the interest of
the street gossip, it seemed that Tom had played his last game of
cricket for the colony of Victoria. Hammersley had triumphed.

THE ARRIVAL OF GRACE

AUGUST 1873–MAY 1874

Richard Wardill's body was found drifting on the Yarra. It had been in the river for eighteen days. On the last day of his life, a Sunday afternoon, Richard Wardill, Victorian cricketer and Melbourne Cricket Club captain, sat down to write a letter of confession. He confessed to defrauding his employer, the Victorian Sugar Company, of 7000 pounds. Wardill, the company's bookkeeper, struggled to cleanse his soul as he wrote his letter: 'I have been a frightful scoundrel but have suffered dreadfully during the last two years and I feel better now I have told you all.' He talked of suicide: 'I had determined to drown myself tonight, but when I went home to dinner the sight of my wife and child sent me to my bedroom and I prayed to God the first time for years . . . While I am writing this I think it better that I should make away with myself but if I do I have been taught that I shall be consigned to everlasting punishment and I dare not.' Wardill had gambled extravagantly; card playing was his weakness and to nurture his illicit habit he had stolen from his employer, forging the company's financial records with a deft hand. Wardill took his confession to the company secretary.

Miserable and tormented by shame, Richard Wardill could barely speak; so depressed was he that the messages to his lips arrived sluggish and disconnected. The first cricketer to score a century in intercolonial matches, and sometime colleague and often antagonist of Tom Wills, was a wrecked man. Wardill asked the company secretary if he might see his wife before going to the police. Soon after entering his house, Wardill took a pencil and scribbled a note: 'I have gone to the Yarra. It is best for all' and placed it in an envelope. He took off his watch, removed several silver coins from his pocket and, walking quietly out of the back of the house, fled into a black Melbourne night.

Wardill lived off Punt Road in South Yarra, only a short distance from the river. The police search had Melbourne gossiping as another day passed without finding Wardill. The Melbourne press speculated on his whereabouts, not all convinced that he had taken his life. The river was not dragged for a body. An unforgiving Melbourne public, weighing up his gambling and fraud, cast Wardill as a villain, some suggesting he had hidden to avoid facing the public shame. There was little generosity in their voices; he had left a young wife and a child. A ferry owner, who took people across the Yarra, later recalled that his dog had barked on the night Wardill disappeared, but on calling out there was no answer, and he then heard 'a noise in the river in the south side – it was something jumping into the river . . . I saw no persons about.'

On 4 September 1873, Richard Wardill's body, soft and swollen and discoloured, was found floating on the Yarra. When the police searched his body they found a penknife, a pair of gloves and a handkerchief.

On a cheerless day, the funeral procession – fourteen public and private vehicles each filled with the friends of the deceased – plodded towards the Melbourne Cemetery. It is possible that Tom Wills attended the funeral, though no information remains to suggest either way. Once in a humorous conversation, Tom remarked about suicide: 'it's against creation to commit suicide tell him if he dies he will be tried for it & if found [guilty] sentenced to banishment for life'. Tom Wills and Richard Wardill had been competitors. Wardill's death made it just a little easier for Tom to make the Victorian team.

Tom remained that winter in Geelong, but he was restless. 'I believe Tom is going to engage in Melbourne again,' was Egbert's view. Now a champion footballer, sinewy athlete and conservative bank teller, Egbert would make his mark with the Melbourne Football Club. But Tom, whose ageing body and mind meant reflexes less sharp and muscles less firm, was unlikely to return as a professional cricketer to Melbourne. Tom was compelled to look beyond that city's confines. He could remain in Geelong, there was safety in that, but he seemed a little bored by the idea, and it stifled his natural disposition to wander.

In early September Tom wired a telegram to the South Australian Cricket Club, offering to coach and play as a professional bowler for two months. He asked for 35 pounds plus travel expenses. It was a modest request, but the South Australians were unable to find the money. The provincial towns buzzed about him, anxious to scavenge a Melbourne cast off – Wills would be a prize to hold aloft. Ballarat, Bendigo, Geelong and Camperdown flirted with him, offering what they could and more. Knowing that he could not rely upon a single club or colony to sustain his fragile income, Tom kept his position in Geelong but also took on coaching in Ballarat and Bendigo.

Tom's younger siblings shuttled between Geelong and Melbourne. Colden Harrison had moved into his new home in the Melbourne suburb of Kew; retired from football but still the game's most formidable voice, he no longer moved with the same alacrity as he tended his garden. Emily was her niggly, offensive self and, if anything, her manner had coarsened over the years: Colden had a harsh time of it. His mother, old Mrs Harrison, still lived in Victoria Parade, Collingwood, and welcomed the Wills family whenever they visited from Point Henry, particularly the sisters Elizabeth, Eugenie and Minnie, who fussed about and cluttered the place when they weren't dancing at balls and visiting friends. Tom was never part of their social engagements; his mind was fixed upon other matters. W.G. Grace, after haggling over price, had at last consented to bring an English cricket team to the colonies.

Tom communicated to the Melbourne Cricket Club his willingness to travel from Geelong to the Melbourne Cricket Ground 'frequently' to coach the local players in preparation for the English, if the MCC could see their way to provide him with a free railway pass. The MCC rejected Tom's offer of assistance.

Tom was desperate to play for Victoria against Grace but he had to undo the insinuations of alcohol abuse and win favour with the committee charged with selecting the team. One of the men on the committee was William Hammersley. The Melbourne newspapers published team lists they thought worthy of meeting Grace, and readers wrote in their opinions. In the final months of 1873, opinions were divided over Tom. Some alluded to the 'unpalatable truths' of his past behaviour: an implied reference to Tom's drunkenness on the cricket field that rendered him untrustworthy. What kind of an embarrassment would Tom be if he swayed heavy in head with grog, and 'shied' all day? What would Grace think of us!? Tom responded, asking in his public letters 'if any of the umpires of the last All England team ever no-balled me?' Those who supported Tom pushed his cause hard, dismissing his heavy drinking and tantrums as 'trifling indiscretions'. Wills had been a magnificent sportsman, even his darkest enemies nodded to that. However, with Hammersley on the committee it was unlikely Tom would be selected.

There was ill-feeling in the colony towards Hammersley; the mood was sympathetic to Tom. In the face of growing public affection for Tom, a peevish Hammersley resigned from the selection committee; he cooled, rethought his position and then retracted his resignation. William Gilbert Grace arrived in Melbourne on 13 December; when the Victorian team was announced on 23 December the name of Tom Wills was absent.

Grace was large, with the steely frame of an ocean steamer. He was young, just turned twenty-five, and had not yet attained that girth so familiar in his later years. Recently married, it would be six years before he gained his medical degree. At the age of eighteen he had scored 224 runs for England against Surrey, and had remained unequalled as a cricketer. A straight-hitting batsman, he made scores not thought possible, took wickets and threw the ball prodigious lengths. He was cricket's first pillar of greatness.

The Grace team was composed of seven professionals and three amateurs. One of the professionals, the short and ageing slow bowler James Southerton, kept a diary. Concise enough to be held comfortably within the palm of one's hand, he poured into it – with Pepys-like honesty on the human state – priceless observations of life as a cricketer with Grace. Southerton was not a true-to-type professional. He spent time at the Theatre Royal in Melbourne, watched Shakespeare's *As You like It* and heard the opera *Faust* performed in Tasmania. While he enjoyed the arts, his comrades – amateur and professional – were about town drinking, 'on the spree'.

The English XI played the Victorian XVIII on Boxing Day. On the morning of the match, the Victorian team fumbled to find a worthy captain. One was found almost by default and the Victorians won the match, surprised and almost apologetic about defeating Grace. Southerton, impressed with the Melbourne Cricket Ground, pencilled in his diary: 'the wicket not to be surpassed in England'.

The English left Melbourne on New Year's Eve, taking the four-hour train trip to Ballarat, north-west of Melbourne. On New Year's Day they met and dined with James Thompson; touring Ballarat on a day said to be '107 in the shade', they were taken down a goldmine. The next day Wills bowled and batted with the Ballarat team against Grace. He followed the team to

Stawell, at the foot of the Grampians, deep into the country of Tom's childhood. The Stawell XXII cricket team, a team of farmers and clerks (with the odd Melbourne professional), defeated Grace. Southerton wrote of the Stawell pitch in his diary that it was the 'worst looking wicket ever seen'. Southerton would have cause to alter his opinion as the tour continued.

Tom latched onto the English team and was their companion over the next three weeks. He had previously prepared the Bendigo, Ballarat and Geelong teams to play against Grace and was warmly welcomed back by the provincial teams. W.G. Grace saw more of Tom Wills than any other Victorian cricketer.

The ruddy features of the English team spoke of more than the flaming sun above could explain. The team was drunk: on the field, off the field and in their sleep. The colonial press struggled to understand and accept this:

> In the first place, they were not in a fit state to play, having partaken too freely of the generosity or mistaken kindness of the Stawellites, who were very anxious to show that their love of mother-country had not diminished ... The cricket ground was surrounded by tall trees, and a halo of dust, raised by the vehicles. The Englishmen said that the shadows from these trees themselves prevented them from seeing the pitch of the ball. Others give a very different reason for their dullness of vision but it is very likely that it was a little bit of both.

Drunk or not, the English left for Warrnambool on the western coast of Victoria at 4.30 a.m. on Sunday 11 January. The local Warrnambool cricket committee had written to Tom, asking if he would come and play for them. They need not have bothered; he was already on his way.

Tom played in all the country matches and his performances suggested that the decision to leave him out of the Victorian team was correct. Every now and then he hit the ball with force or took a wicket with a swinging or bouncing ball but the occasions were increasingly rare. The English players noted his 'shies' but even those occasional throws did little to influence the course of a game. Although the Melbourne journalists cringed at the possible English response to Tom's bowling action, they need not have been concerned. The English simply ignored it.

Tom returned to Geelong and the English team boarded the SS *Otway*, travelling from Warrnambool around Cape Otway to Melbourne. Southerton, who was enjoying the shenanigans of Grace, noted that on board W.G. was nearly drunk 'and amused himself by shooting harmless gulls from the stern and letting them lie in the water'. The English continued by sea from Melbourne and steamed into Sydney Harbour on 21 January. They were met with glasses of champagne. The following day, the team attended a breakfast limited to eighty guests at Tattersall's Hotel in the heart of Sydney. The Bill of Fare recorded that the team dined on fish, pigeon, game pie and duck washed down with unlimited German white wines, claret, colonial wines (Dalwood), champagnes (Piper), liqueurs and amontillado sherries. The team then adjourned to the Albert Ground to practise!

Two months before Grace arrived in Australia, an obscure article had appeared in a Melbourne newspaper suggesting that Tom Wills might coach a team of cricketers in South Australia to play against Grace. What made this brief statement so enticing was not the desire of a team to play Grace, as all of the colonies seemed ready to prostitute common sense to obtain Grace, but where this match would take place. The match was set for a copper-mining town called Kadina on the Yorke Peninsula in South Australia. In early November Tom had begun negotiations with the Yorke Peninsula Cricket Association to be their cricket coach. On 31 January it was announced that 'Mr Wills will most likely be engaged as coach'. His rate of pay was described as 'liberal'.

Before Grace's arrival in Australia, an unseemly battle had been waged by South Australia to lure the English team to their colony. It was assumed that Grace would travel to Adelaide on his homeward voyage and play a team from the capital, but negotiations were slow. Then at the point of signing a contract, the Adelaide cricketers were stung to find that a small cricketing association on the Yorke Peninsula had already signed a contract with Grace to come to South Australia. And most rankling of all to the Adelaide cricketers was that the Yorke Peninsula contract forbade the English to travel to Adelaide to play any kind of match. No one, it seems, could quite believe what was happening. A town on the edge of the desert had nabbed Grace for themselves.

The news was instantly relayed to Melbourne, from where Grace's manager was undertaking the negotiations. One can almost see the smirking faces of the men and women of Melbourne as they boarded their carriages and omnibuses in Collins Street and opened the pages of *The Australasian* and *The Argus* – they must have wondered what on earth Wills and Grace were doing. What madmen went to the edge of nowhere? But the question most often asked by those top-hatted gentlemen in Melbourne was: exactly where was the Yorke Peninsula? And even if you wanted to go there, how did you do so?

•

Tom boarded the steamer *Aldinga* as it docked in Melbourne. From its midship rose two thin funnels, like inverted cigars, that puffed Tom all the way to Port Adelaide, where he was greeted by Julius Ey, the town clerk of Kadina. Together they travelled to Kadina by Cobb & Co coach: leaving Adelaide on Friday morning and due in Kadina that evening, 13 February. An accountant by profession, Julius Ey had in the last few weeks been coaching the Peninsula Cricket XI in preparation for Grace, but his skills were more adept at purchasing and selling shares than facing a cricket ball.

Kadina lay 100 miles in a north-westerly direction from Adelaide and no one who took this trip considered it pleasant. In the rain it was almost impossible to drive along the track – drivers

were celebrated for their feats of getting passengers safely to
their destination. There were five sections to be traversed and
four different sets of horses used to make the journey. The
mallee scrub, the vegetation seen everywhere, was thickest
coming into Port Wakefield where passengers stopped 'to
liquor' and rest. The weather had been dry for some time when
Tom made the trip, so the muddy ruts that often bogged down
coaches did not delay the journey. Beyond Port Wakefield the
coach crossed swamps and the Hummock Ranges. Nearing
its destination, to the north lay the rounded elevation of the
Hummocks and to the south the low flat-topped plateau of the
Yorke Peninsula. The coach turned southwards for its final
leg into the Yorke Peninsula. Tom was set down at Kadina
as scheduled on the evening of 13 February. Cricket practice
started the next day at 2 p.m.

•

The Peninsula, a narrow strip of land with a club-foot at its
base that stretched deep into the Southern Ocean, owed a lot
to the discovery of copper. Fifteen years earlier, a shepherd
had come across the green carbonate ore that signalled the
presence of copper in the soil. Three towns had sprung up
in rapid succession around the copper mines: Kadina, the
unearthly sounding Moonta and the port of Wallaroo – boasting
a combined population of over 12,000 people.

Much of the Yorke Peninsula was hot rock and life-
less. Summer temperatures regularly exceeded 100 degrees
Fahrenheit. The only relief to the unbroken line of baked soil
were dozens of miners' huts; the damp salt could be seen seeping
into and rotting the walls. Littered in profusion were the mines,
black holes in an alien landscape, into whose hungry mouths
miners went daily, digging for copper. And then there were the
smelters: each a fire that breathed deep within the earth and
into which the rock around them was fed, to be worked upon.
From the smelters a thick black excreta rose high into the blue

desert sky – foul plumes of metallic smoke – an unholy mess of the earth's crust and industrial additives. The fumes crept over the desert and out to sea; on days when heavy air sat still above the smoke, the fumes were breathed in, settling as an unnatural taste in the mouths of the people.

For every mineshaft dug, a steeple was erected to serve God. The Bible and copper supported and comforted the peninsula. Sermons were preached: crowds of people were drawn to church, sometimes appearing in such numbers that, unable to find a seat, they were turned away. Crime was petty: the librarian in Moonta was charged with embezzling the sum of 10 pounds. Thanks were given for the smallest of delights: a new school of music had just brought instruction to all three towns. Water was scarce and the sometimes stagnant pools bred disease; typhoid preyed upon the miners. Just before Tom arrived, an epidemic struck and several hundred died and were buried in unmarked graves. It was often the newcomers unused to such water and the Peninsula's children who fell ill and perished.

There was no vegetation to see. The Mallee scrub, stripped and uprooted from the earth, was needed as wood to construct the mines and the buildings above ground. The landscape had mutated, as if a surgeon had excised a patch of skin and replaced it with a foreign covering – what had been natural and right and harmonious was replaced by the artificial. Around the shafts that sunk deep into the ground were the regurgitated offerings from the earth, the cast-off ore thought not to be so valuable, which formed pyramids of rubble all over the fields. There were work sheds, chimneys, blacksmiths, carpenters, steam-driven pulleys cranking this way and that, and miners moving in all directions working underground and on top. Some of the humans who moved around the piles of refuse were just boys scampering between the earth and the shafts: useful, agile and seemingly plentiful.

The mining companies made large amounts of money. The miners, mainly Cornish men, brought their mining techniques and religion with them. Their skin was permanently blackened and flushed in the heat, shining brightly, polished by the sweat of their labours as they worked deep within the earth. They were lean muscular men and worked in groups of three; each wore a papier-mâché helmet on which stood a candle, their only form of illumination underground. In gangs of three they swung their sledgehammers in search of the copper ore. Photographs show their staring eyes, bright, like the blazing furnaces they fed.

The people of Yorke Peninsula were isolated and they dreamed more than most. W.G. Grace's aura was even bigger here than in Melbourne or Sydney. When the local cricket association had secured the contract that compelled Grace to come to Kadina, they believed it was something special about themselves that had induced him. They were deluded, of course. Even if they privately admitted it was only the exorbitant money paid that brought Grace to Kadina, they could lie to themselves that he would see what others could not: that Kadina and its people were special and worthy. And so preparation began for the match.

•

Tom was free to think and behave as he wished, appearing to the Kadinians as not a man prone to verbal remonstration, but rather quiet. Bloated with self-importance, the Yorke Peninsula Cricket Association described Tom: 'Short of GRACE himself, probably no better cricketer could be found in Australia, than WILLS.' To praise Tom was to praise themselves for their cleverness in nabbing him. And he gave them no reason to think otherwise. Sarah Barbor was with Tom in Kadina, but was rarely mentioned. Whether she travelled over with him or came later is unknown, but 'Mr. and Mrs. Wills' were treated as distinguished guests.

Tom felt at home. His easy disposition drew the miners and the people of the peninsula to him. He wrote home to Geelong, boasting of his team of town clerks, doctors, lawyers, amateur thespians and others, as 'a fine lot of men' – an expression of a natural captain with the gifts to inspire the less-talented. Tom was loved and at a meeting of the Wallaroo Bay Cricket Club he was unanimously admitted into the club as an honorary member.

Tom immediately assessed that the heat was their common enemy and reorganised practice to be held at 6 a.m. and early in the evening. Wills travelled between Kadina, Moonta and Wallaroo, bowling and batting. Even at the age of thirty-eight, physical endurance was still a natural asset. His movements were watched carefully and recorded in the local papers. Not a critical word was said of him.

The site of the match was decided by local politics, not by the quality of the ground. The racecourse, midway between Wallaroo and Kadina, was chosen. Julius Ey was to captain the Peninsula team. His brother Theodore, a left-hander and actor in local amateur theatricals, was in the team, as was Dr Herbert, the local doctor. Dr Herbert was president of the Yorke Peninsula Cricket Association, and his portly frame and walking stick were presumably some hindrance when he stooped, bowling his slow underhand deliveries. A banker, a coach driver and an assortment of other individuals made up the team.

Tom was also in charge of giving life to a cricket pitch in the desert – an absurd task. There was no grass and without water the fine dust hardened into a baked crust. High-velocity winds raised the Peninsula dust into the heavens, ascending several miles and travelling as far as the colony of Victoria. So thick was the dust that it prevented players from seeing more than a few yards during a windstorm. It was a finely desiccated dust, as soft and light as the powder on a lady's cheek, and it insinuated itself into every crevice in the town. In ferocious winds, the sand, each particle a grit of flint, skidded horizontally and penetrated the players' faces. When it rained, the earth became a slurry of mud, and gutters and pipes in the town clogged with sludge. Tom did what he could, ordering daily rolling and sweeping of the pitch. The lessons of John Lillywhite and Rugby School were repeated.

Tom was safely distant from Melbourne; no one in Kadina insulted him. Melbourne looked on in disbelief at the cricket preparations as though watching and hearing a fantasy. Melbourne had disgorged Grace, and now the Yorke Peninsula Cricket Association debased themselves with their servility to him.

The months of February and March were an extraordinary period for Kadina. Normally the mining town had little connection with the outside world but now everything swung around the Grace match. English cricket shirts and trousers were imported and sold, as cricket became everyone's game. A local carpenter carved two bats that were picked by Tom as cricket trophies and awarded to local players with the highest score at practice. Tom, buoyant, wrote home to Geelong that all aspects of the local team were improving.

The *Wallaroo Times* announced that in preparation for Grace, the usual weekly delivery of sixty hogshead of beer from Adelaide had nearly doubled; and that the Rev. G.B. Sobbs was coming, 'one of the best preachers in Scotland'. The temperatures were high; all that was needed was Grace.

The English Cricket XI boarded the steamer at Queen's Wharf in Melbourne and headed for Adelaide, drinking as they had done all tour, some to excess. Henry Jupp had been taking 'farewell nips' in the most liberal manner. Jupp, liked by the Australian public, wore his professional status with some charm. An opening batsman from Surrey, he was a short man with narrow shoulders – neatly formed one might say and as steady a batsman as Grace had in the team. Admiring Jupp for his courage, Grace noted in an aside: 'He had rather a liking for a glass of champagne, but objected to dilution.'

On the first evening out from Melbourne, Jupp came on to the deck of the steamer. He was in an excitable, confused and paranoid state. Blaspheming all about him, Jupp thought he saw sparkling 'blue light beacons' dancing around him and accused others of soiling his clothes. He insisted that someone examine his shirt and trousers, and kept his teammates awake asking for the captain every 'five minutes'. Jupp was disturbed for the three days it took to reach Port Adelaide on Friday morning, 20 March, where Dr Herbert, the president of the Yorke Peninsula Cricket Association, had raced to meet the team.

Southerton nursed Jupp all day at the York Hotel in Adelaide, then players took turns to sit by his bed. At one point Jupp leapt from his bed and dashed madly through an Adelaide street but at midnight was 'apparently much better'. He deteriorated again and 'at 2 he commenced to rave and swear . . . and was so evidently mad that Dr Herbert got an order to take him to the hospital'. Jupp was admitted to the Adelaide Hospital at three o'clock in the morning and diagnosed with alcoholism and delirium tremens. Three hours later the team boarded a coach to Kadina hoping to arrive at six o'clock in the evening. Jupp, the opening batsman, remained behind in a 'padded room' in the Adelaide Hospital raving, quite out of his mind. The newspapers reported that Jupp was discharged from hospital the next day; Southerton received word that Jupp had not been discharged, he had 'escaped'.

When Grace arrived at Kadina a crowd of one to two thousand people had gathered around their hotel, many of whom remained to get a glimpse of the English captain. The amateurs of the team lodged at Mitchell's Royal Exchange Hotel and 'the remainder', in reference to the professionals, elsewhere. Elsewhere was not recorded.

On the Sunday night before the cricket match, the long dry period broke suddenly and rain hit the Kadina earth with a determined pulse, washing the dirt into rivulets, down into crevices and eroding what was left to be eroded. By morning the rain settled but a heavy cloud hovered overhead. Grace and his team left their hotel at eleven-thirty in the morning in their coach pulled by a quartet of horses, and arrived at the racecourse where the match was to be played.

Just after lunch, town businesses shut down, mines closed and released their workers, and those who wished, and could afford the 2 shillings 6 pence, made their way to the racecourse. Railway lines from all three towns carried to the ground open trucks filled with spectators, and on the hour poured out their load, much like the copper ore they usually held.

Two concentric fences enclosed the cricket ground. Carriages and horses were strapped to the outer-wire fence. The inner fence, 7 feet tall, was constructed of wood and galvanised iron. Two temporary grandstands, each 100 feet across, rose from the dust and four publican booths, each with a frontage of 80–100 feet, sold refreshments. Water was scarce; beer was abundant.

On the afternoon of 23 March, in front of 1800 spectators Grace led his team onto an open space, the space that had been watered and swept. The ground was irregular and everywhere Grace looked there were stones of all sizes strewn about, lending it the appearance of a lunar world. When he asked the whereabouts of the cricket ground, Grace was told he was standing upon it. Recalling this scene many years afterwards, Grace wrote: 'There was scarcely a blade of grass to be seen, while the whole area was covered with small stones. On the morning of the match a bushel of pebbles was swept up.' Against Grace assembled the local team of twenty-two, including Tom Wills. Dr Herbert batted at number 22, and a Moonta solicitor, an ex-Cambridge man, Thomas Burtt, was chosen as the team's umpire.

A reporter from the Melbourne *Australasian* had been despatched by the newspaper to record this strange match, seemingly for the amusement of Melburnians. He recorded: 'the wicket was chosen . . . There was very little choosing one place was as good, or rather as bad, as another.' There was no tape available to measure the 22 yards; a piece of board was measured out at one yard and then laid on the site of the pitch and turned over end 21 times until the required distance was reached. It was then used to etch the earth's crust to signify the creases. The stumps were unable to be hammered into the ground until more water was poured at their base.

Julius Ey won the toss and Yorke Peninsula batted. Southerton, sniggering at the absurdity of it all, recalled in his diary that after ten minutes the local team changed their minds and asked the English to bat first instead. Grace disagreed and the game continued. As the ball hit the pitch, soft puffs of dust rose from the earth, almost as an afterthought to mark the spot where the ball had landed.

The local team made 42 runs in just under two hours. Wickets and alcohol flowed merrily. Troopers on two occasions quelled drunken behaviour in the crowd. The Peninsula scored 13 runs in their second innings. Tom looked neither like a miner nor a cricketer, making ducks in both innings and taking 2 wickets. The English won by an innings and 9 runs. W.G. Grace later wrote:

> Mr. T.W. Wills, the old Rugbeian, had been coaching the Kadina team for over a month in view of the match, and as he had been instructing them in the game the Kadina people thought a good deal of his prowess, and expected him to do valiantly against us. He made a pair of spectacles – clean bowled in each innings – and after that the Kadina people were interested in him no more.

Three days had been reserved for the match. It was over in two. Grace agreed to play another game on the third day, but at a cost. He wanted a further 110 pounds. The locals paid. After the second game in Kadina, the teams sat at the Royal Exchange Hotel for dinner, an elaborate reception having been arranged to thank Grace and his team. During the meal, Grace announced that he and his team were taking a coach to Adelaide to play one last game. It seems that a loophole had been found in the contract with the Kadinians and that Grace, after all, would earn more money in Adelaide – another 400 pounds – before returning to England. Grace rose from his table and boarded the coach that was waiting outside, leaving the locals with the food still in their mouths.

Grace's callous exploitation of their trusting, small-world pomposity left the locals struggling to come to terms with their misplaced servitude. They had become vulnerable through their determination to impress Adelaide and the English – at a likely cost of over 1300 pounds.

Those two months marked a period of contentment for Tom. There were no hotheaded tantrums; he had worked steadily and in easy comradeship with the miners and townspeople. His manner, in the light of the Grace defection, was lauded. Tom remained in Kadina until the middle of April when he and Sarah made arrangements to return to Geelong.

Tom was formally farewelled on 10 April at the White Lion Hotel where he and Sarah were introduced to the crowded room and Tom was thanked not only for his coaching but for his manner, which was 'most genial, gentlemanly, and social'. A letter of appreciation was then read to Tom, and 'Mr. and Mrs. Wills' were presented with a purse of sovereigns. He responded by offering to come again if they needed him, as long as they gave him 'enough to get bread and butter'. Tom warmed local hearts and sided with them in their dispute with Grace. At that moment, the Kadinians rejoiced again in having 'Short of GRACE himself' probably the best cricketer in Australia in 'WILLS'. Perhaps they convinced themselves that having Tom was better than having Grace. The crowded room was liberally supplied with nobblers and swipes, and towards the end of the evening Tom sang 'an extraordinary song'. We never hear what he sang and why it was extraordinary. Perhaps it was bawdy, so typical of such events, or perhaps it was simply out of character for the cricket coach they regarded as the 'quiet' man.

Tom and Sarah left for Geelong on Saturday 18 April.

After their match in Adelaide, Grace and his team boarded a steamer for England. The steamer docked at King George Sound on the Western Australian coastline where the team went ashore. The isolated harbour, long visited by sealers and whalers, was now a refuge for the Noongar people, who had been reduced to selling trinkets to visiting ships. Southerton disliked King George Sound. When he made a second trip to Australia three years afterwards, he wrote of it as a place where time dragged heavily with only the 'disgusting blacks for amusement'. Grace and his team viewed Australia with condescension and the black figures huddled on the beach at King George Sound reinforced their disdain. Southerton reflected on Kadina in his diary: 'How we managed to pass the day in this wretched hole I cannot tell. Where there is nothing but miners huts to be seen . . .' Tom Wills was recalled in passing, in neutral terms, along with several other players. Southerton gloated about the money that had been made in Kadina, reasserting that the team was at ease with their conscience. Even Southerton, a man of fine intellect and normally a thoughtful diarist, could not resist a smug moment of acquisition as he counted his money and recalled that the Kadina killing had made the Australian trip 'rather a good finish'.

DUST HIM OFF ONCE MORE

MAY 1874–FEBRUARY 1876

In the small world of Geelong, in the winter of 1874, Tom Wills felt confident of his status. From his cottage it was a five-minute stroll to the railway station where he met the visiting football teams that arrived to play against the Geelong Football Club. Since the end of 1865, he had played all his football with the Geelong club.

The Geelong football team played on an expanse of uneven ground that extended from the Argyle Hotel to the Wesleyan Church. The ground was wedged between the Methodists and a public house and was a common pathway for carriages of all kinds. Sheep happily grazed upon it. During the winter, the walking path that ringed the paddock served commendably as the boundary line. Players who fell on the path during a game, for years afterwards recalled its hardness.

Before each match the players of both teams met at the Argyle Hotel for a luncheon, and at points in the game returned to the hotel for 'refreshments'. Mr O'Brien, the generous host of the Argyle Hotel, took upon himself the task of supplying footballers with liberal quantities of champagne, beer, and various colonial and European wines. It was in the hotel that the players changed from their civilian clothes into their football uniforms. The eyes of an admiring small boy watched the players enter and emerge from O'Brien's Hotel, just one of the crowd of spectators who waited for Tom Wills. The image stayed with this boy and over thirty years later he recalled the ageing captain leading his players onto the field.

By 1874 Tom rarely travelled away from Geelong to play football. On Tuesday and Thursday evenings, Tom walked to the Argyle ground to football practice, his presence drawing a larger than normal collection of footballers to the field. In Geelong he was simply called Mr Wills, a formal title that seemed incongruous with the crude and combative sport of football.

Tom played with and against schoolboys from Geelong College and Geelong Grammar. One of the boys from the Grammar school wrote of the early years of football in Geelong:

> Slinging, viz., catching by the neck . . . and throwing to the ground was tolerated . . . jumping on a man's back . . . pushing from behind, or indeed from anywhere . . . was not prohibited . . . Seldom more than two or three free kicks were given during the course of the game, only the most flagrant breaches of the rules, such as tripping, catching hold of a player when he had not the ball, or having possession was . . . Marks were nearly all made against the breast, marking with the hands above the head being seldom tried.

Tom played in numerous positions. At Rugby School he had played as a forward, as a back (also called a 'flier' or 'dodger'), and also as a goal kicker. His early years of football in Melbourne suggested that he followed the ball as captain, and in Geelong he was typically in the ruck, a position that revolved around the centre of the ground where the player moved in a smallish radius, though he was occasionally recorded as kicking a goal.

Tom's views on football were sought after in Geelong. Never shy about self-promotion, Tom let everyone know: 'This manly game was first introduced into the Colony by the writer,

(T.W. Wills) A.D. 1857.' The earliest rules that he, Thompson, Hammersley and Smith devised were, Tom felt, superior to the present laws of the game and he remained interested in the development of the rules. When Tom spoke on the game of football, provincial Geelong listened:

> To prevent accidents, or rather to lessen the chances of them, the writer would suggest that all pushing from behind be abolished, and in no case shall a player run further with the ball in hand than is necessary to obtain a kick . . . this would put a stop to all dodging, and would make the game more scientific, as the captains would have to place their men so as to make them play more to each other. Next to Cricket, it is perhaps the best sport out, being far less dangerous than hunting . . . moreover it requires no severe training, such as boating and pedestrianism does.

As captain of the Geelong team, he had shaped the playing of football over the previous decade. Several years earlier, in the darkest days of winter, Tom had met his team of Geelong footballers and boarded the train to Ballarat. Horace, down from Cullin-la-Ringo, travelled with the team. The competition with Ballarat was sharp. The mob at Ballarat was a nasty bunch. Brawling between spectators and players was not unheard of during football matches in the colony and police were frequently requested to prevent spectators assaulting players. The larrikins were thick in the Ballarat crowd. It was no different in Geelong or Melbourne. Crowds and players in Geelong had previously threatened Tom during his career so he could have expected little better in Ballarat.

It was cold on Wynne's Paddock, the Ballarat ground named after the obliging publican who offered players lunch and drinks. There was nothing like a cold Ballarat day anywhere in the colony of Victoria – reddened and numbed fingers and a ball soaked and burdened by the mud of the paddock. The wind screamed down the middle of the ground when Tom flipped the coin to start the match. He won the toss and the Geelong supporters egged Tom to kick with the wind; he did so taking each advantage over Ballarat. Tom was an ageing footballer, but still the best tactician in the game.

The players assembled on either side of the centre-line prior to the place-kick, which started the match from the centre of the ground. The rain had been steady from morning till afternoon. Wynne's Paddock, a picture of climatic misery, had more puddles than grass and an icy wind skipped about its flanks. The game was bloody – ringbarked shins, bruised bodies and disabled players – the first half being little more than a heave-ho. No goals had been scored when the half-time break was called.

Early in the second half, the Ballarat team, kicking with the gale, was dominating the match. Then the Geelong team adopted a strategy that had not been seen before. A good captain, following the conventional tactics of the day, kept his players in set positions: back players remained in defence and forward players remained near the goals; but on this bleak and windy Ballarat day, Tom and all his Geelong teammates moved to the backline.

The Ballarat team, despite having the ball for most of the half, could not kick a goal because the Geelong players clogged up the goal area. And when the Geelong players grabbed the ball they immediately kicked it over the boundary line to waste time. The Ballarat supporters, regarding the Geelong tactics as unchivalrous, screamed and hissed insults at Tom and his team. As darkness drew in around Wynne's Paddock the game was called off, and at five o'clock, in near darkness, Tom and his players left the field. The knaves of Ballarat ringing the field, faces twisted in anger, booed and swore at the Geelong team. It was understood that Tom had not breached the rules, but his willingness to push his negative tactics beyond the expectations of the time bewildered, then enraged, the spectators. Tom had not changed in over twenty years – a few ugly men and women in the Ballarat mud were never going to intimidate him.

Washed and towelled, Tom and his team combed their bedraggled hair and cheered the publicans Mr and Mrs Wynne for their hospitality. Tom spoke at dinner with characteristic economy; the speeches and drinking were plentiful. Unsteadily, the drinkers and players moved towards the Ballarat train station, where the crowds, by now more good humoured, cheered and sang throaty choruses of 'Auld Lang Syne'. The Geelong team boarded the train, singing their bawdy and comic songs, and journeyed back home, leaving the Ballarat team thinking about the innovative football tactics used that day.

Tom had last captained the Geelong Football Club in 1873. The following winter, his name was seen only occasionally in the player lists for the Geelong club and he played his last game in 1874. He returned to umpiring football, usually as a central umpire but occasionally as a goal umpire. In the 1870s, a central umpire might remain in his civilian clothes if he wished and moved only within a small radius in the centre of the ground, taking care not to overly exert himself. A firm control and an indifference to the insults of players and spectators were indispensable.

During 1874 Tom was re-elected vice president of the Geelong Football Club, a position he had first held the previous year. He involved himself conscientiously with match committees, fundraising committees, and, despite his chronic indebtedness, started donating money and trophies for football competitions. Sometimes these were trophies for winning teams; others were presented to individual players who won football kicking contests.

The local Geelong newspapers respected and often protected Tom, even at this late stage of his football career. On one occasion, the *Geelong Advertiser* chose not to publish a letter from Tom because they feared it would embarrass him. At times he reported on football and cricket matches for the *Geelong*

Advertiser. Letter writing was no longer the compulsion it once was, but a letter from Tom was always worth reading. It took a little more than it once did to motivate him to write a letter; perhaps maturity had taken the edge off his impetuosity or perhaps he felt there was little to rail against in Geelong. But he still spoke about football – at the Argyle Hotel in 1875, Tom Wills, vice president of the Geelong Football Club, lectured 'at some length' on the origin of football in the colony, what he called 'the king of games'. He never relinquished the idea that it was he and he alone who had brought the new game of football to the colony.

Tom continued umpiring football and serving on committees. In the first big game of 1875, Tom's brothers Cedric and Horace came down from Cullin-la-Ringo to play. Towards the end of the 1875 football season, in a match umpired by Tom, spectators roared as Satchwell, a Geelong player, received a free kick in front of goal. Instead of trying to kick a goal, Satchwell was allowed by Tom to hand the ball to Hall, the best goal kicker in the Geelong team, to take the shot. That was unexpected. In the Victorian code, the player who received a free kick in front of goal took the kick for goal; another player was not allowed to take it. At Rugby School the situation was different – the best kicker was always called upon to kick for goal. Tom's Rugby days continued to influence him. There were protests but the Geelong press defended Tom:

> The case in dispute, was where Satchwell was held, and Mr Wills allowed Hall to kick the ball, thereby securing a goal. Most decidedly the central umpire was correct, on the grounds that as an injustice had been done to the Geelong team the captain had a perfect right, as a free was allowed, to give it to the best kicker in the team. The decision of Mr. Wills should have been sufficient, as, being an old Rugby captain, he is perfectly well aware of the laws of football.

The memory of Tom as a Rugby schoolboy had not faded.

•

Money preoccupied Tom's mind. Adelaide, searching for a professional, had consulted James Lillywhite, a cousin of Tom's old coach John. Lillywhite said that in England 'good men can earn from 12 pounds to 20 pounds per week'. Tom wrote to the Adelaide cricketers, as he had done for the past few years, applying for a professional position for the 1874–75 summer. The going pay rate was 3 pounds per week. He still had the skills to be chosen but was overlooked for an obscure professional from Ballarat.

Tom had not been considered for the Victorian intercolonial team since called for throwing in 1872. The year after Tom was called, the Victorians, in a close match, defeated New South Wales. Tom's name, once indispensable, no longer appeared in press reports when possible Victorian teams were discussed. As 1874 drew to a close, he wrote to his friend William Handfield, still honorary secretary at the Melbourne Cricket Club, to ask a favour. Tom offered to umpire the next intercolonial match. It would pay a little, not a lot, but each pound was of value to him. William Handfield was unable to bring Tom good news:

My dear Sir
Your letter of the 7th inst. offering your services as umpire in the forthcoming match between New South Wales & Victoria has been this day laid before the Committee of the Melbourne Cricket Club & I am directed to reply that the Committee have left the selection of the umpire in the hands of the Intercolonial Match Committee.

Tom's letter was either lost, ignored or shuttled amongst committees of the Melbourne Cricket Club as nothing further was heard or recorded of Tom's application. If Tom had been granted the chance to umpire he would have done so alongside the New South Wales umpire: native-born Edmund Barton, a young Sydney barrister and mediocre cricketer who would become Australia's first Prime Minister. New South Wales easily won that match, as they did the following match in March 1875. All the while Tom remained tethered to Geelong, playing for the Corio Cricket Club as their professional. Though Tom was celebrated in Geelong, he seemed discontented with the smallness of the town and kept his eyes fastened on Melbourne, looking for any opportunity that would allow him to return.

In another attempt to earn money, Tom wrote *The Australian Cricketers' Guide for 1874–5*. Geelong was proud of his guide, but in the Melbourne press there was mild derision. They considered it presumptuous of Tom to write a cricketing guide from distant Geelong as he could not have witnessed the 'major matches', which naturally took place only in Melbourne. Tom despatched letters to Adelaide, Melbourne and the country towns advertising his guide; perhaps, at best, he might have made a few pounds.

In the winter of 1875, the Melbourne Cricket Club admitted its lack of talent for the coming summer. It wanted skilled professional bowlers who could bowl, unwearied, throughout the day, and it set about finding them in Australia and England. A letter was sent to the Marylebone Cricket Club in London. Marylebone responded but they were less interested in the Melbourne Cricket Club than the whereabouts of the Aboriginal cricketers 'Mullagh' and 'Cuzens'.

Marylebone asked one further favour from Handfield: to advertise on their behalf in the colonial papers for cricketers to send in their sporting biographies to the Melbourne Cricket Club, which would then be passed on to Marylebone. Only one person in the colony responded to the advertisement: 'The only answer I have received as yet is from T.W. Wills who learnt his cricket at Rugby, and was for many seasons the champion here both with bat and ball – His schedule is enclosed.' Though quarantined in Geelong, Tom's insistent voice was like a distant piccolo, whose thin spare notes never allowed the Melbourne Cricket Club to entirely rest at ease.

It had not been a financial success but the publication *The Australian Cricketers' Guide* placed Tom back before the Melbourne public. In the guide, he pontificated on cricket – an older Tom was no less dissatisfied with the torpor of Victorian cricketers than he had been twenty years earlier. The timing was perfect: Tom's rise in prominence met with the declining fortunes of the Victorian cricket team. To Tom it was hardly a coincidence. His task was to convince the Victorian public and selectors that the best man for the job of captain was languishing in Geelong. The answer he was more than happy to tell the colony was simple: a new captain for the Victorian team was needed. Not some raw, inexperienced, passive captain more concerned about his appearance than being effective, but a leader who would not lose his nerve; who knew what was required. Though Tom did not quite state his own name, no one reading his words could mistake its intent – what Victoria needed was Tom Wills.

Tom made the decision to return to the city of Melbourne and play for Richmond; it seemed a calculated decision to place himself before the Victorian selectors. In late October 1875 he left Geelong to play for and captain the Richmond cricket team. No one took it too seriously until Tom took 5 wickets against the East Melbourne Cricket Club, then voices stirred, raising the remote possibility of Tom's return to the Victorian team after three years' absence.

Tom's manoeuvres had placed him on a list of twenty-four players under consideration for the intercolonial match at the end of 1875. But when the Victorian team was selected, Tom's name was not included. He probably smiled with perverse satisfaction as Victoria lost by an innings and were booed by the Victorian spectators from the MCG. A further intercolonial match was planned for late February in two months' time in Sydney. Tom saw his opportunity.

Before the next intercolonial match, a benefit was held for Thomas Wray, an ailing amateur of the MCC. He had taken

over the position of honorary secretary of the MCC when Tom
was dismissed in 1858. Wray was well liked but was a cricketer
of moderate skills. The benefit was a chance for Tom to show
himself again before the public and for the selectors to redress
what he regarded as their negligence in not selecting him for
the last intercolonial match. Tom captained an older group of
cricketers who had played for Victoria prior to 1865 against a
team of more recent players. The young Victorian team was
captained by Louis Goldsmith – articulate, a barrister and an
all-round cricketer – the type of ideal gentleman Horatio might
have had in mind when he planned Tom's future.

Tom was immediately embroiled in an argument. Goldsmith
was two men short of a complete team, and Tom refused them
permission to have substitute fieldsmen. This was partly due
to Tom's blunt competitiveness, but also due to an earlier
misunderstanding with Goldsmith, in which Tom felt his team
had been slighted. It was poor judgement by Tom to engage
in the dispute. To gain selection into the Victorian team he
simply needed to show a little political awareness. Instead
his uncontrolled competitiveness and inability to tolerate an
opponent's barbs, real or imagined, meant he behaved poorly,
like a bully. His obstinate manner courted little admiration.
Goldsmith refused to complete the match because of Tom's
behaviour.

As a final preparation for the New South Wales match the
Victorians played an eighteen-man team in Adelaide. Tom
expected to go to Adelaide with the Victorian team but fell
ill in early January. His doctor 'pronounced his illness to be
an attack of the epidemic' of scarlet fever. Around the colony
mothers boiled water for their children, cabs and omnibuses
were disinfected, and belladonna, a poisonous plant and physician's panacea, was prescribed, along with broths. The news of
Tom's illness was reported in the press, stating that he remained
in bed for ten days. When there were suggestions that he was
not suffering from scarlet fever, Tom, who it seemed could be

antagonised and rise with indignation even in illness, wrote a
letter to a friend and attached his doctor's report. Tom's letter
was quoted in *The Australasian* newspaper:

> I caught the fever in the M.C.C. pavilion, from Smith
> (Jack, the umpire). He had his house full of it during the
> Intercolonial and the New and Old Intercolonial Champions'
> Matches. Suppose I had a family, what a mess there would
> have been. I had it worse, because I caught cold with it. So
> you will see I shall be unable to do Adelaide, but will be
> fit for Sydney.

Tom in one swipe blamed the MCC and an umpire for his
illness and reassured the colony that he would be fit for Sydney.

In late January the team was picked; Tom was the last man
selected. The match committee was deluded into thinking that
a mummified Wills, with his vain promises, could succeed. The
Melbourne newspapers responded:

> Why on earth the last name, that of Wills, appears in it.
> Of no use as a bat or field, and with a certainty of being
> no-balled for shying if he is put on, there is some sentimental
> notion afloat that as a captain he is peerless.

Louis Goldsmith immediately wrote to the selection committee
and resigned from the team.

But gradually opinions shifted and Tom's return was seen
as offering the colony hope – perhaps the first time in three
years – of a victory. Tom's past victories were warmly recalled
and a return to Victorian eminence was talked of. Facts were
overlooked and hope instilled. Not a bad thing sometimes.
The desperate hopes of the colony were concentrated on Tom.

It took little encouragement to inflate Tom's perception of
his abilities. Dreams are powerful things and Tom's dreams had
been transmitted to the colony. In a letter to a friend he wrote:
'Thursday night I dreamt that we had just won the match on
the Albert ground, and it's not the first time my dream has

come true.' Confidence was everywhere, except with those who believed Tom's selection was an error likely to lead to humiliation. But even those critics might have hoped that the spontaneous growth of expectation might herald a triumph. The anger of a disenchanted public had been replaced by adulation. The noise of expectation steadily rose, deafening his detractors; Tom was elected captain of the team.

On 25 February Tom Wills stepped onto the Albert Ground – a bald man, leading the Victorians. The German band played vigorously; Punch and Judy fought each other as entertainment in the stands; and the umpires walked out carrying umbrellas for shade.

As each wicket fell it was telegraphed to Melbourne; clumps of colonists packed the venues where the results came through, waiting and hoping for the first Victorian win in three years. Tom had won games for the colony in the past when no one thought they could be won.

A young fast bowler for New South Wales, Fred Spofforth, bowled a ball that broke a bat and another that broke a stump. He was criticised for using an overly long run. A glimpse of the future was overwhelming some; the world of Tom Wills seemed old and distant. Tom was the last batsman in the Victorian line up; he scored 0 and 4, and his bowling was worse. He did not bowl in the first innings and, in the second innings, with that universal lack of insight into one's own decline, he bowled more overs than any other Victorian player. At first he regressed to his gentle underhand balls of pre-Rugby School days, a sad anachronism; then, with no wickets falling, he bowled his medium-paced round arm. He still took no wickets. The crowd jeered him – his shuffle to the wicket was a parody of himself. The Victorians lost by 195 runs. Tom tacked slowly off the Albert Ground, without a backward glance. His pride, an indestructible ally of a lifetime, had rendered him blind.

NO ROOM AT THE INN

FEBRUARY 1876–MARCH 1878

The colony had lied to itself before the Sydney match but after defeat took no responsibility for the result and its part in elevating Tom. The articles and letters that condemned Tom might also have been directed towards the journalists and selectors who were seduced by the nostalgia and fed Tom's fantasy. The more bitter the anger towards Tom, the less responsibility anyone else needed to take. In the forgetful eyes of the colony, Tom Wills alone had disgraced them. On 6 March Tom wrote a letter defending himself:

> As captain of the team . . . it can be fully proved that I strove my utmost to bring about a win for the colony that did me the honour to select me . . . And, as far as generalship was concerned, there is not a man in the colony who could have done better, if as well . . . the only error was that I kept on a little too long, and in that particular I could scarce help myself, as most of the bowlers objected to that particular end . . . Surely, sir, when the crack batsmen all get out for next to nothing, it is not the captain that the blame should be attached to.

Tom had little contact with his family when he returned to Geelong; indeed, family letters no longer mentioned Tom and

Sarah. The main flow of correspondence was between Horace and Cedric on Cullin-la-Ringo and their mother at Belle Vue. Horace wrote to Elizabeth:

> I found out the other day that an old blackfellow named Bobby who was shot about four years ago by the troopers for killing a cow of Schofields, was the last of Pa's murderers that was alive, he and four others killed Pa. The particular man had a shrivelled leg we used always [to] think him such a poor harmless old wretch & were sorry when he was shot. If I had only known it before I should have saved the troopers the trouble. The Blacks say they went into the camp & spoke to the white fellows & then they got close to them & sprang onto them & held them while others hit them.

Tom returned to his Geelong routine, which for the past nine months had included weekly meetings of the Geelong Australian Natives' Association (ANA). The ANA was a Friendly Society, formed in Melbourne in 1871, to promote the cause of Australian-born citizens. Members of the ANA donated regular sums of money into a common pool, from which money could be drawn to assist Australian-born colonials who through illness, or other circumstances, were in financial distress. In 1875 at the Black Bull Hotel in Geelong, Tom, sitting alongside Graham Berry, future premier of Victoria, had moved that a Geelong branch of the ANA be created. Tom diligently attended the meetings and made three donations – four, three and ten shillings – over one year. The Geelong branch of this society held its last meeting in July 1876 at the local fire brigade: 'Mr T W Wills, vice president' chaired the last recorded meeting. The reasons for the branch's demise were unstated.

Tom and Sarah moved from Upper Skene Street and bought a 'cottage' of five rooms with garden, in Malop Street East, Geelong. Tom had recently sold at least one block of land in Geelong and it became clear that, despite his income from cricket and the family estate, he was continually in debt. He did not give reasons for his debts but the story had not really changed for over twenty years.

By the late 1870s Tom's throwing had become a private joke even amongst his most ardent Geelong supporters. The parochialism of the town had protected him over the past five years, allowing him to bowl despite a tacit acknowledgement of his throwing. In this provincial environment, away from the metropolis of Melbourne, he was fawned over and remained a sporting idol. The Melbourne press had, for the most part, grown tired of the throwing issue with Wills and, when raised, it was in the form of gentle condescension towards the balding middle-aged man in Geelong. Geelong was singled out as having indulged throwing, which was not tolerated elsewhere. The smug Melbourne press even coined a neologism for throwing the cricket ball, inspired by Tom Wills – a 'Geelonger'. Till the end of his life, Wills was remembered for his 'shying', but with his faster balls no longer a danger to flesh or batting average, he was rarely called for throwing. Although Tom's bowling speed had slowed, and his occasional throwing was less effective, he remained a crafty bowler who, in Geelong, still took wickets.

In September 1876, at the Annual General Meeting of the Corio Cricket Club, Tom received a cricket ball for the club's best bowling average for the past season. He was not, for the first time in several years, elected to an office-bearing position. From this point he played only intermittently with the Corio Cricket Club. As his cricket abilities declined with age, he captained the Breakwater Cricket Club, a lower standard of competition, as well as moving amongst other clubs in the Geelong area. Tom's name was noted with Corio, Breakwater and Kardinia Park cricket clubs. Sometimes he was supposed to play in two different teams on the one day – leaving one club disappointed and angry when he did not arrive.

The recently arrived English cricket team, led by James Lillywhite, travelled from Melbourne to play the Corio Cricket Club in January 1877. Tom Wills' absence from the Geelong team confirmed his decline. Largely relegated to the Breakwater Cricket Club, even at this low level Tom managed to find strife. In January 1877 he was no-balled for throwing – at last Geelong had decided that perhaps he threw the ball after all. It was decreed at a meeting of the Junior Challenge Cup Committee to 'exclude all past or present professional cricketers from Junior Cup matches. This was done with a view to prevent Mr. Wills playing with the Breakwater Eleven.' Tom naturally ignored this exclusion.

In March 1877 a combined Victorian and New South Wales team played the visiting English team at the Melbourne Cricket Ground. That same month James Thompson, one of the co-writers of the first rules of Melbourne football and a fellow colonial cricketer, gave a lecture on cricket to a packed house at the Melbourne Athenaeum. Thompson was dead within three months. Alcohol and bronchopneumonia saw him off at forty-eight.

Tom, nearing forty-two, was willing to play for anyone. Then having seemingly ended his contact with the Corio Cricket Club, he played with them against the 'Bohemians' – a travelling circus of wealthy amateur cricketers – and took 4 wickets. Picked for Breakwater the following week he did not turn up; picked for Corio against Ballarat on 10 March he did not turn up. This was the pattern of his life. After Ballarat won, the *Geelong Advertiser* stated: 'We think that the local players should make every effort to attend matches in which they are picked when the credit of the club is at stake.'

By April 1877 Tom's cosy relationship with the provincial press was gone. His throwing and refusal to abide by the rules of the junior cricket competition produced a sarcastic response in the local press. In April, Tom's team, Breakwater, played the Argyle team for the Junior Challenge Cup. It was the third time the teams had met:

Before the game commenced the Cup-holders lodged a protest against Wills playing with the Breakwater eleven, the cup rules having a proviso to the effect that no cricketer who is, or has been, a professional shall be allowed to play in Junior Cup matches. The Breakwater eleven refused to give way, and the Argyle determined to go on with the game. The action of the Breakwater Club seems inexplicable in the face of the rule referred to, which was carried into law when their representative, and the whole of the delegates for the other junior clubs in town, were present. However, as far as the game has gone, the presence of the gentleman in dispute in the Breakwater team has made very little difference to them.

Wills was captain of the Breakwater team; every aspect of his play was publicly ridiculed and when the match continued the following week Tom was absent. His cricket had become a series of petty disputes in petty games and erratic snatches of cricket of ever-deteriorating standards. He earned small amounts of money wherever he could.

In May 1877 the Victorian Football Association was formed. The Geelong Football Club appointed Tom as one its three club delegates to meet with delegates from other clubs in Melbourne to review the rules of Victorian football. The following week, for reasons unstated, Tom was dropped from the Geelong trio of delegates.

Despite his declining health and ageing body, and his deteriorating sporting life, Tom remained a man with an optimistic, if unrealistic, view of his own future. But he knew that preparations were needed for mortality and with the mind of a man who gave the impression he did not fear it, prepared himself for its inevitability. Tom travelled to Melbourne and visited the legal office of J.R. Hornby in Collins Street to make out his will. In a creased one-page document he described himself, not as the professional cricketer he was, but as a gentleman. Tom's money from the family estate had been invested for him in the names of William Ducker and his brother Cedric, and he received a regular payment from the interest on this money. This interest, if he died, was to be passed on to Sarah Theresa Barbor, whom he referred to as 'my housekeeper' in his will. The principal of 1550 pounds, on the death of Sarah, would remain with Ducker and Cedric. 'All the rest and residue of my real and personal estate for her own sole and separate use and free from the control of <u>her present</u> or any future husband.' There was no religious sentiment in Tom's will and no family member was to receive any of his possessions. Tom signed his will on 22 February 'in the year of our Lord one thousand eight hundred and seventy seven'.

In the early 1870s Sarah was still referred to in family letters as Tom's wife but in the middle and late 1870s her name, along with Tom's, no longer appears in surviving correspondence. Perhaps Elizabeth had become aware that Tom and Sarah were indeed unmarried, something that would have disturbed her religious propriety. When Tom made his will, he appointed Cedric as one of the trustees. If he hadn't already known, Cedric must have realised that the 'housekeeper' was his brother's de facto. It is likely that a combination of Tom's debts and his de facto relationship with Sarah gradually alienated his mother. And distance meant that he saw little of his brothers and cousin Colden.

Tom made plans to leave Geelong and return to Melbourne. With only a dwindling income from cricket and regular payments from the family estate, he was increasingly in need of money to pay creditors. Tom, although comfortable for years in Geelong, was never entirely satisfied with his position. So when the MCC advertised for a secretary at 250 pounds per annum, Tom promptly responded, writing to William Handfield at the Club:

> Seeing by advertisement that applications are to be sent in to you for the Office of Secretary to the MCC I herewith apply for same. I am well up in the duties attached to the office and do not fear <u>work</u>, and I trust that the Committee

will give my application a favourable consideration, owing
to my many years devotion to Colonial cricket.

He then specifically asked Handfield to turn the letter over and
read his brief postscript. Tucked away from his letter, meant
only for Handfield, Tom wrote:

P.S. It is not often that old cricketers through cricket have
a chance of obtaining a billet and even then they are left
in the cold.
T.W.W.

Wills gave voice to a generation of exiled, lonely professional cricketers without shelter and money and, into the void,
questioned the obligation of clubs to their servants. Hammersley
in a reflective article in 1883 portrayed the difficult life of
another professional cricketer, Dick Coulstock, and in so doing
remembered Tom:

I remember this club [South Melbourne] and its ground
well, when its pavilion was a mere shed, in which old Dick
Coulstock lived as 'curator'; if, indeed, such a term could
be applied to the position he filled. He had a cow or two,
and used to sell milk to make both ends meet, for poor
Dick, I think, got very little salary. I often used to have a
chat with him. All alone, except with his big dog Sandy,
poor Coulstock passed the long winter nights there. He
used to complain to me of a pain in his chest at times,
'not much', he said, 'but a curious pain'. One day he was
having a ball or two, and made a sudden movement back
to escape being hit in the chest. The ball, however, did hit
him, and in a quarter of an hour from that time it was all
over with poor Coulstock. Dr. Duret was called in time
to see him and tell him there was no hope. I think Jack
Conway was present when he died; and, if I remember
right, Tom Wills also.

The advertisement for the paid secretarial position with the Melbourne Cricket Club drew forth over fifty responses from around the globe. There were testimonials from loud politicians; earnest theologians; and George Parr, captain of the unbeaten English XI from 1864. Thirty-two applications for the position of paid secretary were read before the MCC selection committee. The letters and their accompanying testimonies remained in the MCC coffers, largely unmentioned in the minutes. Tom Wills did not succeed in his application to return as secretary of the MCC. Curtis Reid, a giant man with a big, thick beard, whom Tom had once helped into the Victorian cricket team, was appointed to the position.

Minute books squeezed emotion dry, leaving the most slender of communications. But there was a sliver there, that within the pavilion there were those who were interested in Tom, perhaps loved him. Out of all the applications, it was Tom's letter that was highlighted when the committee met to discuss the applicants. But he probably never had a chance. No known written response to Tom's application exists.

Tom remained in Geelong, sometimes playing in a match he had been named in but he was just as likely not to appear on the day. On 8 September 1877, he was elected president of the Breakwater Cricket Club and at its Annual General Meeting was one of several members who contributed one pound each to the club's treasury. Two weeks later he was elected as a life member of the club. That evening Tom chaired the meeting at the Eureka Hotel when it was 'resolved that the Club should play its opening match next Saturday, at Richmond Place, below the Elephant and Castle Hotel'. Tom was captain, president and life member and presented the Breakwater Cricket Club with a trophy valued at 2 pounds 10 shillings.

On Thursday evening, 22 November 1877, Tom drove a single-seated buggy along the Queenscliff Road. He had come from the Strawberry Gardens at Wallington and had left Sarah at another local hotel, Coleman's. The Queenscliff

Road was the main route from the town of Geelong to the
seaside settlement of Queenscliff. As darkness fell, Tom's buggy
collided with another buggy drawn from the opposite direction.
His horse was thrown down, cutting its knees; the shaft and
harness, which secured the beast to the buggy, snapped and the
buggy's hood, splash-boards and shafts were splintered and
severely damaged. Tom was thrown to the ground and lay
unconscious on the Queenscliff Road. The report of the accident
was circumspect; no blame was attributed, but Tom having just
left a hotel suggests that he had probably been drinking.

In early 1878, the Supreme Court, under a Writ of Summons,
was after Tom to repay one debt of 64 pounds 5 shillings plus
the cost of legal proceedings. There was a string of other debts,
and angry creditors harassed Tom, demanding their money.

In February, middle-aged Tom was back living in Melbourne.
Cricket was evolving and an Australian cricket team, recently
formed, was preparing to leave for England. On 18 March 1878
the Australian team was in Geelong to play the local Geelong
XXII. Tom had been picked as part of the local team but he
never arrived to play. Once feted and idolised, Tom left Geelong
with no grace and no tribute to his time there. Over these
few months his name sometimes appeared in a cricket match
in Geelong, sometimes Melbourne. Tom Wills did not leave
Geelong at a single moment; rather, he left a piece at a time.

THE EMERALD HILL

MARCH 1878–FEBRUARY 1879

The world was a muddle to Tom. The greatest cricketer of his generation and the man who, more than any other, had influenced the start of the new game of Melbourne football, was broke and on the run. His genius with bat and ball offered him little solace beyond the playing field. Somehow he found his way to the Melbourne suburb of Emerald Hill.

Emerald Hill was a gentle rise of land just south of Melbourne's Yarra River. Wharves and the concerns of ship merchants lined the banks of the Yarra River. The low-lying lands next to the river in Emerald Hill were chronically swamped as water spilled from the Yarra, forming cesspits and stagnant pools. The foul air that rose from these dank pools shrouded Emerald Hill with an aroma that belied its glittering name. It would be another five years before Emerald Hill would become known as South Melbourne.

Back lanes threaded their way behind residences and shops; butchers were everywhere and dairies, often just a single cow, ensured a regular supply of milk. The streets were treeless – it was raw, cleared and semi-industrial, with stray dogs sniffing at the wheels of the cabmen's buggies. The land had been stripped of trees to make way for buildings, and in 1878 workmen and builders were seen all over the suburb.

Emerald Hill was largely working class but there were entrepreneurial men and women who lived in the area's elevated heart – its broad clean streets suggestive of the gentry and professional classes. The heart was St Vincent's Place, a dress circle address modelled on an English square, its fenced parkland ringed by gracious residences. It was near here that Tom and Sarah now lived, probably boarding at 28 Park Street West, a six-bedroom brick residence only two minutes from William Hammersley. They could have walked to the town of Melbourne but everything they needed was within a few minutes' stroll.

Children, lost and neglected, were directed to Emerald Hill. In Park Street the bluestone Protestant Melbourne Orphanage harboured its hundreds of boys and girls. The orphanage sat upon the crown of Emerald Hill, on 10½ acres, commanding views in all directions; its Tudor towers, which brought Emerald Hill closer to the heavens, drew all eyes towards it. On its expansive grounds, the hundreds of waifs played football, cricket and athletics, and an assortment of games that children will contrive amongst themselves on the school ground.

Two years before Tom arrived, over 300 children of the Protestant orphanage lined up for a photograph in front of the bluestone – toddlers to adolescents, pale faces set against the dark of the stone. Each line of faces was like a row of marbles, forty to a line and eight lines high, stretching into the distance until nothing could be seen but the small pale circles that represented a child's face. In Tom's first months in Emerald Hill those children were removed to Brighton, and the Protestant Orphan Asylum in his street gave way to a multitude of labourers and their tools as construction work began on the new town hall.

Tom had lived his life next to cricket and football grounds. From Park Street it was an easy walk to the South Melbourne Cricket Ground where he played his first game of cricket with that club on 19 February 1878. Tom played five matches with the South Melbourne Cricket Club during the early months of 1878. He was no longer a prominent player and it was unlikely that he earned money. A bits-and-pieces player, he batted last and rarely took a wicket. When he did bowl, it was usually his slow balls. If the best cricketers in the area were available Tom would not make it into the team's first XI; he played when others were absent or when a second XI was chosen. If he chucked, no one cared. Not that he was mocked; indeed, he was occasionally praised and his celebrated past as the finest player of his era was remembered. But when the season was reviewed by the club, Tom's name was absent. The secretary of the South Melbourne Cricket Club, and previously its captain, Buck Wheatley recalled in his memoirs:

> I consulted the football committee and asked them if they would agree to play on the SMCC ground provided they received half the profits. They willingly agreed. The cricket club committee objected at first, but I brought expert evidence to prove that the turf on the ground would not be damaged. My old friend Tommy Wills, once captain of Rugby School, informed the committee that football was always played on the great English public school cricket grounds during the winter and top dressed early in the spring. When football was finished with, cricket was then played. The wickets played just the same – in fact, even better – according to Mr. Wills' statement.

Tom had been familiar with this problem of playing the two sports on one ground since his first days at Rugby, knowledge he had gained from John Lillywhite. Football was allowed on the South Melbourne ground and the cricket club flourished. South Melbourne was not the only club to benefit from allowing football upon its cricket ground; Geelong did the same and the money flowed.

Tom Wills was not moribund in Emerald Hill, no matter how many waving hands chased him from Geelong demanding money, and in the months of June, July and August he umpired in the newly formed Victorian Football Association. In the first of

these matches Tom was the central umpire when Carlton played
Albert Park at the South Melbourne Cricket Ground before
1000 spectators. When the match was stopped due to darkness,
Carlton led 3 goals to 1. Umpiring was not easy and after the
match Tom was criticised in the Melbourne press. In response,
Tom wrote what was to be his last public letter. Less florid
than the letters of his youth, and with no classical allusions, it
nonetheless had the hallmarks of oversensitivity and irritability.
Two weeks later he umpired again on the South Melbourne
ground. His brother Egbert was playing for Melbourne that
day and a miserable day it was. A constant drizzle, a muddy
surface, and a wind that blew hard for the 1000 adults and about
500 boys who had wormed their way into the ground – not
necessarily through paying the standard 6 pence admission fee.

In Geelong, the Geelong Football Club defeated the Barwon
Football Club but the match was more notable for the brawling
between spectators and the intervention of the local police
to protect the Geelong team: 'The fighting continued in the
evening when they attacked their Geelong opponents on the
streets.' The following week the championship for the 1878
Victorian Football Association was decided; Geelong defeated
Melbourne. It had been the first winter in over a decade that
the name of Tom Wills had not been a part of the Geelong
Football Club.

Tom held no positions of power at the South Melbourne
Cricket Club. When team lists appeared in the local Emerald
Hill newspapers his name sometimes appeared. His surname
wandered in and out of the brief cricket reports that were tucked
into inconspicuous corners of the newspaper. Only occasionally
were his initials T.W. used for identification. There was once
a time when the name of Thomas Wentworth Wills, Mr T.W.
Wills or Tommy Wills, was impossible to miss, embossed and
emblazoned as the lead on every sporting article in the colony;
now it was uncertain to whom the papers referred. Stripped of
his Christian name he was simply called 'Wills'. At the Annual

General Meeting of the South Melbourne Cricket Club in September 1878, Tom was not mentioned.

On 19 October he travelled to Geelong with the South Melbourne cricket team, a troupe fashioned and welded together under a name that signified unity but was a rickety mix of part-time players. Tom captained the team, scoring 13 runs and taking 3 wickets – they lost. The presence of Tom Wills no longer distorted a game or its reporting, and only older readers appreciated his past victories.

Tom made one last overture to the Melbourne Cricket Club. In October 1878 he sought a position as an MCC ground bowler. A ground bowler was typically a player beyond his peak who provided regular bowling practice for the members. Years earlier Tom would have seen this as a menial position. On 2 October, the secretary Curtis Reid wrote: 'I am instructed by the Committee of this club to inform you that the Bowlers employed on the ground last season have been reappointed and that no addition to their number is considered at present necessary.' But it was decided not to send this letter of rejection and Tom's application was reconsidered at two further meetings. That was highly unusual, considering the lowly position Tom sought. Only after those further considerations was a letter of rejection sent to Tom, on 15 October: 'I am instructed by the MCC committee to inform you that arrangements have been made with reference to bowlers required for the coming season. Under these circumstances your application cannot at present be entertained.' The committee remained mute on the reasons for its decision. Whether it was from a generosity of spirit, pity or genuine regard for his fading skills, the committee minutes did not reveal why Tom was considered several times before his rejection. The last stream of paltry income from cricket was finally asphyxiated.

Tom had not paid the debts he owed, despite repeated warnings and legal directives to do so. In the Geelong County Court in April 1878, Tom was found to owe Mr James Close 13 pounds

1 shilling nine pence. He did not pay and was pursued. By July
the case was in the Supreme Court and Tom was sued by Mr
Close; then a Mary Johnson tracked Tom throughout 1878 for
money he owed her. On 21 November the Sheriff entered 28
Park Street West and, under instruction from the Supreme
Court, confiscated Tom's 'goods and chattels'. The *Geelong
Advertiser* published Tom's name as the subject of a Supreme
Court action. The money to pay Tom's debts would have to
come from selling whatever property and personal estate he
still had in Geelong.

Tom owned several blocks of land in Geelong which he
began selling. Most were sold in early 1878 to try to clear his
debt. When he signed these papers to sell his property, one
of his signatures was notable for its shaky script, evidence
of a tremulous hand. William Ducker helped Tom manage
the sales. Tom was burning his father's and uncle's financial
legacy that had been nurtured by family and friends such as
William Ducker, but he had no other choice. All the property
and buildings he owned in Geelong had to be sold to pay off
those who hounded him. While Tom ran from his past, the
Australian cricket team returned in November 1878 from the
first representative tour of England to a crowd at Circular Quay,
Sydney, estimated at 20,000.

Tom and Sarah moved into 92 Napier Street from nearby
Park Street, and rented a wooden cottage with six rooms on a
large block of land: certainly not one of the smaller houses of
one or two rooms. Despite the recent confiscation of goods to
pay debts, for the purposes of the local Emerald Hill council
Tom still called himself a 'Gentleman' and not 'a cricketer'.
Perhaps by now he was neither.

A temperance hall stood in Napier Street, a moral counterpoint of sorts, not that Tom's mind would have been much
occupied by thoughts of temperance. Also on Tom's street
stood the Roman Catholic Orphanage, which offered care
in the name of St Vincent de Paul. And all around were the

many hotels of Emerald Hill, which had multiplied six-fold in less than twenty years. From his house he could walk to where Napier intersected with Moray Street and look down that street to see the South Melbourne Cricket Ground.

In the summer of 1878–79, the name of Tom Wills was hard to find in local newspaper cricket reports. The South Melbourne Cricket Club sent a second XI to the Kew Asylum in January to play the staff and perhaps an inmate or two; Tom may have played with this South Melbourne team. The name Wills appeared in another, even less significant, team: the Albert Park second XI. It could also have been Tom.

In February 1879, Sydney spectators behaved just as Melburnians expected – they rioted when the Englishman Lord Harris took his team to Sydney. Unamurriman, who nine years earlier Tom had declared would die, was playing against the Englishmen. Unamurriman offered an ageing grace, refinement and the best set of flexible wrists in the team. In February Tom captained a poor-quality South Melbourne team to play Geelong. He took 5 wickets. Then Tom just disappeared from Emerald Hill.

AN ISLAND IN THE SUN

FEBRUARY 1879–MARCH 1880

Tom and Sarah drifted to the shire of Heidelberg, eight miles
east-north-east from Melbourne, and rented a house in Jika
Street. Heidelberg, the place 'near Melbourne' as Tom so vaguely
yet accurately described it, had been prosperous in the 1850s,
but now lay neglected. Its population of just over 500 had not
grown for nearly thirty years. Melburnians, when they thought
of it, remarked upon its rolling hills covered with market gardens
and vineyards. Tom did not plan to stay long. A local girl helped
about the house; fowls, birds and dogs ran about the backyard.

Jika Street was short: a handful of cottages on one side and
a Presbyterian chapel and cheese factory at the street's end.
Opposite their house stood the police station and lock-up, in
a shallow depression surrounded by thickets and greenery, and
beyond this was the Old England Hotel on Buckland Street.
A bend of the Yarra River wound next to Jika Street. From
their backyard Tom and Sarah would have seen the square
brick tower of St John's Anglican Church looking down upon
them, only 50 yards away. Past the tower of St John's was the
Heidelberg Cricket Ground and racecourse.

The coach from Melbourne stopped at the Old England
Hotel each day. As it approached the hotel along the Heidelberg

Road it came to a slight rise from where the village could be seen. The passengers could observe the two-storeyed hotel with its ornate balconies, the hotel's stable and its orchard; to the right of the hotel, beyond the thickets and police building, were the dwellings of Jika Street – just a one-minute stroll from the Old England Hotel. Tom did not need to stray far to satisfy his desires.

The only doctor in the hamlet was the English surgeon John Bleeck, who cared for his patients with his assistant Robert Heward, a former grape grower. Bleeck lived in 'Brockley', one of the more stately residences just around the corner from Jika Street. Tom knew Bleeck; he had cared for the Aboriginal cricketer Bilvayarrimin back in February 1867. Tom also knew D.C. Macarthur, another Heidelberg resident and former president of the Melbourne Cricket Club.

By 1879 Tom rarely heard from his family, and he did not write often. Elizabeth had left Belle Vue and was living in the town of Geelong. His brothers were scattered: Cedric and Horace on Cullin-la-Ringo Station, Egbert at the Bank of Victoria in Melbourne. Egbert and Horace were Melbourne Cricket Club members. Emily and Colden still lived in Kew.

His brothers on the station did not know where to find Tom. Cedric, one of the trustees of Tom's will, wrote from Cullin-la-Ringo to Colden Harrison, and affectionately asked: 'Do you ever hear anything of brother Tom & where he is living?' Over winter and spring, Harrison organised football games on the Melbourne Cricket Ground between footballers from an earlier time and current footballers. Harrison wrote to Cedric, inviting him to participate. Cedric declined; his family was too large to travel. Harrison captained one team and William Hammersley umpired. Whether Tom was invited is unknown but he did not play in the games.

Tom regarded Heidelberg as a place of exile, and hoped not to be stranded too long. He read in *The Age* newspaper of events in Melbourne. Plans were afoot for a team of Australian footballers playing under Victorian Rules to travel to England; the first night games of football were played. In one game, on a cold night in August, Carlton played Melbourne under light towers. The football, painted white, burst and an 'ordinary' coloured football replaced it, rendering the ball virtually invisible to the thousands of spectators, in that 'fitful and unsteady light which the machines gave'. A new white ball was produced and the game completed. Carlton won 3 goals to 1.

In November the MCC held a benefit match for Sam Cosstick. Sam had remained employed as a professional bowler with the MCC; continued to get into scrapes; was ordered out of the pavilion bar for using 'foul and beastly language'; was threatened with dismissal; continued to squirm his way out of trouble and took wickets for the Club. Nothing had changed for Sam.

Life in Heidelberg was still; newsworthy events were few. By the start of 1880 St John's Anglican Church boasted a new reverend, Arthur Joseph Pickering; the local Irish-born constable John Hanlon and native-born Thomas Murphy gave evidence of the cruelty meted out to a horse; and at times a 'wandering lunatic' or staggering drunkard was kept overnight in the police lock-up.

In early January, the Victorians played New South Wales at the Melbourne Cricket Ground and Tom made one of only two trips out of the hamlet to watch the intercolonial match. At the ground he sat in the pavilion next to William Tunks, whom he might not have seen for nearly two decades. Tom was seen chatting, 'hale and hearty', in the members enclosure, presumably telling anyone who might listen how the Victorians should play and shaking his bald head at their lack of practice.

Tom played with and coached the local Heidelberg cricket team. The cricket ground was well known and thought attractive but an absence of water made its care difficult; mud from the local creek that sprang from the Yarra was gathered to fill the holes on the ground; the local council covered the maintenance costs and permitted a small pavilion to be erected. The Heidelberg team travelled by coach and four horses to nearby matches. The team was made up of locals: farmers, gentry, butchers, blacksmiths and cow keepers. On 13 March the Bohemian cricket team travelled to Heidelberg to pay a call. The wicket, still rough and not well flattened, was Tom's ally and his 'chucks' worked sweetly that day. The 44-year-old took 5 wickets. Tom shared the bowling with William Nuttall, a farmer from Banyule, and George Edward Bond top-scored for the locals – 19 not out. Everyone met afterwards at Haliburton Beale's Old England Hotel where the players ate and drank until it was time for the city dwellers to take the long trip home. Tom only needed to make his way 200 yards, past the police lock-up, to reach his bed.

Tom received his regular payment from William Ducker; it was just about the only regular contact he had with family or friends. Money was needed, without which he would have been incapable of caring for himself, yet Tom seemed chatty and pleasant in a letter to Horace at Cullin-la-Ringo. Rapidly moving between topics, superficially buoyant despite his circumstances, it was a glimpse of a distant younger Tom:

> Everything in Victoria is very stagnant at present & for some time back, but it is expected that when the Exhibition is opened at the end of the year things will brighten – The Prince & Princess are expected to be here at the opening so you may guess pretty well that there will be a grand gathering in Melbourne ... I've only been in Melbourne twice since I've been here. I see by todays paper that wool has risen considerably in the Home market. The farmers here are shipping for England quantities of wheat & grain – The frozen meat experiment ... the only news I pick up is from the newspaper (Age) & that's been full of nothing of late but electioneering business. I dont think however that the present ministry will retain Office for any length of

time . . . I should be glad to get news from you sometimes.
Sally [Sarah] joins me in love to all.

Heidelberg was more dream than reality, a tiny green patch
perched on the edge of Melbourne where Tom, in an abstract
sort of way, kept watch on Melbourne but rarely left his isolation
to visit anyone. He had written once that he might like to
travel to Fiji to wander the plantations and join all the other
colonial dreamers. Heidelberg was the closest Tom would get
to that tiny island.

Tom would have noticed the mild tremors in his hands.
His face, which once had the countenance of a prince, was
burdened by the blemishes of a trying decade. His beautiful
constellation of features was eroded. With its sweet rhythm of
intoxication and the mindlessness of hours lost, drink had been
Tom's lifetime companion.

Summer ended. The rains fell hard and Heidelberg steamed
a little; the swaying of perpetual drunkenness might simply
have been the breeze of the South Pacific. 'Have you any fruit
on the station (growing)?' he asked his brothers in Queensland.

THE GATES O' HELL

MARCH 1880–MAY 1880

The last surviving letters from Tom Wills, dated 15 March 1880, reflect the husk of a sportsman, not quite dead but neither fully alive. The handwriting reveals a slight tremulousness – but only just. They were written to Horace and Cedric on Cullin-la-Ringo, which was now burdened by drought and debt. The letters were affectionate but expectant. And what he expected was money – 20 pounds to be exact, just 'to pay off a few debts here'.

Wills had become a beggar within his family, coaxing dribs and drabs of money from his brothers when he pressed them with stories of his ill fortune. From the regular stipend of 3 pounds per week, the methodical Ducker skimmed one pound off the top 'till some old debts are paid off in Geelong'. Heidelberg, Geelong, Melbourne – there was always someone waiting in the shadows to collect money from Tom, from whose fingers coins still slipped with carefree ease.

In his final letter to Cedric, with all self-respect gone, he falsely promised: 'If I get £10 from you I will not trouble any of you again & will repay as soon as I can.' He wailed about his isolation in Heidelberg – 'I'm out of the world here' – and of his rare trips to Melbourne. In a life dulled by the routine

15th. March 188t
Heidelberg

My dear Horace

Many thanks for your
order on Ducker for £10 which
I duly received from him. I
always thought you all lived
at the old head station I never
by any chance hear about the
station at all except a little from
Ducker about the business part
All the family seem to have
scattered all over the Colonies
I am glad to learn from your
note that Sarah & Elliott are
well. When do ... intend to
pay Victoria a visit? I receive
weekly from Ducker £.3.7
one pound he retains till some
obd

of daily existence and numbed by alcohol he dreamt of escaping to Tasmania. But despite moments of characteristic charm in the letters, his incorrigible optimism had faded. His words rang out sadly, from his bleak and constricting world. Empty and fed up, he was adrift.

A listless Heidelberg was made even more so by an autumn that was unseasonably 'warm & sultry'. No doubt it was good drinking weather. Tom and Sarah had been drinking heavily up until Wednesday 28 April, then they both stopped; presumably there was no money to buy more alcohol.

Wills, a heavy drinker for all of his adult life, drank in the predictable manner of all alcoholics. His brain was bathed in alcohol 24 hours a day. When he abruptly stopped drinking, his damaged brain – so long accustomed to alcohol lapping at its edges – recoiled and set his body into alcohol withdrawal. For Tom, this began in the morning when he woke unsettled and with a slight tremor in his hands. Gradually rational judgement was lost.

By Friday 30 April, two days after Tom had ceased drinking, Sarah summoned Dr John Bleeck to treat him but there was little he could do. That night Tom Wills did not sleep. On Saturday morning, Sarah 'was afraid he would do harm to himself' and decided to take Tom to the Melbourne Hospital where he would be treated and kept.

The city's oldest hospital stood like a medieval landmark on Lonsdale Street, set well back from the street. Entry to the grounds of the hospital was through a front gate, where a duty porter sat beneath a porch. His task was to take name, age and details of the illness before granting the patient admission. Once inside, a gravel path led directly to ten stone steps that swept up to the formidable and heavy door, which marked the main entrance to the hospital. On Saturday 1 May 1880, Tom Wills was admitted to the Melbourne Hospital.

The hospital staff promised Sarah Barbor to keep Tom Wills 'under restraint until he recovered'. Tom was taken to

Melbourne Hospital

Ward 21, for males only, where his physician was Dr Patrick
Moloney. Moloney was probably the most interesting of all the
doctors at the Melbourne Hospital, but perhaps not the most
assiduous in his craft. Considered 'gentle and generous', he was
one of the first two graduates in 1867 from the new Melbourne
University School of Medicine. He was more of a poet than a
doctor. A dreamy non-conformist, Moloney counted among
his friends Adam Lindsay Gordon and Marcus Clarke. Many
years afterwards, medical students of the day recalled him as
knowledgeable on all subjects but that, perhaps, medicine was
his point of weakness.

It is hard to know what the increasingly fragile mind of Wills
would have made of this environment. Although his medical
record is brief, it details all the key elements – when he arrived,
his treatment, his mental state, and when and how he departed
the hospital. His doctor wrote, in scratchy ink, stained in several
places by drops of dried blood, that Wills was 'admitted in a semi
Delirium Tremens state . . . tremulous movements of hands'.

190

Thomas Wills aet. 45 –
Admitted 1.3.80.

Hat. Ferri. univ. c̄ Pot. Bromid
et. Tr. Digital m x̄.
2/5 – Patient admitted in a semi
Delirium Tremens state tremulous
movements of hands – was rather
obstinate – refused to remain in
hospital –

Absconded at 5 p.k.

Newspapers and periodicals of the day were littered with references to DTs. Delirium tremens was a condition well known to medical and lay people – it was a commonplace problem. DTs was known to be a short cut to madness. There was no consensus on treatment for DTs but all remedies sought to calm the body and tranquilise the mind's erratic discourse. The medical jottings in Tom's file detailed precisely the DTs treatment of the day: potassium bromide to induce sleep, digitalis to soothe a violent heart, and iron salts to improve nutrition. The medical notes added that Tom 'was very rather obstinate – refused to remain in hospital'. Given Tom's character, the genteel 'rather obstinate' should probably have been as the writer originally intended: very obstinate indeed. Bloody-minded more likely. For a man who lived his life in dispute, DTs gave Wills his full head to rail against all around him. Despite the ministrations of the day, Tom Wills, disconsolate, aggravated and sufficiently disagreeable to excite comment, absconded from Ward 21, at 5 p.m. Saturday evening.

His DTs as yet had not fully exploded – his tremulous hands were the most conspicuous sign of its growing potency. Quick to startle and quick to misjudge, dishevelled and wide-eyed, Wills fled the Melbourne Hospital, slipping past the gate porter. Scampering down Lonsdale Street, he made for the point where Swanston Street cut across Lonsdale. From here a regular coach service, a lone horse pulling a carriage, left two to three times a day for Heidelberg. The trip would take one hour. At 6 p.m. he boarded the coach for home, travelling along the Heidelberg Road, the principal link between Melbourne and the outer hamlet of Heidelberg. At 7 p.m. the coach pulled into Heidelberg, its final stop for the day.

The events of the next twenty-four hours are told through the eyes of the individuals who were with Wills, largely from strangers who were simply passing through at the time. The exception to the parade of walk-on-parts was Sarah Barbor. The bit-players were equally as important for their reflections.

At 9 p.m. Saturday, Anne Heddle (a friend of Sarah's), finding an agitated Tom Wills stalking about the verandah, roused Sarah, who had been asleep. The two women found Tom wildly gesticulating to imaginary persons who taunted him. The shadows about him fashioned themselves into creatures – hideous and deformed. Reluctant to accept the word of those who wished to help him, after some effort Tom was persuaded to enter the house and slip into bed. But he did not sleep or remain in bed. Sarah and Anne, along with the servant girl,

Jennie, kept vigil while Tom stalked the house muttering the threats of a madman.

Prodded by hallucinations, his increasingly violent threats rendered him impossible to deal with, so, at three o'clock in the morning, an anxious Sarah despatched Anne to the police station to fetch Constable John Hanlon. The local lock-up was the usual place to cart drunkards of the district to but Sarah rejected this for Tom, perhaps for reasons of propriety or simply that she did not trust Tom to be out of her sight. As matters unfolded, her decision not to accept this advice was to prove a fatal error. As an alternative, a local labourer – David Dunwoody – was fetched to supervise Tom and, if need be, to physically restrain him. Dunwoody recalled: 'He was quite out of his mind . . . He heard persons speaking to him and was constantly looking under the bed. He tried several times to suffocate himself by holding his mouth and nose.'

As the sun rose on the first Sunday of the month, Tom's condition was unchanged. Auditory hallucinations thumped in his ears and visions from hell sucked the blood from his veins. In his world of swirling misperception he harboured suicidal and murderous intentions. Tormented by delusions of persecution, he saw death as the only escape for himself and, if so, he might as well take Sarah with him. A blasphemous stream of thoughts poured from his mind. In moments of lucidity, he sought forgiveness for his sins. All the while he muttered a soft soliloquy, measured and rational in its madness.

Then, against the tide, Tom seemed to improve on Sunday at around 1 p.m. Always affectionate towards animals, in his last hours Wills walked about the small yard 'feeding the fowls'. At that point of apparent reprieve, Dunwoody informed Sarah, Anne and Jennie that he was leaving briefly for dinner. He carefully put away any knife or instrument that Tom may have turned to fatal use. Satisfied, Dunwoody 'left him in [the] charge of his wife and servant girl'.

Within minutes of Dunwoody leaving the house, Tom returned from the garden. Highly aroused, he immediately scanned the kitchen for a knife. There were none, but Tom saw a pair of scissors resting upon the mantelpiece. He secreted the scissors into the palm of his hand and edged to a slightly more private area, just away from the women. Then in full view, thrusting aside the two women who grasped feebly at his arm, he opened the scissors and plunged them with a ferocity sufficient to pierce the protective hull of his chest three times, directly over his heart. This was no task at all for an athlete such as Wills, for whom the combination of aim and strength was his life's craft. The wound bled only a little from the tiny punctures. He died within minutes.

Constable Thomas Murphy was summoned at 1.15 p.m. With impeccable understatement, the dutiful police officer noted: 'I got the scissors produced they had blood upon them.' On Sunday 2 May at 1.30 p.m. Tom Wills was pronounced dead.

THE SWEETEST MAN

Tom's suicide was the final insubordinate act in an insubordinate life. The day after his death, Egbert visited Jika Street, his dead brother laid out before him. Egbert did not write openly of his grief but he 'felt it very much'. Egbert was thirty but he was still a schoolboy, dreaming of his older brother, the famous and admired Tom Wills – the Tom who was known to all of Egbert's school friends, the footballer and cricketer who travelled to the most fantastic places and who did great deeds. He wrote to Horace, chronicling the last hours of Tom's life. Egbert's final letter on Tom was a love letter of sorts, a letter of adoration, held together by an account of the facts. It was Egbert's moment of grief.

Egbert Wills, Kew, Melbourne, Victoria
to his brother
Horace Wills, Cullin-la-Ringo, via Rockhampton, Queensland

Then all night he spoke in a very queer way he told S that they had to die soon it was no use they both had to go. He then asked S whether she wd rather he killed her or for someone else to do so, he said (pointing to his left side) I'm to be struck here & you in the back – but she took no notice

307

of all this. Then during his ravings in the night he began praying for himself & S to be forgiven for all their sins. In the morning he washed himself & put on all his best things and told S to put on her black dress to be ready for their maker. After he got up in the morning & while S was in a drunken sleep the little girl heard him saying to himself, shall I murder her or not – no I wont. After breakfast he went & fed fowls, his birds & dogs & as he fed each he said, Now that is the last feed you'll get from me, talking & acting to all appearance in a sensible way. He then kept telling S to go and put on her black dress & be ready – while S was preparing the dinner he kept saying, it is no use doing it, neither of us will be here for it. About 12 the old man who was watching him said, Mr. Wills, I am going to dinner. Tom said all right & went into the kitchen where S & the girl were. Before this they had hidden every sharp instrument about the house when in the kitchen the girl saw him pick up & try two small knives but they bent too easily. He then seemed to be looking for a short strong table knife but c<u>d</u> not find it, he then went & stood by the mantelpiece for a few moments then went out of the side door passing S's back. When S looked up she saw him with his arm raised & a siscors in his hand he then struck himself in the chest, she ran & caught his arm then struck twice more falling at the last and on to his elbow. They laid him on his bed & he died in two minutes. He must have touched the heart, he never spoke after he fell.

On Monday 3 May an inquest was conducted at Tom's home, presided over by Dr Richard Youl, the coroner for the city of Melbourne. Dr Youl did not order a post-mortem on Tom nor did he call any medical witnesses for the inquest. There was no autopsy; the cause of death was apparent to all.

Twelve local men were picked as jurors for the inquest; women were banished from the official processes that governed inquests. The jurors filed in to view the body of Wills. His body, still dressed in the clothes of the day before, was carefully laid out on the bed. The first lacquer of death sealed his face. The three puncture wounds were clearly visible through his shirt and vest. Blood had gently seeped from his wounds and marked his clothing. He appeared calm to those who drew around him; a moment of serenity. It was a mischievous illusion – the sardonic grin of death as the muscles of Tom's face tightened around each bone. The jurors who milled about the body included Thomas Davey, the butcher, Edward Studley, the baker, and Daniel Sullivan, the grocer. There was also the blacksmith, the poundkeeper and the plasterer. Thomas Evans, the owner of the house, and George Edward Bond and James Salter, two Heidelberg cricket teammates, stood with them.

Dr Youl questioned the witnesses: Sarah, Anne, the police, the servant girl and the labourer Dunwoody. He questioned them to lay before the twelve jurors all the evidence and to help shape the verdict, though the actual decision was the job of the jurors. The inquest sought to determine how Tom died and to clarify his state of mind prior to his death. And it was this last point, Tom's state of mind, that was the inquest's most critical role in a suicide.

Although religious beliefs on the evils of suicide were less confidently held than they had been in previous centuries, the belief that suicide was bad was still held widely. Suicide was evidence of having strayed from God's path and that the devil had inveigled his way into the heart of the dead man or woman. If an inquest judged a person was not suffering from a mental aberration, it was possible for that person to be found guilty of the crime of self-murder. By 1880 this legal finding was rare but not unknown. There was an increasing view that such findings were cruel to surviving family members and, as a consequence, inquests rarely declared an individual sane at the point of suicide – almost all juries determined that men and women were of 'unsound mind' or 'temporarily insane' when they suicided.

When the twelve jurors gathered around the body of Wills, they concluded that '. . . at Heidelberg on the second of May current the deceased Thomas Wentworth Wills killed himself when of unsound mind from excessive drinking'.

Tom's body remained at his Heidelberg home until Tuesday, the day of his funeral. Heat and air, the embalmer's foe, worked upon Tom's features. Decomposition set in, the odour that curled the nose giving notice of dead flesh.

Although rarely practised by 1880, it was still possible for an inquest to order a night-time burial as a form of punishment. And very occasionally clergy refused to take the funeral service of men and women who took their lives. Tom was not subjected to these practices and William Ducker was entrusted by the Wills family to purchase a gravesite for Tom. He was buried in a 'standard grave' in the Church of England area at Heidelberg Cemetery with a brief service by Arthur Joseph Pickering, the Anglican Minister at St John's Church. On his death certificate Tom's occupation was stated as 'gentleman'.

Tom was buried privately by his family in a manner that was regarded as minimally respectable. His funeral was attended by only a handful of people: his brother Egbert, sister Emily and cousin Colden Harrison; Colden's sister Adela and her son Amos; and Vernon Cameron, a member of the MCC and former colonial cricketer who had played alongside Wills. Sarah Theresa Barbor, alienated from the family, was not present. There was no sentimentality, no record of a church service even though the burial was conducted by a clergyman, no funeral procession or celebration of his life. No constellation of sportsmen lined the streets as Tom was taken to his grave.

His mother Elizabeth did not attend the funeral or, as far as is known, ever visit the gravesite. The understanding was passed down through the Wills family that Tom's mother refused to attend the funeral or visit the gravesite because of her religious beliefs – Tom's suicide, the work of the devil, shamed the family. When a newspaper reporter badgered Elizabeth about Tom's suicide, she is reported as saying words that have condemned her for over 100 years: "'Which son?' she asked. 'Thomas,' said the reporter. 'I have no son called Thomas.'"

It has been said that Tom was buried a pauper. Paupers, poor souls, were thrown into an earthen grave, were not allocated a cube of dirt to themselves but had other bodies tossed on top of them as though burying livestock; they were forbidden the rites of a Christian burial. Although his burial was simple, Tom was not buried a pauper.

The Wills family, for whom Christianity draped every corner of their Victorian household, grappled uncertainly with the suicide. The cavity where Tom once dwelled was smoothed over with the rustle of manners. Family noises were made but above this wash of words there rose an anxiety about respectability. Egbert's wife wrote:

> Fancy last Sunday was the day that poor Tom Wills killed himself – it was dreadful. Egbert was there two days . . . in such a case we are only going into complimentary mourning for a short time. I did not know what to do about it until I went to Mrs. Norcott's & Mrs. Harrison's and they told me what to do. Of course Emy I do not have anything to do with she & Adie [Colden's sister] met at Tom's death but did not speak to each other.

Tom's brothers and his cousin Colden Harrison remembered Tom with affection but there seemed to have been a general understanding that his death would not be spoken about openly. During Tom's life, Elizabeth, sensitive to the opinions of others, had instructed her children to keep Tom's misbehaviour to themselves. The same stricture applied to the family after his suicide and he was barely mentioned in any family correspondence. There was no collective grief expressed in surviving letters; no headstone marked his grave. The women in the

family, particularly Elizabeth and Emily, seemed the carriers
of the shame of the suicide, and wrote nothing about Tom after
his death. It was only the men in the family who wrote about
Tom: Egbert, Cedric, Horace and Colden. And when they did,
it was with love.

Obituaries poured forth in every major newspaper in
Melbourne, the Victorian country papers and in Sydney. Not
a single obituary condemned Tom. They were gentle reflections
upon his life. But for alcohol there was the wrath of the colony:

the curse of these colonies – the demon which has desolated
so many homes, and blasted the fair fame of thousands – got
its hold upon him.

This was printed in *The Leader*. The obituaries accurately and
thoughtfully portrayed his remarkable life. No attempt was made
to avoid the fact of his suicide. Nor was there any public shame
towards Tom, just sadness. Of course, like all obituaries, Tom
was idealised, and there was much to idealise. The colony was
reminded of a colonial life that by then seemed like a distant
land, quaint and old fashioned. Tom was remembered well.

In September, the Melbourne Cricket Club remembered
Tom at their Annual General Meeting and established a public
subscription 'to erect a suitable monument over his grave'.
Hammersley's newspaper *The Australasian* publicised the appeal.
The response was poor. Two months later the minutes of the
Melbourne Cricket Club recorded a one pound donation by a
local club, otherwise there was no mention of the subscription
and the headstone was not erected. Over 100 years later the
MCC returned to Heidelberg Cemetery and rummaged about
in the dirt and weeds to find Tom's grave – a patch of ground
with nothing to signify the man who was buried – and quietly,
privately, the neglect of a century was corrected. The Club paid
for and erected a headstone.

Three years after Tom's death, William Hammersley wrote
of Tom:

He was attacked with softening of the brain, induced by his not taking that care of himself which he should have done, and gradually became irresponsible for his actions, and in a fit of frenzy stabbed himself in the left side with a pair of scissors he snatched from the table. He sleeps quietly in the cemetery at Heidelberg, about eight miles from Melbourne.

Although writing with some sensitivity, Hammersley was still needling Tom in death. When Hammersley wrote of 'softening of the brain' he used a common phrase of the time, which implied a lack of substance and evoked doubts about the person's character or his manner of living. Hammersley made one further reference to Tom, in 1884, while reflecting on Adam Lindsay Gordon, poet and mad horse rider, whom Hammersley chatted to on many occasions at *The Australasian* when Gordon dropped poems in for possible publication. Gordon had killed himself in 1870. Hammersley remembered a wildness and incipient madness common to Gordon and Wills. When Hammersley annoyed Gordon the latter's '. . . eyes flashed fire, his nostrils distended, and I was afraid he would brain me . . . Indeed, I always felt convinced that at times he was not quite right in his mind . . . There was another man well known amongst sporting circles, whom I knew very well indeed, and who came to an end similar to that of Gordon; and curiously enough I detected frequently in him that same peculiar expression in the eyes to which I have alluded.' 'The Evil Eye' he called it.

In all of this, where was Sarah Barbor? She had been with Tom probably from some time in 1864 but was largely a forgotten woman who left no letters and almost no trace of her existence. She and Tom had no children. The traditional sources of consolation – religious faith, sharing memories of Tom with family and friends, condolence letters, the comfort of children – were all denied her. Her relative poverty in a relationship not sanctified by marriage gave her little influence. Almost certainly in the last years of Tom's life the entire family was aware of the ruse of their marriage. In several of Tom's obituaries she was referred to as his housekeeper. Despite this, on Tom's death certificate, Sarah was recorded as marrying Tom at Castlemaine in Victoria. This was untrue. Sarah maintained the illusion of her marriage during the inquest where she was referred to as Mrs Sarah Theresa Wills. Her police statement at the inquest started boldly, defiant in the face of family knowledge of her de facto status: 'The deceased was my husband. His name was Thomas Wentworth Wills. His age was forty four years. He was a gentleman.' Regardless of the perceptions of Tom's family, Sarah was to the end a gentleman's wife.

Sarah was paid money by the family to keep away after Tom's death. Egbert wrote to Horace: 'Tom told S to write & tell Ma & to go to Ducker to arrange her affairs. The proposal is to allow S £100 a year to keep her away.' Horace passed Egbert's letter on to Cedric. It was not made clear whose proposal it was to keep Sarah away, but what seems clear in the confusion of the family's dealing with Sarah, is that Colden Harrison and Tom's brothers handled the matter without malice. In August, three months afterwards, Cedric wrote to Colden Harrison confirming that they would agree to help:

Dear Colden,
Your note of settlement on Tom's 'Housekeeper' duly to hand & what you have done in the matter we thank you for – Horace has not yet seen your note but I will send it out to him first chance – but in the meantime I am quite certain that Horace will agree to what your letter proposes – if not I will be responsible.

Respecting Tom's wishes, Colden Harrison, Cedric, Horace and Egbert undertook to assist Sarah and seemed sympathetic to her plight. The tender asides of Tom's brothers and Colden seem almost whispered and in breach of family ordinance. There are no letters at all that record the thoughts of any of the women of the family on the proposal to support Sarah Barbor.

moments then went out of the side door
passing B.'s back when I looked up
she saw him with his arm raised
+ a scissors in his hand he then struck
himself in the chest she ran & caught
his arm then struck twice more falling
at the last on to this elbow they laid
him on his bed she died in 2 minutes he
must have touched the heart he never
spoke after he fell— Willie E. & I went
out on Monday to see him and arrange
for his burial — He looked very calm
but very much altered decomposition set
in on Tuesday morning, buried at
Heidelberg cemetery Addie & Amos attended a
but as it was all done privately no one
but Cameron was there. I am told B to
write these me + to go to D & Rev to
arrange her affairs. the proposal is to
allow S £100 a year to keep her away—
I send you a paper with Remarks
about Tom.

⟨drawing⟩ wounds 3 through vest & shirt bled
very little.

Your aff Brother
E. S. Wills

Sarah received her money and continued to live in Jika Street, Heidelberg. She maintained the pretence of marriage, calling herself Mrs Wills, but by 1889 she had reverted to her true married name, Mrs Samuel James Barbor, and lived in Simpson Street, East Melbourne, near the Melbourne Cricket Ground. She remained in Simpson Street until she died on 27 September 1906 from a strangulated hernia. Her final resting place was not next to Tom in Heidelberg Cemetery but in the Boroondara Cemetery.

Death is a time of revelation. It was only after her death that Sarah Barbor's full name was revealed: Sarah Theresa Marie Josephine Barbor. Sarah had no money or assets to her name when she died: no real estate, no jewellery or watches, no furniture. There were debts – mainly those incurred from the business of dying: money for the Homeopathic Hospital on St Kilda Road where she spent her final days; her attending doctor at the hospital, Dr Speight; the ambulance that transported her; the 4 pounds for the purchase of her burial plot and the 8 shillings for Reverend Pitt to conduct her funeral service.

A single item noted in her favour, in her meagre will, came as a surprise – Sarah was owed 425 pounds from the estate of Thomas Wentworth Wills. Of all the revelations after her death this was the most unexpected. Despite Tom having bequeathed what was left of his estate entirely to Sarah, she did not receive that money. Sarah did not seek probate on Tom's will. It is possible this was part of her financial agreement with the Wills family that ensured she stayed away from them – the alternative offer of money each year was preferable. But the money Tom had left Sarah had never been touched.

Sarah Barbor left her estate to Sarah Heddle, the spinster and friend with whom she had shared much of her later life. The two had lived together in Simpson Street. Very little is known of Heddle but she did seek probate on her friend's will, fighting hard to retrieve the 425 pounds. Solicitors attempted to unravel the exact nature of the Wills family payments to Sarah

Barbor over the years but, beyond discovering that William Ducker had been placed as a trustee to manage the flow of money, they were thwarted. Till the end, family secrecy was not cracked. In the midst of dry legal notes, there was a cry of frustration from the solicitors: 'The Miss Duckers will give no account in connection with settlement moneys for which the late WF Ducker was Trustee for the late Mrs SJ Barbor.' Whatever secrets the daughters of William Ducker held, they held them close to their Victorian breasts. The details of how much and how long Sarah Barbor was paid by the Wills family was not revealed. The Wills family did not relinquish the 425 pounds easily and they sought legal advice. Sarah Heddle placed an advertisement in *The Argus* of 11 March 1908, to the effect that she was seeking probate on Tom's will. And in April 1909 she was granted probate and presumably received the money Tom had left to Sarah Barbor thirty-two years earlier.

Tom disappeared from family correspondence, apart from occasional reminiscences between his brothers and Colden Harrison. Tom remained within the warm embrace of the memories of Colden, Egbert, Horace and Cedric – no amount of disavowal by the rest of the family seemed to displace an adulation that dated from boyhood.

Horace, perhaps the most gentle of all the brothers, in 1923 recalled Tom – over forty years after his death. What prompted Horace's comments was the discovery of Tom's old cricket cap, the one he wore for Handcock in his 1870 portrait. In 1923 the cap was found by the Melbourne Cricket Club and displayed in a Melbourne sports store: Mayne and Sheppard, Block Arcade. Horace was interviewed about Tom by the *Evening Sun*: 'Tom was a wizard with the ball. I was batting against him once, and he warned me, "Look out, Horace, I'm going to bowl you round your legs." I made a determined attempt to pull him, missed the ball, which turned around me, and I heard the sickening sound of the bails falling.' Horace removed anything unsightly from his mind to leave the brother he wanted to remember and drew a protective circle around Tom. He seemed to understand that Tom was never meant to be constricted by the conventions of life. 'My brother was the nicest man I ever met. Though his nature was care-free, amounting almost to wildness, he had the sweetest temper I have seen in a man, and was essentially a sportsman.'

A CONVERSATION

Tell me a little about yourself.
My name is Lawton Wills Cooke and I live in Melbourne.
I was born in 1920.

How are you related to Tom Wills?
My grandfather Horace was Tom's younger brother. Horace
lived on Cullin-la-Ringo, the family station in Queensland
and then he lived with us in Kew. I went everywhere with my
grandfather until he died in 1928.

Do you have clear memories of Horace?
He was a kindly man. He was loved by the kids in our street.
He always had sweets for them. He used to buy me penny
ice-creams. My mother said he never complained. He used to
wear a grey stetson hat, with a grey ribbon around it; it was
turned up slightly at the sides; very stylish. All the gentlemen
wore them at the time. He used to limp a bit. On the station
he fell once and his revolver went off and a bullet lodged in
his foot. It was never removed. I've still got his pistol from the
Cullin-la-Ringo station and his bullwhip and other bits and
pieces. They're tossed in with the rest of the junk down in the
basement now.

I always remember that, as a treat on Sunday, I was allowed to pop into my grandfather's bed. And he told the most marvellous stories. I guess he spoke of Queensland and Tom. I can't really remember it a lot though. What I remember most about jumping into bed with Grandfather was the smell of pipe tobacco when I crawled into his bed! He always smoked Havelock tobacco. He'd give me two shillings and I'd scoot across two vacant blocks near our house in Kew, buy the tobacco, and race back to give it to him. I loved him dearly. When he died I was heartbroken. I was only eight. I kept thinking where could he possibly be?

Did Horace ever mention Tom?
I don't recall anything. What I remember though, was that my mother used to say, and I heard her say this several times, that Horace thought Tom the most handsome man he had ever seen. A charming man, she said my grandfather called Tom.

When you were a boy, did the family talk about Tom?
Only a little as I recall. I was told that he was a good-looking man in his early days. He was a great ladies' man. I don't know this for sure; it is what came down through the family. We were led to believe he was a philanderer. He was always short of money. He had a lot of drinking mates and was very generous. Mother said he was rather keen on himself, and had a high opinion of himself. My grandfather was always lending him money – that is very well established in the family. I think he was given money to stay out of trouble. I think that they must have been petrified he would do something stupid. I was too young to remember things. I cannot recall them talking about Tom, though my mother mentioned him in later years because she went through the family's private papers. I always gathered in later years from the family that it was a taboo subject. The family had very strong moral and religious beliefs. It was his suicide, you see.

Are you surprised by the interest in Tom?
Yes, quite surprised. Until recent years there was no interest shown by outsiders in approaching the family about Tom. We were always told in the family that it was old Uncle Colden who was the father of football. Colden was held up high in the family, a moral man and a man of tremendous integrity. He was a fantastic athlete. The eulogies at his death were quite remarkable: an enormous funeral. Tom, on the other hand, was buried hastily.

Uncle Colden died a year after my grandfather. I think I was nine years old. Uncle Colden was a fine-looking man. We went often to his family home, 'Molonglo', in Kew. In the last few years he lost his memory and was looked after by his two daughters. We were very close to the Harrison daughters. I don't recall them ever talking about Tom. Ruby and Katie, the two sisters, were very prim and proper. Typical Victorian spinsters. Women of very strong moral and religious belief. Wouldn't put a foot wrong. Dressed simply, very well educated.

I don't remember Uncle Colden talking much about football. He didn't mention Tom. I was too young really. There was great affection between the Harrison and Wills families. Colden, in his autobiography, spoke of Tom with great kindness.

Did Tom leave any items behind after he died?
Just one item that I know of. The Harrison family passed it on. It is a trinket: made up of a gold wicket, a gold bat and a ball made out of something red, it looks like coral. Something that you attach to a watch chain, a fob. It was passed from Alma to my mother and she gave everything to me. I have it somewhere. It is beautifully made, quite unique.

A final word on Tom?
The family never really spoke about him. There's really nothing left to say.

AFTERWORD

TOM WILLS AND THE ORIGINS OF AUSTRALIAN RULES FOOTBALL

During the research for this book I was repeatedly asked the same two questions. Did Tom Wills include features of Aboriginal games in the rules he helped write in the 1850s? And how important was Tom's contribution to the origin of Australian Rules football? Both questions deserve a straight answer.

It has been claimed over the last two decades that Tom Wills played a type of Aboriginal football, or at least observed such a game, while he was a boy living near Mount William in the 1840s. The argument goes that, having experienced this game as a child, Tom incorporated features of Aboriginal games into the early rules of Australian Rules football. Although often presented as factual, no archival evidence has been cited to support these claims.

There are several documented references to early forms of football played by Aborigines in Victoria. The best known of these is Marngrook, described by the Assistant Aboriginal Protector William Thomas in a handwritten manuscript from 1858. More recently, at Cambridge University, an image was discovered from the William Blandowski scientific expedition to the Murray River in 1857, showing young Aboriginal boys kicking and catching tightly rolled plant roots in a manner that loosely resembles Australian Rules football. There are other documented descriptions of Aboriginal football and I have no doubt that more will surface.

James Dawson, a western district settler and a man of fine sensibility and deep humanity, wrote a description of Aboriginal football in his 1881 book *Australian Aborigines*. Dawson was a respected documenter of Aboriginal vocabulary and at the back of his book he compiled a word list. The word 'football' appears in this list as part of the Djab wurrung vocabulary. The Djab wurrung word for football was Min'gorm. Therefore, it is likely that a type of Aboriginal football was played near where Tom lived as a boy or, at the very least, that the local Aboriginal people knew of such a game. That Tom knew of and watched such games is, at best, speculation.

The bigger problem with the argument is the lack of evidence that, when Tom helped write the first rules of Australian Rules football in the late 1850s, any such observation of an Aboriginal game shaped his thinking. Certainly, Tom left no evidence to support this. No source during his lifetime, or afterwards, suggests that he incorporated any aspect of Aboriginal games into early Australian Rules football. None of the first rule writers of the Australian game – Tom Wills, James Thompson, William Hammersley and Thomas Smith – mentioned Aboriginal games as an influence. All my research points to Tom Wills having been almost solely influenced by his experience at Rugby School, with two other factors having an effect – the physical environment of Melbourne's parklands and the rules of other English Public School football games, such as those played at Eton, Harrow and Winchester. From these starting points, the game of Melbourne football evolved.

As for the second question, it was Tom's cousin Colden Harrison who recalled in words made famous over the years: 'But when T. W. Wills arrived from England, fresh from Rugby school, full of enthusiasm for all kinds of sports, he suggested that we should make a start with it. He very sensibly advised us not to take up Rugby although that had been his own game because he considered it as then played unsuitable for grown men, engaged in making a livelihood, but to work out a game of our own.'

In the years before and soon after Tom's death, there was little attempt to understand the origins of the game. It is often said that Tom's suicide led him to be written out of, or at least played down, as a significant figure in the game's history. I don't think this was the case at all. Not a great deal was written about Tom, or indeed the other important figures in early Melbourne football, because it took time for a historical perspective to develop. Tom's suicide had nothing to do with that. As a historical perspective on football's origins developed over the latter part of the nineteenth century and early twentieth century, the name of Colden Harrison was elevated to a position of pre-eminence. But Tom's name was never forgotten and, after Harrison, it was Tom Wills who was most often recalled. During this period, the contributions of James Thompson, William Hammersley, James Bryant, Thomas Smith and others were more often than not overlooked.

By the late twentieth century, with more research, it was understood that while Harrison's role was vital over a long period, his name did not appear as a writer of the 1859 rules and did not appear in the first games of 1858. With this correction, the name of Tom Wills emerged as the most significant figure. But the roles of James Thompson and William Hammersley were also particularly important. Thompson's skill as a writer and his access to *The Argus* as a forum helped spread knowledge of the game, and his jousts with Tom Wills over the early rules were important in shaping the game's trajectory. The same can be said of William Hammersley, a man whose witty prose shines through decades of newspaper articles. James Bryant, the professional cricketer whose role was perhaps neglected more than any other, provided a place to meet to discuss the rules, the provision of equipment and entrepreneurial skills. His play on the field also deserves recognition.

So where does Tom stand in all of this?

A small cohort of men in the late 1850s, without much organisation or hierarchy, established the beginnings of the game. Tom Wills was one of them, and, to my mind, was the most extraordinary and inspiring figure of them all – the most important man in the origins of Australian Rules football.

Australian Rules football owes its defining features – emphasis on handling the ball, marking the ball, the importance of kicking, the shape of the ball, receiving a free kick after marking the ball and much more – to the Rugby School rules that Tom Wills brought to the Richmond Paddock.

It would be wrong to think that Tom simply introduced Rugby School rules without considering the need for change. He particularly liked the Rugby School rules but wrote of the dangers of throwing men to the ground on the parklands around Melbourne; this forced a different view of the required rules. Although the earliest games resembled Rugby School football, they were distinct from the beginning.

No new game is conceived of by one man and seen through by one man. By disposition, Tom, with his mind of loose strings, was never going to sit down and oversee any game's development in any conventional way. That would hardly have been Tom. In fact, it is likely that no player at the time looked any further than the immediate problem of sorting out rules for the next weekend's game.

Tom Wills was the first football captain of the Melbourne Club, the first recognised leader of men on the field and the possessor of the finest innovative tactical mind. His name is the first signature on the first known set of rules penned in 1859. His exposure to cricket and football being played on the same ground at Rugby School was critical in the development of both games in Melbourne. And he was the first to articulate clearly and in public, in his 1858 letter, the key requirements for the formation of a foot-ball club. He was the colony's best footballer, best captain and most original thinker. And he stands alone in all his absurdity, his cracked egalitarian heroism and his fatal self-destructiveness – the finest cricketer and footballer of the age.

Charles Box, the nineteenth-century English commentator on cricket, considering the sporting brilliance he saw around him, wrote, almost reluctantly: 'Genius: this word, though hardly applicable to cricket, is insisted upon by some, therefore has to be recorded.'

Indeed it does.

NOTES

Please note that all quotes from letters remain unchanged, except where the addition of punctuation or a word was necessary for clarity and ease of reading. 'Sic' has been avoided wherever possible, assuming the reader will understand that irregularities in spelling are part of the authentic reproduction of the correspondence.

These notes have been selected to give the source for quoted material where it is not clear within the text, or to give extra information where the finding might appear contentious, or where the additional information is interesting in itself. Full details of publications mentioned in the notes can be found in the selected bibliography. More detail on sources can be found in my fully footnoted doctoral thesis, 'Tom Wills: In From the Cold, the Life of a Nineteenth-Century Sporting Hero', Victoria University, 2008.

FINDING TOM WILLS

Page xiv: Newspaper sources were unclear about whether or not Tom had been admitted, so finding his in-patient notes was a wonderful discovery. Unbeknown to me at the time, most Australian hospital records did not keep clinical files as far back as 1880, or such records had been destroyed over the years.

Page xvii: The death of the boy was recorded in the Evans House archives. Scarlet fever and other infectious illnesses were common.

Page xvii: Letter from Tom Wills to his brother Cedric, May 1870.

CHAPTER 1: THE FAVOURED SON

Page 3: Jane Wallace was convicted in Dublin. She was a servant. She arrived in Australia aboard the *Catherine*. Michael 'Weir', black haired with hazel eyes, a leather dyer, arrived in Australia aboard the *Three Bees*. Elizabeth's date of birth has recently been confirmed as 3 October 1817. The date was found in her daughter Eugenie's birthday book.

Page 3: Not all the girls were orphans; many had one parent but women with children struggled to support their children because of the difficulty of finding employment in the colony. The school was largely under the care of clergy during Elizabeth's time there. The main building of the Orphan School remains in Parramatta and has undergone several transformations over the years. Recently restored, one can still walk about the gardens and down to the river as a young Elizabeth might have done.

Page 4: The fate of Elizabeth's other sister remains unknown.

Page 4: Quote regarding school, *Currency Lad*, 17 November 1832.

Page 4: Elizabeth's lined handwriting book is a slim volume in the possession of Lawton Wills Cooke.

Page 6: Edward Wills' obituary, *Sydney Gazette*, 18 May 1811.

Page 6: The archival documents that describe Edward Wills, his crime and punishment are in the possession of Lawton Wills Cooke and Terry Wills Cooke.

Page 6: George Howe was transported as a convict to Australia and arrived in 1800. Sarah had one child to George Howe, a daughter Jane who married Captain John Harrison. Jane was the mother of H.C.A. Harrison.

Page 7: The events between Horatio and his stepbrother Robert Howe can be found in the *Sydney Gazette*. Horatio explained that his older brother Thomas had arranged the apprenticeship but that while Thomas was away, Robert Howe altered the nature of their working relationship. At some point during his absconding, Horatio spent time at sea. Many years afterwards, as a Victorian parliamentarian, he recalled his days on board a vessel in the Pacific.

Page 7: William Charles Wentworth studied at Cambridge University and won second prize for the poem 'Australia' for the Chancellor's gold medal. Horatio co-opted two lines of Wentworth's poem to head each issue of the *Currency Lad* newspaper.

Page 7: Judge's comments, the *Sydney Gazette*, 15 February 1828.

Page 8: *Currency Lad* quotes, 24 November 1832 and 19 January 1833.

Page 8: The details of the purchase of land in 1837 on the Molonglo were recorded in the *Government Gazette* but Horatio's exact movements are unclear during the years 1835 and 1836. This lack of information about the family's movements raises questions about where Tom was born; there are no archival documents yet found that pinpoint this precisely. The best evidence is from a recollection made by William Hammersley in 1869, based on notes apparently given to him by Tom, indicating that he was born in the Molonglo region. Horatio is recorded as taking sheep in preparation for Burra Burra as early as the start of 1836 and most likely earlier and, although the few letters around this time indicate that he did not yet own land, it seems likely that he and Elizabeth were in the vicinity preparing to settle. In the period before Horatio settled on the Molonglo he spent time on both his brother's (Thomas Wills) estate and his sister's (Eliza Antill) estate on the outskirts of Sydney. It was through the latter that he received mail. The date of Tom's birth – 19 August 1835 – is based on numerous family letters which state it clearly. Tom was baptised by Rev. J. McGarvie and the handwritten certificates give Tom's birth date as 19 December 1835 and 19 December 1836. The background to Horatio's choice of his son's Christian names has been passed down through the family oral history.

Page 9: Letter from Eliza Antill, 24 January 1839, to her brother Thomas Wills in Port Phillip. Horatio regarded himself as the family doctor. Family correspondence of 4 July 1873 recalled that Horatio 'used to always take on the doctoring if any of the household got ill and would sit up all night if necessary'. The nature of Tom's illness was not specified in letters but was most likely to have been an infectious disease. Why Horatio left the Molonglo River run is unclear. The family recollection was that perhaps licensing fees were a problem on Burra Burra. Horatio's brother Thomas had overlanded the previous year to the district of Port Phillip. Horatio followed, heeding Dr Redfern's advice.

CHAPTER 2: A BOY IN A TENT

Page 10: There were several Djab wurrung clans near Mount William. Djab wurrung is pronounced with a silent 'w'. The same sound in the language could be transcribed with either a hard sound like 'd' or softly with 't'. The same guideline applies to the letters 'b' or 'p'.

Page 11: Robinson made over twenty journeys into the four districts of the Aboriginal Protectorate and kept extensive notes. The protectorate was abolished in December 1849. For more material on the history and customs of the protectorates, see works by Ian Clark listed in the bibliography.

Page 12: Quotation from Robinson's journal, 27 January 1840.

Page 12: Quotation from Robinson's journal, 20 May 1841.

Pages 12–13: Robinson's interaction with Elizabeth Wills and his recording of the accusations against Horatio can be found in his journals from July 1841. There is a further accusation that Horatio killed an Aboriginal man and woman.

Page 13: Parker's observations are from *Memoirs of Edward Stone Parker*.

Page 13: Letter to Governor Latrobe from Horatio Wills, asking for increased protection, March 1842. La Trobe was a close acquaintance of Horatio's older brother Thomas in Melbourne.

Pages 14–15: The diary is an extraordinary document, its uncensored contents giving a clear understanding of the role of religion in Horatio's life. Tom never expressed overwhelming views about religion although his occasional comments suggest that he believed in Christianity, or at least that the lessons of his father had taken sufficient root so that he could mouth them when required.

Page 16: Brickwood's role in education is best tracked through the several Melbourne newspapers in the 1840s and in his obituary. He was such an important figure in early Melbourne that when he died in France in 1902, the major Melbourne newspapers reported it.

Page 16: Tom played in other cricket games around this time; surviving letters recall the young Tom playing with a schoolboy team against the Melbourne Cricket Club and lunching with the members of the MCC. Brickwood's position as vice president of the MCC is confirmed in the Melbourne Cricket Club archives.

Page 16: *Port Phillip Herald*, 21 December 1848.

Page 18: Horace Wills reflecting upon his brother, *Evening Sun*, 7 December 1923.

Page 18: Comment by H.C.A. Harrison on Tom, *Running with the Ball: Football's Foster Father*, Mancini and Hibbins.

Page 19: Tom's first letter from England, 7 August 1850, is scrawled simply and large, reflecting the mind and writing style of a boy. He promised to write a more detailed account of the voyage but if such a letter exists, it has not yet been found.

CHAPTER 3: COCK OF THE SCHOOL

The descriptions of school life have been gathered from the letters, journals and books found in the Temple Reading Room, Rugby School. The school was a community within the township and quite distinct from the people and life around it. The boys sometimes wrote quite disparaging comments about the 'townies' and the maids who served them in their houses and who helped out around the school.

Page 20: Letters from *Tom Burn's Schooldays*; these letters are only some of the Rugby School collection of the time.

Page 21: The letters by Wills make no mention of Goulburn although the headmaster often features in other boys' letters.

Page 21: Berdmore Compton's somewhat dry biography emphasised the religious aspect to Goulburn's life.

Page 21: The assessment of Evans was written by one of Tom's fellow housemates in 1854, in 'Arthur Stanton: A Memoir', Reading Room at Rugby School.

Pages 22–3: The description of Mrs Townsend and beer was in *Tom Burn's Schooldays*.

Page 24: Tom recalled this time at Rugby School in notes he sent to William Hammersley which the latter recorded in *The Australasian*, 8 May 1869.

Page 24: Descriptions of fagging were in *School Experiences of a Fag*, an almost masochistic description of life at Rugby School. Despite this, Melly regarded his experiences, on the whole, as positive. Charles Kemp, Tom's fellow student, regarded Melly's account as 'a faithful picture of the school'. Tom wrote his comments on fagging in a public letter in *Bell's Life in Victoria*, 28 November 1857.

Page 25: Tom's description of the swans comes from his letter which he has dated 4 June 1851, although a study of the letter suggests that this was the incorrect date. Most likely some, if not all, of the letter was written on 5 July 1851.

Page 26: This letter has many spelling errors, and is a rambling scrawl. Although Tom has dated it Saturday 4 June 1851, this is an incorrect date. By examining the cricket match he refers to, Kent versus England at Lord's, it is most likely that some of the letter was written on Saturday 5 July 1851 and the match he refers to played on Monday 7 July. He would have watched Fuller Pilch, Felix, Clarke, Haygarth, Wisden – the great cricketers of the day.

Page 27: The Great Exhibition celebrated progress in art, science and industry. It was a huge event with exhibits over 19 acres and up to 42,000 people visited each day.

Page 27: Tom's comment about strawberries comes from the letter mentioned above, most likely written 5 July 1851.

Page 28: Letter from Tom to Horatio, 18 August 1851, rivals the size of any newspaper broadsheet; Tom has crammed the pages with cricket scores.

Page 29: Letters from James Alexander to Horatio Wills, 30 July 1851. Also 11? October 1851, 13 February 1852.

Page 29: Letter from Tom to Horatio, 18 August 1851.

Page 29: In 1852, W.W. Follet Bright Esq. of Trinity College, Cambridge, an old Rugby boy, initiated an annual athletics event for prize money. The part about beating Tom in the mile race comes from a letter from David Hanbury in *Tom Burn's Schooldays*.

Page 30: Winter stripping of the grounds, *Bell's Life in London*, 10 October 1852 and 15 October 1854. 'The annual match between the first Eleven against the next Thirteen (with John Lillywhite) was commenced on the 23rd ... A new ground will be made during the winter at a cost, it is said, of £500, for football and cricket.' The issue of playing cricket and football on the same ground was debated in England as it was to be in Australia.

Pages 30–2: I spent about two weeks at Rugby School, Cambridge and Lord's. On my final afternoon at Rugby, archivist Rusty Maclean realised that the old pavilion might hold something of value. It was boarded up and we entered wearing the obligatory hard hats for safety. After some looking, we found the painted cricket honour boards. In the gloom, the name I first found was that of another Tom, the barrister Thomas Hughes, author of *Tom Brown's Schooldays*, who captained the School XI. Since my visit the Green Pavilion has been restored and I believe that guided tours of the school now mention Tom Wills as an old boy, noting his cricket prowess and his role in creating the game of Australian Rules football.

Page 32: It was never made clear in the newspapers what aspect of the delivery was thought unfair – whether the delivery was over the shoulder or if the arm jerked. See *Bell's Life in London*, 26 December 1852.

Pages 32–3: John Lillywhite's letter defending Wills and Harman, *Bell's Life in London*, 16 January 1853. Lillywhite was appointed as the school's first professional cricket coach in 1850.

Page 33: Letter from Horatio to Tom, 1 May 1853. Horatio's story of the young boy who questioned Tom's whereabouts is interesting. Despite the accusations of having killed Aborigines in the early 1840s, there is a sense of Horatio's warmth not only towards his son but also towards the Aboriginal boy. Even more, Horatio seems to look upon the suggestion of kinship between Tom and the Aborigines of Mount William with satisfaction.

CHAPTER 4: THE GOVERNOR'S DISPLEASURE

Page 35: The Barby Hill run was recorded in the Evans House archives, 29 October 1853. The boys recorded the names of the hares and hounds, the time for each runner, and a brief description of weather conditions, the course and notable events.

Page 36: The exceptional running ability of Tom was recorded in *Rugby School Hare and Hounds*, a record of runs with descriptions that are extraordinary for their detail. Running had a relatively short season and was seen as virtuous, not exciting the boys as much as football and cricket.

Page 37: Cheese, beer and bread was the accepted trilogy of delights at the various public houses where runs concluded. This was written about quite openly in boys' journals and histories at the time with no attempt at secrecy, so it is something that masters and parents must have been well aware of. The issue seems to have been of concern to masters when drinking was not moderate.

Page 37: Archibald Tait, later Bishop of Canterbury, had good reason to be concerned about pestilence – he and his wife lost five daughters to scarlet fever.

Page 37: The quotation about the filth in the town was taken from John Mannering's thesis, 'An Appraisal of Sanitary Reform in Rugby 1849–1875'.

Pages 37–8: Experience of house brew comes from 'House Sketches', *The New Rugbeian*, Vol. II., No. II, November 1859. Although it is clear that the boys brewed beer, the sanctions around its consumption were not clearly stated other than the need to drink in moderation.

Page 38: Quote from *Tom Burn's Schooldays*, p. 77.

Page 38: Letter from Charles Kemp to his mother, 19 March 1854.

Page 38: Alcohol was commonly mentioned in relation to sports. One example, from Thomas Hughes' *Tom Brown's School Days*, is a telling reference to drinking while playing football, hinting at Hughes' disapproval of the practice. During the half-time break, fruit vendors distributed oranges as they wended their way through the players. The seniors, 'past oranges and apples', placed ginger beer bottles innocently to their lips, but something stronger was being swallowed. Hughes made no bones about alcohol's drain on a sportsman's prowess – 'One short mad rush, and then a stitch in the side, and no more honest play; that's what comes of those bottles.' Although not written as an historical tract, there seems little doubt that Hughes was describing his own experiences at the school.

Page 40: This monthly school report has sometimes been mistaken as being from Tom's period at Brickwood's School in Melbourne. Comparison of the names of boys in this report and with the names of boys enrolled at Rugby School confirms its origins and that it was most likely written in 1853.

Page 40: Form system taken from the 1854 Summer book of lists; there were slight variations especially in subdivisions. It is possible to track Wills' academic progress through 'Rugby School Lists 1850–1855' and other archives from the time. Tom was still in the lowly Remove when Horatio criticised him in his letter of 1 May 1853.

Pages 41–2: Letter from Horatio to Tom, 1 May 1853.

CHAPTER 5: GENIUS

Pages 43–4: *Bell's Life in London*, 12 November 1854 and 3 December 1854. Before this, there is no trace in the archives relating to Wills playing football, although he is likely to have played very soon after his arrival in 1850. It is worth noting that early Melbourne footballers recalled players who, while running with the ball and dodging others, were given licence to extricate themselves from tacklers. One of the critical points to take from the *Bell's* match descriptions is that Tom Wills was noted – there were large numbers of boys in these games and only very occasionally was anyone mentioned by name.

Page 45: The playing out of games over many widely separated days and by a large number of players was similar to the early games of Australian Rules football in the 1850s. In Rugby School football, if a player ran the ball over the goal line, that team could then try to kick a goal, or they could score by kicking during the course of play governed by detailed rules. No points were awarded for simply carrying the ball across the line at the end of the field of play. Rather, this allowed a try for goal by then kicking the ball.

Pages 46–7: *The New Rugbeian*, November 1860, Vol. III, no. II: a typical schoolboy reflection. The boys wrote extensively about football in their school magazine and were protective of its rules, disliking outside criticism of the way the game was played at the school.

Pages 47–8: Letter from Sarah Alexander to Horatio Wills, 10 May 1854.

Page 48: Watson, in 'Ye Annals of Evans'. Another boy, John Paddon, is recorded in the school register as dying at the same time, although the cause is not specified.

Page 49: The stranger who wrote to Tom was Rev. Stonehouse, 6 April 1855.

Page 50: This was the first of an annual game still played to this day between Rugby School and Marlborough College. Wills recalled the match fourteen years later with a clear memory for detail: '[I] got them all with slows', a reference to the eleven wickets he took. This quote comes from a biographical piece by William Hammersley, *The Australasian*, 8 May 1869.

Page 50: *The Times*, 30 June 1855.

Page 50: Daguerreotype of Tom, *Evening Sun*, 7 December 1923.

Page 51: The description of the celebration was in *Ye Annals of Evans House*, in the Evans House archives.

Page 52: 'Poor Edward', as Aunt Sarah Alexander called Tom's uncle, took his life not long after studying law, according to family history.

Pages 52–3: Tom Wills played the following games:

- For the Marylebone CC and Ground v Cambridge, 15 & 16 May 1856 at FP Fenner's Ground, Cambridge. University won by 26 runs.
- For Magdalene College v Quidnunce, 17 May 1856 at Parker's Piece, Cambridge. Tom top-scored in both innings for the College and took 3 wickets.
- For a Cambridge 16 v United England XI at Lord's, 9–11 June 1856. In the report of this game, *Bell's Life in London* said that Tom was 'one to come', that is, he was expected to enrol at Cambridge.
- For Cambridge v Oxford at Lord's, 16 & 17 June 1856.

The match where he played for Magdalene may be the source of the story of his enrolment at this college but review of the University *Almanack*, 1857, reveals that he was one of three given players, that is, not belonging to the college.

The Map Room at Cambridge Library shows Fenner's on the SE outskirts of Cambridge with Magdalene on its NW fringe. Fenner's cricket ground in Tom's time had the shape of a dilapidated quadrangle, a roomy 500 by 600 feet. The annual game against Oxford was a sporting high point of the year and *Bell's Life in London* noted that Wills 'threw a ball from long leg' and ran out a 'Mr. Lane'. In this match he also took one wicket with his fast round-arm action. The unusual manner in which Wills was allowed to compete, in that Cambridge was one man short, has been repeatedly referred to by cricket texts. At times there are suggestions that the rules were passed over to allow him to play.

Page 53: Quote regarding the 4 lb. bat, *The Australasian*, 8 May 1869.

Page 53: A further clue on the reasons for Tom's return to Australia came over 40 years later in 1898, when an anonymous letter was written to the English press, and then published in the school magazine *The Meteor*, 19 March 1898. The writer recalled Tom's vexed relationship with Horatio: 'It was intended by his father that he should go from Rugby to one of the Universities, and afterwards study for the Bar, but having led a sort of nomadic life when a youth in Australia, he could not bring himself to study for professional work, therefore returned home . . .'

CHAPTER 6: THE SHRINKING AND EXPANDING WORLD OF TOM WILLS

Page 57: I Zingari, a club borne from irreverence and played by those of independent means, was formed in England. Social qualifications were important. Its colours of black (out of darkness), red (through fire) and gold (into light) were its trademark.

Page 60: Hammersley's comments regarding 'the queerest match' were made in *Sydney Mail*, 18 August 1883.

Page 61: The two quotes from Tom are from *Bell's Life in Victoria*, 7 February 1857.

Page 63: Letter from Cedric to Emily, 27 March 1857.

Pages 64–5: *Bell's Life in Victoria*, 1 August 1857.

Page 68: One type of seizure – complex partial seizures – classically produces symptoms where sensory perception is altered, the world and self are experienced in an altered fashion and thinking is clouded. But Tom's symptom's were never referred to again, and with this limited information it is virtually impossible to make any definitive statement as to what was happening to him at the time of this letter.

Page 69: Tom's thinking, at times, was similar to what is known to occur in people with bipolar illness, characterised by episodes of elevated and depressed mood. (This description is a simplification of the many permutations of this illness, for the purposes of these notes.) Between episodes the person may have a normal mood level. Sometimes people can become psychotic; that is, they may experience hallucinations or delusions. Without more evidence, it is virtually impossible to say that Tom suffered from this illness but a variant, albeit a less severe variant, is not an unreasonable hypothesis.

CHAPTER 7: APPLAUSE, PROSPERITY, SOCIAL ACQUAINTANCE

Page 70: The chapter title is taken from the 1858 notebook of Matthew Arnold, with a foreword by his daughter E. Wodehouse, in which he wrote 'the 3 things that support genius: prosperity, social acquaintance and applause'. Tom had all three during his last period in England and early years in Melbourne.

Page 70: Richard Twopeny, *Town Life in Australia*, pp. 3, 20.

Page 71: Horatio's comments on the Mongolians appeared in *The Argus*, 28 September 1857.

Page 72: The best way to get a feel for how the MCC operated at this time is to read, page by page, the minute and letter books, and the vast amount of material in the archives at the MCC – truly a national treasure.

Pages 72–3: *The Cricketer's Guide of Australasia, 1857–8*, in their annual review of the season, make a most interesting Australian comment in reference to a game played between Gentlemen and Players: 'We cannot allow any remarks on this match to appear without recording our opinion on the want of taste displayed in drawing the above invidious distinction in the two elevens selected. It may be considered unobjectionable in England, but in these colonies such notions ought not to be tolerated, as they tend to prevent that general equality amongst cricketers which the nature of the game is calculated to engender.' Although this statement gives the impression that this division was uniformly disliked, there were other indications that such a separation between amateur and professional in the colony of Victoria was expected by some.

Page 75: Letter from Tom Wills to George Marshall, 3 November 1857. Marshall regarded this letter as important and held on to it for almost a decade. Then in 1866 he submitted it to the MCC as evidence that he was still an honorary member. The MCC returned it to Marshall saying that Tom Wills' letter only applied for 1857–58. This is one of many pieces of evidence highlighting the difficult position of the professional cricketer.

Page 75: Letter supporting Gideon Elliott, *Bell's Life in Victoria*, 13 February, 1858.

Page 76: The letters to and from William Tunks were an unexpected find in Sydney at the NSW Cricket Association. They give a different picture of a young Tom Wills who, at least at that point in his life, had some awareness of broader political matters. The two letters from Wills are dated 4 and 15 October 1857; and from Tunks, 9 October 1857.

Page 78: Tom's letter, *Bell's Life in Victoria*, 26 December 1857.

Page 81: *The News of the Week*, 15 January 1858.

CHAPTER 8: FOOT-BALL

Page 83: The sly comment regarding Tom having drunk 'lemonade' was made in *The Argus*, 20 April 1858. Euphemisms and puns for the drinking of alcohol abounded in nineteenth-century newspapers; generally speaking, discussion of the effect of alcohol upon players was not open.

Page 84: Tom's letter of complaint about the way in which the Victorians were treated appeared in *The Cornwall Chronicle*, 3 March 1858, and his comments regarding Launceston were broadcast widely when he returned to Melbourne.

Page 85: The unflattering description of Horatio was in *The Argus*, 2 March 1855. William Strutt, the colonial artist, sketched Horatio in parliament and offers a view of Horatio that is more forgiving that those of the political satirists of the day. In Strutt's images, Horatio cuts a stylish figure; Horatio's moustache, thick and broad like a broom, rests on a plump face; tiny spectacles rest upon his nose; and his luxuriant hair flows, not unlike his son's. One would not have thought it from his correspondence, but the man of pedantic bent was full of grace, and with his slightly ruffled curly hair, was almost bohemian. In one sketch, Horatio is at ease reclining against his bench, next to Dr Evans, editor of the Melbourne *Herald*. In another, Horatio is drawn leaning forward, intent, hands clasped upon his knees. About him are William Stawell, Charles Sladen and Ebeneezer Syme, *The Age* proprietor.

Pages 85–6: Description of the St Kilda Cricket Club dinner was in *Bell's Life in Victoria*, 1 May 1858.

Page 86: Tom's rebuke of the MCC appeared in *Bell's Life in Victoria*, 26 June 1858.

Page 88: Letter urging formation of a rifle club was in *Bell's Life in London*, 4 March 1855.

Page 89: It is not clear which team wore which colour. Although the Scotch–Melbourne Grammar match was the first recorded match in the newspapers, it was not the first football match of the year. There were two earlier games played by Bromby's students: one against St Kilda Grammar and another against the St Kilda Club.

Page 90: Bromby's journal was accessed, with permission, through the Melbourne Church of England Grammar School. Bromby took a keen interest in the boys' sports though he wondered at one point if he was allowing too much time for the boys to practise football. In the month before the match, Bromby read and wept over the account of Rugby School life, *Tom Brown's School Days*.

Pages 90–1: 'No rules' quote from *The Pioneers of Port Phillip*.

Page 91: Recollections of Wills was in 'Old-time footballers', *The Australasian*, 9 September 1922. Other details of playing football and cricket were given, suggesting the recollections were accurate.

Pages 91–2: In many ways the article in *Melbourne Punch*, 30 September 1858, sums up the game of football in 1858 – most similar in style to Rugby School football yet different, with Tom Wills as the leading figure in the game.

THE TREE OF LIFE

Pages 93–4: Frederick McCoy was chosen as the first professor of natural science at the University of Melbourne which opened in 1855. McCoy's *Prodromus of the Zoology of Victoria* attempted to describe the fauna in the colony. The Pink Lady is featured in this work. The year in which the rules of Melbourne football were penned, 1859, was also the year in which Charles Darwin published *The Origin of Species by Means of Natural Selection*. Darwin described how new species could be shaped by a new environment and so adapt and survive. He used the metaphor of a tree of life to describe how these new species were like new branches of a tree – distinct but connected to a central trunk. In a similar fashion the game of Melbourne football did not arise without a precursor, but was connected to the games the players brought to the Richmond Paddock, the most important of which was Rugby School football. But like the new species in the colony, the game adapted to its physical environment and cultural isolation.

CHAPTER 9: TO BOWL WITH THE GODS

Page 95: Tom had made his decision to leave the Melbourne Cricket Club well before his ousting as its honorary secretary. In early September, he represented the Richmond club in a meeting at the pavilion to discuss the changed laws on bowling.

Page 96: Thompson wrote his article just over one year later, *The Argus*, 29 February 1860.

Page 96: Tom was appointed to the organising committee for this intercolonial cricket match against NSW.

Page 100: An often forgotten man in the evolution of Australian Rules football, Jerry Bryant was important in the early years for providing a venue and materials for meetings, as well as taking part in games. There is no evidence that Tom or anyone else set about playing football or devising rules under instructions from the Melbourne Cricket Club. Whether the Melbourne Football Club was actually formed in 1858 is uncertain and there is continuing debate as to whether 1858 or 1859 should be regarded as the year of the MFC's beginnings.

Pages 100–1: It can be argued that other men may have been there at Bryant's Hotel, but the evidence from Wills, Smith, Hammersley and Thompson, when they recalled the day, suggests that it was only these four men.

Smith does mention that Alex Bruce, a signatory to the rules, was added to the group afterwards. Smith's recollections are in *The Australasian*, 26 February 1876.

Page 101: Hammersley's recollections about the background to forming a committee and his reference to Tom favouring Rugby School football are in the *Sydney Mail*, 25 August 1883.

Page 101: Undated letter from Tom to Horace.

Page 103: Thompson's amusement and exasperation over of the shape of the ball and Tom's antagonistic manner was in *The Argus*, 14 May 1860. There was a similar controversy in England concerning the shape of the ball. James Thompson, after Wills, was probably the most significant person in the evolution of the new game of Australian Rules football. As a journalist, he wrote more about the early game than anyone else and his cricket guides contained definitions and guidelines.

Page 103: The first games of football in Geelong that we know of were in 1859. By 1860 Glencross-Smith was already playing for two clubs in the Geelong region. Glencross-Smith knew Harrison and the other Wills boys well.

Page 104: In the very early days of football there were hints of Wills' aggression on the field. On one occasion, his father noted that he was laid up at Mrs Harrison's 'very much hurt at football in Melbourne'. It was common for boys to play alongside men and Wills would not have been alone in encouraging the connection with Melbourne schools, a pattern replicating his Rugby School experience where it was common for schoolboy teams to play adult men in cricket. During one such Melbourne game, a small boy 'smuggled the ball away from Wills'; the boy was pursued, fell and dislocated his wrist but no blame was attached to Wills. In August 1859 there were further suggestions that Tom had injured another player. He wrote to defend himself, saying that he was completely free of blame for the accident.

Page 104: *Bell's Life in Victoria*, 7 July 1860.

Page 105: Letter regarding Colden, from Tom to Cedric, 15 May 1860.

Page 105: I found the book on property law at the same time as Tom's textbooks at Minerva Creek.

Page 105: Letter from Horatio to Elizabeth, 25 September 1859.

Page 106: Thompson wrote of 'a tardy apology' in *The Argus*, 5 December 1859. Tom responded in *Bell's Life in Victoria*, 10 December 1859. And finally Thompson ended it in *Bell's Life in Victoria*, 24 December 1859.

Page 107: Hammersley's recollection of Tom suffering from sun exposure, *Sydney Mail*, 15 September 1883. The description at the time was in *The Argus*, 23 January 1860.

Pages 107–8: Letter from Emily to her brothers, 15 February 1860.

Page 108: Tom on the bowling law, *Bell's Life in Victoria*, 26 June 1858.

Page 109: Thompson on Tom, *The Argus*, 3 April 1860.

Pages 109–10: Tom on the MCC and bowling rules, *Bell's Life in Victoria*, 7 April 1860.

CHAPTER 10: A FATHER CALLS FOR HIS SON;
EXPECTATION IS FULFILLED

Page 111: Letter from Horatio to his boys in Germany, January 1861. There were two letters found with similar material, one dated 7th, one 8th.

Page 111: Letter from Cedric to his sisters, 13 June 1860.

Page 112: Letter from Tom to Colden, written from Mr Alex Anderson's property near Skipton, 1 October 1860.

Page 112: Letter from Horatio to his boys in Germany, 7/8 January 1861.

Page 112: Letter from Tom to Cedric, 15 May 1860, on giving up cricket.

Page 113: The committee to manage the visit of the English team contained names of influence and all were known to Tom: T.F. Hamilton the president of the MCC, George Coppin MLC, Sir George Stephen and William Haines. It was rumoured in Melbourne that Tom Wills had agreed to return from Queensland to play against the English and the committee agreed to pay his costs from Queensland: 'there is an *on dit* that not even the allurements of squatting in Queensland will deprive us of the valuable services of Tom Wills'.

Page 113: Letter from Tom to brothers in Germany, 23 August 1860, on heading bush; letter from Tom to Cedric 15 May 1860, claiming the law won't pay.

Page 114: Letter from Tom to Cedric, 15 May 1860, on unnamed woman.

Page 115: The details surrounding the arrival in Moreton Bay and their preparation for departure can be found in the *Moreton Bay Courier*. The paper mentioned Horatio had five drays although later Horatio said he had four.

Pages 117–18: Letter from Horatio to boys in Germany, March 1860.

Page 118: Letters from Cedric to his mother and sisters regarding attitudes towards Aborigines, 2 January 1860 and 10 March 1860. There is some doubt about the year but 1860 seems most likely.

Page 118: Letter from Egbert to his father and sisters, 1 July 1860, also 13 July 1860.

Page 118: Letter from Horatio to his boys, 7/8 January 1861.

Page 119: The Select Committee of Inquiry of the Queensland Parliament into the Native Mounted Police Force, 1861, gives further details of the violent methods used to 'disperse' Aborigines.

Page 119: Horatio's letter to his boys, 12 July 1860. The word 'rifles' is difficult to interpret in the original letter and seems to have two 'f's. The context suggests that the word is rifles. The same letter details hearing footsteps.

Page 119: Letter from Horatio to boys, 7/8 January 1861, demanding he be pleased with them.

Pages 119–20: Letter from Horatio to Elizabeth, 18 July 1861.

Page 120: Letter from Horatio to Elizabeth, 6 October 1861.

Page 121: Jimmy Baker and a man called Aubrey went with Tom to get the drays. Jimmy Baker was the overseer's son. The name Aubrey is also spelt Albery and Albury in the accounts.

CHAPTER 11: THE PRIDE OF QUEENSLAND

Note that the killings took place on Kairi Aboriginal land. It is difficult to say any more than this as details of the event are scarce.

Pages 122–3: Letter from Tom to Colden, 24 October 1861.

Pages 123–4: Report on campsite from *Rockhampton Bulletin*, 9 November 1861; also the *Moreton Bay Courier*, 11 November 1861.

Page 124: Letter from Tom to Colden, 24 October 1861.

Page 125: There is no evidence that Tom Wills was a part of the Gregson party that killed Aborigines in this initial retribution. In Gregson's memoirs, he noted that they came across 'hundreds of them in the camp . . . at the first alarm they were quickly out of sight. We then set to work collecting and burning the spears and other weapons which occupied us for an hour or more . . . We then made our way back to Rainworth where we found a section of Native Police on their way to the scene.' An article printed in the *Try Excelsior News*, Vol. 3, No. 10, The Try Boys Society, June 1896, gives a version of this with more details of killings. It is difficult to know how accurate this is but the figure of 30 dead tallies with the official communication from Governor Bowen. It is reproduced in *Currency Lad*, 1998.

Page 125: Herbert, the Colonial Secretary, responded to Tom's letter of 26 October on 12 November. He passed on sympathy and assurances of further Native Police support, 'I beg to assure you that the Government feels the warmest sympathy with the sufferers by the most atrocious outrage . . . deeply regrets that although the Natives had been visited by the Native Police twice within the three weeks previous to the murder the Blacks should nevertheless have succeeded in what must have been a most unprovoked and deliberate attack.'

Page 128: Letter from Elizabeth to her boys in Germany, 21 December 1861.

Page 128: *Queensland Guardian*, 30 November 1861. The newspaper reports do touch upon the sensitivity of the timing of their interest in procuring Tom. But given Tom's isolation and the recent deaths this still seems an extraordinary idea to get Tom to play for Queensland.

Pages 128–9: Letter from Elizabeth to Cedric, 9 November 1863, on 'horrible blacks'. Also from Elizabeth, 20 November 1861.

Page 129: Letter from Cedric to Tom, 17 February 1862.

Page 129: See letter from Herbert, Colonial Secretary, to Rockhampton Mayor, 12 November 1861: 'The Government feels deep sympathy for those who have suffered and who are endangered by the cold blooded and unprovoked hostility of the natives and will use every effort to protect life and property against their attacks.' Herbert was supportive of the Macdonald retribution party. One official letter suggested that Horatio, at least to the administrative eye, was regarded as too lax in keeping the Aborigines at bay. John Jardine wrote to the commander of the Native Police detachment on 23 October 1861: 'A private party led by Mr P.F. MacDonald also starts tomorrow for Wills Station for the purpose of recovering the lost sheep – protecting the survivors of the party and cooperating with your force . . . You will also most likely meet Mr Patrick with his Detachment there . . . it is most likely that

Mr Patrick with his Section has ere this dispersed the perpetrators of the murders with the other Blacks in the vicinity, but I need not remind you that this is a case demanding the strongest measures and the most prompt and energetic action on the part of the Native Police ... I do trust it will prove a warning to the settlers generally as against allowing the Blacks up to the stations and admitting them to too much familiarity.'

Page 130: Letter from Emily to brothers, 21 November 1861. There are two versions of this letter.

Page 130: The official response from England also suggested concern about excessive retribution. See letter, Newcastle, Secretary of State for the Colonies to Governor Bowen, 8 March 1862. 'I cannot dismiss from my mind the impression produced by the Report on the Native Police Force which you have recently forwarded to me recording that in not very distant times these Natives were in some parts destroyed indiscriminately by strychnine, and that even now common destruction of men and women is by no means unknown ... The first lesson of importance which a savage ought to learn from a civilized Government is the difference between discriminating justice and indiscriminate vengeance ... I do not know why the Australians should be incapable of learning this lesson and I hope the Government of Queensland is not incapable of teaching it. When this is done and not till then I shall entertain some hope that the Colony under your Government may be an exception to that unhappy law which seems to prohibit the occupation of the same country by the Anglo-Saxon and the Aboriginal. I shall of course have much pleasure in supporting as far as I properly can your application to the Society for the Propagation of the Gospel for a Missionary teacher.' Governor Bowen sent a despatch to London in December 1861 and recorded that about thirty Aborigines died in the initial retribution. Following this Lt Cave pursued the Aborigines and many were killed either by gunfire or in fleeing over a precipice.

Horatio's death was a public fulcrum for debate on broader issues of land, squatters and Aboriginal dispossession. *Sydney Morning Herald*, 5 November 1861: 'the intrusion of a sheep establishment upon a country still occupied by its Aboriginal inhabitants is commonly unresented by them at the first moment of arrival'. *Queensland Times*, 15 November 1861: 'In all our dealing with the aboriginals of Australia they have been treated as if they possessed no rights; their lands have been taken from them, and they have been driven from one place to another, and hunted about much in the same style as the kangaroo ...' *The Argus*, 13 November 1861: 'Instructions have been issued for the despatch of a large force of native police to the scene of the outrage, ... This horrible butchery has had no parallel since the awful massacre at Hornet Bank, some years ago, which will long live in the recollection of the settlers in that district. In this case we shall probably never learn the origin of the attack, the merciless savages having performed their barbarous work so thoroughly that no survivor is left to tell the bloody tale.'

Page 130: The terms 'inoffensive' and 'harmless' were typical of the types of words he used.

Page 130: While not condoning the murder of Horatio Wills, Dutton was an advocate for Aboriginal rights. He was critical of the Queensland Native Police whose violence he claimed precipitated Aboriginal retribution. Dutton claimed to have warned Horatio about the need for guns but that Horatio had dismissed his advice. Dutton did not single out Tom Wills nor indeed his father for criticism beyond the latter's alleged carelessness. Dutton's views found voice in numerous letters to the Queensland press. There was official support for Tom's claims regarding Dutton. See letter from Manning to Tom Wills, Norwood, 20 January 1862: '. . . Mr Dutton, who persists in affording his protection contrary to the repeated remonstrances of the NP officers and others who are equally cognizant of the fact. I am to inform you, in reply, that the present is not the first occasion on which Mr Dutton's conduct in this respect has been brought under notice . . . trusting solely to the vigilance and determination of the NP to drive back as far as possible the treacherous and vengeful savage.'

Page 130: Tom to Colonial Secretary, 6 January 1862.

Page 131: Letter from Tom to Elizabeth, 17 June 1862.

Page 131: Criticism of Horatio, *Sydney Morning Herald*, 19 November 1861.

Pages 131–2: Letter from Tom, 21 November 1861, published in *Rockhampton Bulletin*, 7 December 1861.

Page 133: Hammersley on Wills, *Sydney Mail*, 15 September 1883.

Page 133: 'Old Wills' attitude, Gregson's memoirs.

Page 133: Tom on 'the natives', *Queensland Times*, 28 January 1862.

Page 134: Cedric, in *Daily Record*, Rockhampton, 9 November, 1912. Also see Jesse Gregson's papers in the Mitchell Library. These include his comments about his early dealings with the Aborigines and the native police force; he mentions Tom Wills several times as a noted cricketer and that Tom was left to look after the stock after the murders. The fifth part has a commentary by James Nisbet which is scathing of Cedric's version of events.

Pages 134–5: Letter from Tom to Elizabeth, 17 June 1862.

Page 135: Letter from Emily to her brothers, 21 November 1861.

Page 135: Letter from Tom to Elizabeth, 8 June 1862.

Pages 135–6: da Costa, J.M. Irritable heart.

Page 136: Letter from Emily to her brothers, 23 December 1861.

Page 137: Letter regarding Tom on dream, undated but appears to be from 1864. Tom mentioned on several occasions from this point his acting as a shepherd and the loneliness of station life. This quote is taken from a later example and appeared in the *Geelong Advertiser*, 19 October 1863.

PART TWO

Page 139: Quote from William Hammersley, 8 May 1869.

CHAPTER 12: GOD PRESERVE ME FROM A
SYDNEY MOB

Page 142: Letter from Tom to Elizabeth, 26 July 1862, on Roope.

Page 142: Letter from Tom to Elizabeth, 8 June 1862, on Roope and alcohol. Roope remonstrated with Tom that not enough respect was shown to his father's memory and charged Tom with allowing the blacks too close to Cullin-la-Ringo. Tom haughtily dismissed Roope's concerns.

Page 142: Letter from Tom to Elizabeth, 8 June 1862, on Roope being too slow.

Page 142: Catherine Roope's diary, 1 July 1862.

Page 142: Letter from Tom to Elizabeth, 17 June 1862, on doing everything.

Pages 143–4: Letter from Tom to Elizabeth, 17 June 1862, on doing Horatio's work.

Page 144: Letter from Tom to Elizabeth, 26 July 1862, on escaping a snake.

Page 144: Letter from Tom to Elizabeth, 8 June 1862, on the mountains.

Page 145: Letter from Tom to Elizabeth, 26 July 1862, bragging.

Pages 145–6: Letter from Tom to Attorney-General, 30 October 1862.

Page 147: Tom played three matches with the Albert Club in early January. He played cricket in Melbourne for the rest of January.

Page 148: Letter from Emily to Tom, 1 December 1862.

Page 149: Marshall was also known to enter disputes over similar incidents in club matches in Melbourne.

Page 149: Ernest Docker, who later entered law, was invited years afterwards to talk about colonial cricket. His thoughts on the riot were found in the archives of the NSW Cricket Association (uncatalogued).

Pages 150–1: Letter from Tom, *Sydney Morning Herald*, 14 February 1863.

Page 152: Letter from George Glencross-Smith to Cedric, 11 February 1863.

Page 152: The Albert Cricket Club met and pondered if Tom should be expelled as a member. They resolved not to do so, but censured him for his behaviour in the intercolonial match.

CHAPTER 13: LEAVING CULLIN-LA-RINGO

Page 153: Catherine Roope's diary, 24 January 1862, on the Anderson sisters. The Roope diary offers a personal insight into the running of Belle Vue, not always flattering to the children of Horatio and Elizabeth Wills. Catherine Roope's gossipy manner tended to put her offside. Neither she nor Elizabeth ever made reference to their days in the Female Orphan School at Parramatta. Her husband, William, was probably the reason Catherine remained close to the family over the years as he was trusted by Horatio and Elizabeth. In contrast to his wife, he was measured and balanced in his views.

Page 154: Letter from Tom to Cedric, February 1863, boasting.

Page 154: Letter from Emily to Cedric, February 1863, on cricket over courtship.

Page 154: Letter from Alex Anderson to Tom, 13 November 1863.

Pages 154–5: The two surviving letters (undated, and 13 November) from Julie Anderson to Tom are from 1863. The phrases used are from both. Sadly, no letters to Julie Anderson remain though clearly Tom wrote many. The two letters from Julie leave little doubt that she was besotted with Tom and would have welcomed marriage.

Page 155: Letter from George Glencross-Smith to Cedric, 1 May 1863.

Page 156: Letter from Elizabeth to Cedric, 21 July 1863. The topic of medicine was a common theme in the letters of the Wills family and dated back to Horatio's interest in the subject, being concerned primarily for the welfare of his children.

Page 156: Letter from George Glencross-Smith to Horace, 26 May 1863. Glencross-Smith wrote of the trip to Queensland: 'I licked Tom playing putting rings on a peg in the steamer.' When George Glencross-Smith returned to Victoria he kept Tom and Cedric aware of football. Of one game on the Richmond Paddock, he wrote that football was deteriorating in Melbourne. And in a letter to Cedric on 10 September 1863, he wrote of the Richmond Paddock: 'we played on the ground outside the Melbourne cricket ground. It was in good order, but rather hard ... remember me to Tom.'

Page 157: Letter from Elizabeth to Tom, 18 August 1863.

Pages 157–8: Letter from Tom, *Brisbane Courier*, 17 October 1863.

Page 159: The match between NSW and Queensland was eventually played, but after Tom had left Cullin-la-Ringo; he did not play in the match.

Page 160: Emily to Cedric, 17 December 1863.

Page 160: Letter from Tom to Cedric, 21 December 1863, on Rockhampton.

Page 162: Letter from Sarah Alexander to Tom, 14 April 1864. Whatever misdemeanours Tom committed in life, there is no doubt that Aunt Sarah was terribly fond and protective of Tom and her image of him was that of a schoolboy not of a sportsman. Nonetheless, I think it is reasonable to read into this letter that she had some inkling of his waywardness and saw all cures within the fold of Christianity. Tom remembered his aunt's care and remained affectionate and respectful towards her.

Pages 162–3: Letter from Elizabeth to Cedric, 12 January 1864. Morris was a bank manager and trustee of Cullin-la-Ringo. Tom's misbehaviour in this instance came as a complete surprise to the family. His mother's letters suggest that whatever occurred, it had happened only recently.

Pages 163–4: J.H. Norcott to Cedric, 17 November 1863.

Page 164: Letter from Elizabeth to Cedric, 21 February 1864. Although Elizabeth makes the claim that marriage would settle Tom – a timeless hope for those around an unsettled individual – there is little discussion about marriage prospects and what the family thought of Julie Anderson in the lead-up to the broken engagement.

Page 165: Letter from Tom, in *Otago Daily Times*, 19 and 20 February 1864. It is surely a measure of Tom's impetuosity that, finding himself in another country, he could write such a letter. The normal boundaries and cultural expectations that might make a person reconsider, were insufficient to stop him firing off the letter.

Page 166: Letter from Elizabeth to Cedric, undated, 1864, on Horace.

Page 166: Letter from Elizabeth to Cedric, 21 February 1864, on Tom and work.

Pages 166–7: Letter from William Ducker to Cedric, 20 February 1864.

Page 167: Letter from Horace to Cedric, 29 February 1864.

Page 167: Letter from Elizabeth to Cedric, 3 April 1864. This, and the above letters, are painful to read, even now, and indicate Elizabeth's disillusionment with her son while still endeavouring to admire and protect him for other aspects of his character. Tom's brothers, while noting that things tended to go missing when Tom was around, reveal no anger or resentment.

Page 168: Letter from Emily to Cedric, undated, 1864.

Page 168: Letter from Elizabeth to Cedric, 3 April 1864.

CHAPTER 14: THE MAN WITH NO CLOTHES

Page 169: Although Tom had been at Cullin-la-Ringo since October 1861, his time in charge of the station was limited. He remained in charge from the time of Horatio's murder for only 3 months until William Roope arrived in December 1861. He was again in charge when Roope left in June 1862 until Cedric arrived later that year. It tells us a great deal that Cedric, who turned eighteen in December 1862, was placed in charge over Tom. This was largely because Tom spent little time on the station from the start of 1863.

Page 169: Letter from Tom to Cedric, 2 April 1864.

Page 170: Letter from William Ducker to Cedric, 4 April 1864.

Page 170: Letter from Elizabeth to Cedric, 18 October 1864.

Page 170: Letter from Emily to Cedric, 24 June 1864. Despite Emily obviously knowing the details of Tom's behaviour, the letters in which she documents them have either not survived or have not yet been found.

Page 170: Letter from Emily to Cedric, 26 September 1864. After Emily's priceless comments on her brother's behaviour after he leaves the station she becomes estranged from Tom. Tom, on the other hand, remains fairly neutral towards his sister.

Page 171: Letter from Emily to Cedric, 24 June 1864.

Page 171: The 'bad woman' mentioned by Emily comes as such a surprise and it is difficult to know at first how to make sense of it. The relative absence of surviving family correspondence during the second half of the 1860s, particularly with respect to Tom, makes interpretation harder. Certainly by 1870, Tom's 'wife' is mentioned fairly regularly but there is a gap from this statement by Emily in 1864 until 1870. Tom never married anyone – neither Sarah nor anyone else – during his life. If the woman mentioned is Sarah Barbor, it is likely that most or all the family considered Tom to be married for a period of time. Emily's brief comment could also be interpreted to mean that the children conspired to keep Elizabeth in the dark about this woman's existence. The possibility that Emily was making reference to a woman other than Sarah Barbor needs to be considered although no other woman's name ever appears linked with Tom from this date. The matter is further complicated that in a 'singles versus married' game of cricket played in 1867 in Melbourne, the press included Tom as a single person. Certainly this was a family where the need to maintain propriety was thought to be paramount, so that what was known was not always written about, at least by Elizabeth. I think the most important conclusion that can be drawn is that, regardless of the secrets within the family, at least some of the family considered Tom to be married in 1864. It is worth noting that although the family later on used the term 'wife' to describe Sarah, and Sarah also called Tom her 'husband', at no stage did Tom ever call Sarah his 'wife', as far as is known. She was either Sally (Tom's name for her) or a 'housekeeper'.

Page 172: Letter from George Glencross-Smith to Cedric, 25 May 1864.

Page 172: Letters from Tom to Cedric, 24 September and 14 November 1864.

Page 173: Letter from Tom to Cedric, 14 November 1864.

Page 173: Letter from Elizabeth to Cedric, late April 1864.

Pages 175–6: Elizabeth to Cedric, 21 February 1865.

Page 176: The other person at the meeting to argue for a cross bar was O'Brien.

Page 177: The *Bell's Life* reference to Tom leaving Melbourne is noteworthy because it indicates clearly that on the field of play, virtually from the first games described, Tom was regarded as the finest captain and tactician in the colony.

Pages 177–8: Article on smoking, *Yeoman*, 13 September 1862.

Page 178: Letter from Egbert to Horace, 15 December 1865. The finding of this letter was a breakthrough in my research. Written just after the school year had ended, adolescent Egbert wrote of Tom without any self-conscious attempt to conceal Tom's behaviour on the field. It remains the clearest evidence (although there is quite a deal of circumstantial evidence) that at times Tom played cricket while drunk.

CHAPTER 15: HAVE NOT THESE BLACKS NAMES OF THEIR OWN!

Page 183: On the 'excessive payment' to Tom, Horace later remarked in relation to his coaching the team: 'I hope Tom makes good use of his money.'

Page 183: Letter from Tom to Horace, 11 September 1866. An inkling into what friends of the Wills thought after the killings was in another letter from George Glencross-Smith, 30 March 1863: 'I am sorry to see that the blacks have [been] near your station again and I hope that you keep a good guard against them as they are very sly and cunning . . .' Wills' attitude to the local Aborigines has been portrayed in a romanticised way; his boyhood affinity with Western District Aborigines is at times superimposed onto his relationship with Queensland Aboriginal tribes, with little evidence to support this view.

Page 184: Letter from Tom, *Geelong Advertiser*, 5 December 1866.

Pages 184–5: Tom Wills and the Aboriginal cricket team, in the *Geelong Advertiser*, 11 December 1866. The evidence is clear that Tom's knowledge of the Djab wurrung language, which was largely shared with the Jardwadjali, was remembered and used extensively on tour. At Lake Wallace, Tom captained the team in three practice matches against local white teams. They lost the first and won the next two. Before they left for Melbourne, Sugar, one of the Aboriginal cricketers, died.

Page 187: Andrew Newell's letters capture more powerfully than any public document the reaction to Tom's coaching the black team. These private letters were not altered or censored in any way as public letters might have been. It seems that Newell was an MCC member.

Pages 187–90: Handfield of the MCC recalled the game nearly ten years later in correspondence to the Marylebone Club: 'I bowled (slow underhand twists) had the pleasure of disposing of 8 wickets for 9 runs in the first innings, and 5 for 21 in the second – Mullagh in this match made 14 and 42, in first rate style and Cuzens obtained most of the wickets (fast round) of the MCC.' The MCC won by 9 wickets but it was really the batting of Wardill making 45 that set up the victory. Cuzens took 7 of the 11 wickets to fall of the MCC. Wills scored 4 and 25. Mullagh scored 16 and 33.

On the third day the Aboriginal team contested a day of athletics. Colden Harrison appeared: 'The contrast between the two jumpers was most striking, Mr Harrison's tall muscular figure, with his well developed powerful understandings, set off in the tight fitting pants, being so opposite to Tarpot's short figure and wiry legs; but the darkie jumped beautifully, and with very little apparent effort, especially when doing the long jump . . .' At 3 p.m. the governor was introduced to the cricketers by Tom Wills.

Page 190: Letter from Elizabeth to Cedric, 4 December 1866. Of all the family members one might have expected some anger from Tom's mother. But instead, her comments on the Aboriginal team sit comfortably between her thoughts on Cedric's birthday and shearing sheep.

Page 190: Letter from Horace to Cedric, 13 January 1867. Also see letter from Horace to Cedric, 22 January 1867, when he mentions in passing that the Aboriginal team is playing in Geelong and the letter from Horace to his mother and sister Emily, 9 February 1867: 'I see by the papers that the Black Cricketers are going to play in Sydney on the 21st of this month.'

Page 191: Letter from Horace to Sarah Beswicke, 16 April 1871.

Page 191: Letter from Elizabeth to Horace, 10 January 1867.

Page 192: A number of different spellings have been used for the Aboriginal team over the years. Even within this contract, which appears to be a copy of the original, the spelling varies. In this book I have elected to use the Aboriginal names rather than the adopted European names for the players, using this contract as reference. I am aware that the name for Mullagh is different in other sources but it seems to me that this contract is the closest we have to what was understood to be his Aboriginal name.

Page 196: The arrest was reported in the *Richmond Australian*, 12 January 1867. It is notable that such a potentially embarrassing and damaging incident was reported only in the Richmond press and not copied more widely throughout the colony. Only on one occasion did Tom refer to drinking amongst his team. He was reported to have said that he was concerned about the excessive drinking of two of the Aboriginal players.

Page 197: Jellico, *Hamilton Spectator*, 23 January 1867.

Page 197: Hammersley, *Bell's Life in Victoria*, 20 May 1865.

Pages 198–9: Public letter to Tom, *The Empire*, 27 February 1867.

348

Page 199: Rugby School mention of the cricket tour, *The Meteor*, 12 April 1867.

Pages 199–200: Tom, Yellana and Bullenchanach were part of the Victorian team that played Tasmania in Melbourne in the middle of January. The Tasmanians won by 5 wickets. Wardill was captain, not Wills.

CHAPTER 16: A LOT OF BLACK SAVIDGES A PLAYING AGAINST XTIANS

Page 202: The title for this chapter comes from Mrs Jones, the nosy, noisy busy-body commenting on life in the colonies in *Sydney Punch*, 23 February 1867.

Page 202: The early part of the NSW leg of the Aboriginal cricket team tour, particularly the arrest of Tom Wills, has always been a mystery to historians and other writers – until now. A review of a variety of Victorian and NSW newspapers gave separate pieces of information but together articulated a reasonably clear story. But then I accidentally came across key minutes of the NSW Cricket Association when trawling through vast amounts of their archival material, and for the first time it was clarified that Tom had been manoeuvring to manage the team on his own and was in direct competition with Gurnett. Once I had this information, interpreting the newspapers became much easier.

Page 203: It seems that the team did not leave Melbourne in time to play on the Domain because, unfortunately for Wills, after he made the travel arrangements a proposed match between Victoria and Tasmania was postponed to a later date. This may have been a critical factor in his not being able to arrive in Sydney in time.

Page 203: Wills' breach of contract, *Sydney Morning Herald*, 18 January 1867.

Page 204: There are also suggestions that William Hayman was briefly held this day as well. Although Hayman's name does not appear in the archives kept by the NSWCA which suggest that Tom arranged the Domain match, Hayman's name is mentioned in Victorian newspapers as assisting in the failed plan to play on the Domain.

Page 204: Gurnett's letter, *Sydney Morning Herald*, 25 January 1867.

Page 206: In his handwritten diary, Lawrence details many aspects of his touring with the Aboriginal team but, disappointingly, gives no details or insights into Tom, the team, or his personal relationship with Tom. At several points the fact that Tom's key role had been completely overlooked gives the impression that Lawrence has deliberately, unfairly and inaccurately excluded Tom from the discussion.

Page 206: Parody of Aborigines, *Sydney Punch*, 16 March 1867.

Page 207: Inquest on Bilvayarrimin (Watty), 15 May 1867.

Page 208: Letter from Thomas Kennedy to H.R. Barclay, Superintendent of Police, Portland, 15 August 1867.

CHAPTER 17: MR WILLS TAKES A JOB

Page 213: Letter from William Handfield to Tom Wills, 21 September 1867.

Page 213: Naturally Tom did not play cricket with only one club – that had never been his preserve. He also played with Geelong and was elected that club's vice president.

Page 215: Letter, William Handfield to Tom Wills, 25 March 1868.

Page 217: Praise for Tom, *The Australasian*, 6 July 1867. Occasionally Tom wrote about the tactics used by opponents or their behaviour. When Jack Conway led his Carlton team to Geelong, to play upon the paddock near the Argyle Hotel, Conway left the field after a dispute and Tom wrote to the press. Sometimes Tom played around the centre, other times as 'goal keeper', an older position in Australian football much more akin to a soccer position. Sometimes he kicked goals. By the end of the decade he was umpiring some matches in South Melbourne at the foot of Clarendon Street.

CHAPTER 18: TOMMY WILLS! TOMMY WILLS!

Page 218: Disagreement over captaincy, *The Leader*, 6 March 1869.

Page 219: Frank Allan described, *Sydney Mail*, 25 August, 1883.

Pages 219–20: Tom's letter, *The Leader*, 3 April 1869.

Page 221: Tom frustrating the committee, 6 April 1869, Match and Ground Committee, MCC archives.

Page 221: Disputes within the MCC were common and not only with professional cricketers. On several occasions when amateurs misbehaved or exhibited drunkenness, they were chastised and sometimes lost their membership of the club. The professionals generally exhibited a surly manner when confronted and questioned by the amateurs, often hinting at, but only occasionally openly expressing, disrespect. Tom occupied an unusual position, wedged between his past life as an amateur cricketer and his professional career.

Pages 221–2: Cosstick's letter, *The Australasian*, 8 May 1869.

Page 222: Letter from William Ducker to Cedric, 20 September 1869.

Page 222: After his return to the MCC, a meeting of the MCC committee elected Tom, Wardill and Hammersley to the match committee for the intercolonial.

Page 223: Letter from Tom to Elizabeth, 2 February 1870.

Page 223: The first part of the quote regarding the percentage of insanity is from a lecture by Dr Graham Edwards, in which he quotes Manning. See 'Sunstroke and Insanity in Nineteenth Century Australia'. The second part regarding drinking comes from Frederic Norton Manning, 'The Causation and Prevention of Insanity'.

Page 223: Marshall, *The Australasian*, 18 January 1867.

Pages 223–4: Letter from Tom to Elizabeth, 2 February 1870.

Page 224: An assessment of the assets and liabilities of the estate of Horatio Wills, as of 31 December 1868, showed that Tom owed the estate 36 pounds and 6 shillings.

Page 224: On Tom and Twopenny bowling, *The Australasian*, 26 February 1870.

Page 225: Letter from William Ducker to Tom, 1 August 1870.

Page 226: Three months before his death Handcock was admitted to Castlemaine Hospital, 24 May 1871, with cancer.

Page 226: Hugh Trumble purchasing the portrait of Tom Wills, *The Australasian*, 8 December 1923.

Page 227: Tommy Wills song, *Melbourne Punch*, 20 May 1869.

THE ART OF FORGERY

Page 229: *The Life and Adventures of Valentine Vox, the Ventriloquist*, Henry
  Cockton, Ward, Lock and Co., London, 1840.

CHAPTER 19: SATAN'S LITTLE HELPER

Page 230: Hammersley, *The Australasian*, 5 April 1873.

Pages 230–1: Letter from Elizabeth to Horace, 4 January 1871.

Page 231: Elected captain of the Victorian team, Tom was chosen as part of the
  intercolonial match committee along with R.W. Wardill, Dan Wilkie,
  William Handfield and Vernon Cameron.

Page 231: *The Australasian*, 4 February 1871.

Page 232: Tom's professional engagement with the MCC was to have ended
  on 6 March, but was extended by the club by a further three weeks as
  more matches were to be played. Notably, the East Melbourne Cricket
  Club, which for some time had desired to beat the MCC, had requested
  that if Tom played it would field 15 players to compensate but if he
  was not to play then 11 players would take the field.

Page 232: *The Cricketers' Guide* was Tom's first guide. Such guides had previously
  been written by amateur cricketers so for Tom to write this as a professional was significant. Again, his approach was more in keeping with
  a man who perhaps did not quite fit into the mould of a professional.

Page 233: Anonymous letters, *The Australasian*, 1 April 1871.

Page 234: As the season came to its end Wills wrote to the MCC. He had
  first written to the MCC before the match against NSW asking if he
  'would be paid during the time of his absence at Sydney'. There was
  no response; we assume this was granted. Then on 31 March the MCC
  debated whether, 'a bonus of 5 pounds be given to Mr TW Wills for
  his excellent play in the match with NSW'. The vote was split; no
  money was given. He wrote again 'claiming payment for two days
  service as bowler, one day's play in the last cup match, and two days as
  umpire in the match with Tasmania'. Complaints about non-payment
  or disputes needed to be handled delicately, which was not Tom's style,
  but he managed tolerably. On 24 April a further letter was read, some
  considerable time after he had completed his contract with the MCC,
  and he complained that he had been led to understand that he would
  receive a bonus for making over 50 runs in the NSW match. After
  a long debate, some of his requests were acceded to and he received
  3 pounds on the basis that he not ask for more money. Each pound
  was grudgingly given.

Page 234: Letter from Horace to Elizabeth, 18 June 1871.

Page 235: Letter from Horace to Elizabeth, 18 June 1871.

Page 237: Hammersley, *The Australasian*, 21 October 1871.

Page 237: Wills' response, *The Leader*, 28 October 1871.

Page 238: Elizabeth, in an undated letter, gives a brief description of Tom and
  Sarah's house, its yard and its closeness to the football ground. Although
  Tom is still not commonly mentioned in letters, the impression from
  this letter is that he was regarded well by his mother.

Page 238: 'Discarded' Tom was elected as cricket captain of Geelong in 1872 and in that year was on the committee of management and the match committee. The team practised each Wednesday at 4 p.m.

Page 239: Wardill's letter, *The Argus*, 1 December 1871.

Page 239: Tom on lost-ball variations, *Geelong Advertiser*, 21 December 1871.

Page 240: Hammersley on superior English connections, *The Australasian*, 23 December 1871.

Page 240: Tom challenged any man in the colony at single-wicket for 25 pounds a side, *Geelong Advertiser*, 25 December 1871. Two weeks later in early January he upped the amount but no one played him.

Page 241: The best cricketer in the colony, *The Leader*, 13 January 1872.

Page 241: Curious set of meetings, *The Argus*, 22 March 1872.

Page 241: System of throwing, *The Leader*, 30 March 1872.

Page 241: Tom Wills was the first cricketer in an intercolonial match to be called for actually throwing a cricket ball. In an earlier incident, a Tasmanian bowler had been called for raising his arm above his shoulder but not actually throwing the ball.

Page 242: Letter from Tom, *The Leader*, 27 April 1872.

Page 242: 'Darkies', *Geelong Advertiser*, 6 May 1872; 'ludicrous', *The Argus*, 7 May 1872.

Page 243: On Tom's good fortune, *Geelong Advertiser*, 22 August 1872.

Page 243: Letter from Tom Wills to William Handfield, 27 January 1873.

Page 244: Hammersley, *The Australasian*, 11 January 1873.

Pages 245–6: Tom's letter, *The Leader*, 18 January 1873. Tom quotes Hamlet, who is musing to his friend Horatio, not long before Hamlet's death. It is tempting to think that Tom wondered about his own fate and that, regardless of this spat, he and Hammersley were answerable to powers more significant than their own. Or perhaps his use of the quote was nothing more than another flashy classical allusion learned at Rugby twenty years previously, and not matched by deeper considerations.

Pages 246–7: Hammersley, *The Australasian*, 25 January 1873.

CHAPTER 20: THE ARRIVAL OF GRACE

Pages 248–9: The material on Wardill's death was included in his inquest papers.

Page 249: Letter from Tom Wills to Emily, 28 June 1859. The tone of Tom's writing when he penned the suicide remark was lighthearted but it nonetheless tells us that this is almost certainly what Tom was taught as a boy and young man, just as Richard Wardill revealed. Similarly it informs us that this was almost certainly a view held by at least some members of his family, and particularly by his mother.

Page 250: Letter from Egbert to Cedric, 8 September 1873. Tom was also elected as an honorary member of the Queen's Park Cricket Club in Geelong.

Page 251: Tom's letter re no-balling, *The Leader*, 12 July 1873.

Page 253: Drunkenness of the English team, *Geelong Advertiser*, 16 January 1874. Other more satirical accounts in journals such as *Melbourne Punch* portrayed Grace and the cricketers as reclining in couches having had too much hospitality and food for their own good.

Page 254: The original Bill of Fare is held by the NSW Cricket Association.

Page 254: Tom's rate of pay, *Wallaroo Times*, 31 January 1874.

Page 258: No better cricketer than Wills, *Wallaroo Times*, 25 February 1874.

Page 258: Sarah's Christian name was not used; rather she was an appendage to Tom as 'Mrs. Wills'. There was no suggestion other than that she was Tom's wife.

Page 260: Dilution quote, from *Cricket*, W.G. Grace.

Pages 260–1: Southerton gives a graphic moment-by-moment account of Jupp's illness in his diaries. There was a question raised as to whether the correct diagnosis was delirium tremens given Jupp's miraculous recovery to play in Kadina. It may not have been, but regardless of the exact nature of his illness there was a casual acceptance of his alcoholism and possible delirium tremens.

Page 261: The original plan had been for the XI to take a steamer directly from Adelaide to the Yorke Peninsula, for which the Peninsula Cricket Association had previously paid the XI's fare. But Grace, in light of a rough passage from Melbourne, asked that they be taken by coach to Kadina. Dr Herbert offered every courtesy; to the point of self-denial and against his better judgement. In response to Grace's request, Dr Herbert organised a coach trip for the XI and the Association paid their way. It was the first clear sign that Grace and his team were contemptuous of the local people on the Peninsula.

Page 262: Grace on leading his team onto the ground, *'WG': Cricketing Reminiscences and Personal Recollections*, p. 99.

Page 262: Report, *The Australasian*, 4 April 1874.

Page 263: Grace on Wills, *Cricketing Reminiscences*, p. 100.

Page 264: Extraordinary song, *Wallaroo Times*, 15 April 1874.

Page 265: Southerton's diary.

CHAPTER 21: DUST HIM OFF ONCE MORE

Page 267: Memories of early football in Geelong, *The Grammar School Quarterly*. Also in this article, Egbert Wills noted that the ruck position (a position Tom played in) was located in a small radius about the centre of the ground.

Pages 267–8: Tom's views on the introduction of football, *The Australian Cricketers' Guide for 1874–5*. The earliest years of football are difficult to track with accuracy because of the absence of evidence. Tom says he introduced the game in 1857; while the well-known Scotch College and Melbourne Grammar match in August 1858 was not the first game of football, it was clearly the first described in the press. Given that Tom was incredibly particular in matters of sport and saw himself as someone who knew its history well, I suspect that when he states '1857' that is exactly what he meant. However, no archival documents have been found as yet that show his attempts at football in 1857. His comment about the earliest rules devised by himself, Thompson, Hammersley and Smith might refer to the famous meeting at the Parade Hotel in May 1859 but there was also an indication in the press that a committee of unnamed men met in 1858, supporting Tom's recollection of the game being played in 1857.

Page 269: Four years after the Geelong–Ballarat game, a similar situation with 'unchivalrous tactics' applied when Geelong played Barwon. The Barwon team used Tom's tactic of deliberately kicking the ball out of bounds. Ironically it was Tom – showing rare diplomacy – who was called in to quell the dissent of the Geelong players.

Page 270: Tom was elected to the position of vice president of the Geelong Football Club in 1873, 1874, 1875 and 1876. It is sometimes claimed that Tom played 210 games of which 172 were with Geelong but it is impossible to know how many career games Tom played given the spasmodic reporting of games.

Page 271: Report of Tom speaking at the Argyle Hotel, *Geelong Advertiser*, 11 October 1875.

Page 271: Geelong press' defence of Tom, *Geelong Advertiser*, 6 September 1875.

Page 272: Letter from William Handfield to Tom Wills, 8 December 1874.

Page 273: In September 1874 Tom had been elected as secretary of the Corio Cricket Club. In March 1875 he was elected as captain of CCC. For the 1874–75 season Tom topped the Corio batting averages. He was also re-elected secretary to CCC in September 1875.

Page 273: Tom's response to the MCC request was in a letter from William Handfield to R.A. Fitzgerald, 10 August 1875, MCC Archives.

Page 276: Tom's letter, *The Australasian*, 22 January 1876.

Page 276: The Melbourne newspapers' response to Tom's selection, *The Leader*, 22 January 1876.

Pages 276–7: Tom's dream was reported in *The Australasian*, 22 January 1876.

CHAPTER 22: NO ROOM AT THE INN

Page 278: Tom's letter appeared in *The Australasian*, 11 March 1876.

Page 279: Letter from Horace to his mother recalling the murder of his father fifteen years previously, 18 April 1876.

Page 279: Tom's involvement in the ANA went against the grain of what I expected to find at this point in his life. The standard treatise is that Tom, in chronic debt, was not capable of acts other than on the sporting field. But Tom was not only involved in the ANA – a society to promote welfare and charity towards the native-born – but he moved that the local Geelong branch be initiated as well as contributing money. This is a clear link to the influence of his father who could only have smiled at his son's determined effort to promote things Australian. Geelong ANA Minute Book, 1875–76.

Page 279: Tom sold land in 1875 but still had property left at this time. William Ducker was involved in virtually all these financial and real estate transactions.

Page 281: Junior Cup, *Geelong Advertiser*, 5 February 1877.

Page 281: Although Tom was not elected to an office-bearing position of the CCC, he was on the general and match committees. He first played for and captained Breakwater in October 1876, and continued in quite prominent administrative positions for the Geelong Football Club up to and including 1876. In April 1876 the Annual General Meeting of the Geelong Football Club was held at the Argyle Hotel and Tom was elected vice president and on to the match committee. He donated a silver Challenge Cup – 'the bowl is an emu's egg, the cover to it being surmounted by a ball, on which stands a footballer' – for competition between Geelong, Ballarat and the teams of the Western District. Tom held a position of prominence within the club and chaired meetings during the season. Tom's brothers Egbert and Horace retired from the Geelong Football Club. The first club match was held in June and played on the Argyle Ground. Tom was the central umpire. By 1877 his role was greatly diminished.

Pages 281–2: The Junior Challenge Cup is reported in *Geelong Advertiser*, 9 April 1877.

Page 282: On 12 April 1877, the 18th Annual meeting of the Geelong Football Club was held at the Argyle Hotel. Tom attended as one of the club's vice presidents.

Pages 283–4: Tom's letter to the MCC, written in blue ink with his characteristic backward sloping script, was dated 19 September 1877, and written from Geelong.

Page 284: Hammersley's article was in the *Sydney Mail*, 29 September 1883.

Page 285: I found many applications for the secretarial position stored in the MCC archives. Some were from prominent individuals, which, to me, highlighted the significance of Tom's letter being mentioned in the minutes. Most of the other letters were not referred to at all.

CHAPTER 23: THE EMERALD HILL

Page 289: Buck Wheatley's was one of the few archival documents I was unable to review due to restricted access to the South Melbourne Cricket Club archives. However I spoke to Dr Robert Grogan, author of *Our Proud Heritage: A History of the South Melbourne Cricket Club from 1862* (South Melbourne Cricket Club, 2003), who found Wheatley's notes. The transcription is Dr Grogan's.

Page 290: Tom's last public letter was in *The Leader*, 15 June 1878. He umpired at least four matches as part of the new Victorian Football Association in the middle of 1878. In June he umpired a match between Carlton and Albert Park at the South Melbourne Cricket Ground; Melbourne Football Club and Albert Park at the South Melbourne Cricket Ground; and Albert Park and St Kilda. In August he umpired a football match between Carlton and Ballarat at the East Melbourne Cricket Ground, watched by 1200 spectators.

CHAPTER 24: AN ISLAND IN THE SUN

Page 295: Letter from Cedric to Colden Harrison, 7 March 1879.

Page 296: Report of the night match was in *The Australasian*, 16 August 1879.

Page 296: Tom is first recorded playing with the Heidelberg club in November 1879.

Pages 297–8: Letter from Tom to Horace, 15 March 1880.

CHAPTER 25: THE GATES O' HELL

Page 299: Tom wrote letters on 15 March 1880 to both Horace and Cedric.

Page 302: It would seem from the description of 'semi Delirium Tremens' in Patrick Moloney's casebook that the syndrome was not fulminant at that point.

CHAPTER 26: THE SWEETEST MAN

Pages 307–8: Letter from Egbert to Horace, 9 May 1880.

Page 311: Elizabeth's words on her son were related to me by Terry Wills Cooke, as oral family history.

Page 311: Letter from Mary Wills to Bella, 9 May 1880.

Page 313: Hammersley on Tom Wills appeared in the *Sydney Mail*, 15 September 1883. Ironically Hammersley was said to have died of 'softening of the brain'.

Page 313: William Hammersley wrote about the 'Evil Eye' in *Victorian Review*, May 1884.

Page 314: Letter from Egbert to Horace, 9 May 1880; letter from Cedric to Colden, 18 August 1880.

Pages 317–18: The interview with Horace appeared in the *Evening Sun*, 7 December 1923.

EPILOGUE

Page 321: The pin described by Lawton is the one Tom received after the Victorian victory in the 1860 intercolonial cricket match against NSW, clearly described by Tom's sister Emily. The players received their pins at Cremorne Gardens near the Richmond Paddock.

AFTERWORD

For more detail, see G.M. de Moore, 'Tom Wills, Marngrook and the evolution of Australian Rules football', in *Crossing Boundaries*.

SELECTED BIBLIOGRAPHY

A more comprehensive list of references used for this book can be found in my PhD thesis, 'In from the Cold: Tom Wills – A Nineteenth-Century Sporting Hero', 2008, held at Victoria University.

My PhD was the result of ten years of research. I tracked down over 150 published letters, either written by Tom Wills or others who make significant comment on him, in nineteenth-century newspapers across Australia, England and New Zealand. Over 500 archival items on the Wills family were found in collections in several countries, including 300 letters written by members of Tom's immediate family. While many of the private letters were in the Wills family collections, I have also read material scattered in public collections across Australia. In addition, there were dozens of other pieces of archival evidence that tracked the path of Tom Wills and the genealogy of the Wills family, and that gave context to Tom's life. My research uncovered many hitherto unknown items.

Listed below is a selection of the main sources I used.

PRIMARY DOCUMENTS RELATING TO TOM WILLS
Letters and documents in the Wills family collection, particularly the letters
    collated by Terry Wills Cooke, Tom Wills and Lawton Wills Cooke;
    the Wills family archives at the State Library of Victoria; baptism
    papers, death certificate, will and inquest of Thomas Wentworth Wills;
    medical admission notes of Tom Wills. The Melbourne Hospital, Dr
    Moloney, Males, No. 21 Ward, from 2/1/1880–1/5/1880.

INFORMATION ON RUGBY SCHOOL
The following material was located at the Temple Reading Room, Rugby
    School:

'A Victorian Schoolboy: Tom Burn's Schooldays; From the School Letters of Thomas Harris Burn, 1841-1852', Andrew Robert Burn (ed).

Census figures for Evans and Cotton House, 1851.

Evans's House Football Book, MDCCCLIV-LXI, Hutchinson's House Football Book, MDCCCLXII.

Evans House Score Book, MDCCCLI-LVII.

Letters of Charles E. Kemp.

Monthly report of Rugby School students, c. 1853.

New Rugbeian 1858-1861, Whittaker and Co., Crossley and Billington (school magazine).

'News from Rugby School', Summer 2005, p. 14.

Pamphlets of Rugby IV.

Price House Score Book, MDCCCXLIX-L.

Programme of Rugby School Athletic Games, 1852.

Reproduced paintings of Rugby School: G. Barnard, E. Harwood, H. Fellowes.

Rugby School, Cricket Scores, 1831-1893 (Foreign and Bigside matches), A.J. Lawrence, Whittaker and Co., 1894.

Rugby School Lists 1850-1855, printed by Crossley and Billington.

Rugby School Register, 1842-1874, Volume 2, revised and annotated by Rev. A.T. Michell, printed for subscribers by A.J. Lawrence, 1902.

The Crescent, Rugby, an Arnoldite Publication, Third Series, Part 1, 1867.

The Meteor (school magazine), 1867, 1868, 1873, 1874, 1880, 1881, 1898.

The Rugbaean, 1850-1852 (school magazine).

The Rugby Magazine, 1835, 1836.

The Rugby Miscellany, Whittaker and Co., 1846, no single author.

'Ye Annals of Evans', unpaginated.

INFORMATION ON CULLIN-LA-RINGO

Official letters to and from Tom Wills in the aftermath of his father's murder and his subsequent management of the station can be found in the Queensland State Archives.

SPORTING ARCHIVES

Charles Lawrence's diary, Bernard Whimpress, South Australian Cricket Association.

James Southerton diaries, Trent Bridge Library.

Melbourne Cricket Club Archives:

    MCC Letter books: 1863-83, 1891-1901.

    MCC Minute books: 1847-52; 1859-81; 1891-93; 1922-25.

    Minutes of the IC committee 1859-61.

New South Wales Cricket Association:

    NSWCA Minute Book, 1857; October 1866-May 1875; July 1875-80.

    Trustees of the Outer Domain Minute Book, 5 January 1857-16 May 1876.

    Bill of Fare, Complimentary breakfast to the All England Eleven at Tattersall's Hotel, Sydney, 22 January 1874.

South Australian Cricket Association:
    Minutes, 31 May 1871–5 February 1875.

OTHER ARCHIVES

Aboriginal Protectorate Weekly, Monthly, Quarterly and Annual Reports
    and Journals; E.S. Parker, 1842 reports.
Australian Natives' Association, Geelong Minute Book, 1875–76.
Agreement between W.R. Hayman Esq., Unamurriman and others, and
    W.E.B. Gurnett relating to engagement of cricketers on 8 January 1867.
John Bromby diary, transcribed, Melbourne Church of England Grammar
    School.
Female Orphan School, 1817–32, Parramatta Heritage Centre Archives,
    Authority of NSW, AO Reel 2777, Admission Book.
Jesse Gregson, memoirs and related papers, Mitchell Library.
Inquests on Richard Wardill and Bilvayarrimin (Watty).
Letter from R. Brough Smyth to the Honourable Chief Secretary, 14
    October 1867.
Letter from Thomas Kennedy to H.R. Barclay, Superintendent of Police,
    Portland, 15 August 1867.
Letter from R. Brough Smyth to The Honorable James McCullock, Chief
    Secretary, 12 February 1867.
Letters of Andrew Newell, Royal Historical Society of Victoria.
State Records of South Australia regarding Henry Jupp, GRG 78/49
    Admission Register for Adelaide Hospital 1840–1900.
The Thirty Third Annual report of the Committee of Management of the
    Melbourne Hospital, Fergusson and Mitchell, 1881.

THESES

Blaskett, Beverley, 'The Aboriginal Response to White Settlement in the
    Port Phillip District, 1835–1850', Masters thesis, History Department,
    University of Melbourne, July 1979.
Cooke, Simon, 'Secret Sorrows: A Social History of Suicide in Victoria,
    1841–1921', PhD thesis, University of Melbourne, History Department,
    1998.
Critchett, J.F., 'A "Distant Field of Murder": Portland Bay District Frontiers
    1834–1848', PhD thesis, Faculty of Arts, University of Melbourne,
    1988.
Daws, A.G., 'The Origins of Australian Rules Football', Honours thesis,
    History Department, University of Melbourne, 1954.
Mannering, John, 'An Appraisal of Sanitary Reform in Rugby 1849–1875',
    Honours thesis, West Midlands College of Higher Education, 1985.
Mitchell, A. M., 'Temperance and the Liquor Question in Later Nineteenth
    Century Victoria', Masters thesis, History Department, University of
    Melbourne, 1966.
Stephens, Tracey, 'Societal Reactions to Suicide in Victoria, 1882 and 1892',
    Honours thesis, History Department, University of Melbourne, 1988.

BOOKS

Batchelder, Alf, *Pavilions in the Park: A History of the Melbourne Cricket Club and its Ground*, Australian Scholarly Publishing, 2005.

Billis, R.V. & Kenyon, A.S., *Pastoral Pioneers of Port Phillip*, Stockland Press, 1974.

Bird, J.T.S., *The Early History of Rockhampton*, The Morning Bulletin, 1904.

Blainey, Geoffrey, *A Game of Our Own: The Origins of Australian Football*, Black Inc., 2003.

Bouwman, R., *Glorious Innings: Treasures from the Melbourne Cricket Club Collection*, Hutchinson Australia, 1987.

Christie, M.F., *Aborigines in Colonial Victoria 1835-86*, Sydney University Press, 1979.

Clark, Ian D. (ed.), *The Journals of George Augustus Robinson, Chief Protector, Port Phillip Aboriginal Protectorate*, vols I–IV, Heritage Matters, 1998.

Clark, I.D., *Scars in the Landscape: A Register of Massacre Sites in Western Victoria 1803-1859*, Aboriginal Studies Press, 1995.

Clark, I.D., *That's My Country Belonging To Me: Aboriginal Land Tenure and Dispossession in Nineteenth Century Western Victoria*, Heritage Matters, 1998.

Cockton, Henry, *Valentine Vox, the Ventriloquist*, Ward, Lock and Co., c. 1840.

Compton, Berdmore, *Edward Meyrick Goulburn*, John Murray, 1899.

Dawson, James, *Australian Aborigines, Melbourne, Sydney and Adelaide: George Robertson, 1881*, Facsimile edition, Australian Institute of Aboriginal Studies, 1981.

de Serville, Paul, *Port Phillip Gentlemen*, Oxford University Press, 1980.

de Serville, Paul, *Pounds and Pedigrees: The Upper Class in Victoria 1850–80*, Oxford University Press, 1991.

Fairfax, W. (ed.), *The Cricketer's Guide of Australasia, 1857-8*, Fairfax and Co., 1858.

Flanagan, M., *The Call*, Allen & Unwin, 1998.

Grace, W.G., *Cricket*, J.W. Arrowsmith, 1891.

Grace, W.G., *'WG': Cricketing Reminiscences and Personal Recollections*, James Bowden, 1899.

Gregory, A., *The Ever Open Door: A History of the Royal Melbourne Hospital 1848-1998*, Hyland House, 1998.

Grogan, Robert, *Our Proud Heritage: A History of the South Melbourne Cricket Club from 1862*, South Melbourne Cricket Club, 2003.

Hammersley, W.J. (ed.), *The Victorian Cricketer's Guide, 1861-2*, Sands & McDougall, 1862.

Harrison, Brian, *Drink and the Victorians*, Faber and Faber, 1971.

Hess, R. & Stewart, B. (eds), *More Than a Game: An Unauthorised History of Australian Rules Football*, Melbourne University Press, 1998.

Hibbins, Gillian M., *Sport and Racing in Colonial Melbourne: The Cousins and Me: Colden Harrison, Tom Wills and William Hammersley*, Lynedoch Publications, 2007.

Hope Simpson, J.B., *Rugby Since Arnold: A History of Rugby School from 1842*, Macmillan, 1967.

Hughes, Thomas, *Tom Brown's Schooldays*, Ward Lock & Co., 1911.

Macrory, Jennifer, *Running with the Ball*, CollinsWillow, 1991.

Mancini, A. & Hibbins, G.M., *Running with the Ball*, Lynedoch Publications, 1987.

Maudsley, Henry, *The Pathology of Mind*, Macmillan, 1879.

Melly, George, *School Experiences of a Fag at a Private and a Public School*, Smith, Elder & Co., 1854.

Morrison, Edgar, *Early Days in the Lodden Valley: Memoirs of Edward Stone Parker, 1802–1865*, The Editor, 1965.

Mulvaney, D.J. & Harcourt, R., *Cricket Walkabout: The Australian Aborigines in England* (2nd edn), Macmillan in association with Dept. of Aboriginal Affairs, 1988.

Perrin, L., *Cullin-La-Ringo: The Triumph and Tragedy of Tommy Wills*, Les Perrin, 1998.

Priestley, Susan, *South Melbourne: A History*, Melbourne University Press, 1995.

Russell, George W.E., *Arthur Stanton: A Memoir*, Longmans, Green and Co, 1917.

Smith, R. & Williams, R., *W.G. Down Under: Grace in Australia 1873–4 and 1891–2*, Apple Books, 1994.

Strutt, William, *Victoria the Golden: Scenes, Sketches and Jottings from Nature*, with a narrative by Marjorie Tipping, Library Committee, Parliament of Victoria, 1980.

Thompson, J.B. (ed.), *The Victorian Cricketer's Guide, 1858–59*, Sands & Kenny, 1859.

Thompson, J.B. (ed.), *The Victorian Cricketer's Guide for 1859–60*, Sands, Kenny & Co., 1860.

Twopeny, Richard, *Town Life in Australia*, Penguin, 1883.

Welsh, A.R., *Rugby School Hare and Hounds: Description of the Big-Side Runs*, A.J. Lawrence, 1902.

Whimpress, Bernard, *Chuckers: A History of Throwing in Australian Cricket*, B. Whimpress, 2002.

Whimpress, Bernard, *Passport to Nowhere: Aborigines in Australian Cricket, 1850–1939*, Walla Walla Press, 1999.

Whimpress, Bernard, *W.G. Grace at Kadina: Champion Cricketer or Scoundrel?* B. Whimpress, 1994.

Wills Cooke, T.S., *The Currency Lad: A Biography of Horatio Spencer Howe Wills, 5 October 1811 to 17 October 1861 and the Story of His Immediate Family 1797 to 1918*, T. S. Wills Cooke, 1998.

Wills, T.W. (ed.), *Australian Cricketers' Guide 1870–1*, J&A McKinley, 1871.

Wills, T.W. (ed.), *The Australian Cricketers' Guide for 1874–5*, Henry Franks, Printer, 1875.

Wilson, Philip. St. John., *The Pioneers of Port Phillip: The Story of Early Melbourne for Boys and Girls*, Robertson & Mullens Ltd, 1934.

CHAPTERS OF BOOKS

Blaskett, Beverley, 'The level of violence: Europeans and Aborigines in Port Phillip, 1835–1850', in *Through White Eyes*, Janson, S. & Macintyre, S. (eds), Allen & Unwin, 1990, pp. 77–100.

de Moore, G.M., 'Tom Wills, Marngrook and the evolution of Australian Rules football', in *Crossing Boundaries*, R. Hess (ed.), Maribyrnong Press, 2005, pp. 5–15.

de Moore, G.M., 'The tree of life: Tom Wills, Rugby School and the evolution of Australian Rules Football', in *Rugby History: The Remaking of the Class Game*, Bushby, M. & Hickie, T.V. (eds), Australian Society for Sports History, Studies No. 22, 2007, pp. 113–19.

Flanagan, Martin, 'Sport and Culture', in *The Alfred Deakin Lectures: Ideas for the Future of a Civil Society*, ABC Books, 2001, pp. 327–35.

Murphy, Leonard J.T., 'Patrick Moloney', in *Occasional Papers on Medical History Australia*, Forster, F., Attwood, H. & Gandevia, B. (eds), Medical History Society, AMA, Victorian Branch and Medical History Unit, University of Melbourne, Victoria, 1984, pp. 1–33.

ARTICLES

Atkinson, F. P., 'Treatment of Delirium Tremens', *Australasian Medical Gazette*, May 1883, pp. 178–9.

Barrett, James, 'Some incidents in the history of the Melbourne Hospital from 1879–1883', *The Melbourne Hospital Clinical Reports*, vol. I., no. 2, November 1930, pp. 97–110.

Barry, J.V., 'Suicide and the law', *Melbourne University Law Review*, vol. 5, no. 1, May 1965, pp. 1–16.

Black, J., 'On Delirium Tremens', *Australian Medical Journal*, April 1856, pp. 119–24.

Clutterbuck, J.B., 'Delirium Tremens', *Australian Medical Journal*, vol. 16, December, 1871, pp. 358–61.

Cutts, Dr., 'Softening of the brain', *Australian Medical Journal*, vol. 7, 1862, pp. 122–4.

da Costa, J.M., 'On irritable heart: A clinical study of a form of functional cardiac disorder and its consequences', *The American Journal of the Medical Sciences*, January 1871, pp. 17–52.

de Moore, G.M., 'The sons of lush: Tom Wills, alcohol and the colonial cricketer', *Sport in History*, vol. 25, December 2005, pp. 354–74.

de Moore, G.M., 'The suicide of Thomas Wentworth Wills', *Medical Journal of Australia*, vol. 171, December 1999, pp. 656–8.

de Moore, G.M., 'Tom Wills and the adventure of the lost cricket ball', *Baggy Green*, vol. 8, no. 1, November 2005, pp. 62–72.

de Moore, G.M., 'Tom Wills and birth of Aussie Rules', *Inside Football*, July 2006, p. 12.

de Moore, G.M., 'Tom Wills, Satan's little helper: A case study of throwing in nineteenth-century Australian cricket', *The International Journal of the History of Sport*, vol. 25, no. 1, January 2008, pp. 82–99.

Edwards, G.A., 'Sunstroke and insanity in nineteenth century Australia', 3rd National Conference on Medical History and Health in Australia, Adelaide, November 1986.

Grow, Robin, 'Nineteenth century football and the Melbourne press', *Sporting Traditions*, vol. 3, no. 1, November 1986, pp. 23–37.

Hammersley, W.J., 'Personal reminiscences of the late Adam Lindsay Gordon', *Victorian Review*, May 1884, pp. 66–9.

Hibbins, G.M., 'The Cambridge Connection', *International Journal of the History of Sport*, vol. 6, no. 2, September 1989, pp. 172–92.

Manning, F.N., 'The Causation and Prevention of Insanity', *Australian Medical Pamphlets*, vol. 10, 1880, pp. 1–17.

Patel, V. & de Moore, G.M., 'Harakiri: A clinical study of self-stabbing', *Journal of Clinical Psychiatry*, vol. 55, 1994, pp. 98–103.

Various, 'Recollections of football by Old Boys', *The Grammar School Quarterly*, July 1902, pp. 18–26.

NEWSPAPERS AND PERIODICALS

The following is a list of nineteenth-century newspapers and periodicals that contained information on Tom Wills and background to his life and times:

England: *Bell's Life and Sporting Chronicle London*; *The Times*, London; *Midland Counties Illustrated News*; *Midlands Sporting Chronicle and National Register of Sports*; *The Rugby Advertiser and Central England News*; *Rugby Recorder and Local Advertiser*; *Sheffield Times*; *Sheffield and Rotherham Independent*.

New Zealand: *Daily Southern Cross*; *Lyttleton Times*; *New Zealander*; *New Zealand Herald*; *Otago Daily Times*; *Otago Witness*; *The Press*; *Weekly News*.

New South Wales: *Bathurst Times*; *Bell's Life in Sydney and Sporting Reviewer* (to Oct 1860) then *Bell's Life and Sport Chronicle* (to Dec 1870); *The Bulletin*; *Currency Lad*; *The Empire*; *The Era*; *Evening News*; *The Field*; *Illawarra Mercury*; *Illustrated Sydney News*; *Illustrated Sporting Life and Pastoral Register*, Sydney (Sept 1866–June 1867), changed title to *Sydney Sporting Life* (Sept 1866–June 1867); *Life*; *Maitland Ensign*; *Maitland Mercury and Hunter River General Advertiser*; *Maitland Weekly Post*; *Newcastle Chronicle*; *Newcastle Chronicle and Hunter River District News*; *Newcastle Despatch*; *Newcastle Morning Herald and Miners' Advocate*; *Newcastle Pilot*; *NSW Government Gazette*; *Northern Times* (Newcastle); *Sydney Afternoon Telegram*; *Sydney Gazette*; *Sydney Mail*; *Sydney Morning Herald*; *Sydney Punch*; *Town and Country Journal*.

Queensland: *Brisbane Courier*; *Daily Record*, Rockhampton; *Moreton Bay Courier*; *North Australian*, Ipswich; *Queensland Guardian*; *Queensland Times*; *Rockhampton Bulletin*; *Toowoomba Chronicle and Queensland Advertiser*.

South Australia: *Adelaide Advertiser*; *Adelaide Observer*; *Bell's Life in Adelaide and Sporting Chronicle*; *Express and Telegraph*; *Illustrated Adelaide Post*; *South Australian Advertiser*; *South Australian Register*; *Walleroo Times and Mining Journal*; *Yorke's Peninsula Advertiser and Miners' News*.

Tasmania: *Cornwall Chronicle*; *Hobart Mercury*.

Victoria: *The Age*; *Ararat Advertiser*; *The Argus*; *The Australasian*; *Australasian Sketcher*; *Ballarat Courier*; *Ballarat Evening Post*; *Ballarat Star*; *Bendigo Advertiser*; *Bendigo Independent*; *Bell's Life in Victoria and Sporting Chronicle*; *Daily Telegraph*; *Evelyn Observer*; *Evening Star*; *Evening Sun*; *Examiner and Melbourne Weekly News*; *Geelong Advertiser*; *Geelong*

Chronicle; Geelong Register; Gippsland Mercury; Gippsland Times; Hamilton Spectator and Grange District Advertiser; The Herald; Illustrated Australian News (Melbourne); *Illustrated Melbourne Post; The Leader; Melbourne Punch; Mercury and Weekly Courier* (Collingwood and Fitzroy); *Mount Ararat Advertiser; News of the Week; The Observer; City and Suburban Advertiser* (Collingwood); *Pleasant Creek News* (Stawell); *Port Phillip Herald; Port Phillip Gazette; Port Phillip Patriot; Richmond Australian; Richmond Guardian; South Melbourne Record; The Sun; Warrnambool Standard; Weekly Age; Weekly Times; Yeoman and Australian Acclimatiser* (Melbourne).

PICTURE CREDITS

Page ii: Oil painting of Tom Wills, 1870. This most recognisable of images hangs in the MCC Museum. Artist, William Handcock. Courtesy of Melbourne Cricket Club Museum collection.

Page xviii: Studio portrait of Tom most likely taken in the year after he returned to Australia, c. 1857. Courtesy of Terry Wills Cooke.

Page 4: A recently discovered image of young Elizabeth at the time of her marriage. She was sixteen years of age. Courtesy of Terry Wills Cooke.

Page 5: 'Graceful manners distinguish the well bred.' Fifteen-year-old Elizabeth wrote these lines in her writing book from Mrs Jane McGillivray's Boarding School, Parramatta, during the period in which she was being courted by Horatio. Courtesy of Lawton Wills Cooke.

Page 17: Lexington, Mount William. Courtesy of Terry Wills Cooke.

Page 22: 'The School from the Close', George Barnard, 1852. Barnard's painting reveals teachers, wives and children sauntering along the dirt path that rings the playing fields; the school clock tower hovers in the distance; capped boys play football in multiple knots on a field that sprawls undefined; a trio of defenders stand in front of the H-shaped Rugby goals; all players don long white trousers whose upper edge is cleanly defined by the sparkle of a shiny thick black belt. The chapel is obscured but to the left of the main school building. Courtesy of Temple Reading Room, Rugby School.

Page 31: Rugby School Athletic Games were a feature of the school sports year and attracted crowds of town dwellers who observed the events. Tom sent this home to his parents with his notes all over the record detailing his achievements. When he returned to Melbourne, Tom wrote to the press to try and institute a similar athletic event in the colony. Courtesy of Terry Wills Cooke. Photograph by Greg Elms.

Page 41: This Monthly Report was for many years mistakenly attributed to Tom's time at William Brickwood's school in Melbourne. By examining the names of the boys and the Rugby School register, it almost certainly came from 1853 at Rugby School. Although it looks impressive, Tom was several years older than a number of boys in this group. Courtesy of Lawton Wills Cooke.

Page 44: 'Football at Rugby', E. Harwood, 1859. Harwood's painting reveals small bands of boys attired in long white pants playing on Big-Side. Teachers circumnavigate the close; the ball is more spherical than oval and the landscape less denuded of trees than it is today. The painting is set after the elm leaves had fallen. The unpainted wooden H-shaped goals can be seen to the right. It was common for families of the masters to watch the boys play. The chapel can be seen through the trees in the distance. Courtesy of Temple Reading Room, Rugby School.

Page 50: Daguerreotype of Tom at the time of leaving Rugby School, 1855. This was kept by his brother Horace and reproduced in the *Evening Sun*, 7 December 1923. Courtesy of State Library of Victoria.

Page 56: Belle Vue, Point Henry. Courtesy of Terry Wills Cooke.

Page 59: Bradshaw's original scorecard of the 1857 intercolonial cricket match. This was Tom's first intercolonial match, less than a month after he had returned from England. The scores are printed on silk. Courtesy of Terry Wills Cooke.

Page 63: Studio portrait of Horace and Cedric Wills, 1859. The two boys idolised Tom. The gap in years between the younger boys and Tom resulted in a relationship that really was never between two equals. The boys, until the end, looked up to their older brother. Courtesy of Terry Wills Cooke. Photograph by Greg Elms.

Page 65: Studio portrait of Emily Wills, c. 1855. Her severe facial expression matched her niggly and difficult temperament. Courtesy of Terry Wills Cooke.

Page 67: Tom's wild and wonderful 1857 letter to Emily written from 'The Parade'. Courtesy of Lawton Wills Cooke.

Page 80: 1858 intercolonial match between Victoria and NSW at the Melbourne Cricket Ground, coloured lithograph. Victoria won this match and Tom was an instant colonial hero. Note the tiny MCC pavilion in the background with its gable end pieces. Beyond this is the Richmond Paddock. Tom is preparing to bowl. In the foreground, highlighted as part of the artistic technique of the day, are important Club and colonial men. Courtesy of the Melbourne Cricket Club Museum Collection.

Page 88: Wood engraving, Robert Bruce, from the *Illustrated Melbourne Post*, 27 July 1866. The caption in the newspaper was: 'Winter in Australia: Football in the Richmond Paddock'. The Richmond Paddock, next to the Melbourne Cricket Club, was the site of many of the early games of football. Note the shape of the football and the two goal posts with small flags atop each. To the sides are two kick-off posts. In the background is the MCC pavilion. Courtesy of State Library of Victoria.

Page 93: 'Jolimont, from the hill beyond the Yarra Yarra', pencil drawing by Edward La Trobe Bateman, 1854. This is Richmond Paddock. Courtesy of State Library of Victoria.

Page 96: The 1860 intercolonial match. Courtesy of Melbourne Cricket Club Museum Collection.

Page 98: Victorian cricketers 1859. Looking more like buccaneers, they are, from left: Gideon Elliott, Barton Grindrod, George Marshall, James Bryant and Tom Wills. Courtesy of Melbourne Cricket Club Museum Collection.

Page 102: The first known written rules of Melbourne football as conceived at the Parade Hotel, next to the Richmond Paddock. Tom's name is listed as the first of the rule writers. Courtesy of Melbourne Cricket Club Museum Collection.

Page 112: Horatio Wills. Courtesy of Terry Wills Cooke.

Page 127: Telegram about Cullin-la-Ringo in the aftermath of the killings. This was a critical telegram as it confirmed Tom's safety. Courtesy of Terry Wills Cooke. Photograph by Greg Elms.

Page 136: The envelope of a letter written by Tom to his mother, July 1862. To reach Belle Vue from Cullin-la-Ringo a letter passed through Rockhampton, Brisbane, Sydney and Melbourne before reaching Geelong and then Belle Vue. Note that Belle Vue, Point Henry, is simply described as 'near' Geelong. Courtesy of the Wills family.

Page 138: Tom Wills, c. 1863. This previously unpublished image was a real find during the research. It was found amongst a pile of old photographs at Minerva Creek, Queensland. The image was found on a *carte de visite*. These were calling cards, popular at the time. Fellow cricketers joked how Tom was fond of using his *carte* and implied that he had a high opinion of himself. Courtesy of Tom Wills.

Page 144: Elizabeth Wills. Courtesy of Terry Wills Cooke.

Pages 158–9: Cullin-la-Ringo in the 1880s. Courtesy of Terry Wills Cooke.

Page 167: Horatio's gravesite. Courtesy of Terry Wills Cooke.

Page 186: Tom Wills and the Aboriginal cricket team – his ten black magistrates – outside the MCC pavilion, December 1866. Courtesy of the Melbourne Cricket Club Museum Collection.

Pages 188–9: Aboriginal cricket team, December 1866, outside the MCC pavilion. Tom appears quite casual and the lines of his body are those of a natural athlete. W.E.B. Gurnett is at the centre of the image with the top hat. Courtesy of Mitchell Library, SLNSW, Sydney.

Pages 194–5: Copperplate contract that bound the Aboriginal cricketers and William Hayman to William Gurnett. Although the press at the time mentioned that Tom signed the contract, there is no mention of Tom in this contract. Courtesy of State Library of Victoria.

Page 200: Wood engraving that appeared in the *Australian News for Home Readers* (Melbourne), 27 December 1866. This image was based on a series of separate photographs sent to Melbourne as publicity for the tour. Sugar died before the team reached Melbourne. Courtesy of State Library of Victoria.

Page 228: Henry Cockton, *The Life and Adventures of Valentine Vox, the Ventriloquist*, Ward, Lock and Co., c. 1840. Author's copy. Photograph Greg Elms.

Page 235: Egbert and Horace Wills. Courtesy of Terry Wills Cooke.

Page 298: Tom's signature from his last letter, just under two months before his suicide. Courtesy of Terry Wills Cooke.

Page 300: Tom's last letter to Horace. Courtesy of Terry Wills Cooke.

Page 302: Melbourne Hospital, c. 1880. Courtesy of Royal Melbourne Hospital archives.

Page 303: Patrick Moloney's casebook, no. 21 Ward, 2 January 1880–1 May 1880. These clinical notes, though brief, outline precisely Tom's mental state and his treatment. Courtesy of Royal Melbourne Hospital archives.

Page 315: Egbert's letter to Horace describing in detail the final hours of their brother's life. Courtesy of Lawton Wills Cooke. Photograph by Greg Elms.

ACKNOWLEDGEMENTS

First and foremost I want to acknowledge the descendants of the Wills family. Within their keeping they have archival documents that I regard as national treasures. Terry Wills Cooke, his wife Marian and their daughter Sarah took me in as a boarder on several occasions in the kindest way possible. Terry's family history, which he was completing as I started my work, was vital in allowing this project to develop. Without it I would have stumbled at the beginning. Terry, thank you for your willingness to share your knowledge and many bottles of fine white wine over dinner. Lawton Wills Cooke and his wife Lynette in Melbourne offered urbane conversation, fine coffee and repeated assistance while I rummaged about their cellar looking for material. During the 2000 Olympics I had the opportunity of spending one week with Tom Wills at Minerva Creek, Springsure. It was a week I will never forget. Tom was a wonderful and knowledgeable host; he showed me the site of Horatio's grave and the massacre site, and took me about, freely giving up a great deal of his time.

Thank you to Allen & Unwin for considering that the idea of a biography on Tom was worth doing. In particular, thanks to commissioning editor Andrea McNamara for answering Patrick Gallagher's query, 'Who is Tom Wills?' correctly, and for her intelligence, professionalism and support over the final year of writing. I've not written a book before and at each step I have learnt a great deal, but perhaps none more so than when I was presented with the copyedited manuscript. Patricia Cortese's attention to detail and her ability to keep all the threads of Tom's life together was invaluable and greatly appreciated. For the second edition Angela Handley, Editorial Manager, Allen & Unwin, coordinated everything. I thank her for her efforts and skills.

Literally hundreds of people have assisted me over the decade it has taken to research the life of Tom Wills. Many more were recipients of my phone calls and letters, which usually started off: 'You don't know me, but

I am looking for information on a man called . . .' Living in Sydney posed a problem as most of the material was in Victoria and Queensland. However, I grew to believe it was an unexpected geographical advantage in that I was not swamped by local stories or prejudices about Tom Wills. Nonetheless, it meant many trips to Victoria. Peter Gill was my 'right hand man' over many years, diligently gathering everything I requested.

Thanks to the following individuals who gave advice or information on Tom Wills and different aspects of his times that I used in the book: Jeremy Ashton, Alf Batchelder, Bob Brenner, Neil Carter, Richard Cashman, Richard Christen, Ian Clark, Colin Clewes, Michael Collins Persse, John Cordner, Graham Edwards, Peter Ellis, Martin Flanagan, David Frith, Warwick Franks, Stephen Green, George Griffiths, Robert Grogan, Robin Grow, Gillian Hibbins, Liz Huf, Sally Hopwood, John Kean, Ivo Kelaart, Carol Liston, Sandy McFarlane, Howard Milton, Bernard Nicholson, John O'Hara, Sacha Orive, Roger Page, Susan Priestley, Jonathon Richards, Jackie Ristau, John Rose, Kay Rowan, Greg Ryan, Rick Smith, Russell Stephens, Kenly Simpson, Bernard Thompson, Leo Tidey, Warwick Torrens, Derek Ufton, Ray Webster, Bernard Whimpress and Jan Worthington.

Les Perrin's early contributions to the study of Tom Wills, particularly his research on Tom's time in Queensland, were important to this book.

The archival collection at the Melbourne Cricket Club is without doubt the finest collection of sporting material I came across. There were numerous staff members who gave me assistance. I would particularly like to thank Andrew Paterson, Jean Johnson, Jennifer van Dam, Margaret Birtley, Patricia Downs, Alison Ware, Rex Harcourt, David Studham and Trevor Ruddell.

Libraries – large and small – have been my 'home' for ten years. As a psychiatrist, I spent plenty of time observing the goings on in libraries, their little colonies of people and the many visitors who wandered in and out. Libraries, I discovered, are sanctuaries for many – academics, historians, octogenarian family history researchers and the homeless. Many thanks to the staff at the State Library Victoria; Mitchell and General Reference Libraries of NSW; State Library of South Australia; State Library of Tasmania; Queensland State Library and John Oxley Library; Central Queensland University Library; National Library, Canberra; Bendigo Library; Brownless Medical Library, Melbourne University; Baillieu Library, Melbourne University; Wellington and Auckland Municipal Libraries; Cambridge University Library; Magdalene College, Cambridge; Rugby Municipal Library; British Library, London; Lord's Cricket Library. The smaller Sydney libraries were comfortable and accessible places where much writing occurred. A few – Hurstville, Oatley, Penshurst and Rozelle – were constant companions.

I would specifically like to thank Brenda Heagney, former librarian at the Royal Australasian College of Physicians, who started me on my way when she suggested that I try the Royal Melbourne Hospital archives to see if they had the clinical notes on Tom Wills' admission in 1880. It turned out to be the first step of a long journey. At the Royal Melbourne Hospital I was assisted by Gabby Haveaux who showed me the pile of admission books in which I found Tom's medical notes.

The staff at the following institutions were helpful: Public Records Office, Victoria; Public Records Office, Tasmania; Queensland State Archives; Temple Reading Room, Rugby School where Rusty Maclean and staff provided me with much previously undiscovered material; staff at Winchester and Harrow for assisting me in my study of their nineteenth-century football games; Collindale Newspaper repository in London; London Metropolitan Archives; Victorian Cricket Association; New South Wales Cricket Association; Hocken Library; Wellington Museum.

The staff at the following historical and heritage centres answered letters and phone calls, and gave me their time when I visited: Ararat and District, Geelong Heritage Centre, Heidelberg, Midlands Historical Society, Royal Historical Society of Victoria, Skipton, South Melbourne, Victorian Police Historical Unit and Queanbeyan.

Thanks to the many people with whom I 'camped' as I travelled about, including Ray and Charles Smith who put me up and offered plenty of fine Scotch whisky in Brisbane. I spent a delightful day at Trent Bridge, Nottingham, flicking through notes and reading the handwritten diaries of James Southerton, and eating a sandwich with Peter Wynne-Thomas. Thanks to Beryl Armstrong who provided me with material on Tom's role in the Australian Natives' Association.

Thanks to Rob Hess, supervisor of my PhD project upon which this book is partly based, for his help in the important task of academic rigour.

To Ian Johnson, former MCC secretary, for giving me an opportunity many years ago. In a similar vein, thanks to Anne Deveson.

To my parents, Des and Eileen, for putting me up whenever I travelled to Melbourne and came back weary, late at night by train, after another session at the State Library; and to my brothers Dirk and Glenn for memories of footy and cricket in the streets of Merlynston as a boy. Many times in the gloom of an archival vault, somewhere in the world, it was these memories that kept me going.

I have dedicated the book to my wife, Heather, and my children, Eve and Willem. Without them nothing would have been done, nor would it have been worth doing.

INDEX

Page numbers in *italics* refer to illustrations